Given all of this, one might suppose that we would write off children altogether and leave them to their own devices until they reach the "age of reason." But of course we do not do that, for we must willy-nilly see them as tomorrow's citizens, albeit often with dismay, and we are deeply committed to them, but our commitment all too often has a strange flavor consisting of part scorn because they must be classed with the Great Excluded, and envy because they can violate the joyless principles of the Puritan Ethic and get away with it, a crime we would all dearly love to commit.

— Natalie Babbitt
Publishers' Weekly, July 19, 1971
Copyright, Xerox Corporation

"Because the major content of repression is the child, the contemporary revolution on behalf of the repressed—black or poor, feminine or natural or undeveloped—becomes unavoidably the revolution of the child."
—James Hillman, "Abandoning the Child," *Eranos*, 40 (1971), 372.

Cover design
by Jan Bakker

Wenzel Hollar (Bohemian, 1607-1677) after Pieter van Avont (Flemish, 1599-1652).

Christ and St. John as Infants with Child Angels, c. 1650. Etching 12.7 x 20.5 cm. G. Parthy, *Wenzel Hollar: Beschreibendes Verzeichniss seiner Kupferstiche*, Berlin, 1853, no. 495.

Hollar, one of the most popular and prolific printmakers of the seventeenth century, has taken the theme of the Holy Cousins from a drawing by his friend van Avont, who specialized in prints of playing children. St. John kneels and tenderly embraces his cousin, the hair shirt which he was to wear in the desert draped around his pudgy body and the water bowl with which he baptized Christ at his feet. Child angels at the left play with a cross and a kneeling lamb tethered with a string—both of which symbolize Christ's sacrifice. Christ and St. John as infants was a popular subject in Western Art, especially in the north, where they are usually shown playing under the supervision of their mothers Mary and Elizabeth, often with the Instruments of the Passion serving as toys.

William H. Wilson

Children's Literature

Volume 3

Journal of The Modern Language Association Seminar
on Children's Literature and
The Children's Literature Association

Temple University Press
Philadelphia

Editors: Francelia Butler and Bennett A. Brockman

Advisory Board: Martin Gardner, John Graham, William Moynihan, William Rosen
Book Review Editor: Barbara Rosen
Assistant Editor: William E. Sheidley
Consultant for the Library: Charity Chang
Consultants for Publishing: Edward G. Fisher and Cliff Ewert
Consulting Editors: Jan Bakker, Marcella Booth, Rachel Fordyce, Narayan Kutty
Consultants for The Children's Literature Association: Anne Jordan and Jon C. Stott
Editorial Assistants: Deborah A. DeRose, William A. Dickerson, Joan Somes

Editorial correspondence should be addressed to:
  Editors, *Children's Literature*
  English Department, U–25
  University of Connecticut
  Storrs, Connecticut 06268

Manuscripts submitted should conform to the second edition of the Modern Language
Association *Style Sheet*. An original and one copy are requested. Manuscripts should
be accompanied by a stamped, self-addressed envelope.

Temple University Press, Philadelphia 19122
© 1974 by Francelia Butler. All rights reserved

Published 1974
Previously published in Storrs, Connecticut as *Children's Literature: The Great Excluded*
Printed in the United States of America

International Standard Book Number: 0-87722-078-6 cloth; 0-87722-077-8 paper
Library of Congress Catalog Card Number: ~~75-21550~~ mc 78 -2585

Second printing, 1975

Contents

Reviews

Varia

The Editor's High Chair

Last summer, on a grant from the Research Foundation of the University of Connecticut, I visited eight European countries to try, among other things, to determine the extent to which children's literature is studied in the faculties of language, psychology, philosophy, or history of European universities.

The results were disappointing. Students of pedagogy and library science continue to make important contributions which those in other disciplines cannot make as well if at all. But those in liberal arts faculties decline to undertake studies for which they are uniquely qualified. When asked about research into children's literature at an important European university, a professor of English declared impatiently that a playground was the best place for such an investigation.

He was partly right, of course. Important things about children and their literature are to be learned from children at play. But especially in the United States there are indications that scholars in the humanities and social sciences are becoming aware of the importance of the field as an area that repays critical literary examination and provides rich data for the historian, philosopher, sociologist, art historian, and psychologist. It is possible that this burgeoning interest reflects the theories of Freud and Jung about childhood: scholars are beginning to see that it is good to pay more attention to the influences to which children are exposed, including literary influences. Perhaps a balanced study of the literature will develop in which all interested scholars will participate. If children's literature is studied as part of the experience of the whole personality of both child and adult, and as a manifestation of complex cultural phenomena, valuable discoveries which will positively affect future generations will be made.

In this issue of *Children's Literature* we have an article by James Hillman, Director of the Jung Institute in Zurich. Dr. Hillman, a practicing depth psychologist, has been a Terry Lecturer at Yale University, in a series which has included such distinguished psychologists as Erich Fromm and Carl Jung. If his Jungian theories gain wide acceptance, the literary experience of children could be revolutionized.

A feature of Volume One continued in this volume is also of special interest: a list of topics for research which are suitable not only for student papers but in many cases for scholarly investigation as well. We especially feel that the values communicated by the literature need more intensive analysis than currently available.

Finally, the editors are happy to note the rapidly expanding national and international circulation of the journal. We are particularly gratified that scholars like Professor R. Gordon Kelly, of the University of Pennsylvania Graduate School of American Civilization, have praised the journal's pioneer role in the serious scholarly study of the field. Our hope is that an ever growing body of scholars, including students, critics, librarians, writers, and educators, will find it an important resource and an indispensable forum for their research.

Francelia Butler

A Note On Story

James Hillman

From my perspective as depth psychologist, I see that those who have a connection with story are in better shape and have a better prognosis than those to whom story must be introduced. This is a large statement and I would like to take it apart in several ways. But I do not want to diminish its apodictic claim: to have "story-awareness" is *per se* psychologically therapeutic. It is good for soul.

1) To have had story of any sort in childhood—and here I mean oral story, those told or read (for reading has an oral aspect even if one reads to oneself) rather than watching story on screen—puts a person into a basic recognition of and familiarity with the legitimate reality of story *per se*. It is given with life, with speech and communication, and not something later that comes with learning and literature. Coming early with life, it is already a perspective to life. One integrates life as story because one has stories in the back of the mind (unconscious) as containers for organizing events into meaningful experiences. The stories are means of telling oneself into events that might not otherwise make psychological sense at all. (Economic, scientific, and historical explanations are sorts of "stories" that often fail to give the soul the kind of imaginative meaning it seeks for understanding its psychological life.)

2) Having had story built in with childhood, a person is usually in better relation with the pathologized material of obscene, grotesque, or cruel images which appear spontaneously in dream and fantasy. Those who hold to the rationalist and associationist theory of mind, who put reason against and superior to imagination, argue that if we did not put in such grim tales in early impressionable years, we would have less pathology and more rationality in later years. My practice shows me rather that the more attuned and experienced is the imaginative side of personality the less threatening the irrational, the less necessity for repression, and therefore the less actual pathology acted out in literal, daily events. In other words, through story the symbolic quality of pathological images and themes finds a place, so that these images and themes are less likely to be viewed naturalistically, with clinical literalism, as signs of sickness. These images find places in story as legitimate. They *belong* to myths, legends, and fairy tales where, just as in dreams, all sorts of peculiar figures and twisted behaviors appear. After all, "The Greatest Story Ever Told," as some are fond of calling Easter, is replete with gruesome imagery in great pathologized detail.

3) Story-awareness provides a better way than clinical-awareness for coming to terms with one's own case history. Case history too, as I have pointed out in *The Myth of Analysis* (Northwestern Univ. Press) and in *Suicide and the Soul* (Harper's Colophon), is a fictional form written up by thousands of hands in thousands of clinics and consulting rooms, stored away in archives and rarely published. This fictional form called "case history" follows the genre of social realism; it believes in facts and events, and takes all tales told with excessive literalism. In deep analysis, the analyst and the patient together re-write the case history into a new story, creating the "fiction" in the collaborative work of the analysis. Some of the healing that goes on, maybe even the essence of it, is this

collaborative fiction, this putting all the chaotic and traumatic events of a life into a new story. Jung said that patients need "healing fictions," but we have trouble coming to this perspective unless there is already a predeliction for story-awareness.

4) Jungian therapy, at least as I practice it, brings about an awareness that fantasy is the dominant force in a life. One learns in therapy that fantasy is a creative activity which is continually telling a person into now this story, now that one. When we examine these fantasies we discover that they reflect the great impersonal themes of mankind as represented in tragedy, epic, folktale, legend, and myth. Fantasy in our view is the attempt of the psyche itself to re-mythologize consciousness; we try to further this activity by encouraging familiarity with myth and folktale. Soul-making goes hand in hand with deliteralizing consciousness and restoring its connection to mythic and metaphorical thought patterns. Rather than interpret the stories into concepts and rational explanations, we prefer to see conceptual explanations as secondary elaborations upon basic stories which are containers and givers of vitality. As Owen Barfield and Norman Brown have written: "Literalism is the enemy." I would add: "Literalism is sickness." Whenever we are caught in a literal view, a literal belief, a literal statement, we have lost the imaginative metaphorical perspective to ourselves and our world. Story is prophylactic in that it presents itself always as "once upon a time," as an "as if," "make-believe" reality. It is the only mode of accounting or telling about that does not posit itself as real, true, factual, revealed, i.e. literal.

5) This brings us to the question of content. Which stories need to be told? Here I am a classic, holding for the old, the traditional, the ones of our own culture: Greek, Roman, Celtic, and Nordic myths; the Bible; legends and folk-tales. And these with the least modern marketing (updating, cleaning up, editing, etc.), i.e. with the least interference by contemporary rationalism which is subject to the very narrowing of consciousness which the stories themselves would expand. Even if we be not Celtic or Nordic or Greek in ancestry, these collections are the fundamentals of our Western culture and work in our psyches whether we like it or not. We may consider them distorted in their pro-Aryan or pro-male or pro-warrior slant, but unless we understand that these tales depict the basic motifs of the Western psyche, we remain unaware of the basic motives in our psychological dynamics. Our ego psychology still resounds with the motif and motivation of the hero, just as much psychology of what we call "the feminine" today reflects the patterns of the goddesses and nymphs in Greek myth. These basic tales channel fantasy. Platonists long ago and Jung more recently pointed out the therapeutic value of the great myths for bringing order to the chaotic, fragmented aspect of fantasy. The main body of biblical and classical tales direct fantasy into organized, deeply life-giving psychological patterns; these stories present the archetypal modes of experiencing.

6) I think children need less convincing of the importance of story than do adults. To be adult has come to mean to be adulterated with rationalist explanations, and to shun such childishness as we find in fairy stories. I have tried to show in detail how adult and child have come to be set against each other: childhood tends to mean wonder, imagination, creative spontaneity, while adulthood, the loss of these perspectives ("Abandoning the Child," *Eranos Jahrbuch,* 40 [1971]). So the first task, as I see it, is restorying the adult—the teacher and the parent and the grandparent—in order to restore the imagination

to a primary place in consciousness in each of us, regardless of age.

I have come at this from a psychological viewpoint, partly because I wish to remove story from its too close association with both education and literature—something taught and something studied. My interest in story is as something lived in and lived through, a way in which the soul finds itself in life.[1]

Footnote

[1]Some short works relevant for the point of view presented in this note: J. Hillman, " 'Pathologizing' and 'Personifying' " (Yale University Terry Lectures, 1972), in *Art International*, 17, nos. 6 and 8 (Summer and Oct., 1973); M.L. von Franz, *Creation Myths* (Zurich: Spring Publications, 1972) and J. Hillman, *Pan and the Nightmare* (Zurich: Spring Publications, 1973).

S. Rosamond Praeger (1867-1954). *The Philosopher.* Collection Ulster Museum, Belfast.

Narnia: The Author, The Critics, and The Tale

Walter Hooper

Before the recent revival of fairy tales got fully under way, C.S. Lewis's seven Chronicles of Narnia were treated a little like "hand-me-down" clothes which are passed down from big to little children and are immediately given up when the little ones outgrow them. Now that people are returning to the old distinction between stories which can only be read by children and those which can be enjoyed by people of all ages, the Narnian books occupy a position on something like a "Jacob's Ladder" and are continually being passed up and down from young to old, from old to young, depending on which member of the family discovers them first. Of the million copies of the Chronicles sold in England and the United States last year, about half were bought by college students.

Professor Tolkien's *Hobbit* and *Lord of the Rings* grew out of the stories he told his children, but Lewis, who was a bachelor for most of his life and knew little about children, wrote fairy tales simply because he liked them himself and because he found them the best art-form for what he had to say. As scholars of the past, both men knew that the association of fairy tales and fantasy with children is very recent and accidental. Fairy tales gravitated to the nursery when they became unfashionable with adults. It surely marks an important recovery that they are coming back—indeed *are* back—into fashion with whoever likes them of whatever age.

Asked how he came to write the first Chronicle of Narnia—*The Lion, the Witch and the Wardrobe*—Lewis said: "All my seven Narnian books, and my three science fiction books, began with seeing pictures in my head. At first they were not a story, just pictures. The *Lion* all began with a picture of a Faun carrying an umbrella and parcels in a snowy wood. This picture had been in my mind since I was about sixteen. Then one day, when I was about forty, I said to myself: 'Let's try to make a story about it.' "[1]

Though Lewis had probably forgotten it, there is some evidence which would seem to indicate that the initial impetus behind his Narnian stories came from real children.

In the autumn of 1939 four schoolgirls were evacuated from London to Lewis's home on the outskirts of Oxford. It was his adopted "mother," Mrs. Moore, who mainly looked after the evacuees, but Lewis shared the responsibility of entertaining the young visitors. On the back of another book he was writing at the time, I found what I believe to be the germinal passage of the first story of Narnia—*The Lion, the Witch and the Wardrobe*. It says: "This book is about four children whose names were Ann, Martin, Rose and Peter. But it is most about Peter who was the youngest. They all had to go away from London suddenly because of the Air Raids, and because Father, who was in the army, had gone off to the War and Mother was doing some kind of war work. They were sent to stay with a relation of Mother's who was a very old Professor who lived by himself in the country."

I've been told by a neighbor who used to see them across her back fence that the schoolgirls did not remain very long in Oxford, and I've never been able to discover whether Lewis wrote any more of the story at this time. The next we hear of the book is from Chad Walsh who says that, when he visited Lewis in the summer of 1948, he talked "vaguely of completing a children's book which he had begun "in the tradition of E. Nesbit.' "[2] Then, on the 10th of March, 1949, Lewis read the first two chapters of *The Lion, the Witch and the Wardrobe* to his friend, Roger Lancelyn Green, who is the only person to read all seven stories in manuscript. Spurred on by Lancelyn Green's encouragement, *The Lion* was completed by the end of the month. More "pictures" or mental images—which Lewis said were his only means of inspiration—began forming in his head and the next two stories, *Prince Caspian* and *The Voyage of the "Dawn Treader,"* were completed by the end of February, 1950. Before the year was out he had written *The Silver Chair* and *The Horse and His Boy* and made a start on *The Magician's Nephew.* The final installment, *The Last Battle,* was written two years later.

Lewis is generally thought to have been the best-read man of his time. Though this, in itself, would not insure readable books, the combination of his vast learning, his superior abilities as a prose-stylist, and his rich and vivid imagination have resulted in the Narnian books being first, though not foremost, extremely well-written adventure stories. What has led people to read the stories over and over again—what I'd say is the foremost reason for their success—is, I think, quite simply their "meaning." Before going into this, however, I should glance at the unpleasant reactions of some adults to the Narnian books.

Objections to the books are rare. When they've come, it's usually been from schoolmistresses and professional educators for whom the delicate unreality which they call the "whole child" seems to bear little resemblance to the children most of us meet. They claim that the Narnian battles and wicked characters frighten children and give them nightmares. I believe there is no better answer to these charges than that given by Lewis himself in his defense of fairy tales in his essay "On Three Ways of Writing for Children." While agreeing that we must not do anything (1) "likely to give the child those haunting, disabling, pathological fears against which ordinary courage is helpless," he was strongly opposed to the notion that we must keep out of the child's mind (2) "the knowledge that he is born into a world of death, violence, wounds, adventure, heroism and cowardice, good and evil":

> The second would indeed be to give children a false impression and feed them on escapism in the bad sense. There is something ludicrous in the idea of so educating a generation which is born to the Ogpu and the atomic bomb. Since it is so likely that they will meet cruel enemies, let them at least have heard of brave knights and heroic courage. Otherwise you are making their destiny not brighter but darker. Nor do most of us find that violence and bloodshed, in a story, produce any haunting dread in the minds of children. As far as that goes, I side impenitently with the human race against the modern reformer. Let there be wicked kings and beheadings, battles and dungeons, giants and dragons, and let villains be soundly killed at the end of the book. Nothing will persuade me that this causes an ordinary child any kind or degree of fear beyond what it wants, and needs, to feel. For, of course, it wants to be a little frightened.[3]

Another bit of adverse criticism comes from Mr. David Holbrook in his article "The Problem of C.S. Lewis" found in *Children's Literature in Education,* No. 10 (March, 1973), pp. 3-25. The article is what booksellers call "Curious," and has convinced me that, though there is a problem, it is most certainly not Lewis's. Mr. Holbrook says:

Taking clues from the philosopher of surrealism, Gaston Bachelard, from psychoanalysis, and from my work on Sylvia Plath, I believe that C.S. Lewis's Narnia stories have their origins in the fact of his life that his mother died when he was a baby. I believe that this left him a psychic hunger—to be nurtured by the mother he had lost. It left him . . . needing to find his way *into the other world where the mother was*: the world of death.

How do we get there? Since we came into the world through mother's body, we could go back there, through her body: and the Wardrobe is her body (or, to be more specific, her birth passage). But also symbolized is the need *to be seen as ourselves* as we seek *to find ourselves in* the mother's eyes: in the front of the wardrobe is a mirror, and the path to "other worlds" is through reflecting pools. Going "through the mirror" (as in *Alice,* or in some of George MacDonald's stories) is *going through the mother's eyes* into the other world where the dead mother is, she who can help one to BE. This is, or course, a quest for *birth* . . .

But now another problem arises. If we go into that other world of death where the mother is, we shall perhaps encounter a mother who has not been humanized by us, as a mother normally is, over the long years of knowing her as a child. She may be the all-bad, all-hate mother we were capable of phantasying as an infant. In Kleinian terms, she may be "bad breast" split off from wholeness. She may be what Melanie Klein called the "castrating mother."

Lewis never, of course, read this, but I recall a conversation we had about the same kind of thing. The difficulty, he said, about arguing with such Freud-ridden sheep is that *whatever* you say to the contrary, no matter how clear and obvious to a sensible man, the Freudian uses it to support what he's already decided to believe. Or, as Lewis says elsewhere, they argue in the same manner as a man who should say, "If there were an invisible cat in the chair, the chair would look empty; but the chair does look empty; therefore there is an invisible cat in it. A belief in invisible cats cannot be logically disproved, but it tells us a good deal about those who hold it."[4] I can find no chink in Mr. Holbrook's article whereby the light of reason might get through. As his sexual imagery goes on perpetuating itself, I have the sensation of observing a hydra that will go on sprouting heads whether you strike them off or not. Besides pointing out that Lewis was ten years old when his mother died—and so hardly a baby—the only thing I can say about Mr. Holbrook's article is that, were he given a lie-detector test to discover whether or not *he* believes what he's written, I feel sure he wouldn't pass.

Lewis was much gratified by the extraordinary success of the Narnian books. Of the many fan-letters he received, he seemed most pleased with those from children. Whereas adults usually wanted to know where he got his "ideas," children—not being required to write learned articles—let the stories act on them more directly.

To the many children who pleaded with him to write more stories, Lewis's answer was usually the same as that he gave me: "There are only two times at which you can stop a thing: one is before everyone is tired of it, and the other is after!" Almost all wrote of their love for Aslan, the Creator and ruler of Narnia. Last year an eleven-year old, Lucy Fryman, from Texas was so anxious to talk to someone who had known Lewis that she addressed the following words to his life-long friend, Owen Barfield:

> I have read Mr. Lewis's books. I got so envoveled in them all I did was eat, sleep, and
> read. I wanted to write to you and tell you I understand the books. I mean about the

sy[m]bols and all...I know that to me Aslan is God. And all the son's and daughter's of Adam and Eve are God's children. I have my own philosophies about the books. If it is possible I would like to meet you. None of my friends (well some of them) liked the books. I tried to explain to them but they don't understand about symbols. I never really did until I read the books.

I think it'd be inaccurate to say that most readers make the instant connection, as Lucy did, between Aslan and God. Lewis wanted it to happen naturally, or not at all. When another little girl asked what Aslan meant in the last chapter of *The Voyage of the "Dawn Treader,"* when he tells the children that in their world they must learn to know him by "another name," Lewis answered:

> As to Aslan's other name, well, I want you to guess. Has there never been anyone in *this* world who (1) Arrived at the same time as Father Christmas (2) Said he was the Son of the Great Emperor (3) Gave himself up for someone else's fault to be jeered at and killed by wicked people (4) Came to life again (5) Is sometimes spoken of as a Lamb (at the end of the "Dawn Treader")? Don't you really know His name in this world?[5]

Lewis used a capital "H" in the "His" above because Aslan is Christ. In another place he explained the reason for his reticence in saying no more than this: "Why did one find it so hard to feel as one was told he ought to feel about God or about the sufferings of Christ? I thought the chief reason was that one was told one ought to. An obligation to feel can freeze feelings . . . But supposing that by casting all these things into an imaginary world, stripping them of their stained-glass and Sunday school associations, one could make them for the first time appear in their real potency? Could one not thus steal past those watchful dragons? I thought one could."[6]

Professor Tolkien once told me that he thought the Christian elements in the Narnian stories too "obvious." But I think this is because he not only knew the Bible better than most of us, but began by knowing what Lewis was "up to." Judging from what I hear, only about half Lewis's readers guess that Aslan is meant to be Christ—and that half is made up about equally of children and adults. I side with Lewis in not wishing to attract the attention of those "watchful dragons," but as the Narnian books are, whether I like it or not, undergoing very detailed analysis, I offer the following comments about what I think the Christian elements in them are. This requires, first of all, clearing up a linguistic difference between Lewis and his readers.

It's about as natural as sneezing for moderns to call something an "allegory" when it has a meaning slightly different from, or other than, the one the author gives it. In this sense you can "allegorize" practically anything. The reason why Lewis and Tolkien claimed that their books are not allegories is that they were using the ancient definition of the term: by allegory they meant the use of something real and tangible to stand for that which is real but intangible: Love can be allegorized, patience can be allegorized, anything *immaterial* can be allegorized or represented by feigned physical objects. But Aslan and Gandalf are already physical objects. To try to represent what Christ would be like in Narnia is to turn one physical object into another (supposed) physical object—and that is not, by Lewis and Tolkien's definition, an allegory.

There are those who consider Satan the "hero" of Milton's *Paradise Lost,* by which they mean, not that he is in any way good, but that he's the best drawn character in the poem. Long before Lewis wrote the Narnian stories, he explained in his *Preface to Paradise Lost* (ch. xiii) why it is so much easier to draw a bad Satan than a good God:

> To make a character worse than oneself it is only necessary to release imaginatively from control some of the bad passions which, in real life, are always straining at the leash; the Satan, the Iago, the Becky Sharp, within each of us, is always there and only too ready, the moment the leash is slipped, to come out and have in our books that holiday we try to deny them in our lives. But if you try to draw a character better than yourself, all you can do is to take the best moments you have had and to imagine them prolonged and more consistently embodied in action. But the real high virtues which we do not possess at all, we cannot depict except in a purely external fashion. We do not really know what it feels like to be a man much better than ourselves.

In talking with Lewis about his almost unbelievable success in picturing the divine Aslan—Who is a million times more interesting than any of his equally convincing bad characters—I found him reluctant to take any credit, pointing out that Aslan pushed His *own* way into the books. Not only has Aslan received the highest praise of anyone or anything in the books, but, perilous compliment though it may sound, I think most readers (of which I am one) have been unable to divorce Aslan from Christ. Though it is a contradiction in terms, some love Him even more than His Original. I'm reminded of a little boy here in Oxford who chopped through the back of his wardrobe and half-way through the bricks of the house to get to Him. Aslan is not a "reinterpretation" of Christ, as I think *Jesus Christ Superstar* is meant to be. He is, as Lewis says, "an invention giving an imaginary answer to the question, 'What might Christ become like, if there really were a world like Narnia and He chose to be incarnate and die and rise again in *that* world as He actually has done in ours?' "[7] But some of us, on meeting absolute goodness, discover it to be too strong for us. I remember Lewis reading an article in which the writer referred to Aslan as "smug," and I know this pained him. "Do you think Aslan 'smug'?" he asked. I think I replied that what would sound perfectly ordinary coming from God would sound deranged coming from a mere man. The humanitarians may think *us* unkind for holding clear and definite beliefs, but they can hardly expect the Creator of all worlds to qualify every statement with "so it seems to me" or "in my opinion."

The closest parallel between Aslan and Christ comes in *The Lion, the Witch and the Wardrobe* where Aslan offers His life to save Edmund. This is very similar to Christ's vicarious death on the cross, but if the analogy is pressed too closely it will be discovered that nowhere—not even here—does Lewis provide us with a geometrically perfect equivalent of anything in the Bible or Christian doctrine. Lewis hoped that by seeing Aslan die on the Stone Table we'd not only be better able to grasp the significance of what happened in the actual history of this world, but see that it was a very good thing in itself and in the context Lewis gave it.

Not only is "disguise" part of Lewis's intention, but it is also essential to see that what is in one book or world cannot be the same in another book or world. What "Miss T" eats does not remain as it was but *turns into* "Miss T." The instructions Aslan gives Eustace and Jill on how to discover Prince Rilian is meant, I think, to reinforce the importance of following Christ's commandments. On the other hand, if, while reading *The Silver Chair,*

16

we're thinking only of Christ's instructions to the rich young man recounted in St. Mark 10: 17-21, we'll have missed what we are meant to be attending to in Narnia. It's afterwards, minutes or hours or perhaps even years afterwards, that the two worlds are to be joined in our minds. But even if that juncture *never* takes place, we will have benefited enormously from *The Silver Chair,* for it is part of the success of a great author that the sense of his book not depend on the reader knowing the original source of its ingredients.

Is there any good to be had from source-hunting? My belief is that when teachers come across children who feel they have solved a "puzzle" by discovering that Narnia is the name of a place in Italy, that Aslan is the Turkish word for lion, the teacher should lead him away from the suspect realm of anthropology to true literary pleasures by showing him how one thing becomes a *different* thing in another book. For instance, it's not enough to say that the immediate source of Shakespeare's *Romeo and Juliet* is Arthur Brooke's extremely ugly *Tragical History of Romeus and Juliet:* we need to show him what a completely different use Shakespeare made of the story if we are to help him appreciate the latter's genius.

More than most books, the Narnian tales are specially rich hunting grounds for scholars. In chapter xiii of *The Voyage of the "Dawn Treader"* the children find three Lords of Narnia fast asleep under an enchantment, round a table spread with exotic foods supplied by a beautiful Princess. On the table is the cruel-looking knife with which the White Witch killed Aslan. The Princess' father, Ramandu, appears but is unable to speak until a bird lays a live coal on his lips. Among the many possible "sources," other than Lewis's own imagination, for these elements are those we all know about. There is Rip Van Winkle; there is the passage in I Kings 17:6 which tells how ravens fed Elijah with "bread and flesh in the morning, and bread and flesh in the evening." The Knife recalls King Pelles' sword which struck the Dolorous Blow. The bird takes us back to Isaiah 6:6: "Then flew one of the seraphims unto me, having a live coal in his hand,which he had taken with the tongs from off the altar: and he laid it upon my mouth." It is inevitable that a man so widely-read as Lewis should have remembered all these things—but they, neither collectively nor individually, are what *his* story is about.

Besides their obvious parallels, the Narnian books are suffused throughout with moral teaching of a quality which I don't believe anyone, whatever his beliefs, could fairly object to. The tales are not, as might be imagined, built around moral themes which were in the author's mind from the beginning, but grew out of the telling and are as much a part of the narrative as scent is to a flower. I heard an expert on children's literature say the other day that writers are going back to moral themes—and cited "pollution" as the supreme example. None of us objects to a clean world, but the morality of Lewis's books goes far deeper and touches on levels of human understanding rarely attempted even by those who write for adults. An especially good example occurs in *The Voyage of the "Dawn Treader"* (ch. x). As Lucy searches the Magician's Book for the spell which will make the Dufflepuds visible, she comes across a spell which will let you know what your friends say about you. Not even wishing to avoid this dangerous thing, Lucy says the magical words and hears her good friend, Marjorie, say very unkind things about her to another person. Later, when Aslan discovers what poor heart-broken Lucy has done, He says, "Spying on people by magic is the same as spying on them in any other way. And you have misjudged your friend. She is weak, but she loves you. She was afraid of the older girl and said what she does not mean." "I don't think I'd ever be able to forget what I heard her say," answers Lucy. "No, you won't," replies Aslan.

Are there many of us who have not found, like Lucy, that such a dangerous course, once taken, forbids return? I've never seen the enormous difference between what our friends *say*, and what they really *think*, about us so unforgettably portrayed.

In *The Last Battle,* which won the Carnegie Medal for the best Children's Book of 1956, and is the most theological of all the books, Lewis uses a stable door as the way out of Narnia. Those familiar with Lewis's beliefs can understand how characteristic it is that he will not allow his readers to camp too long on any of his earthly creations. As we must, in reality, pass on, he will not write "and they lived happily ever after" till it is safe to do so. It is certainly not safe to do so at the beginning of *The Last Battle,* which is, in my opinion, the best-written and the most sublime of all the Narnian stories, the crowning achievement of the whole Narnian creation. Everything else in all the other six stories finds its meaning in relation to this book. Not that one can't enjoy the other stories separately; but, as Lewis would say, you cannot possibly understand the play until you've seen it through to the end. Lewis insists on taking us to the end—and beyond.

If *The Last Battle* is re-read less often than the other fairy tales this is probably because the first eleven chapters, which take place in the old, familiar Narnia, are so extremely painful to read. Almost everything we have come to love is, bit by bit, taken from us. Our sense of loss is made more excruciating because we are allowed—even encouraged—to believe that things will eventually get back to "normal." We feel certain that the King, at least, will not be deceived by Shift's trickery: but he is. When Eustace and Jill arrive we know it will only be a matter of time until all is put right. Yet, despite their willingness to help, there is so little they can do without the help of Aslan. And where, by the way, *is* He? Our hearts warm within us as Jewel the Unicorn recounts the centuries of past happiness in which every day and week in Narnia had been better than the last:

> And as he went on, the picture of all those happy years, all the thousands of them, piled up in Jill's mind till it was rather like looking down from a high hill on to a rich, lovely plain full of woods and waters and cornfields, which spread away and away till it got thin and misty from distance. And she said:
> "Oh, I do hope we can soon settle the Ape and get back to those good, ordinary times. And then I hope they'll go on for ever and ever and ever. *Our* world is going to have an end some day. Perhaps this one won't. Oh Jewel—wouldn't it be lovely if Narnia just went on and on—like what you said it has been?"
> "Nay, sister," answered Jewel, "all worlds draw to an end; except Aslan's own country."
> "Well, at least," said Jill, "I hope the end of this one is millions of millions of millions of years away." (ch. viii)

So do we all. Yet a few minutes later Farsight the Eagle brings word that Cair Paravel, the high seat of all the Kings of Narnia, has been taken by the Calormenes. And, as he lay dying, Roonwit the Centaur asked the King to remember that "all worlds draw to an end and that noble death is a treasure which no one is too poor to buy" (ch. viii).

Lewis's didactic purpose ought to be clear to those who are conversant with orthodox

Christianity. He uses his own invented world to illustrate what the Church has been teaching since the beginning, but which is becoming more and more neglected or forgotten. Namely, that this world will come to an end; it was never meant to be our real home—that lies elsewhere; we do not know, we cannot possibly know, when the end will come; and the end will come, not from within, but from without.

Most of the events in *The Last Battle* are based on Our Lord's apocalyptic prophecies recorded in St. Matthew 24, St. Mark 13 and St. Luke 21. The treachery of Shift the Ape was suggested by the Dominical words found in St. Matthew 24:23-24:

> If any man shall say unto you, Lo, here is Christ, or there; believe it not. For there shall arise false Christs, and false prophets, and shall shew great signs and wonders; insomuch that, if it were possible, they shall deceive the very elect.

The Ape almost—almost—succeeds in deceiving even the most faithful followers of Aslan. First through trickery and, later, when he becomes the tool of Rishda Tarkaan and Ginger the Cat, in propounding his "new theology": the confusion of Aslan and the devil Tash as "Tashlan." As the monkey Shift is a parody of a man, so his "theology" is a parody of the truth. We are prepared for ordinary wickedness in an adventure story, but with the advent of the "new theology" we move into a new and dreadful dimension where ordinary courage seems helpless.

When it seems quite certain that Eustace and Jill will soon die fighting for Narnia, they speculate as to whether, at the moment of their death in Narnia, they will be found dead in England. Frightened by the idea, Jill begins a confession which she breaks off mid-sentence. "What were you going to say?" asks Eustace. She answers:

> I *was* going to say I wished we'd never come. But I don't, I don't, I don't. Even if we *are* killed. I'd rather be killed fighting for Narnia than grow old and stupid at home and perhaps go about in a bath chair and then die in the end just the same.   (ch ix)

From that point onwards Lewis lets go the full power of his imagination, and we are carried relentlessly forward into what is truly the *last* battle of Narnia, in front of the Stable. There the King, the children, and the remnant of faithful Narnians are either slain or make their way inside. The Stable has become none other than the way into Aslan's Country, and, drawing out this brilliant piece of symbolism, Lewis has Jill say in a moment of selfless appreciation: "In our world too, a Stable once had something inside it that was bigger than our whole world."   (ch. xiii)

What is a little confusing, but which is partly explained in chapters iv and v, and fully cleared up in the last chapter, is that all (except one) of the "friends of Narnia"—Digory Kirke, Polly Plummer, Peter, Edmund and Lucy Pevensie, Eustace Scrubb, and Jill Pole—died together in a railway crash in England. They are reborn in glory and, inside the Stable, Eustace and Jill meet all the others. The exception is Susan Pevensie who, "no longer a friend of Narnia" (ch. xii), has drifted of her own free will into apostasy. Liberal clergymen and other "kind" but mistaken people, preferring the temporary passion of Pity to the eternal action of Pity, have found the absence of Susan a reason for calling Lewis "cruel." But they are well answered in *The Great Divorce* where, explaining why those who have chosen Hell shall not be allowed to veto the joys of Heaven, he says: "Every disease that submits to a cure shall be cured: but we will not call blue yellow to please those who insist on still having jaundice, nor make a midden of the world's garden for the sake of some who cannot abide the smell of roses."[8]

With a terrible beauty that almost makes the heart ache, and which is perhaps only matched by Dante's *Paradiso,* Aslan goes to the Stable door and holds His Last Judgement. Those who are worthy pass in, the others turn away into darkness. Inside, the children watch as Aslan, fulfilling the apocalyptic prophecies of the New Testament, destroys Narnia by water and fire and closes the Stable door upon it for ever.

After this dazzling feat of the imagination, one might reasonably expect that Lewis could not help but let us down in "unwinding" his story. He knew that the merest slip of the pen could have cast a shadow of incredulity over all that went before, and he proceeded very cautiously in opening the children's eyes to where they are. The question was how do you portray Heaven? How make it *heavenly*? How "wind" *upwards*?

The answer lay in finding—and then trying to describe—the difference between the earthly and the eternal world. Years before, writing about the difference between allegory and symbolism, he said:

> The allegorist leaves the given—his own passions—to talk of that which is confessedly less real, which is a fiction. The symbolist leaves the given to find that which is more real. To put the difference in another way, for the symbolist it is we who are the allegory. We are the "frigid personifications"; the heavens above us are the "shadowy abstractions"; the world which we mistake for reality is the flat outline of that which elsewhere veritably is in all the round of its unimaginable dimensions.[9]

Symbolism, as described here, was not for Lewis a fanciful bit of intellectualism. He believed that Heaven is the real thing of which earth is an imperfect copy. His problem was not only of finding some way to illustrate this, but to describe the heavenly life in such a way that it would not seem a place of perpetual negations. In his essay "Transposition," he suggests that we think of a mother and son imprisoned in a dungeon. As the child has never seen the outer world, his mother draws pencil sketches to illustrate what fields, rivers, mountains, cities and waves on a beach are like:

> On the whole he gets on tolerably well until, one day, he says something that gives his mother pause. For a minute or two they are at cross-purposes. Finally it dawns on her that he has, all these years, lived under a misconception. "But," she gasps, "you didn't think that the real world was full of lines drawn in lead pencil?" "What?" says the boy. "No pencil-marks there?" And instantly his whole notion of the outer world becomes a blank . . . So with us. "We know not what we shall be"; but we may be sure we shall be more, not less, than we were on earth.[10]

Lewis had a knack of making even the most difficult metaphysical concepts understandable and picturing the otherwise unpicturable. In order that his readers will feel as comfortable in the world beyond the Stable door as the children in the book, he brings in homely details such as the fact that Narnian clothes felt as well as looked beautiful and (I'll never forget how much Lewis disliked "dressing up") the even more pleasant fact that "there was no such thing as starch or flannel or elastic to be found from one end of the country to the other" (ch. xii). Then, as the children and many of the animals they have come to love follow Aslan further into the country, their sense of strangeness wears off till it eventually dawns upon them that the reason why everything looks so familiar is because they are seeing for the first time the "real Narnia" of which the old one had only been a "copy." As they rejoice in this discovery, Lord Digory, whom we first met as old Professor Kirke in *The Lion, the Witch and the Wardrobe,* explains the difference between the two, adding "It's all in Plato, all in Plato: bless me, what *do* they teach them at these schools!" He is referring, of course, to Plato's *Phaedo* in which he discusses immortality and the unchanging reality behind the changing forms.

One other little detail, overlooked perhaps by the majority of readers as it is blended so perfectly into the narrative, concerns the manner in which resurrected bodies differ from earthly ones. The children discover that they can scale waterfalls and run faster than an arrow flies. This is meant to be a parallel to the Gospel accounts of Christ's risen body: though still corporeal, He can move through a locked door (St. John 20:19) and ascend bodily into Heaven (St. Mark 16:19).

When the children reach the Mountain of Aslan they are joined by all the heroes of the other six books, Reepicheep the Mouse, Puddleglum the Marsh-wiggle and a host of other old friends. Uneasy that their joy may yet be snatched from them, and that they may be sent back to earth, they turn to Aslan who answers the question in their minds: "Have you not guessed?" He says, "The term is over: the holidays have begun. The dream is ended: this is the morning."

After that we are told that "He no longer looked to them like a lion." Lewis is here referring to the passage in the Athanasian Creed which states that Christ is both God and Man "not by conversion of the Godhead into flesh: but by taking of the Manhood into God." This means that Aslan was transformed into a Man—which Manhood He keeps for all time. "The things that began to happen after that," says Lewis, "were so great and beautiful that I cannot write them"—and, of course, neither can I or anyone else.

There has never been a book written, I fancy, in which the assumptions of the author were not present, implicitly or explicitly. Even the most blameless stories of child-life have at their base beliefs about something or the other. There is no such thing as not believing *anything.* One who does not agree with Christianity must agree with something else. Will it lead to better ends than those pre-figured in Lewis's books? I have read many modern works of literature about which I am forced to say "I admire the workmanship, but deplore the sentiments"; but only of the Narnian Chronicles can I unhesitatingly say, "This is beautiful, and this is right."

Footnotes

[1]C. S. Lewis, "It All Began With a Picture . . . " in *Of Other Worlds: Essays and Stories,* ed. Walter Hooper (London, 1966), p. 42.

[2]Chad Walsh, *C. S. Lewis: Apostle to the Skeptics* (New York, 1949), p. 10.

[3]"On Three Ways of Writing for Children," in *Of Other Worlds,* p. 31.

[4]C. S. Lewis, "Friendship," in *The Four Loves* (London, 1960), p. 73.

[5]Quoted in Kathryn Lindskoog, *The Lion of Judah in Never-Never Land* (Grand Rapids, 1973), p. 16.

[6]"Sometimes Fairy Stories May Say Best What's to be Said," in *Of Other Worlds*, p. 37.

[7]*Letters of C. S. Lewis*, ed. W. H. Lewis (London, 1966), p. 283.

[8]C.S. Lewis, *The Great Divorce* (London, 1945), p. 112.

[9]C. S. Lewis, "Allegory," in *The Allegory of Love* (London, 1936), p. 45.

[10]C. S. Lewis, "Transposition," in *They Asked for a Paper* (London, 1962), p. 178.

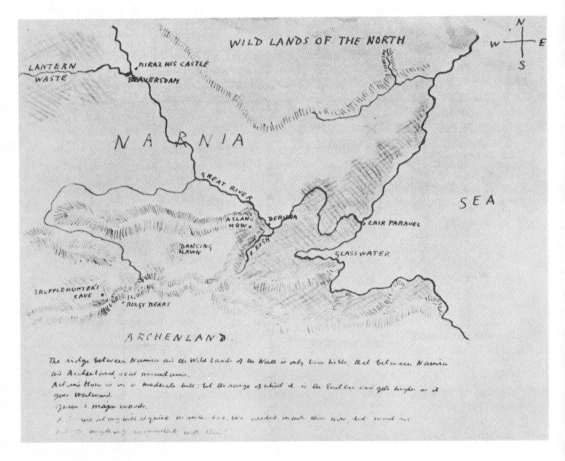

C. S. Lewis, Map of Narnia. Bodleian Library, Oxford, MS. Eng. lett. c. 220, fol. 160. Copyright—Trustees of C. S. Lewis Estate.

Pinocchio: Archetype of the Motherless Child

James W. Heisig

Carlo Collodi's *The Adventures of Pinocchio* has to stand, along with Lewis Carroll's *Alice's Adventures in Wonderland,* L. Frank Baum's *The Wonderful World of Oz* and J.M. Barrie's *Peter Pan,* as one of the few truly classic pieces of children's literature. For whatever the fate of these authors has been in academic circles—where Carroll has understandably proved the most exciting of the lot—many of the characters they created have become independent entities with lives of their own, free of the vagaries of literary taste and opinion. They seem to have escaped the written page, disowned their makers and become part of the very fabric of twentieth century civilization, in much the same way as the fairies, heroes and ogres found in the folktales of the brothers Grimm, Perrault, Basile and Hans Christian Andersen have returned to the hearths, the taverns and the nurseries from which they were originally gleaned. To some extent theatrical productions, films, cartoon animations and the vast market of children's books have contributed to this process. Yet the resultant success could not have occurred were it not also for a certain profound and universal psychological appeal, transcending the powers of commercialism. A study of *Pinocchio* may, I think, shed some light on the dark forces of enchantment at work in such tales.

Carlo Lorenzini was born in Florence in 1826, the first of nine children. His father was employed as a cook by the marchesi Garzoni. His mother, a cultured woman of rich sensitivities, worked as a seamstress and chambermaid to the same household. At sixteen years of age Carlo entered the seminary at Val d'Elsa, probably with the financial aid of the marchese since his parents were short of funds at the time.[1] There he studied Latin, scholastic philosophy and theology, graduating with honors four years later. Feeling unsuited to an ecclesiastical career, however, he left the seminary and turned to journalism, a profession in which he was to exploit his biting but inoffensive wit to earn himself a place of respect as a critic and political commentator.[2]

Lorenzini interrupted his apprenticeship with the *Rivista di Firenze* in 1848 to fight alongside his fellow Tuscans in the war against the Hapsburg Empire. Upon his return he was made secretary of the Tuscan Senate and shortly thereafter founded a journal of political satire, *Il Lampione.* In 1849 he was promoted to secretary first class in the provisional government of Tuscany, a post which he resigned after the restoration of Austrian rule. Not surprisingly his journal was soon suppressed. In 1853 he initiated another journal, *Lo Scaramuccia,* devoted to the dramatic arts. What little political comment he could work into its pages had to be carefully disguised to avoid the ubiquitous eye of the censors.

In April, 1859, Piedmont again declared war against Austria and Lorenzini abandoned his flourishing career—between 1850 and 1859 had published a number of books on a wide variety of subjects—to fight as a volunteer on the plains of Lombardy. He returned after the Peace of Villafranca and was named secretary of the Prefecture of Florence.

There he remained until 1881, inaugurating a number of significant educational reforms during his term of office. In 1860 he reopened *Il Lampione,* picking up where he had left off eleven years before. In that same year he published a little book in defense of the unification of Italy, *Il sig. Albèri ha ragione,* which carried for the first time the pseudonym of Collodi—the name of a small town near Pescia where his mother had been born and where he had spent so many happy holidays as a young child.

What turned Collodi to children's books was, ironically, the pressure of gambling debts. With his creditors growing impatient and his usual income too meagre to meet their demands, he contracted to translate three of Perrault's *contes* and a selection of fables from de Beaumont and d'Aulnoy. The collection appeared in 1875 as *I racconti delle Fate.* Soon afterwards he put his pedagogical skills to use to update a well known children's reader, which he published in 1876 under the title of *Giannettino.* The success of these ventures led Collodi, now over fifty years old, to write a number of other textbooks for children on reading, geometry, grammar and arithmetic. The last of these appeared in 1890; in October of that year, while preparing an outline for yet another children's book, Collodi died suddenly and without warning.

It was during these last years of his life, in which Collodi had dedicated his talents almost exclusively to children's literature, that the figure of Pinocchio was born. In 1881 Ferdinando Martini, an established publisher and author, began a children's magazine called *Giornale per i bambini,* which had immediate success, reaching a subscription of some 25,000. Collodi, who had recently retired from public office, was among the first to be invited to write for it. His need for money and the solicitations of the editor, Guido Biagi, prompted him to overcome his habitual laziness and put pen to paper. Some time later Biagi received a packet in the mail with a manuscript bearing the title "La storia di un burattino" and the following message: "I am sending you this childishness to do with as you see fit. But if you print it, pay me well so that I have a good reason to continue with it." In fact it took a good deal more coaxing both from the editor and from children who had grown fond of the little wooden puppet and his adventures, before Collodi agreed to see the project to the end.[3] Two years later it appeared as a complete book whose sales quickly soared to a million copies in Italy alone.[4]

It is difficult to know just how to classify *Pinocchio* in terms of literary genre. Strictly speaking we cannot treat it as a folktale since it was not handed down from tradition but rather originated in the creative mind of its author. On the other hand, it would be equally unfair simply to class it as a piece of imaginative fantasy for children, since the little wooden marionette who wanted to become a real boy has *become* something of a folktale tradition over the years. What is more, there is much in Collodi's style which betrays a close affinity with the household tale and the apologue. And the problem of classification is further complicated by Collodi's introduction of certain social and political criticisms into the text which add an element of contextual reality foreign to the folktale. In short, *Pinocchio* seems to fall on the borderlands between a number of literary forms and therefore lends itself to a variety of interpretations, no one of which can be taken as exhaustive.

The unusual blend of fantasy and reality which so many critics have observed in

Pinocchio stems in part, I think, from Collodi's intention to recover in imagination his lost childhood. The course of his career having been run, he now seeks in his mature years to relive his past creatively and thereby to pass judgment on it, to evaluate its influence on his personality. Indeed the very fact that he chose the role of a storyteller to achieve this anamnesis supports such a view, for already as a lad Collodi was beloved for his ability to fascinate other children with his stories. His brother Ippolito tells us that "he did it so well and with such mimicry that half the world took delight and the children listened to him with their mouths agape."[5] Moreover Collodi knew well enough that other character traits which had established themselves in his youth continued to mark him throughout life and into old age. His nephew writes that Carlo's career in government was distinguished "neither by zeal nor by punctuality nor by subordination" (P. Lorenzini, p. 986). He was an individual bordering on eccentricity, largely self-taught and always distrustful of status and rank. A true Florentine in spirit, Collodi was ever ready to mock what he saw about him, though always with affection and good humor (Biagi, p. 97, Morganti, pp. 12f). These same qualities, by his own admission, were dominant in his childhood. The picture he paints of his early days at school as prankster and clown leave little doubt on the matter: eating cherries in class and stuffing the pits in his neighbor's pockets; catching flies and putting them into someone else's ears; painting figures on the trousers of the lad in front of him; and in general causing frustration to his would-be teachers.[6] The fact that this short autobiographical sketch was done in Collodi's last years after the completion of *Pinocchio* maintains our thesis that the book was an introspective venture. It does not take much effort to see in the puppet a mirror-image of the independent, indolent and self-reliant little Carlino who refused to listen to his elders.[7] Yet there is something suspicious about Collodi's conclusion in that sketch, namely that he abandoned his impish ways and became a good boy, obedient and respectful towards his teachers. To some purpose imagination seems to have distorted memory so that his own life story might turn out as Pinocchio's had.

Unlike the adventures of Wendy Darling, Alice and Dorothy, the adventures of Pinocchio do not begin in the real world and progress to the fanciful. From the very outset we move in a land without time or geography. The color of Collodi's landscapes is of course unmistakably Tuscan, as Baldini has pointed out;[8] but it is so *typically* depicted that it is meant to be "everywhere and nowhere." Likewise there is an apparent disregard for season and time. It snows and rains to fit the occasion; fireflies appear months ahead of their season; the muscatel grapes are ripe in the middle of winter (see Ch. 20, 21).[9] The spoken idiom and certain details of social structure and fashion belong to the lower and middle bourgeoisie of nineteenth-century Italy. Yet the story and its principal themes belong to that universal time which its opening words recall: "Once upon a time . . ."[10]

Further, unlike Alice's "wonderland," the "wonderful world" of Oz and "Neverland," there is no dream-like quality to Pinocchio's world. The fantastical elements are always kept in check by the realistic environment. The miracle of a living puppet is balanced by Pinocchio's subservience to the nature of a little boy, just as the anthropomorphisms of the animal characters must submit to the laws of nature. Even the Blue Fairy, who works some splendid feats of disappearance and transformation, is nevertheless powerless against the superior force of Pinocchio's free will and susceptible to sickness. Indeed every trace of magic or surrealism is set against a backdrop of reality where magic is the exception and not the rule (Fanciulli and Monaci, pp. 216-218).

At the same time the book is full of factual inconsistencies of the sort frequent in fairy-tales but uncommon in authored children's books.[11] For example, since Pinocchio does not go to school as he should he is unable to read the simple signs at the carnival, and yet somehow he succeeds in deciphering the more difficult text on the tombstone of the beautiful child. He has no ears, having escaped Geppetto's workshop before they could be added, and yet hears perfectly well. (It is conceivable, let it be noted, that Collodi may have intended a bit of irony here, because it is Pinocchio's inability to "listen" which causes him so much trouble.) Or again, Collodi seems to have forgotten that he gave his puppet a bread-crust hat and paper jacket for all the weathering that meagre wardrobe is made to suffer. That such slips are due merely to the carelessness of the author, who could after all have later corrected them, is unlikely. Even without their help the blend of the realistic and the fantastic would be dominant in the story.

Perhaps no aspect of *Pinocchio* is more striking than the role which animals play in the story. In the words of one commentator, it is "a veritable Noah's ark . . . with the typical apologal function of betraying and translating the various dispositions of mankind" (Bernabei, p. 593; Baldini, p. 120). Crickets, rabbits, dogs, apes, donkeys, birds and fish of various sorts; not to mention the fox, the cat, the eel, the snake, the snail, the fire-fly, the crab, the marmot, the calf and the little goat—all these characters and more figure in the world of Pinocchio as naturally and unpretentiously as if they were human. It may be the case that by means of such animal projections the child is led to recognize traits of personality and signs of virtue and vice which are as yet indistinguishable to him, or at least only vaguely discernible, in the adult world about him.[12] If this is so, then from the very outset *Pinocchio* is a didactic venture, and the blend of fantasy and reality serves the higher purposes of a moral fable.

If *Pinocchio* is a fable in narrative, it seems to be one with a fundamentally conflicting moral to it, and this for reasons again of the mixture of fantasy and reality. The lesson for children is clear and forthright. Hardly is Pinocchio taught to walk before he runs away in disobedience; as a result he burns his feet and has to be repaired. Repentance is short-lived, however, and he takes off self-reliantly again and again, piling up a history of lies and broken promises, and involving himself with shady characters who promise to fulfill all his desires without his having to go to school or do a stitch of work. In consequence of his misdeeds Pinocchio is nearly used for firewood, is hung by the neck on an oak tree, finds his nose grown to immense proportions, loses his money to the fox and the cat and goes to prison, is caught in a trap and tied up as a watchdog, is forced to beg for food, spends a second term in jail, is almost fried as a fish in a pan, is transformed into a donkey, is sold to a circus and then to a man who decides to make a drum of his hide after drowning him, and is finally swallowed by the great shark. The moral is obvious: evil comes to those who disobey their elders. "Woe to little boys who rebel against their parents . . . . They'll come to no good in this world and sooner or later will live to regret their actions bitterly." Both the episodic style of the moral and the underlying metaphysic (virtue rewards, vice punishes) are close to the thought-patterns of the young child. It is, as Chesterton has wisely noted in his autobiography, the most spontaneously appealing world to the child who knows too little of hypocrisy and cunning to reject such moralizing.[13] And perhaps the appeal of *Pinocchio* to older generations simply indicates a desire to return to that purity of ideals which one once enjoyed as a child at play in imagination.

Together with this unambiguous advice to children to obey authority we find Collodi's lighthearted but subtler mockery of civil authority. Three times it happens that innocent parties are cast into prison: Geppetto for chasing after Pinocchio, Pinocchio for being robbed of his money and again later for staying to help a wounded friend. In the town of Fools' Trap,[14] the judge is a giant gorilla wearing gold-rimmed glasses without lenses and his police are great bulldogs. When a general amnesty is proclaimed by the mayor, Pinocchio manages to escape prison with the others only by admitting that he is a criminal, since the jailer wants to keep him locked up because of his innocence. Such parody works deceptively to undermine trust in lawful authority on the part of the young child, and hence stands in contradiction to the surface moral of the story. More importantly, it seems to suggest that in the *real* world there is no justice; that only in the world of *fantasy* does good come of good, evil of evil. On our earlier hypothesis this tension can be traced back to Collodi's intention to recapture his youth and its ideals as a means of reflecting on his past life with its political concerns. But the conflict is not Collodi's own; it is a paradigm of our very human condition.

We are compelled, therefore, to see in Pinocchio more than merely the ghost-image of Collodi. In the same way that Pinocchio learns the harsh truths of life through experience by leaving his father-creator behind and venturing out into the world alone, so also does he escape the control of Collodi himself. It is a phenomenon familiar to the writer. John Fowles, for example, pauses in Chapter 13 of his brilliant study of Victorian England, *The French Lieutenant's Woman,* to reflect on the autonomy his characters had achieved: "Perhaps you suppose that a novelist has only to pull the right strings and his puppets will behave in a lifelike manner . . . . It is only when our characters and events begin to disobey us that they begin to live." In the case of Pinocchio this lifelikeness means, however, not the concretization of an individual figure, but rather his universalization. Pinocchio represents man, *homo viator.* In the suggestive phrase of Benedetto Croce, "The wood of which Pinocchio is carved is our very own humanity."[15] This insight needs to be understood in turn on two levels.

On the first level, Pinocchio appears to us, in the words of one commentator, as "the personification of our very own natural tendencies" (Bernabei, p. 595; cf. Morganti, pp. 26, 29) and, more importantly, as the personification of a life-myth which brings those tendencies into harmony one with another. This Collodi achieves by depicting Pinocchio's progress as a quasi-Socratic version of the way to virtue. He learns the lessons of life not from abstract classroom theories, but from direct experience, the frequent repetition of which ends in true conversion. His latent sentiments of loyalty and altruism surface only as he slowly learns the need to trim his frenzied passions for independence and the sweet life. He is victimized by wicked and evil men not because of any real wickedness on his own part, but because of ignorance; and he disobeys his elders since he does not yet know any better. In short, Pinocchio's travels lead him from an ignorance of ignorance to a knowledge of ignorance and thence to a self-conscious trust in the wisdom of age and tradition. In contrast to the cat and the fox whose hypocritical masquerade brings them finally to misfortune, Pinocchio's innocence is educated by his adventures in a world (unlike that of Voltaire's *Candide*) where happiness is ultimately guaranteed to the pure of heart.

Of all the animals who assist in Pinocchio's self-education, the Talking Cricket merits special attention. As every schoolboy knows, he represents "conscience," the wee inner voice of warning, the bond between law and responsibility. At their first encounter Pinocchio falls into a rage with the "patient little philosopher" and flattens him to the wall with a wooden hammer from Geppetto's workbench. But the Cricket cannot be so easily disposed of and his ghost appears later in the story to haunt Pinocchio, though his advice is again ignored. Still later the Cricket is called in by the Blue Fairy for his opinion on the ailing puppet, whether he be dead or alive. And here, true to his function as a *psychic* censor, he refuses to say anything abouth Pinocchio's *physical* well being, but simply denounces him as a disobedient little rogue who is going to be the death of his good father by and by. It is only at their final meeting that Pinocchio addresses him as "my dear little Cricket" and follows his counsel. Thus Collodi embodies in the figure of the Talking Cricket the imperative to trust in those inner promptings of the mind which curtail and yet finally protect one's independence.

Morganti summarizes the paradigmatic role of Pinocchio on what I have called this first level simply and accurately: "Collodi gives a place of value to the basic human goodness of the child and to his or her right to self-determination in the process of education. To adults, the child seems but a puppet . . . without a will, who must follow blindly the will of his educators."[16] The conflict in the moral of *Pinocchio* which was pointed up earlier, therefore, cloaks a deeper irony in the book. It is not merely the case that children seem to be required to have faith in an older generation which often turns out to be corrupt; but also that true maturity is a function of individual insight which cannot be learned except through personal experience and reflection. Likewise, when Collodi concludes his sketch of school memories with the advice that students should obey their teachers, we can only presume that he is writing tongue-in-cheek, perhaps somewhat fearful of enunciating his own life-myth into a general principle.[17] In *Pinocchio* its signs are more apparent, though many have overlooked them and consequently have not understood the reasons (however mistaken) for which the book was condemned as immoral (Morganti, pp. 25,50f).

Pinocchio stands before us as a reflection of our human condition on another level—one is tempted to say a "deeper" level to stress its greater distance from consciousness, though not necessarily to imply a greater importance as well—which complements and balances the level of moral self-affirmation. To appreciate this we may consider the figure of the Blue Fairy, who can serve as a sort of psychopomp into the nether world of primordial, archetypal images. To ignore her, or to dismiss her as a mere *dea ex machina* who directs the fate of Pinocchio to a happy ending in typical fairytale fashion,[18] is in my view radically mistaken and a distortion of the textual evidence of Collodi's finished tale.

The Blue Fairy, it will be remembered, first makes her appearance as a beautiful child with blue hair who lives in the mysterious House of the Dead, where she awaits the funeral bier to carry her off. She speaks without moving her lips and watches helplessly as the murderers abduct Pinocchio. In the following episode we discover that the beautiful child is really a Fairy who has lived in the woods for a thousand years and commands an assembly of animals to do her bidding. It is she who makes Pinocchio's nose to grow, in order to teach him a lesson about telling lies. Then, having grown fond of him, offers the proposition: "If you want to stay with me, you can be my little brother and I your good little sister." Pinocchio agrees but only on condition that he can be with his father as well. The Fairy explains that she has already made arrangements for Geppetto to join them; and that if Pinocchio is really anxious to meet him, he need only take the path through the forest and he will find him on his way. Of course, things turn out otherwise; and when Pinocchio eventually returns to look for the Fairy he finds only a tombstone whose epitaph tells him that she died meantime of sorrow, abandoned by her little brother Pinocchio. Shortly thereafter he encounters the Fairy again, this time mysteriously grown into a good peasant woman. At first she tries to hide her identity, but when she sees the depth of his affection for her, reveals to him that whereas she had been his little sister previously, now she is "a woman who could almost be your mother." Whereupon Pinocchio begins to call her "mamma." His mischievous ways part them a third time, after which he returns with his usual fervent purpose of amendment. But before long Pinocchio's foolheartedness gets him in further trouble, and this time their separation is final. He sees her for the last time, though only for a brief moment, in the audience of a circus where he is performing as a donkey. She appears later in the form of a beautiful little goat with blue-colored wool who tries, in vain, to save him from the giant shark. The next news that comes to Pinocchio is that she is lying sick in bed, "gravely ill, struck down by a thousand misfortunes and without so much as enough to buy a crumb of bread." In his grief he vows to work double-time to help her, to which purpose he stays up half the night at work. When he falls asleep the Fairy appears to him in a dream and tells him that as a reward for his goodness she is going to make him a real boy. And with this miracle the adventures of Pinocchio come to a close.

Now there can be little doubt about the central role which the Blue Fairy enjoys in Pinocchio's life-story. As soon as he meets the beautiful child, his aimless wanderings begin to have an object: he wants to be with her. She proves inspiration and goal enough temporarily to conquer his innate distaste for school and even to forget about his father. For it is she who promises to make him a real boy, something Geppetto could not do. As Collodi himself suggests, she is something *like* a little sister; or later, something *like* a mother. More than that he does not seeem to know. Indeed one feels that as the story progresses, the author does little more than *record* the activities of the Blue Fairy, who spontaneously suggests the part she will play in Pinocchio's process of development.

At this point we are obliged further to clarify our original hypothesis and to see *Pinocchio* as an involuntary autobiography which covers not only Collodi's childhood and his public career, but his private adult life as well. He never married, though it seems he sired a "secret" daughter (Morganti, p. 16), who would thus have been, for all practical purposes of reputation, "dead" like the beautiful child who could not communicate by word of mouth. But note the immediate transformation which the symbol undergoes once it has been introduced into the story. The child returns Pinocchio from the threat of death

29

which he had incurred by choking on the money he refused to give up; and then she teaches him a lesson about lies, those with short legs (which do not carry one very far) and those with long noses (which are apparent for all to see). The connection with Collodi's gambling habits and the daughter he tried to keep hidden by deceit could not be clearer. The symbol becomes his savior both financially (the writing of the story provided him with an income) and psychologically (by reflecting him to himself).

The transformation continues and the child soon becomes the idealization of Collodi's own mother, for whom his respect seems to have been constant and unfailing, as hers had been for him.[19] The link between the images of child and mother can only be guessed at. Perhaps, because rumor has left us little or no information about the mother of Collodi's daughter, it is the filial love—in the one case given, in the other received—which was more important to him than matrimonial love. In any event, the final import of the story is clear: Geppetto gives Pinocchio his body, but the puppet must search elsewhere for his soul, which he eventually finds in the healing power of a mother's love.

Here again *Pinocchio* as the story of man-writ-small rises to the stature of man-writ-large. Willy-nilly Collodi has fallen into a world of symbols whose psychic roots touch more than the personal history which occasioned them in the first instance, and even more than the typical human problems of ethical maturation considered earlier. In a word, Pinocchio has now to be understood as *archetype of the motherless child.*

Pinocchio's own description of the Blue Fairy—"She is my mamma, who is like all those good mothers who love their children deeply and never lose sight of them . . . "—tells only half the tale. Bernabei intimates the double entendre by referring to her description as the *Blue* Fairy: the color of her hair makes her as unmistakable to the puppet as each mother is to her children; but it is also the color of heaven, the seat of Providence, the mother of all. Thus Bernabei finds it natural that she disappears at the end of the story "since the rightful place of *that* mother is in heaven rather than on earth" (p. 599; Fanciulli and Monaci-Guidotti, p. 220). The point is well taken, though others less familiar with feminine forms of the divinity in the history of religions and myth, and in particular within the Judaeo-Christian tradition, might object to the inference.

To characterize Pinocchio mythologically as an archetypal motherless child is to classify his adventures psychologically as a quest for that which can transform a man from within, heal his divided self, and restore him to a state of primordial wholeness. For as the ego emerges from its embryonic identity with the mother's womb, it finds itself in a state of ambivalence. On the one hand the expansion of consciousness and the affirmation of autonomy are highly desirable; on the other, the comforts of unconsciousness and the bliss of ignorance are less threatening.[20] Pinocchio's search for a mother is a symbol of this fundamental dividedness. At one moment we see him stubbornly following his own will in deliberate disobedience of the Blue Fairy; at the next, eschewing all temptation to freedom in a frantic flight to her protecting arms. He is a puppet of contrary forces not yet integrated into his nascent ego. It is only after his final adventure with the giant shark, in which he successfully demonstrates mastery over himself, that Pinocchio assumes the form of a hero and the Blue Fairy disappears as an external reality. He ceases to be a puppet and becomes a real boy; she ceases to be a projection and becomes a dream-figure of the *scintilla divinitatis* dwelling within. The solution to the moral conflict met on the first level is therefore confirmed here on the second: personal consciousness and social obligation are harmonized through self-reflection, through union with but not absorption into the place of one's origins, the Great Mother, the realm of the unconscious.

Numerous other images and motifs in *Pinocchio* suggest similar mythological and psychological parallels which would add support to this interpretation of the tale. I would like briefly to consider two of them by way of illustration.

Let us first look at the unusual circumstances surrounding Pinocchio's birth. Master Cherry the carpenter wants to make a table-leg from an ordinary piece of wood, when he hears a voice crying out from it in protest. "Can it be that someone is hidden inside?" he asks himself, and hastens over to the house of his friend Geppetto, who has coincidentally been dreaming up a plan to make a puppet of wood and travel about with it to earn a living. Cherry parts with his log and Geppetto sets to work to carve himself a little marionette, with no further objections from the wood.

The scene immediately brings to mind Michelangelo's neo-Platonic *concetto* theory of art. According to this theory the true artist is one who discovers. He sees in a block of stone, for instance, an inner form which is hidden to the non-artist. His handiwork consists merely in chipping away what is extraneous in order that that form become visible to all. This theory is incarnated in Michelangelo's famous *Prigioni* in Florence's Academy of Fine Arts, figures struggling to get free of the rock which seems to hold them fast. This is also the image which Collodi creates—perhaps wittingly, being a Florentine himself and well acquainted with the art and theories of Michelangelo—in having the puppet *in potentia* (i.e. in a state of relative unconsciousness) cry out from a simple piece of wood, "a log like all the rest." From the very outset, then, the principle of self-realization, according to which everything must deveop after its own ideal, not as a *product* of environmental tools and forces but as a *project* of consciously exercized free will, is articulated in mythopoetic imagery.

The creation of man out of wood is a theme found in a number of mythical traditions. For example, we read in the *Popul Vuh* of the Quiché tribes of southern Guatemala of the gods first creating man out of clay and, finding them blind and stupid, sending a flood to destroy them. Next they carved manikins out of wood; but these creatures had no heart, lacked insight and were forgetful of their creators. They too were destroyed by flood. And so on, until a satisfactory man was made.[21] The parallel is striking (all the more so in that it is nearly impossible that Collodi could have known of it) and shows us the other side of the coin to Pinocchio's creation.

Both in *Pinocchio* and in the Quiché myth the relationship between creature and creator is so symbolized as to accentuate a broken rapport and its eventual restoration. If the wooden manikins turn out contrary to the expectations of the gods, so does Pinocchio show his independence in a manner which brings grief to his poor father. And just as the gods need to experiment with the work of creation in order to achieve success, so does Collodi, dissatisfied with what he has made of his own life, need to recreate himself in the figure of Pinocchio, who in turn has to be cast aside like dead wood to give way to a real boy. In each case the creature, intended as a *reflection* of its creator's best qualities, reveals itself rather as a *distortion*. Its freedom, or capacity for self-formation, frustrates the plans of the gods and requires the redemptive work of a new creation.[22] In other words, if we may dissolve the relationship between Pinocchio and Geppetto into psychological language, man must acknowledge the relativity of consciousness vis-à-vis the accumulated wisdom of tradition if he is to achieve true self-realization; and conversely the keepers of tradition must beware fashioning a society which does not respect the essential freedoms of its individual members.

Secondly, let us consider the figure of the giant shark who swallows first Geppetto and then Pinocchio. Geppetto, we recall, has set off in a little skiff to look for his son. Meantime Pinocchio has nearly succeeded in catching his father up, but arrives at the seashore only in time to see him hopelessly out to sea. He dives in after him and swims to exhaustion until the waves cast him ashore on a sandy island beach. When he awakens a friendly dolphin tells him of the terrible shark who roams these waters and who has probably swallowed good Geppetto. Much later in the story, Pinocchio, now a donkey, is thrown into the sea to be drowned, but miraculously emerges his former self. "It must have been the sea water," he exclaims. "The sea works such extraordinary changes." (Later he tells how the Blue Fairy had sent a school of fish to eat away his donkey's flesh and set him free again.) Pinocchio then swims away to escape the farmer who had purchased him as a donkey, and is soon swallowed by the sea monster, "the Attila of fish and fishermen." When he awakens from the shock he finds himself in "a darkness so black and thick that it seemed to him that he had been dipped head first into an inkwell." Seeing a faint light in the distance, Pinocchio follows it and finds his father, who had been living in the shark for two years. That night they escape through the open mouth of the shark who sleeps with his jaws ajar because he suffers from asthma and heart murmurs. Lifting Geppetto onto his shoulders, Pinocchio swims ashore, with some final help from a passing tuna. He then labors day and night for five months to support his failing father, at the end of which time he becomes a real boy and Geppetto is restored to good health.

The religious and mythical motifs at work here are immediately evident to the reader. Pinocchio's adventure with the giant shark calls to mind stories like that of the Hebrew prophet Jonah or the Algonquin warrior Hiawatha, both swallowed by sea monsters from whose bowels they emerge as heroes.[23] This same motif is re-enacted ritually, with remarkable similarity of detail, among certain New Guinea tribes in their ceremonies of initiation.[24] In addition various structural parallels are to be found in baptismal and penitential rites from a wide variety of religious traditions too numerous to mention. Pinocchio's transformation into a real boy takes the form of a double cleansing. First, the outer animal shell, the weaknesses of the flesh, is eaten away by a school of fishes. Second, the "old man" is devoured by the sea monster and is replaced by a "new man" spiritually reborn. In each instance the change occurs through the dark forces which dwell beneath the waters, the realm where the Blue Fairy is in command. It is she who sends the fish and who lures Pinocchio into the mouth of the giant shark in sirenic fashion by appearing as a little goat on a white rock. In other words, the imagery must be seen as a further elaboration of Pinocchio's archetypal character. By confronting the unconscious the ego is confirmed and enabled to embrace social tradition and personal freedom in one saving act of self-realization. Thus the whole magic lantern of adventures is swept up into this one final heroic gesture of Pinocchio carrying the aged Geppetto on his back across the sea to dry land.

If we are moved and enchanted by the story of Pinocchio it can only be in virtue of some underlying affinity with the material upon which the author has drawn for his tale. In struggling to recover his lost childhood through the symbols of imagination, Collodi refracts the reader's gaze inwards to the often faint and nearly imperceptible truths of his own nature. This process takes three forms, as we have seen. First, it plays fantasy against reality, giving us an insight into the loss of idealism through continued contact with the bitter truth of man's injustice to man. Second, it plays the deeds of desire against the deeds of duty, giving us an insight into the contrary forces out of which responsible self-realization is forged. And third, it plays security against transformation, which gives an insight into man's need to yoke himself to a rhythm transcending the superficialities of the present moment. We are all of us, motherless children, whose task is to integrate our becoming with our origins. *

*Several weeks after my text was written, Glauco Cambon''s *"Pinocchio and the Problem of Children's Literature"* (published in this journal, Vol. 2, 1973, pp. 50-60) came into my hands. If I understand Dr. Cambon correctly, I can only register amazement that our distinct points of view have yielded such similar conclusions. The question of literary genre which I have handled summarily he deals with at length; and most of the psychological themes which I have tried to describe in detail he condenses marvellously *en passant.*

Footnotes

[1]This information is provided by Carlo's nephew, Paolo Lorenzini, who incidentally denies the rumor that it was Carlo's mother who made the decision to place him in the seminary ("Il Collodi," *La Lettura*, November 1930, p. 985).

Unless otherwise indicated, the remainder of the biographical data was drawn from the following sources: Torindo Morganti, *Carlo Collodi* (Florence: Marzocco-Bemporad, 1952); Luigi Santucci, *Collodi* (Brescia: La Scuola, 1961); G. Fanciulli and E. Monaci, *La letteratura per l'infanzia* (Turin: S.E.I., 1949), pp. 209-21.

[2]The best of his journalistic writings have been collected by Giuseppe Rigutini in two volumes, *Note Gaie* and *Divagazioni critico-umoristiche* (Florence: Bemporad, 1892).

[3]Cf. Guido Biagi, *Passatisti* (Florence: La Voce, 1923), pp. 112-14.

[4]Numerous "sequels" to the story appeared later, including one by Collodi's nephew Paolo, though none of them ever achieved the renown of the original *Pinocchio*. Morganti lists the most important in Italian (p. 44). The first English edition, translated by M. A. Murray, appeared in 1892 and remains the best in print. Due to certain inadequacies and omissions, however, I have provided my own translations throughout this essay.

[5]I. Lorenzini, "Collodi," *Il Giornalino della Domenica*, I, 23 November 1906.

[6]Cf. "C. Collodi" in Stanley J. Kunitz and Howard Haycraft, *The Junior Book of Authors* (New York: H. W. Wilson, 1951), pp. 74-76.

[7]P. Lorenzini, pp. 985-6. Note also that Collodi makes Pinocchio a confirmed story-teller who recounts his adventures, though not always very accurately, to any willing listener.

[8]Antonio Baldini, *Fine Ottocento* (Florence: Le Monnier, 1947), pp. 120f. Baldini's theory, developed in his essay "La ragion politica di 'Pinocchio'," is that Collodi wanted to create a utopic Tuscany, cleansed of all moral and political strife, an ideal for which he had long struggled as a journalist (pp. 118f, 122-124). That Collodi had such visions is possible, even likely; but that he was expressing them in *Pinocchio* is a notion that overlooks too much of the non-political character of the book.

[9]Cf. Mario Bernabei, "Commento a Pinocchio," *Rivista pedagogica*, 30 (1937), p. 597.

[10]Cf. Max Lüthi, *Once Upon a Time* (New York: F. Ungar, 1970), pp. 47f.

[11]Amerindo Cammilli, who edited the critical edition of *Pinocchio* (Florence: Sansoni, 1946), notes in his introduction nearly twenty such inconsistencies.

[12]To my knowledge, Santucci has been the only commentator to sense this deeper psychological significance of these projections. See his *La letteratura infantile* (Milan: Fabbri, 1958), p. 32; and his *Collodi*, p. 54.

[13]*The Autobiography of G. K. Chesterton* (New York: Sheed and Ward, 1936), p. 40. It is this truth which the late Professor Tolkien has raised to epic proportions in *The Lord of the Rings*.

[14]It is difficult to find an English equivalent to the Italian *Acchiappacitrulli*. Literally it means "where the innocent (both legally and mentally) are caught red-handed."

[15]"Pinocchio," *La letteratura della nuova Italia* (Bari: Laterza, 1939), Vol. V.

[16]Morganti, p. 25. This I also take to be the reason for Pietro Mignosi's conclusion that *Pinocchio* represents in children's literature what Kant's *Critique of Practical Reason* does in the literature of philosophy. "Il pregiudizio della letteratura per l'infanzia," *L'educazione nazionale* 6:2 (October 1924), pp. 25-26. Cf. A. Michieli, *Commento a Pinocchio* (Turin: Bocca, 1933), pp. 156-158.

[17]It is interesting that Colloci is reported by Ermenegildo Pistelli to have forgotten whether or not he wrote the concluding sentence to *Pinocchio* ("What a fool I was when I was a puppet . . . . and how happy I am now that I have become a real little boy!"). Pistelli suggests that these words may have been added by the editor, Biagi, at the suggestion of Felice Paggi, general editor of all children's literature dealing with moral themes. See Pistelli, *Eroi, uomini e ragazzi* (Florence: Sansoni, 1927), p. 250.

[18]This is, for example, the view of Santucci (pp. 53, 59), who stresses her concreteness and lack of similarity with the fairies of Perrault. Morganti (p. 39) also denies the Blue Fairy any symbolic value.

[19]Cf. P. Lorenzini, p. 986. I have not been able to determine the date of her death, in connection with his assumption of "Collodi" as a pen-name in 1860.

[20]In this regard, see Erich Neumann, *The Origins and History of Consciousness* (Princeton University Press, 1954), pp. 39ff.

[21]*Mythology of All Races*, ed. J. A. MacCullock (Boston: Marshall Jones Co., 1916-1932), 11.163f. An almost identical version of the same creation myth is found among the Dyaks of Borneo (9. 174-175).

[22]P. Bargellini has argued that the main characters of the story can best be understood in terms of Christian theology: Geppetto = God; Pinocchio = man; the Blue Fairy = the Virgin Mary. The movement of the story is then seen to progress along the lines of salvation history: fall, covenant, messianic hopes, redemption, resurrection. *La verità di Pinocchio* (Brescia: Morcelliana, 1942).

Such a theory is not without its supporting evidence, both in the grander themes of the book and in certain specific details. It seems more likely, however, that Collodi has fallen into a mythopoetic genre more basic than that of Christian theology. Then too, Collodi himself was not a church-going Catholic and even showed certain signs of outright impiety on occasion, a fact which caused his mother not a little grief (see P. Lorenzini, p. 986). This should not lead us to conclude as Michieli has (pp. 158f) that the absence of deliberate religious beliefs renders *Pinocchio* somehow imperfect and incomplete.

[23]Walt Disney's famous animation of *Pinocchio* (probably the most successful of all the folktales and children's stories he has brought to the screen) depicts the giant shark as a whale named Monstro, thus recalling the widespread mistranslation of the biblical sea monster (*tannin*) in the story of Jonah. The escape scene in the Disney version is also of great interest. Pinocchio builds a fire which produces so much smoke that Monstro is forced to cough up his prisoners. An exact parallel occurs in a Maori myth where the hero, Nganaoa, finds his parents in the belly of a whale and builds a fire to set them free. *Mythology of All Races*, 9.69. See also Stith Thompson, *Motif-Index of Folk-Literature* (Bloomington: Indiana University Press, 1966), F.911.4.

For an interesting commentary on the profound personal repercussions of *Pinocchio* for Disney himself and their effects on the finished product, see Richard Schickel, *The Disney Version* (New York: Simon and Schuster, 1968), pp. 225-27.

[24]James George Frazer, *Balder the Beautiful* (London: Macmillan, 1966), 2.239-241.

Heroic Quintuplets:
A Look at Some Chinese Children's Literature

Thomas A. Zaniello

Once upon a time there were two fairy tales, one American, the other Chinese. Although worlds apart, the two tales recount ostensibly the same events: how five look-alike Chinese brothers, each of whom has a different superhuman power, circumvent a death sentence decreed for one of their number. My texts are the American *Five Chinese Brothers* (1938) by Claire Huchet Bishop, with illustrations by Kurt Weise, and the anonymous Chinese *Five Little Liu Brothers* (1960), with illustrations by Wang Yu-Chuan (in English translation from the Foreign Languages Press in Peking).[1]

Both versions of the tale begin with one of the brothers getting into trouble and end with all of the brothers avoiding punishment; both sets of brothers (with one exception) have the same superhuman powers: one can swallow the sea, a second has a neck that can resist the executioner's axe, a third can stretch his legs to any length (and can therefore survive being thrown from great heights), and a fourth cannot be burned. In the American version, the fifth brother "could hold his breath indefinitely," while the Chinese fifth brother, called "The Know-All," can "speak the languages of all birds and animals."

The significant difference between the two tales lies not in the varying roles of the fifth brother but in the *source* of the brothers' difficulty and its *resolution*. In the American version, the brother who can swallow the sea tries to help a little boy who wants to go fishing. The brother sucks up the sea so that the little boy can roam the sea-bed at will. The little boy refuses to return at the pre-arranged signal and is drowned by the sea-waters as they rush out of an exhausted Chinese brother. This first brother is arrested and condemned by a judge for killing the boy, but before each attempt at execution, a different Chinese brother takes his place. Of course, the brothers survive all attempts at execution and the judge who condemned him (them) originally releases him (them), assuming that he (they) must be innocent, since execution is impossible.

This rather kindly looking and permissive judge is replaced in the Chinese version by a nasty, marauding "big official" from the city. The "big official" begins the Chinese version by leading a hunting band of his men into the countryside of the five Chinese brothers. Brother "Know-All" warns his sheep and all the other animals of the forest to hide. The "big official" suspects his bad luck in the field is due to Know-All and he orders this brother to be thrown into a cage with a tiger. Know-All quickly befriends the tiger; the enraged official orders a new execution. The brothers' drama of exchanging places begins, as in the American version, but with certain crucial differences.

In the Chinese version there is no judge and no trial; the brothers are not given permission by a judge to visit their mother to say farewell (and thereby exchange places easily), but each night the brother escapes from the autocratic official; and finally, the Chinese version has a happy ending only *after* the violent death of the "big official" and his retinue when they attempt to throw overboard the brother who can swallow the sea. This brother swallows the sea and spits it out on the stranded official and his men:

> He sent the billows and rolling waves and drowned the big official and his men in the turbulent water. At dusk the water became very tranquil and peaceful. Only an official's hat floated on the calm surface of the blue, blue sea.

The Chinese version of the fairy tale reflects—like all the other English translations of Chinese children's books available to us—[2] situations and issues typical of a developing communist society.[3] There is an overt, sometimes violent class struggle, which in the *Five Little Liu Brothers* is between the country folk and the city's ruling elite; there is, in addition, a special representative of the people who are struggling to survive at the bottom of society; in this Chinese tale, the representatives are the superhuman brothers, the heroic quintuplets.

The five Liu brothers are typical heroes of a recent phase of Chinese socialist culture—the early 1960's—insofar as we can judge from published translations from Peking.[4] The development of such popular heroes in socialist literature and art, a function of Marxist aesthetic theory, has been, since at least the 1920's, one of the characteristic features of Marxist culture, not only in the socialist countries (especially the Soviet Union and China), but also in Marxist movements in the United States.[5] The question of the kind of popular hero or heroine who should appear in literature and art is linked not only to certain key problems in socialist aesthetics but also to political and cultural questions. In the 1930's, for example, the questions of "socialist realism" (the realistic projection of a developing revolutionary society in artistic forms) and the "typicality" of socialist heroes (heroes who represent the revolutionary potential of society) dominated Marxist thought not only in the Soviet Union but wherever the "international" of writers with Marxist and leftist orientations met and debated. The Chinese, one of the peoples today most self-conscious about projecting its heroes, have their own version of the typical heroes of socialist culture, heroes whom they characterize as models of conduct. Questions of socialist literature and culture must, for the most part, be considered also as questions of politics.

This close relationship of politics and art elevated Chairman Mao's *Talks at the Yenan Forum on Literature and Art* (1942) to its influential and popular position. Although Mao's statement is the result of his specific resolutions on critical controversies in the Chinese Marxist cultural movement of the late 1930's and early 1940's, it functions in Chinese culture today as a general sourcebook of aphorisms with wide-ranging practical application.[6] Mao argues in the *Talks* that "people are not satisfied with life alone and demand literature and art as well." Why? He continues:

> Because, while both [literature and art] are beautiful, life as reflected in works of literature and art can and ought to be on a higher plane, more intense, more concentrated, more typical, nearer the ideal, and therefore more universal than actual everyday life. Revolutionary literature and art should create a variety of characters out of real life and help the masses to propel history forward. For example, there is suffering from hunger, cold and oppression, and also there is exploitation and oppression of man by man. These facts exist everywhere and people look upon them as

commonplace. Writers and artists concentrate such everyday phenomena, typify the contradictions and struggles within them and produce works which awaken the masses, fire them with enthusiasm and impel them to unite and struggle to transform their environment.[7]

Mao's thesis is essentially that of the Soviet socialist realism school of the 1930's, although he does not refer to socialist realism explicitly. The implication of Mao's words is clear: literature, including children's literature of course, is not only a cultural manifestation, but part of the political arena as well.

Chinese children's literature available to us in translation comes from two distinct periods. The first is the main period of Soviet influence, in terms of the cultural life of China, which ended in the early 1960's. Second, there is the explosion of popular heroes in literature, art, and other cultural forms during the mid-1960's period which the Chinese call the "Great Proletarian Cultural Revolution" or, more simply, the "Cultural Revolution."

The Cultural Revolution is clearly the definitive event of the 1960's not only for China's cultural life but for her political struggles. The beginning of this Revolution is variously dated: 1963, the year in which Chiang Ching, Mao's wife, criticized traditional Peking Opera as bourgeois, is sometimes emphasized. But 1967, when the head of Peking University was publicly criticized in a poster, is also significant.[8] Partly a reaction against the development of non-collective practices in the political-economic sphere—such as workers receiving individual bonuses and peasants cultivating individual plots of land—the Cultural Revolution most often represented critical attacks on leading members of China's cultural elite. The main criticism directed against the high-level intellectuals was that their theoretical articles were weak Marxism and that they, like their Soviet counterparts, in practice permitted many examples of non-socialist art to flourish. Chiang Ching summarizes this criticism in the pamphlet *On the Revolution in Peking Opera* (1964) when she writes that the operatic stage is dominated not by characters representing workers, peasants, and soldiers, but by "emperors, princes, generals, ministers, scholars and beauties, and on top of these, ghosts and monsters."[9]

Children's literature apparently did not remain exempt from these cultural and political struggles. It is in terms of the "heroic" image that children's literature reflects the changes of the Cultural Revolution. The *Five Little Liu Brothers,* with which I began this study, is a pre-Cultural-Revolution tale of heroes; another earlier fairy-tale, *The Golden Axe* (1958), edited by Yang Chu and illustrated by Li Tien-hsin, tells of Chen Ping who works for Skinflint Wang. Chen Ping meets a mysterious old man one day on his way to chop wood; the old man then rescues Chen's iron axe which had fallen into a stream. The old man had first offered Chen silver and gold axes, but Chen refused each offer, saying that they were not his axes. Struck by his woodsman's tale, Skinflint deliberately goes back to the stream and throws the iron axe in. The old man appears again, offering Skinflint first the iron, then the silver, and finally, the gold, axes: Skinflint denies owning the first and keeps the last two, only to fall into the stream himself and disappear. The moral?

And how about Chen Ping? He returned home and every day went to the mountain

38

to cut wood with his wonderful iron axe. He gathered so much wood that he earned enough to keep his mother and father and himself as well, so they had a very happy life. [10]

These last lines are accompanied by an illustration, in traditional Chinese style, showing Chen's beautiful, rustic (but individual) home, his parents in the yard, and Chen, who approaches his home from a mountain road with his wood cuttings.

Both pre-Cultural-Revolution tales deal with supernatural events and employ super-heroes (human beings with superhuman powers). Although both tales are about class struggle—country boys against a "big official" and a greedy boss—the dilemma in each case is resolved by individual exploits which permit a single family to live happily ever after.

It is perhaps unfair to generalize on the basis of these two early tales (even if they are two of the very few officially released translations). But if we compare these early tales to children's books published and released during the Cultural Revolution, the change in heroic images is obvious. The Cultural Revolution stories usually deal with young children in service to other people, fighting for a collective goal, often (but not exclusively) with revolutionary or guerilla war themes. The children depicted in the tales live humanly but act heroically. One tale, *Secret Bulletin* (English version, 1965), describes the underground activities of two urban youngsters who mimeograph a newspaper. One of the children tries to be heroic in the face of suspicious Kuomintang (i.e., the enemy) policemen; he succeeds: "I stood my ground like a hero."[11] In another encounter with a Kuomintang spy he fails, exposing his secret mission, and is rescued by his brother and a comrade from the newspaper. His comrade (younger, and a girl) draws the obvious lessons: it is better to work in a group, for the individual tends to show off and make mistakes. Here, significantly, we have the *heroine* with the best lines; *Secret Bulletin*, like other children's books in China, generally avoids sex-typing.

Some of the other Cultural Revolution tales are on war themes—such as *It Happened in a Coconut Grove* (English version, 1965), on the anti-Japanese struggles—but most deal with themes of service to the child's community; the titles are self-revelatory: *Brave Little Sheperd Chaolu* (1963; English version, 1964), *Hunting with Grandad* (English version, 1965), *The Little Doctor* (English version, 1965).[12] One characteristic tale, *I Am on Duty Today* (English version, 1966), is a very didactic story about Tung-tung, narrated by another youngster, both of whom are about six or seven years old. The two youngsters, helping out in a nursery, are the only children in the story who wear what appears to be the red arm band of the Red Guards (the general name of the many different revolutionary youth groups). The narrator is always self-conscious:

> After our nap we have refreshments.
> Tung-tung passes the sweets, I take round the biscuits.
> The large and good ones I give to the children,
> And keep the small ones for myself.[13]

In addition, the narrator emphasizes the Cultural Revolution themes of service to the people and the heroic images of soldiers (often the only force for stability during the hectic period of the Cultural Revolution):

> Now is the time for drawing.
> Today I do not draw flowers and birds
> Or high mountains and streams,
> But a little soldier hero.
>
>   .   .   .   .
>
> We wake [from naps] and get up from our beds,
> And dress ourselves carefully.
> "Let me comb your loosened plaits."
> It is good to help each other.[14]

The Cultural Revolution tales for children have an emphasis similar to mass-circulation pamphlets about "model" heroes which, in narrative and in "comic" book form, are read by adults and children. The role of a model in all of these popular forms of literature reflects other spheres in Chinese life. As Roger Howard, an English writer who has worked and studied in China, points out in his analysis of Maoist political decision-making, the "method of formulating a policy for a course of action is not meant to be obeyed but to be used as an example or the Chinese say, as a 'model'," which is not to be copied directly but is to be "reconstructed" in a new situation depending upon "specific local, technical, professional and personal conditions."[15] In terms of the heroic image in all forms of literature, the model approach develops a "competition" among those who selflessly contribute to the collective; in Howard's words: "Each model, styling himself on another model and adding his own particular character, builds up a many-faceted scheme of revolutionary correctness."[16]

If this "modeling" process seems too overtly political and didactic, we are certainly not missing the point of most Chinese children's literature. Such literature rarely operates symbolically or psychologically, but instead copies a reality which either existed (revolutionary war against oppressors of the upper classes or invading nations) or is developing (revolutionary struggles against internal enemies or selfishness). The ideology, however artfully or charmingly developed, is nonetheless overt.

Footnotes

[1] My principal texts: Claire Huchet Bishop, *The Five Chinese Brothers* (1938; Scholastic Book Services: New York, 7th printing, 1967); and *The Five Little Liu Brothers*, illus. Wang Yu-chuan (1960; Foreign Languages Press: Peking, 3rd ed., 1964). There is available, from Weston Woods Studios (Weston, Conn.) an enjoyable and faithful color-film version of Bishop's book. I have traced two other versions of the "American" form of the tale, both resembling in most details Bishop's book: "The Five Queer Brothers," in Lim Sian-tak, *More Folk Tales from China* (New York, 1948) and in *Tales of Wonder: A Fourth Fairy Book*, ed. Kate Douglas Wiggin and Nora Archibald Smith (Garden City, 1928). The latter version has the additional detail of the brothers' concealing "their peculiar traits" (p. 41), thereby employing a mechanism which eliminates any cynic's observation that the brothers' neighbors might have "given them away."

2   Most of the Chinese materials translated into English in paperback or pamphlet form are not available in libraries but can be purchased in inexpensive editions from one of the offices of China Books and Publications, an import firm located at the following addresses: 2929 24th St., San Francisco, Calif. 94110; 900 W. Armitage Ave., Chicago, Ill. 60614; 95 5th Ave., New York City, N.Y. 10003.

3   I am aware of the difficulties in the use of the words "communist," "socialist," and "Marxist," and I have therefore attempted to limit their meanings in the following manner: "communist," to describe (as the Chinese most often do) the kind of *society* they wish to have or the *party* they do have; "socialist," to describe the *economy* of a country which has eliminated private enterprise; and "Marxist," to describe an *ideology* or *tradition* of thought. I admit, however, that this is a thorny thicket of definitions. I hope that in each case the context should keep the reader from being pricked.

4   We are dealing here with a special problem in access: in a socialist country, one does not order books directly from this or that private publisher but in effect from state organs. However, a recently available English translation (not done by the Chinese) of Chinese "comic books" which serve both adults and children - *The People's Comic Book*, trans. Endymion Wilkinson (Anchor Press: Garden City, 1973) - indicates quite clearly that both in content and form the materials translated by the Chinese for our consumption are typical of the materials the Chinese themselves read.

5   I have given the background to this paragraph in my paper, "The Popular Hero in Socialist Culture and Marxist Aesthetics," presented at the 3rd Annual Conference of the Popular Culture Association of America, Indianapolis, April 13, 1973.

6   See D.W. Fokkema, *Literary Doctrine in China and Soviet Influence 1956-1960* (The Hague, 1965), pp. 11-27, for an account of the Communist authors whom Mao implicitly criticizes in his *Talks*.

7   Mao Tse-tung, *Talks at the Yenan Forum on Literature and Art* (1942; Foreign Languages Press: Peking, 1965; 4th ed. and 3rd revised trans., 1965), p. 19.

8   Joan Robinson, *The Cultural Revolution in China* (Penguin Books: London, 1969), pp. 49, 18. Because the Cultural Revolution did not affect all state bureaus at the same time, a 1958 book may be reprinted in 1965 (*during* the Cultural Revolution), as was *The Golden Axe* (see note 10, below), yet seem clearly out of character with the mood of the Cultural Revolution, because the policy of the publishing bureau had not yet changed.

9   Chiang Ching, *On the Revolution in Peking Opera* (Foreign Languages Press: Peking, 1968), p. 2. Her speech was actually delivered in 1963 at a festival of operas.

10   *The Golden Axe*, ed. Yang Chu, illus. Li Tien-hsin (1958; 4th ed., 1965; Foreign Languages Press: Peking, 1965), no page number.

11   Kao Shao, *Secret Bulletin*, illus. Hua San-chuan, ed. Shanghai Juvenile Publishing House (Foreign Languages Press: Peking, 1965), no page number.

12   Yeh Tan, *It Happened in a Coconut Grove*, illus. Lin Wan-tsui, ed. Shanghai Juvenile Publishing House (Foreign Languages Press: Peking, 1965); Chiang Nan, *Brave Little Shepherd Chaolu*, illus. Han Shu-yu (1963; 2nd ed., 1964; Foreign Languages Press: Peking, 1964); Chao Fu-hsing, *Hunting*

with Grandad, illus. Yang Yung-ching, ed. China Juvenile Publishing House (Foreign Languages Press: Peking, 1965); and Chang Mao-chiu, *The Little Doctor*, illus. Yang Wen-hsiu, ed. Shanghai Juvenile Publishing House (Foreign Languages Press: Peking, 1965).

13   Yang Yi and Liang Ko, *I Am on Duty Today*, ed. Shanghai Juvenile Publishing House (Foreign Languages Press: Peking, 1966), no page number.

14   Yang Yi and Liang Ko, *I Am on Duty Today*, no page number.

15   Roger Howard, "Thinking and Changing," *China Now* (publication of the Society for Anglo-Chinese Understanding, London), June, 1972, p. 11.

16   Roger Howard, "Heroes in Art and 'Real Life'," *China Now*, November, 1970, p. 9.

Children's Literature in Austria

Eva M. Lederer

Critical interest in juvenile literature in Austria and attempts to improve the quality of reading materials available for children go back at least as far as 1902, when the Vienna Society for Adult Education began publishing an annual list of recommended children's books.[1] This compilation was based on very carefully formulated selection criteria along literary and pedagogic lines. Soon, various other organizations dedicated to the same purpose started to issue similar lists of their own.

At the present time, the market of children's literature in Austria seems to be fairly well dominated by the "Austrian Children's Book Club" *Österreichischer Buchklub der Jugend.* Founded in 1948, this "non-partisan, mutual-interest" organization has as its express purpose the furthering of good juvenile literature and the elimination of poor reading materials. Since its establishment, the Club has expanded very rapidly and by 1972 reached a total of some 900,000 members, or about 90% of all Austrian school children.

Membership, which is by subscription only, is organized and administered by the teachers in the public schools. This is thought to be the most efficient method for reaching a maximum number of children. For an annual fee of 15 Austrian Schillings (about $1.00), members are entitled to four coupons a year which enable them to purchase four Book Club selections in any book store at a 25% discount. They can choose among about 150 listed titles, both paperback and hardcover, issued by Austrian publishers and comprising both Austrian authors and translations from other countries. In addition, children receive a yearbook, graded according to age level, with excerpts and illustrations from recommended titles, plus illustrated lists of choices which are supposed to help in building a home library. The parents of each member also receive a parents' yearbook, "Your Child Comes to You,"[2] comparable to a PTA magazine. There are two versions: one for parents of children from four to ten, and the other from ten to fifteen. These publications contain articles on various aspects of raising children, on juvenile reading habits, etc., and include lists of recommended titles, both of literature for the children and on educational problems for the parents.

The founder and central moving force behind this organization is Dr. Richard Bamberger, Professor at the Pedagogical Institute of Vienna, who since 1947 has specialized in children's literature, the development of good reading habits in young people, reading research, and the training of primary teachers in the field of children's literature. Within the framework of the Book Club he established, in 1965, the International Institute for Juvenile Literature and Reading Research,[3] of which he is director. The emphasis of the Institute, which is dedicated to theoretical research, is mainly pedagogical. In cooperation with the Book Club, it issues a quarterly periodical, "Young People and Books,"[4] aimed at and distributed without charge to teachers and administrators of the Book Club. This magazine offers a few professional articles on the teaching of reading and similar topics, news of the Book Club, and a large section of about 50 reviews of new children's books. These reviews are printed on individual detachable index cards to permit easy filing, and provide detailed information as to genre, plot, locale, time period, and age level. Also graded as to literary value, reading difficulty, and plot interest, they provide a very handy tool for school teachers and children's librarians.

In addition, the Institute also issues two other publications. The first of these, *Bookbird*, is an English-language quarterly which purports to be "an international survey of theoretical and practical work in the service of good books for children and young people, and . . . a medium for introducing books of international interest for people working with children."[5] In keeping with the main interest of the Institute, the emphasis is largely pedagogical rather than literary. Contributions are written by professors at teacher training institutions in various countries. The magazine reports on trends, activities, and meetings in the field of reading and education all over the world, surveys prize-winning books of various countries, reviews professional literature, etc.

The other publication, *1000 und 1 Buch* ("A Thousand and One Books"), issued annually, is a brief annotated list of recommended children's titles, divided according to age groups and genre, and rated as to literary value, content interest, and reading difficulty. The selection is directed at teachers, librarians, youth leaders, and parents, and is arrived at cooperatively by the selection board of the Institute and a committee on child development of the School of Developmental and Educational Psychology at the University of Vienna. The choices include a wide variety of titles from all over the world.

There is evidently a very close relationship between the Book Club and the public school system on the one hand and the Austrian publishing industry on the other. The fifteen or so Austrian children's publishing houses depend heavily on the recommendations of the Club. It is also a somewhat closed corporation, since non-Austrian publishers are excluded by the selection committees for the Book Club and for the children's book awards presented by both the Austrian national government and the city of Vienna.[6] To be sure, there are other children's books published and sold outside of the framework of the Book Club, but its importance and its influence are obvious. It is also interesting to note that *Bookbird, 1000 und 1 Buch,* and the various yearbooks of the Book Club are all published by the Verlag für Jugend und Volk, Vienna, one of the Austrian children's book publishers. In addition, there is some evidence of governmental support, through the tie-in with the public school system and the fact that the Honorary President of the Book Club is Dr. Fred Sinowatz, Secretary of Education of the Austrian Federal Government.

The Austrian national awards and the city of Vienna prizes have been offered annually since 1955 and 1954 respectively. They are awarded to living authors and illustrators of Austrian birth or origin whose books have been published by Austrian publishers (or Viennese ones, in the case of the City Prizes).

It is interesting to compare these awards[7] with the titles listed in *The Best of the Best,*[8] a selection of the most worthwhile children's books from 57 countries, drawn from the holdings of the International Youth Library in Munich. There is considerable agreement between these titles and the book prizes as well as, to a more limited extent, the Book Club selections.

The greatest numbers of coinciding titles appear in the 7-9 year and 13-15 year age groups. All except one title in each of these categories on the *Best of the Best* lists also received the State and/or City prizes. They include probably the best and most popular and prolific children's authors of the country: Vera Ferra-Mikura, Mira Lobe, Käthe Recheis, the poetess Christina Busta, Richard Bamberger (as editor of fairy tale collections), Winfried Bruckner, Fritz Habeck, Herbert Tichy, and Othmar Franz Lang. Books by most of these authors were also chosen as Book Club selections, although not always the same titles. In the 3-6 year and 10-12 year categories, only two of the titles in *Best of the Best* have been honored by an award or selected by the Book Club: Marlen Haushofer's *Müssen Tiere draussen bleiben?* and Peter Fuch's *Ambasira.* Most of the other titles, however, were reviewed and recommended in one of the aforementioned Book Club journals. Many of the authors listed in *The Best of the Best* such as Franz Braumann, Karl Bruckner, Auguste Lechner, Gerhart Ellert, Georg Schreiber, and Max Stebich, were awarded prizes for other titles. The discrepancy in these two age groups, especially in the 10-12 year category, may not be due so much to differences in selection criteria or standards as to the stronger emphasis on international and inter-cultural content which is the motivating force of the International Youth Library.

The Book Club *recommendations* cover a wide range of works, from classics, translations, and anthologies to newer titles for all ages, and include those honored by the State and City Prizes. Only occasionally, however, does the Book Club *selection* coincide with the prize awards, and then usually in the young children's category. Judging from the limited evidence of the yearbook excerpts and the lists, the Book Club selections on the whole do not tend to be chosen primarily for literary value, but rather for the contributions they could make to the child's reading progress and learning experience. On the younger levels, especially, they tend to be didactic, and to tie in with obvious religious and moral teachings. They are often reminiscent of "Golden Books," and are strongly oriented along the lines of family stereotypes: mother—kitchen, father—work, grandmother—story telling, and so forth.

This definite pedagogical orientation is reflected in the Book Club's general attitude toward children's reading. Books are meant for school and learning, rather than for pleasure or fun. Though the city libraries have story-telling hours, there is no summer reading program. "Don't make the children read in the summer—let them relax," seems to be the prevailing attitude.

Research being conducted in the field of children's literature in Austria is primarily relegated to the teacher training institutes and to departments of educational psychology and education at the universities. As a field for literary research, the subject is largely ignored by the liberal arts faculties of the universities. A study of the professional articles in *Jugend und Buch* and *Bookbird* clearly reveals this trend, and I was unable to discover any articles on the subject by Austrian academicians in other periodicals.

It might be interesting to compare this state of affairs with the situation in West Germany, especially since articles in the various Book Club publications are frequently written by German authors and often refer to the status of children's literature in the Federal Republic of Germany. According to Dr. Hans Giehrl, Professor of Education at the University of Regensburg, the predominantly pedagogical orientation also holds true in West Germany, where only isolated lecture courses or seminars dealing with children's literature are held by faculty members in the disciplines of language or literature.[9] Apparently, such research is being conducted mainly because of the interest of a few individual instructors. Two special institutes have been set up for study in this field: The Institute for Juvenile Book Research at the University of Frankfurt, directed by Dr. Klaus Doderer, and the Children's Literature Institute of the Teachers' College in Worms. On the whole, Giehrl feels that training and research in juvenile literature is spotty, varies greatly from state to state, and is restricted mainly to primary rather than secondary school teachers. There is, however, some evidence of interest in finding new criteria for literary criticism of children's books, in literary-sociological and socio-linguistic questions, in political aspects and social criticism, in the "anti-authoritarian" children's books, in the preponderance of "trivial" (pop) literature, and in the study of genres rather than the body of literature as a whole, in addition to the obvious stress on the use of children's literature for the teaching of language and reading.

In another article, Dr. Alfred Clemens Baumgärtner, Professor of Language Arts Methodology at the Justus-Liebig University in Wiesbaden, discusses new trends in picture book production in West Germany.[10] It is interesting to note that in Germany, as well as in Austria, a large new market for "educational" books has been created as a result of the pre-school boom. It is apparently no longer enough for a children's picture book to be attractive and entertaining, it must be "educational" as well.

On the other hand, there also seems to be a small but influential "anti-authoritarian," politically motivated movement in the German Federal Republic, initiated by collectives and student activist groups who have been writing and publishing children's books. As far as I have been able to ascertain, Austria does not show any evidence of a parallel movement or influence.

Baumgärtner also describes a growing trend in West Germany to accept the comic book form, to work with it, and not to regard it as the antithesis to "good" literature. Again, this tendency has no apparent counterpart in Austrian book production. The only marginal similarity is found in the use of the paper booklet format for inexpensive graded reading series, such as "The Golden Ladder" and "The Great Adventure."[11] These are abbreviated versions of hardcover editions, anthologies, originals by popular authors, a few translations of excerpts from classics issued by the Austrian Book Club. Except for the colorful cover, they have only rather uninspiring black and white illustrations and are not particularly attractive. They would not be likely to have the same appeal as the imaginative use of the comic book format in a few of the newer German publications, described by Baumgärtner.

On the other hand, the Austrian Children's Book Club performs a very useful service by providing valuable guidance to parents and teachers, and by making juvenile books available to children at a considerable discount. Some of the titles issued by the Club are written by authors of considerable renown and many of them are profusely illustrated in color by such excellent artists as Susi Weigel, Romulus Candea, and Emanuela Wallenta. On the whole, however, the literary quality of children's books in Austria does not seem to be at quite the level of recent juvenile literature in other countries, nor as sophisticated as its pedagogical design.

Footnotes

[1]Herman L. Köster, *Geschichte der deutschen Jugendliteratur*, Monograph Series, ed. Walter Scherf (Munich-Pullach: Verlag Dokumentation, 1968 [c. 1927]), pp. 444f.

[2]*Dein Kind kommt zu dir*, published jointly by the Austrian Book Club and the Austrian Parents Organization for Public Schools.

[3]Internationales Institut für Jugendliteratur und Leseforschung, Vienna.

[4]*Jugend und Buch.* Vierteljahresschrift für Leseerziehung und Jugendliteratur, Vienna.

[5]Advertising leaflet issued by *Bookbird*, International Periodical on Literature for Children and Young People (Vienna: Verlag für Jugend und Volk).

[6]Österreichische Staatspreise für Kleinkinderbücher, Kinder- und Jugendliteratur, awarded by the Austrian Federal Ministry of Education; and Kinder- und Jugendbuchpreise der Stadt Wien, presented by the Office for Culture, Education, and School Administration of Vienna.

[7]Prizes awarded up to 1968 are listed in *Preisgekrönte Kinderbücher. Children's Prize Books*, ed. by Walter Scherf. Internationale Jugendbibliothek. München-Pallach: Verlag Dokumentation, 1969.

[8]Internationale Jugendbibliothek München, *The Best of the Best*, ed. Walter Scherf (New York: R.R. Bowker, 1971), pp. 15-16.

[9]Hans Giehrl, "Children's Literature in the Teacher Training Programme of the Federal Republic of Germany," *Bookbird*, 11 (1973), No. 1, 23-26.

[10]Alfred C. Baumgärtner, "Neue Tendenzen in der Bilderbuchproduktion in der BRD: Intelligenzförderung, Politisierung, Comics," *Jugend und Buch*, 1 (1973), 10-15.

[11]*Die goldene Leiter*, a series published jointly by Verlag für Jugend und Volk, Vienna, and Österreichischer Bundesverlag, Vienna; *Das grosse Abenteuer*, a series published jointly by Österreichischer Bundesverlag, Vienna, and Verlag für Jugend und Volk, Vienna.

The Travail of Jewish Children's Literature

Leonard R. Mendelsohn

Ethnic interests control a significant segment of current children's literature. This fad is readily reflected in conferences and conventions, in journals, in book reviews, and advertisements. Black literature, once the principal ethnic mode, now must share the stage with tales and traditions of Chinese, Chicanos and Chippewas, Poles and Puerto Ricans, Apaches, Italians and Eskimos. No group is too remote or numerically insignificant not to appeal to the outranging appetites of the general reader, and classroom reading fare often resembles a literary soup line ready to serve up all kinds of minority customs and adventures. Peculiarly inconspicuous in this harvest of cultures are the Jews, the people of the Book themselves. Jews, unlike some groups currently enjoying expanded literary coverage, are a people long associated with the production of books, and yet they make only a feeble contribution to the present ethnic extravaganza.

The offerings in Jewish children's literature are impressive neither quantitatively nor qualitatively. A recent issue of *Judaica Book News*, a semi-annual periodical devoted to blazoning anything in print which is even remotely Jewish, lists some twenty-five titles under the heading "New and Forthcoming Books: Books for Young Readers." Ostensibly this might appear to be a respectable amount for a twice yearly listing, but the editors of necessity made the subject quite elastic in order to secure sufficient numbers to allow children's literature to qualify as a legitimate category.

Among the titles considered juvenile Judaica are a book on the Crusades; a study of the Arab world in the twentieth century; a biography of Felix Mendelssohn (who was not a Jew); a volume comparing ten religions; and a story describing certain archaeological finds. All of these books bear only the most ephemeral relationship to things Jewish. If the crusades, the Arabs, and a composer with a Jewish grandfather are directly relevant to Jewish literature, then by the same standards books on suburban white America would be of immediate relevance to blacks, and sexist literature of considerable appropriateness to everyone interested in women's liberation. Some other titles on the list are more nearly related to Jewish concerns but are hardly evidence of any creative flourish. Among these marginal literaria are a pop-up book on Noah's ark, some retellings of three Bible stories, a reissue of the Children's Passover Haggadah, and biographies of Helena Rubenstein and David Sarnoff.

There is of course a biography of Eliezer ben Yehudah and his fanatical but successful struggle to revive Hebrew as a spoken language, and there is *The Upstairs Room* by Johanna Reiss which recounts the adventures of two young Dutch girls in hiding from the Nazis, an apparent expansion of the Anne Frank tradition. But the remainder, including two quasi-textbook studies of Judaism, Jewish holidays and Israel, and two picture books catering to the fashion for nostalgia by depicting bygone eras of Jewish life in America, are hardly very exciting literary ventures. And allowing for inevitable omissions, therein lies the bulk of what might be generously labeled Jewish literature for children during one half year.

While it may be argued that I have selected but a single issue, and that the catalog, if complete and accurate, may simply reflect a particularly lean year, almost any librarian, bookseller, educator or concerned parent will confirm that the famine in Jewish children's literature is one of long standing, so long in fact that it is difficult to recall good times. The recently published *Encyclopaedia Judaica* (1971) devotes some fifteen full pages (including several of charts and illustrations) to an article on children's literature, but the assemblage is noteworthy for the paucity of familiar authors and memorable titles. True, there are such notables as Israel Zangwill, Chaim Nachman Bialik and Isaac Leib Peretz, but neither Zangwill's *Prince of Schnorers* nor Bialik's *Tales of King Solomon* can rate as classics comparable with *The Wind in the Willows, The Wizard of Oz* or *A Child's Garden of Verses.* Possibly the most famous achievement by a Jewish author in the field of juvenile literature is *Bambi* by Felix Salten (1869-1947), a Prague born Austrian writer and theater critic. But the scope of Jewish literature would have to be expanded beyond its already absurdly loose dimensions to incorporate this woodland fantasy within the genre. The stimulus of awards for the best writing in the field of Jewish children's literature has prompted increased activity and a greater output, but the quality still ranges from mediocre downward.

Surely the sorry state of Jewish children's literature cannot be blamed on a shortage of competent Jewish authors. The phenomenon of an American Jewish novel with Roth, Bellow, Malamud and others, or the holocaust literature, particularly some distinguished work by Elie Wiesel, suggest that talent is available. Nor can it be said that the Jewish tradition cannot provide provocative material for its writers, for there are copious treasuries of narratives, and there is a lengthy history extending through centuries and civilizations, replete with social dilemmas and an intriguing gallery of complex personalities—all inviting literary expansion. Furthermore it is obvious that numerous writers have tried their hand at developing these materials as literature for children, though without any notable achievements. It would seem natural that a conflux of talent and such resources should produce a flowering of children's literature. But the promise of these fortunate conditions has simply not been fulfilled.

If reasons for the inadequacy of Jewish children's literature are to be found, they are most likely to be discovered in problems deriving from a basic incompatibility of traditional Jewish materials and vernacular literatures. Each time a good English model is used to display a Jewish theme, the result is invariably poor parody or an outright flop. There have been, for example, several ventures into Mother Goose land trying to versify Jewish identity by adapting some of these immortal lyrics. The ludicrous outcome may be sampled in a book entitled *Rhyme-land for Jewish Children* (New York, 1951).

> Doodle-doodle-doo!
> What does our *Chazzen* (cantor) do?
> He sings for me and you,
> Doodle-doodle-doo!

Or the following treat for Jewish young:

> *Shammos* be nimble,
> *Shammos* be quick,
> *Shammos* light all the Chanukah *licht* (lights).

(The *shammos* is the candle which kindles all the others in the Chanukah candlelabrum.)

Presumably parents and their offspring are to delight in ethnic paraphrase and then to awake and sing things Jewish. Gone are the fun, the verve, the tight rhythms and the catchy rhymes of the English verse treasury, and in their place are uninspired scatterings of Hebrew and Yiddish terminology, all totally lacking the depth, mystery and spirit of the concepts they purport to represent.

Another plum from the same garden of Jewish delights dwells on Passover.

> Bye, Baby Bunting,
> *Abba's* (Daddy's) gone a hunting,
> The *Afikomen* must be found,
> If you saw where I hid it—
> Sh—don't make a sound.
> (The *Afikomen* is the last of the matzoh consumed at the ritual Passover meal.)

Such culture straddling is a sad characteristic of Jewish children's literature. Not only does this rhyme lack the warm mood and lyric facility of its model, which succinctly links the baby's snug and secret world with the father's less innocent occupation in a more apparent realm, but in its place we have nothing of the copious inspiration of the Passover celebration, only a pair of ethnic terms, a Hebrew word for father and a mention of the search for the *Afikomen*. And these terms are void of any poetical appropriateness or suggestiveness, at least in the context in which they appear.

While the examples I have chosen might be egregiously bad, they are unfortunately representative, and they suggest a reason for the sad state of Jewish literature for children in English as well as other vernaculars: the audience to which the writing is directed is primarily one which identifies with English childhood classics. Models and attitudes are essentially those of the vernacular tradition, and the Jewish elements are for the most part intrusions upon the established forms and the linguistic ease of this tradition. Conversely, Jewish concepts could hardly discover, in this western atmosphere, soil suitable for fruitful development. If true Japanese cuisine requires kimona clad waitresses, bamboo dividers, and mats upon the floor to capture its inherent flavor, then a literary tradition with its own customs, terminology, and idioms cannot thrive where it is merely grafted onto existing conventions. Cantalopes are nice, but they are rather freakish growing on pear trees.

The unhappy lyrics cited above are not reserved for collusions of Mother Goose and poetasters. Even a sophisticate like Jessie Sampter failed to create any suitable lyrics for Jewish children. The Reform movement, which proudly proclaims its cultural affinities with the West, and which brandishes standards of proper immersion in the vernacular, selected three poems from Sampter's collection, *Around the World in Rimes for the Jewish Child,* for inclusion in its *Union Hymnal.* Later these poems with their musical setting were reprinted in the *Union Songster: Songs and Prayers for Jewish Young* (New York, 1960). Two of these poems are banal, if not misleading, translations of traditional blessings. The third is presumably a child's view of the Sabbath:

The Sabbath light is burning bright,
Our prettiest cloth is clean and white
With wine and bread for Friday night.

At set of sun our work is done,
The happy Sabbath has begun,
Now bless us Father everyone.

English speaking Jews, whatever their education, have immense tolerance for the aesthetically precious. Bad quality is so commonplace in the market for Jewish children's literature that it is often not recognized for what it is. All critical faculties of the Jewish reading public have been discretely anesthetized.

Without prolonging the examples of futility, it should be at least partially apparent that the Jewish literary venture never attains authentic expression in an English setting. The English format might be ideal for relating experiences of Jews as a minority group encountering a dominant culture, e.g. themes of alienation, prejudice, fading cultural ties, inability to find one's place, and similar topics relating to the perpetually displaced person. These circumstances are not unique to Jews, however, but are shared by most minority groups which strive to retain some identity while at the same time endeavouring to adapt to new and emerging cultural patterns. Perhaps it is this universality of the Jewish experience in the West which accounts for the widespread popularity of the American Jewish novel. Our North American melting pot has established literary avenues for expressing such impacts and collisions, but the singular encounter with one's own tradition in an environment undiluted by reference to another culture is not to be found in the options of English literary conventions. English literature is well suited for *Portnoy's Complaint, What Makes Sammy Run,* and *Howl,* but not for recording the experiences of Rabbi Akiva, the mind of the Baal Shem Tov, the indigenous portrait of the Chassidim in Williamsburg, or even the emotions engendered by Passover, Succoth, and other Jewish festivals. Perhaps it is this intense self-consciousness, this unresolved soul-searching, which erodes any stable base on which a children's literature could develop.

At this point several reasons for the pathetic condition of Jewish children's literature have emerged.

(1) The conventions and terminology of the indigenous Jewish experience are not adaptable to the established English literary models. Writing thus becomes a process of grafting rather than of developing.

(2) Writers are painfully self-analytic and agonizingly self-conscious because they are at home neither with their subject nor with the dominant culture.

(3) Such instability cannot provide the framework for an ongoing indigenous literature.

These conditions which confront the Jewish writer are hardly conducive to the creation of authentic literature of any kind. The Jewish culture is, in the minds of many writers, either directionless, moribund or both. Authors like I.B. Singer display artistic talent, and they deal with backgrounds and subjects familiar to Eastern European Jews, but they are quite conscious of their subjects as a world which no longer exists and of themselves as aliens to Jewish values and scholarship. Perhaps the situation would be analogous to Ibsen in his later period; with all of his Scandinavian settings, his writings would not be in the strict sense considered Norwegian literature. They are more properly classed with exile literature than with a particular national or cultural development. And almost all of Jewish children's literature also belongs to this category. These circumstances alter the writer's stance, making him in Ibsen's case a creator of ideas rather than the spokesman for a culture. In the case of Jewish writers, the alteration has been far less favorable, as they have become not writers at all but rather translators of a culture they improperly understand since they are forever alien to it.

Of course the Jewish tradition does exist as a total and creative milieu to a number of people to this day. There are, for example, a number of Yeshivas, classical Jewish academies, where students devote full time to the study and practice of Jewish learning. There are colonies of Chassidim and solidly traditional Jewish communities such as the one in Monsey, New York. (I am referring to groups committed to living traditional values and not simply to predominately Jewish neighborhoods as those in Great Neck, N.Y., Brookline, Mass., or Cote St. Luc, Quebec, which lack virtually any significant Jewish institutions or practice.) Ideally, representatives of groups living in a committed Jewish atmosphere would produce a substantial and meaningful children's literature. But the output from these areas of promise is not of significant promise for several reasons. First of all, many of these people, particularly those who are the most knowledgeable, are totally committed to traditional Jewish scholarship, and this has prevented them from becoming linguistically competent in the English language. A second reason, however, is even more central to this sustained non-productivity. Even if they would be competent to express themselves in English (and indeed some of them are), they would choose not to do so for reasons central to Jewish thought. If they are concerned with reaching children, they turn their energies towards making the original texts of the Pentateuch, the Talmud and the Midrash more intelligible to the young. The idea of creating an independent literature would be unthinkable, as their principle objective is to involve students directly with the holy writings and to enable them to maintain total involvement with these writings—to the exclusion of all else. Creativity would manifest itself largely in the form of effective communication with students, or in relating oral narratives which would illustrate passages from the texts currently being studied. (It should be mentioned that there is in fact a large body of oral literature which is still being colorfully and profoundly narrated by these scholars, particularly among Chassidim.)

Another reason for the unwillingness of competent scholars to engage in creative writing for children is the most crucial of all. There is conscious distrust of creative arts among almost all traditional Jewish scholars, and this distrust is explicitly communicated to their adherents. This distrust extends not only to secular literature, but to personal artistic creativity in religious literature as well. It would, for example, be forbidden for a Jew to dramatize Moses receiving the Law, because we have no records of Moses' emotion at this moment, and we have no detailed accounts of his body movements or his actions. In contrast with the medieval Christian tradition where it was a permitted and even encouraged practice to embroider saints' lives to inspire the faithful, Jewish scholarship frowned upon personal embellishment no matter how pious the motivation might be. Even the so-called commentaries are in fact traditional verbatim expositions of a received tradition and not matters of personal opinion. The Midrash and the Aggadoth, often inaccurately translated "legends" were recorded line by line by people who refused to alter any detail. A phenomenon such as the medieval English stage with its emergence of certain character types, a garrulous wife for Noah and a devil as a comic figure, would be unthinkable in traditional Jewish scholarship. Significantly enough, there has been little Jewish drama until modern times, and *Fiddler on the Roof* represents as serious an achievement as has been created in English. The Yiddish theater, its ghetto types and Jewish themes notwithstanding, is more related to vernacular European letters than to Jewish tradition. And Jewish children's drama to this day is too silly to discuss.

A further reason for the opposition of competent Jewish scholars to creative writing derives from the concept of *bitul Torah,* the negation of Torah learning. According to Jewish Law, every Jewish male is obligated to devote every available moment to involving himself with studying the received body of Torah precepts. To consume time with developing personal fantasies would most certainly be considered a serious violation of this edict. Personal creative ventures are thus roundly discouraged. The fact that those competent to generate a literature for children are solidly opposed to any such venture does not bode well for any substantial children's literature in the future. Although their opposition is most certainly legitimate and is supported by Jewish Law, it promotes the sad irony that the Jewish quarters of the bookseller's stalls must be furnished by the unknowledgeable and that the people of the Book will never have their scholars as their spokesmen.

Traditionally Jewish children's literature was and is the unabridged Pentateuch, the unedited Talmud and the Midrash. There were compilations of the narrative sections of the Talmud, the most famous of which, *Eyn Ya'akov* (The Fountains of Jacob) appeared in several editions for children. But these editions were always in the same words and in the identical syntax as the original text. The only difference was that the narrative portions, exclusive of the lengthy Talmudic discourses, were bound together. A separate body of Jewish literature specifically directed at children appears in most cases only as outgrowths of Jewish encounters, invariably negative ones, with outside elements. This is to say that if Jews had been left in their own homeland, or in their own ghettos, and had little if any exchange with the outside world, there would be but a negligible output of children's literature, and the literary interests of children would continue to be satisfied by the unaltered Pentateuch, by the Talmud and Midrash and by the vast body of oral narratives.

A separate literature for children invariably coincides with movements. Thus the first great outpouring of a Jewish children's literature accordingly was prompted by the Haskala (Enlightenment) movement, the Jewish equivalent of rationalist fervor sweeping Europe in the eighteenth century. The Haskala movement was a secularist push towards greater assimilation with the surrounding European cultures. The *maskilim,* (literally, "rational ones") as the proponents of Haskala were called, worked towards a breakdown of traditional Jewish schools and of Jewish scholarship, attempting to substitute in its stead the study of secular cultures. Aaron Wolfsohn Halle's *Avtalyon* (1790) related Bible stories in simplified Hebrew prose. His purpose, like that of Judah Leib Ze'ev, was to westernize Jewish learning, and to accomplish their objective they wrote for the Jewish young. Their adaptations of Hebrew texts put Jewish tales in line with those of Hans Christian Andersen (whose stories were published in Hebrew translation by Judah Goor), where the fancy and the imagination would be supreme. David Zemosc of Breslau translated J.H. Campe's version of *Robinson Crusoe*. The study of such works was of course totally counter to the whole philosophy of Jewish learning. The authors of Jewish children's literature were clearly attempting to wean Jewish youth away from their traditional modes and materials of study. Thus a literature for children became identified as a negative element, and the intention of its authors confirmed the traditional opposition to personal literary ventures.

In an effort to stem the waxing influence of the Haskala, a number of traditionalists took pen in hand in order to provide the growing number of young readers with material along traditional lines. Nonetheless, the distrust of creative writing lingered, and the best of the writings of the traditionalists was never of a particularly high literary quality. Dr. Marcus Lehmann, a German orthodox rabbi and a distinguished scholar, wrote such books as *Bustenai* and *Unpaid Ransom*. They were translated into a number of languages from the original German, and the English translations are still in print today. His material is taken largely from factual accounts of Jewish history, but they are highly romanticized and are stylistically unpolished. His position as an author was assumed not out of any personal desire to write, but as a polemic to provide a sense of traditional Jewish values in a market already flooded by reformers and *maskilim*. Thus even the traditional books for children were prompted by the Haskala movement.

In a sense, all Jewish children's literature has been polemic, generated either by a conscious effort to turn young minds to the vernacular or to keep them in the fold. The battle still rages, and it has left the field of Jewish children's literature a scarred battleground instead of a fertile pasture. There is simply no *Wizard of Oz*, no *Tom Sawyer*, and no *Little Women,* i.e. the type of literature where a child can dwell within the artistic milieu and live within the tale itself. And with few exceptions, even adult literature is dominated by polemicists, by sociologists of the Jewish phenomenon, and by human interest buffs in search of anything that appears circumcized. Such self-consciousness about Israel among the cultures has devastated any efforts at serious literary ventures for Jewish children, and until Jewish writers can come comfortably to terms with their own tradition, and on its own terms, the prospects of a meaningful Renaissance of Jewish letters for children is not very likely.

Until that utopian era when Jewish writers can draw upon an undiluted Jewish tradition we must be content with such polyglots as Weilerstein's *Adventures of K'tonton*, a Jewish Tom Thumb who nearly encounters tragedy in bread dough his mother is baking for the Sabbath, or the *World Over Story Book,* some well-intentioned though stylistically bland recountings of the Jewish past. Nixxan Mindel, it should be added, is making a serious effort to adapt the Chassidic oral narrative art to a series of children's books. But for some time to come Jewish interests appear doomed to be represented by the dilemmas of Jewish children who seek to preserve the life of a carp in the bathtub to keep him from becoming gefilte fish.

Jewish children's literature suffers from the fact that, traditionally, Jewish children have never needed it. It was thus the result of movements and was therefore consciously polemic and propograndistic. It never found a comfortable unself-conscious environment in which to grow. Since its initial impetus was to lure Jewish children away from their traditions, it deliberately adopted foreign terminology. When the more traditionally oriented literature arose in reaction, it too found that the models had to be taken from secular cultures. Jewish literature is usually written by authors who are not significantly grounded in Jewish scholarship. Conversely, those who are scholars frequently lack the linguistic competence to undertake the author's role in the vernacular, or they are dominated by a distrust of creative writing in general, insisting as they do upon the Torah and the Talmud as the singular texts for Jewish students of all ages. Furthermore, the traditional mode of delighting children by means of tales is still largely an oral mode. Given these difficulties, it will be surprising to find among the already overworked presses anything that will excite the interests of the connoisseurs of Jewish literature, and the ethnic buffs will have to skip the Jews, or smile condescendingly at the feeble efforts of those who are by fact and reputation a highly literate people.

Greek, 4th Century. Collection Delphi Museum.

Literature for the Children of Greece*

Alexandra Placotari

In ancient days, in this part of the world, one might say that children were rocked to sleep with tales from Homer. Later on, Homer became their schoolbook, their history, their geography, in a way even their Bible. But it is not so today. How could it be? The world has changed, and above all the language has changed so much in these nearly three thousand years that, although most of the words of modern Greek are derived from the same roots and quite a number of them have come down unchanged, it takes a scholar to read a Homeric text and enjoy it with ease. So Homer is now taught in the last two classes of our gymnasium, our secondary school. In the lower classes children read myths from Homer, or even translations of pieces into modern Greek. Educational systems have changed, and although the West still loyally sticks to the ancient Greek sound mind/sound body principle, the school curriculum has had to be altered to meet the requirements of our time. In the following paragraphs, I shall try to sketch the beginnings and progress of modern Greek literature for children.

When we speak of modern Greece, we Greeks have in mind a date—1821—when the Greek War of Independence against the Turks began. The Turkish yoke had lasted for nearly 400 years. It was cruel, devastating. The War was long, full of reverses, thoroughly depleting. It was undertaken by an exhausted and impoverished people, and when it ended and the Greeks won their independence, they were still more exhausted and impoverished. Schools had been closed down by the Turks since their occupation of the country following the fall of Constantinople. In large centers of population some schools reopened and managed to function through thick and thin, but in the more distant districts, in the isolated corners of Greece, schools were non-existent for years and years, so that a very great percentage of the population was doomed to illiteracy. Yet the light had not gone out completely. Tradition never dies, and this land has a long tradition and history, and what a history! So the fire kept burning secretly. At first it was a mere flicker here and there, but soon some enlighted individuals began to think what should be done to stir up the flicker to a flame: to educate the young, to raise the morale of the people, to prepare for liberation. In the beginning a village priest, here and there, secretly gathered the children of his community in the church or in his home and taught them how to read and write. To avoid attracting the attention of the Turkish gendarmes, the teaching was carried out after nightfall. A song came down to us from those times, sung by the children as they went to school. It runs like this, in a rough translation:

> Bright moon,
> Light me on my way
> As I walk to school
> To learn to read and write
> All God's good things
> Sewing and embroidery
> And what God wills.

The schoolbook was the book of Psalms, from which the children memorised their prayers. Often the teacher-priest was a man of only rudimentary education, but sometimes he was a monk who had studied at a monastery school at the University level. The monks who left their monasteries and went among the people teaching and preaching believed that this was a better way of serving their God. Schools were for centuries thus connected with the Greek Orthodox Church, and the people's faith in Christian belief was a great support to them in their hard times.

For hundreds of years education in Greece was a matter of a handful of people who were earnestly interested in educating the nation. There was no ministry of education, no support whatever from the Turkish authorities. On the contrary, it was to their interest that the Greek people remained illiterate. As for books, the Greeks did what they could with what they could find. Myths of Aesop or other Greek myths, some lives of the saints, or a popular biography of Alexander the Great were passed from hand to hand. No printing presses were allowed. One or two attempts to smuggle a printing press into the country were found out and smashed by the Turks, and the smugglers were severely punished. But Greeks who lived abroad and who by dint of hard work had made a fortune, assisted as best they could. In 1670, two Greeks, the Glyki brothers, put up a printing press in Venice. In 1686, another Greek, Sarros, also set up a press in Venice. They began to publish at first a negligible number of books, but soon hundreds and hundreds of them, as schools grew in number and there was an increasing demand. Such was the ardor and zeal and then perseverence of these few people, that their efforts bore fruit: when in the spring of 1821, the War of Independence broke out, the nation was ready for it.

As soon as the War was over and a national government was established, primary education became compulsory, and the fight against illiteracy began seriously. But at this early stage one can hardly speak of literature for children. Attention was concentrated on essential schoolbooks and rudimentary knowledge. It was again a few individuals, enlightened people, who gave thought to books which, besides teaching, would give pleasure to the child. For instance, in 1858 there appeared a book written by Leon Melas, twice minister in the Greek government and a distinguished lawyer, and afterwards a wealthy businessman in London, who later in life concentrated his energy on the education of the Greek youth. He published in 1858 a book in which the central figure, the old man, narrates in a simple, relaxed manner various myths and short tales mostly taken from ancient Greek sources. The book makes very pleasant reading and could be read today with as much ardor as it was in its time, if it were not for its language, which is rather old fashioned. Melas followed up this first book with several others for young people, among them his *Little Plutarch*.

Melas was one example of a number of expatriate Greeks who went abroad, made money, and spent their leisure time writing books, translating Homer and the classics into modern Greek, and helping in various ways towards the cultural education of the Greek youth. Another was Alexander Pollis who translated Homer into modern Greek verse of the demotic type. But what is equally important, he wrote poems for children, in an unusually fresh and simple manner, not at all like the pedantic, didactic poems that children read in their schoolbooks, but real, enjoyable things, with genuine lyricism, and sometimes a lot of humor. He wrote them originally for his own grandchildren, but soon they became universal.

Another expatriate Greek, Argyris Extuliotis, gave us a translation of the *Odyssey,* and still another, Dimitrios Vikelus, a nephew of Melas who worked with him in London, wrote literature for the young. His story, a simple narrative on a subject taken from the time of the War of Independence, was and still is widely read; I remember shedding "black tears" over it. But Vikelus did more than just w r i t e books for children and translate such foreign works as Anderson's tales into Greek. When he settled in Athens he founded an Association for the Diffusion of Useful Books, useful, that is, for educating the young. A number of cheap editions of books (like present-day paperbacks) were published yearly. And each year a larger number of them came out.

These are only the beginnings of literature for children. During the second half of the 19th century we have some good examples of poetry for children by Tantahdes, and also by his student, Sizyenos, who wrote short narrative poems, telling some mythic adventure in ballad form, and some very good short stories. They all showed a new attitude towards literature for children, shifting away from the ordinary rhetorical tone of the moralistic type. They followed the general trend toward a better education and a more modern conception of how it should be planned.

In 1879 a periodical appeared especially for children and young people. It was edited by Nicolas Paperdopoulos at first, and later by some of our most outstanding writers. Owing to its excellent management and good material, it was very widely read and it exercised a great influence on young minds. It was read not only by children in Greece but by the Greek children all over the wrold. Its contributors were well-known writers or scholars seriously interested in education, as well as in children and young people. Many budding writers made their first appearance in its pages. This periodical began at first as a monthly, but soon, owing to the great demand and to its popularity, it became fortnightly and then weekly. Its title meant "The Moulding of the Young." The range of its material was encyclopedic. Through its pages views were exchanged, problems were discussed between young and old. It was a kind of nursery for growing talents and intellects. It continued publication for over 60 years, and were it not for the German occupation it would not have stopped. After World War II it was republished in a new form under new management, but it was short-lived. The world had changed. Children and their tastes had changed.

On the whole the last decades of the nineteenth century were very significant for Greek literature and education in general. A crucial concern was our linguistic problem.

Some scholars thought that Greece, having set the standards for western civilization, should use in writing the language in which our ancestors wrote. Ignoring the fact that a living language changes continually, they thought that the language spoken by the people was unclear. There were also those who believed that we could not go back, and that a language is not vulgar, but people sometimes are, and that we should write the language we speak. The strife that began many years ago is still going on, although its intensity is somewhat abated. Writers of literary books now write without exception in the spoken language. But can you imagine a child just beginning to learn to read being taught that the word for egg or fish was one thing, while people speaking used different ones. Clearly this hampered the education of young children. Even Paperdopoulous' periodical, when it first appeared, was written in this artificial or "pure" language as it was called. But the editors, as would be expected of them, gradually passed on to the currently spoken language. The generations that found intellectual food in its pages have become the writers of today, some of them of world-wide fame. The standard was definitely rising.

In 1917 the educational problem was again taken up by a group of intellectuals and scholars, who launched a new program for schools, following which new schoolbooks had to be written. It was then that one of our best writers, Papemtonious, wrote a reader for the fourth form and called it *The High Mountains.* He was a highly cultured man, a journalist, a writer of both prose and verse, and an aesthete. He also wrote poems of a very high quality for children. In *The High Mountains,* a group of children from the town decide to spend their summer vacation on the mountains, and although when living in town these children are irresponsible and rather spoiled by their parents, once up there and on their own, they change. They become responsible, they organize themselves, and run their camp with success. There is no lack of adventure. They often have to face difficulties and adversities yet they manage to overcome them. The book is interesting, exciting; it teaches much without being pedantic. It is written in a beautiful demotic—Papemtonious was above all a stylist. Though it is no longer a school reading book, it is still very widely read for its narrative interest. And as for Papemtonious's poems for children, they can still be found in the school books of today.

A prose writer, a woman this time, Penelope Delta, has also given us literature for children of a very high standard. Her first book appeared in 1909, *For the Fatherland.* The following year she published *The Tale Without a Name,* a dramatic version of which was staged in the winter of 1972, and in 1911 she published a historical novel, *During the Time of the Bulgarsheyer,* a story taken from Byzantine history. In 1925 she published *The Life of Christ* and in 1937 *The Secrets of the Marshes,* another historical novel. This is not all, because she wrote also novels for children on worldly subjects. She is the Greek writer for children par excellence and as yet unsurpassed. Her books are still best sellers; they are worthy, inspired with true patriotism not the rhetorical kind, and celebrate high ideals. A true patriot herself, Penelope Delta found the German occupation so unbearable that in 1940 she committed suicide.

Since the war, literature for children in Greece has entered a new period. It is part of the general trend towards new ideas and methods, the tendency to take the child more seriously, the will to assist him in his development. Antigone Metaxa, another woman writer, concentrates rather on the younger children of the nursery years or the first school years. For her work she relies on Greek books and tales, on foreign literature and translations. She organizes a regular "Children's Hour" on the radio, with songs and stories and plays which children all over Greece listen to. Later she has these songs and stories published. Parents are advised to buy the books and get into the habit of offering books to children on festive occasions. The business of literature for children is beginning to look up, but publishers are still hesitant; they buy the manuscripts from the writers for a mere pittance, and show great unwillingness to risk money for these publications. Only when a writer with a name tries writing a book for children do they accept it without much ado. But for the rest there is still little encouragement.

In 1956, however, a group of women writers met in Athens with the intention of getting better acquainted with one another and with their work. At first their meetings were mere social gatherings, but soon they found that this was hardly what they really wanted. One member, Mrs. Rena Karthaion, had a bright idea; books for children, the right books for children. It was decided to encourage writers of children's books to keep on writing, to help them to publish, and to inform parents about good literature for children. To this end, the first thing they did was to find donors for prizes and then set up a competition for the best story or book of poems or play for children. A rich friend offered a small sum. A publisher or two promised to publish the book that won the prize and so it went on year after year; and manuscripts poured in in ever growing numbers, and the quality of writing improved. The association of women writers is still going on with this work, and, what is more, publishers are even thankful, because they can finally know what book is worth the expense of publication.

In 1966 another group of women founded the Circle of Greek Children's Books, with similar aims as that of the Women's Writers' Association, but with an eye toward what was going on in the world outside Greece. The Circle, as the Greek National Section of The International Board on Books for Young People, partakes in IBBY's activities. It had a member of its board chosen as member of the Andersen Jury. This provides a contact with other countries for first-hand information about all activity concerning literature for children. The Circle also sets up its own prizes every year, such as the prize for the best tale of the year awarded by the Mayor of Athens, and several prizes for works on nature. The Circle prides itself especially on its award for the best illustrations of a book for children. Until recently it was difficult to get a good printer to illustrate a book for children, unless it were written by an author who had already made a name. Now the prize encourages young artists to produce children's books of merit.

To sum up, I must say that a new genre of literature is blossoming in Greece. Literature for children is becoming a fashion. Every year adds several good books for children to the publications list, and a number of talents come to the fore with these books, some of them very good, good enough to compete with the best writing anywhere, which is a great encouragement to us all.

*An address arranged by Professor Barbara Walker and delivered in Athens, July 14, 1973.

Contemporary Children's Literature in Norway

Ingrid Bozanic

More directly than most, Norwegian children's literature has its origins in an oral tradition of folktales and songs, and its written beginnings in a collection of folk-tales. The definitive collection of Norwegian folk-tales, *Norske Folkeeventyr,* assembled by Peter Christen Asbjörnsen and Jörgen Moe, appeared about 1850. The work was directly inspired by the great success of the Grimm brothers' collection of German folktales called *Kinder und Hausmärchen;* in its retention of local dialect it was undoubtedly also influenced by a current upsurge of romantic nationalism in Norway.

Asbjörnsen and Moe's collections consists of *sagn* or legends connected with historical events or specific places, and of *eventyr* which are the completely fictional stories sometimes called *märchen* or fairy tales. It is the *eventyr* with its trolls, princesses and treasures that has made the Norwegian folktales popular all over the world.

Besides the obvious trolls it is difficult to identify the peculiarly Norwegian elements in an *eventyr* that make it differ from variants in other countries. George Webbe Dasent, who translated Asbjörnsen and Moe's tales into English as *Popular Tales from the Norse* in 1858, made the following observations in his introductory essay:

> These Norse Tales we may characterize as bold, outspoken, and humorous, in the true sense of humor. In the midst of every difficulty and danger arises that old Norse feeling of making the best of everything, and keeping a good face to the foe. The language and tone are perhaps rather lower than in some other collections, but it must be remembered that these are the tales of "hempen homespuns. . . ."[1]

Dasent has mentioned the major characteristics of the tone of Norwegian folktales: sharp objectivity, common-sense, a basic or earthy quality, and a keen sense of humor.

Although Asbjörnsen and Moe's collection was not specifically for children, it quickly became popular with the younger audience. Even today, *Norske Folkeeventyr* is probably the work of literature which is most well-known by children. In the later nineteenth century many collections of poetry, songs and tales were assembled especially for children, and in 1888 the first picture book for children appeared—Elling Holst's collection of songs and rhymes called *Norsk Billedbok for Barn.* There followed the so-called "golden age" of Norwegian children's literature when excellent animal and family stories were written by such authors as Jörgen Moe, Sigrid Undset, Bernt Lie, Hans Aarud, Gabriel Scott, Barbara Ring, and Dikken Zwilgmeyer. Although these novels were original works, they usually dealt with country life and their tone was similar to that of the *eventyr.* They presented a literary version of the national folk revival and remain favorite classics today.

Asbjörnsen and Moe's collection appeared in the context of a national movement to establish *Landsmaal,* the spoken language of the people, on an equal footing with the literary and scholastic language which was derived from Danish. That language problem has never yet been resolved, and affects the whole question of literature for children. There are two officially acceptable variants of Norwegian—*Bokmål,* which is the language derived from Danish, and *Nynorsk,* which is the consolidation of country dialects called *Landsmaal.* Both languages are required of all children in school; yet until recently nearly all books were published in *Bokmål,* which was difficult reading for children who spoke *Nynorsk* at home. Only recently have many books for children been published in both dialects, and *Nynorsk* is developing a literature of its own especially for very young children.

This language problem has intensified the tendency to base modern literature for children on traditional oral literature and song; perhaps as a consequence, the radio has been of great importance in the development of children's literature. For many years there has been a program on Norwegian radio called *Barnetime* (The Children's Hour) which consists primarily of funny ballads and songs presented by their authors. Many of these programs have later been adapted into books, records, and (more recently) television programs. Three out of the four major Norwegian writers for children, Alf Pröysen, Thorbjörn Egner and Anne—Cath. Vestly, entered the field of children's entertainment by composing and singing ballads on the *Barnetime.* In turn, television and radio are constantly drawing on the resources of children's books for their material.

In 1973 the Norwegian school television launched a series of programs based on interviews with children's writers. The authors talk about themselves and their writings and then tell a story or read from their works. On one program the author Anne-Cath. Vestly told an *eventyr* of her own composition about a traditional sea monster called a *draug.* There is quite a difference between a wizened old storyteller of the nineteenth century and a *Barnetime* performer of today, but they are both part of an oral narrative tradition in Norway that still provides material for children's books.

Another contributor to the *Barnetime,* Alf Pröysen, is probably the Norwegian children's author most well-known abroad. In addition to many excellent collections of songs, Alf Pröysen is the author of the Teskjekjerringa series which is called *Mrs. Pepperpot* in English. These are stories about the adventures of a little old lady who often shrinks to the size of a teaspoon or a pepperpot in the English version. In many ways they resemble the Norwegian *eventyr* more than they do other modern children's fantasies about miniature people, such as Mary Norton's *The Borrowers* or T. H. White's *Mistress Masham's Repose.* To begin with, Mrs. Pepperpot is a rather unorthodox main character or heroine for a children's book; but a wily old hag who tricks her husband, neighbors, and animals is traditional *eventyr* material. The tale "Kjerringa mot Strömmen" (The Women Against the Current) is only one example of an obstinate or willful wife in Norwegian folk-tales. Also typical is the lawless and amoral tone of the stories where anything goes as long as it benefits Mrs. Pepperpot. Mrs. Pepperpot's miniature size brings to mind the *eventyr* "Tommeliten" (Thumbkin) and "Dukken i Gresset" (Doll in the Grass). Her ability to understand the language of the animals is common in many Norwegian folk-tales. The books do not have one continuous plot but are episodic, and at the end of each episode Mrs. Pepperpot emerges triumphant and laughing. The stories tend to be wry and satirical.

Alf Pröysen's other stories for children include *Den Grönne Votten* which is the history of the adventures of a green mitten and *Sirkus Mikkelikski* in which the mistreated animals in a small circus revolt and decide to train the circus keepers.

Another *Barnetime* contributor whose writing is clearly influenced by Norwegian folk-tales is Thorbjörn Egner. His original works include the tale of the two tooth trolls *Karius and Baktus,* the adventures of three cheerful thieves and their tyrannical aunt in *The Singing Town* and a story about a community of woodland animals called *Klatremus og de andre dyrene fra Hakkebakkeskogen.* Although they excavate in people's teeth rather than dig for treasure in mountains, Karius and Baktus are just as disreputable and gleefully malicious as other Norwegian trolls. The animal story is a series of episodes in which an industrious mouse and a carefree mouse manage to outwit the sly old fox who pursues them. All of Thörbjorn Egner's books are fulled with delightful ballads and are characterized by a cozy sense of humor and a secure and positive attitude toward life.

In addition to his own stories Thörbjorn Egner has edited many collections of his own children's songs. He has also translated, illustrated, and to some extent rewritten foreign children's books, such as Hugh Lofting's *Doctor Doolittle,* A. A. Milne's *The House at Pooh Corner,* a story of H. G. Wells' called *Tommy and the Elephants* and some of Astrid Lindgren's books. Among contemporary Norwegian children's writers Thörbjorn Egner's influence is the most far-reaching because he is responsible for editing, writing, and illustrating many of the reading books for Norway's schools.

There are also a number of minor authors who have used characters from *eventyr* in their books but the result has not always been successful. Olav Aukrust wrote in the early 1950's quite a few picture books about hobgoblins and small trolls. Among them were *Tuftesteggen, Nisser og Små Troll, Risen og Jutelfjellet* and *Nidgards-Truls.* Anka Borch's *To Små Fjösnisser, Trollet i Nasafjellet* and *Huldra i Byen* are all rather uninspired stories about trolls and their kin. The most imaginative and successful use of *eventyr* material in recent years is Reidar Brodtkorb's *Rokkesteinen.* It is about a troll boy, only a hundred years old, who becomes part of a modern Norwegian farm family, and encounters difficulties. *Tisledevollen* by the same author tells of a small boy who loves *eventyr* so much that magic begins to happen all around him. Chr. Kittelsen's picture book *Huttetu* and Nils Johan Rud's *I Eventyrskog* are both also derived from Norwegian folk-tales.

Not all Norwegian children's fiction is in collections of songs, folk-tales, or fantasies. There are many fine realistic stories about children and animals. Even these novels, however, are characterized by the simple, direct, and humorous tone of the folk-tales and often show a somewhat romanticized view of Norwegian life.

Although the third *Barnetime* writer, Anne-Cath. Vestly, has composed ballads and written stories with elements of fantasy, she is primarily renowned for her realistic fiction for young children. She has little international reputation as yet, but is important because in the last decade she has written over twenty children's books that enjoy tremendous popularity in Norway. Although there are four different series—Aurora, Ole Aleksander, Lillebror og Knerten and Mormor, the books are all very much alike. They deal with the every day adventures and family life of young children. Ann-Cath. Vestly's books, full of humorous scrapes and minor tragedies, are similar to

Beverly Cleary's Ramona stories or Maria Gripe's *Hugo and Josephine*. Although the stories are perhaps a bit too precious and insipid for an adult taste, Anne-Cath. Vestly's books are avidly read and enjoyed by Norwegian children.

Unlike Alf Pröysen, Thorbjörn Egner and Anne-Cath. Vestly, who share certain similarities in background, subject and style, Aimée Sommerfelt is out of the mainstream of Norwegian children's literature. Aimée Sommerfelt's best books deal with the hardships of children in foreign countries or with the problems of aliens in Norway. The great prizewinner *The Road to Agra* is the story of the adventures of a poor Indian boy who travels to Agra with his half-blind little sister in hopes that they will find someone to cure her blindness. Its sequel *The White Bungalow* is about this same boy and how he wants to become a doctor. In *My Name is Pablo* a poor shoe-shine boy in Mexico struggles to survive until a Norwegian family takes interest in him.

Aimée Sommerfelt's other books take place in Norway. *Miriam* is about a Jewish girl and her family in Norway during World War II. The problems of an Italian immigrant family who try to become part of a small Norwegian community are the subject of Aimée Sommerfelt's most recent novel *Den Farlige Natten. No Easy Way* is a rather flimsy story about a girl who wants to become an actress in Oslo in the middle of the last century.

Aimée Sommerfelt's books are a series of events or adventures that force the protagonist to come to terms with himself and his environment. A display of courage and selflessness is necessary before he can achieve his goal. The overall theme of Aimée Sommerfelt's work is the need for human understanding and cooperation, but at times she overdoes it. The tone of her writing can become too noble and lofty and the plot situations are often a bit strained and implausible. For example, the impact of *The Road to Agra* is nearly spoiled by the appearance of the cute UNICEF nurses and doctors at the end of the book. An over zealous attempt to make *Den Farlige Natten* "relevant" detracts from what is otherwise a wonderful story about children who become friends through their common love and desire to save a hunted dog. In some ways *Miriam* is the most successful of Aimée Sommerfelt's novels because it is the least tainted by an excessively moral tone or an implausibly happy ending.

The strength of Aimée Sommerfelt's writing lies in her perceptive characterization of early adolescents and her ability to tell an absorbing story. She is one of the very few Norwegian children's authors who examines in depth the emotions and thoughts of her characters.

The discussion of Aimée Sommerfelt's writing and her somewhat unsuccessful attempts to make her books "relevant" brings one to the main question about current Norwegian children's literature. A surface glance would seem to indicate that the literature does not come to grips with the modern world and its problems in the way that Swedish or American children's literature does or at least tries to do.

Although some of these "socially aware" books are available in Norway, Norwegian children seem to prefer reading rather simple, naive and perhaps old-fashioned books about happy families and animals. There are many adventure stories about sport competitions and expeditions in the wild. Series books about Indians and detectives are also very popular with children although not highly repected by teachers and librarians.

There is a marked absence of complex fantasy and science fiction, of books about children with personal or communal problems and of contemporary and "relevant" teenage books. This general trend in the type of children's books available occurs not only in the Norwegian books but also in those translated from other languages.

A closer look will show that in many ways these books do relate meaningfully to the life of a Norwegian child. Norway does not have the extensive and major social problems of poverty, racial conflict or drug abuse which beset other countries. Norwegians seem in many ways hesitant to give up their romantic conception of Norway and to abandon themselves completely to modern life. By the same token, Norwegian children seem to remain children longer than is usual in America, perhaps because of closer family life, fewer social problems, less television, or a later start at school. Children spend most of their free time outdoors, participating in sports and games or helping on the farm. Although the children's literature available in Norway is limited in quantity and subject, it seems to satisfy the needs and interests of its readers.

Footnote

[1]George Webbe Dasent, *Popular Tales from the Norse* 2nd ed. (New York: E. P. Dutton & Co., 1859), p. 81.

The Psychological Origins of Fantasy for Children in Mid-Victorian England*

Ravenna Helson

Between 1850 and 1870 the following works of fantasy for children were published in England: *The King of the Golden River* by John Ruskin, *The Rose and the Ring* by William Makepeace Thackeray, *Granny's Wonderful Chair* by Frances Browne, *The Water Babies* by Charles Kingsley, *Alice in Wonderland* by Lewis Carroll, *The Magic Fishbone* by Charles Dickens, *Mopsa the Fairy* by Jean Ingelow, and *At the Back of the North Wind* by George MacDonald. The very number of these books and the eminence of most of the authors reflect an interest in children's books which had never occurred in any other time or place.

The thesis of this essay is that these works of fantasy for children reflect experiences of inner conflict, growth, and renewal of the sort Jung described as accompanying the individuation process and that the intensity of these experiences, and also their themes and characters, may be understood in relation to the particular social conditions of mid-Victorian England. Since fantasy lends itself to the depiction of unconscious forces, these books afford a rather direct source of information about relations between the ego and the unconscious more than one hundred years ago.

The fact that these books were for and about *children* is another aspect of interest. The importance of the child has been taken for granted for several generations. In the last decade, however, attitudes on topics such as childlessness and abortion have been reevaluated, and there is an increased awareness of the fact that there have been long periods in history when children were scarcely mentioned.[1] As it is now of interest to consider why the status of a child might *not* be important in a society, so is it also of interest to consider why the idea of the child *did* become important, and why eminent English writers and scholars began to produce works of fantasy "for children" about 1850.

After presenting briefly what several social historians have set forth as the salient characteristics of the mid-Victorian period, I shall review Jung's observations about the archetype of the child and its role in the individuation process. Then I shall attempt to show how these concepts, in the context of the times, contribute to an understanding of themes and symbolic structure.

Although works of fantasy for children can be treated objectively with content analysis and statistical techniques,[2] the method to be used here consists in an objective listing of the "population," and, in principle, the systematic discussion of all members thereof. In the present case, the population consists of all original works of fantasy which were written for children, published in England between 1850-1870, and are still circulating in libraries of the San Francisco area. In the interest of brevity, I shall omit the stories of Dickens, Browne and Ingelow: the first because it is more superficial than the rest of the group, even though it supports my general argument; and the books by Browne and

*This study was supported by a grant from the National Endowment for the Humanities.

Ingelow because social conditions impinged differently upon men and women, and exposition will be simplified by confining the books considered here to those written by male authors. I shall discuss Thackeray's *The Rose and the Ring* briefly, only pointing out why I think its characteristics are different from those of the rest of the group. The four remaining fantasies, those by Ruskin, Kingsley, Carroll and MacDonald, show considerable variety, though all are representative works of the period.

Characteristics of the Mid-Victorian Period[3]

Perhaps the first important fact about the Mid-Victorians is that they felt their world was "demonstrably getting more comfortable and running without too much friction."[4] Britain led the world in commerce and manufacturing, and enjoyed a peace which her dominant position tended to insure. Within the country tensions had lessened. Many Englishmen were prospering, and many others had accepted the philosophy that personal and social inequities were remediable through resourceful effort and "will." Model houses, water-closets, gas-lighting, railway excursions and other modern conveniences had become better, more numerous, or cheaper. Material advantage, social class and social mobility were absorbing interests of the age. High value was placed on being a gentleman, or if not that, on being respectable and self-reliant.

Being respectable and self-reliant involved considerable suppression of wayward or self-indulgent impulse, and these virtues were reinforced by a redefinition of sex roles. The masculine role offered power and the opportunity for achievement in return for self-discipline, initiative and rational effort. The woman's role was to provide moral and emotional support at home. Mario Praz suggests that changes in fashions reflect the sex-role transformation that took place. In the early 1800's men's clothes were designed to be appealing to women, and "women and men harmonized in the same vivid palette."[5] But by the mid-Victorian period men had adopted the uniform of dark suits and black ties, and women wore fashions which testified, as Veblen pointed out, to sumptuousness and conspicuous leisure. Middle class women had no place in the world of work, and "work dominated people's lives to an extent that nowadays, in an 'advanced' industrial economy, is scarcely conceivable."[6]

Religious dedication and evangelical zeal were outstanding characteristics of the period. Perhaps they helped to express, nurture, and channel dissidence, as Harold Perkin suggests.[7] At any rate, the moral seriousness is well represented among the authors of the books to be discussed, three of whom were ministers or had taken church orders—Kingsley, MacDonald, and Dodgson (Carroll). Although religious mores and the economic ideal of self-reliance or self-improvement were both important factors in mid-Victorian stability, they sometimes came into conflict with each other. The new possibility of using one's will and effort to bring about personal profit and social advancement "bit deep," and some of the most successful men, such as Dickens and Thackeray, grossly overworked themselves from these desires. Denunciation of greed and selfishness was common in literature, and is conspicuous in the fantasies to be discussed.

Tension was associated not only with suppression of impulse and moral conflicts but also with adjustments to urbanization, population increase, accelerated tempo of life, pressure of work, social mobility, specialization, and new ideas and intellectual doubts about man, God, and society. "The one distinguishing fact about the time," says Walter E. Houghton in *The Victorian Frame of Mind,* "was that it was seen as an age of transition. Never before had people seen their age as that of transition from past to future."

The numbers of intellectual specialists, writers, and professional men were increasing rapidly, and so was the exercise of disinterested intelligence in the public interest. Victorian men of letters, such as Ruskin and Kingsley among the authors to be considered here, tried to understand *all* of the new forces, to interpret *all* of the new ideas, and to both advise and speak for their countrymen. Perhaps these men felt the strain of transition even more than most other Englishmen.

The high birth rate was an important part of the expansive impetus of the age, and much Victorian idealism centered around the home and mother. Houghton suggests that the Victorian "cult of love" may have been a compensation for excessive concentration on the ego and intellect. It has been facetiously remarked that the Victorians thought they invented the family. In a sense they did, because to accept Houghton's idea, the use of family feeling to compensate for stressing impersonal or selfish ego processes *was* new. Although the father's will was supreme, and supported by law, boys were brought up to hold women in great respect, and their love and affection was least discordant in the feeling for woman as mother. Children were important too, partly because the new possibilities for rising—or falling—in the social scale made middle class parents take their children's development and education more seriously. But beyond this, as Trevelyan says, "enlarged *sympathy* with children was one of the chief contributions made by Victorian England to real civilization . . . Children's books, of which the pleasure was intended to be *shared* with grown-ups, was a characteristic invention of the time" (my italics).[8]

In sum, the mid-Victorian period was one in which there were material gains, an optimistic spirit, and an emphasis upon living up to high and rather rigid standards. The supporting matrix of traditional ways, meanings, and relationships had become attenuated. The age was marked by strict suppression of impulse, by an accentuation of specialized competence in men, and by tender feeling in women. Unpleasant restrictive or predatory ego-qualities developed, but so did compensatory emphasis on family relationships. There was especially the feeling of transition, of moving from an essentially feudal past, through a confusing present, to something new. These were ideal conditions for activating what Jung called the individuation process and the archetype of the child.

Individuation and the Child Archetype[9]

In modern western society, said Jung, there is an overdevelopment of the conscious part of the personality. After a personal crisis or after long-sustained effort to achieve or to meet heavy environmental pressure, the unconscious of an individual may, as it were, take advantage of the wounded or exhausted ego to try to restore the balance of the personality. When this happens, the individual is sometimes overwhelmed by the unconscious, or the ego may bestir itself to wall out the unconscious more completely than ever. In other cases, the ego is not inundated, but simply "irrigated"; there is increased awareness—sometimes highly dramatic—of the forces of the unconscious, and of the collective projection of these forces as societal compulsions. Out of the increased awareness of what hitherto has been excluded from consciousness, one begins to act from a less egocentric base and to become a "whole" person. This is the process of individuation, the encouragement of which is the goal of much Jungian analysis, especially with persons in middle and later life.

The experiences which accompany the process of individuation vary with the age and sex of the individual, and with the particular life history and culture. Nevertheless, in dreams, fantasies, and drawings some core symbols recur. Among these are the child, birth, and rebirth. The depleted, ego-weak individual may begin by thinking himself "childish," or feel himself drawn into old childhood pretensions, guilts and anxieties. But "the child motif represents not only something that existed in the distant past but also . . . a system functioning in the present, whose purpose is to compensate or correct, in a meaningful manner, the inevitable one-sidedness and extravagance of the conscious mind" (9. 162). Though the reality is often different, the *symbol* of the child represents simplicity, naturalness, receptivity, and the potential of growth, in contrast to the adult ego processes of calculating, accumulating, retaining, mastering, and maintaining an admirable persona by suppressive means. Just as the infant is born from the womb with life and inevitable maturation before it, a "nascent state of consciousness" emerges from the conflict of conscious and unconscious with the promise of personality expansion and enrichment. It is the special mission of the archetypal child to explore or reveal the unconscious, or to find a way of integrating conscious and unconscious, as a child may bring together father and mother into a family unity.

The King of the Golden River

In 1840 the young genius John Ruskin was living with his parents recuperating from a severe illness which followed a disappointment in love. By the age of twenty-one he had written papers on various aspects of natural history and architecture. He had won the Newdigate prize for poetry at Oxford, and had already begun his defense of the romantic painter Turner. He was spurred on in this high level of activity by his abnormally strict, doting, and ambitious parents.

A girl of twelve, Effie Gray, came to visit the family. According to Ruskin's biographer Collingwood, she

> challenged the melancholy John, engrossed in his drawing and geology, to write a fairy tale, as the least likely task for him to fulfill. Upon which he produced, at a couple of sittings, *The King of the Golden River,* a pretty medley of Grimm's grotesque and Dickens' kindliness and the true Ruskinian ecstacy of the Alps.[10]

Most historians and biographers accept this description of the book, based indeed upon Ruskin's own few words about it. However, Roger Green says that "the story is rather more than a medley and has a charming originality which keeps it as fresh as the mountain air which seems to rush through it and give it its real inspiration.[11]

Let us recall the story briefly, thinking of it in terms of the individuation process and the archetype of the child. Gluck, the child, is an orphan mistreated by his two greedy and stingy older brothers. Jung remarks that the archetypal child often appears as an orphan or as abandoned because he belongs neither to conscious nor unconscious, and he is mistreated because the "nascent attitude" is threatened by coercive and restrictive ego attitudes.

Gluck befriends a curious and mysterious visitor whose cloak never stops dripping water, but the older brothers reject him harshly. The visitor returns at midnight, devastates the valley in which the brothers live, blows the roof from the older brothers' bedroom, and leaves his calling card—Southwest Wind, Esquire. The unconscious seeks admittance, and when deprived of access, shows its destructive power.

Rain falls on the valley no more. In other words, repression has led to a loss of affect, of vital potential. In their effort for survival, the brothers throw Gluck's mug into the fire to be melted down, but in their absence the molten mug speaks, and turns into a little king. He had been imprisoned in the mug by the power of a stronger king, but now he tells Gluck that whosoever casts three drops of holy water into the great river at the top of the western mountain will have a wealth of gold. Here is the little old man in fairy tales who, in a time of suffering, gives advice, based on the wisdom of both conscious and unconscious. The western mountain probably signifies manhood. The "king of the golden river" would seem to be showing the way to mature generativity and selfhood.

When the brothers hear Gluck's strange story, they are eager to undertake the mountain journey. The rest of the story, with its dramatic use of setting, conveying the imminence of unconscious forces, tells how the greedy, selfish brothers fail in the quest and are turned to black stones. In his loving generosity, Gluck succeeds, the river changes it course, and the valley is fertile again.

From one point of view, the terrible fate of the brothers is an example of the Victorian's "excremental vision."[12] In fact, much of the imagery of the story could be interpreted as a struggle between "pregenital and genital modes." Jung himself had two impressive visions as a child that could be described incontrovertibly, the one as phallic and the other as excremental.[13] However, he saw the body-zone symbolism in relation to larger psychic and religious processes of meaning, healing, and growth.

If the Jungian interpretation has merit, it is clear that Ruskin wrote this story at least as much for himself as for Effie Gray. If she had not asked him for a story, he would not have written it, and indeed he did not publish the story until ten years later, anonymously, after the stories of Hans Christian Andersen were translated into English and original fairy stories had begun to make a place for themselves. And, of course, if John Newbery and others had not developed a middle-class market in children's books, the story would very likely not have been published at all. Still, to elicit the tale required something more than Effie's request and Ruskin's familiarity with Grimm. The story came rather quickly, I believe, as an expression of Ruskin's then-active need for, and experience of, the archetype of the child. That the vision of the generative personality was partial, and not actualized in all areas of life, is clear when one remembers that he later married Effie Gray, and that the marriage was annulled six years later as having never been consummated. And yet Ruskin did become one of the very great Victorians.

The King of the Golden River is the only outstanding fantasy of the nineteenth century to lack a female character. Perhaps this fact is attributable to the author's dominant, overpossessive mother and to his youthful need for relationship to the masculine archetype of the king.

The Water Babies

The writing of *The Water Babies* in 1863 presents a set of circumstances quite different from that of *The King of the Golden River*. Charles Kingsley was 46 years old at the time. Although subject to spells of depression, he was happily married, a busy preacher, social activist, expositor of the new science, chaplain to the queen, and a novelist whose *Hypatia* and *Westward Ho!* were so popular that close friends thought his head had been turned. In 1860 he had been appointed to the Regius chair of history at Cambridge. This was not a happy appointment because he had not been trained as a professional historian.[14]

One day, according to Rose Kingsley, his daughter, his older children reminded him that though he had written *The Heroes* for them, the book he had promised to write for the baby, Grenville, had not yet been produced. "He made no answer, but got up at once and went into his study, locking the door. In half an hour he returned with the story of little Tom. This was the first chapter of *The Water Babies* written off without a correction." The rest appeared in installments in *Macmillan's Magazine* and made quite a sensation. Mrs. Kingsley said it was the last fiction he wrote with ease and as a labour of love, because "his brain was getting fatigued, his health fluctuated, and the work of the Professorship, which was a constant weight on his mind, wore him sadly" (Kendall, p. 117).

The combination of narcissism, pressure of work, threat to the ego and middle-age fatigue is, in Jung's view, very likely to set in motion corrective processes. Certainly *The Water Babies* illustrates many of the observations made by Jung in describing the phenomenology of the child archetype.

Little Tom, an orphan, is mistreated by the greedy, crude, cruel Mr. Grimes. They go to clean the chimneys of the mansion of Sir John, but Tom gets lost in the chimney passageways and comes down by mistake into a little girl's room. She is clean and white, in contrast to himself. Away he runs, chased by the squire and all his ménage, who think he has stolen something. This section suggests a harsh super-ego, childhood sexual curiosity, reentry into the mother's body, voyeurism and perhaps sex-identity conflicts. The author had several brothers and one younger sister. He had been a conscientious child who preached sermons at the age of four and also suffered from "brain fever" and nightmares. One of Kingsley's impassioned ideas was that sexual nature is *not* intrinsically evil, that celibacy is *not* a higher form of life than monogamy. Little Tom, dirty but innocent, seems a part of this complex of ideas.

Tom escapes and disappears into a river, where he encounters a wide variety of under-water creatures. Water, of course, is the most common symbol for the unconscious, and eels, lobsters, fish, snakes, etc., commonly symbolize our natural instincts and impulses. After some soul's progress, Tom arrives at the mouth of the river, where he is able to see many other water babies, though they have been with him all along. He goes with them into the ocean, and attends an ocean school under the tutelage of two great female authorities. When his rebelliousness and bad moods cause him to grow prickles, he is put into the charge of a little girl, Elsie. Later, he is sent on a pilgrimage, first to Mother Carey's fount of life, where old creatures are changed into new ones, and on "to do something he does not want to do," which is to try to help Mr. Grimes. On his return, he and Elsie fall in love. Their vision is enlarged; they see that the several magical women in the story are aspects of the same moving spirit throughout nature. Elsie takes Tom home with her, and at the end of the book, he "is now a great man of science, and can plan railroads, and steam-engines, and electric telegraphs, . . . and knows almost everything about everything. . . . And all this from what he had learned when he was a water-baby underneath the sea."

Harvey Darton called *Water Babies* a "museum piece" because it is replete with Kingsley's quintessentially Victorian views on many subjects and contains satirical references to many controversies of the time.[15] However, Kingsley himself wrote to his friend Maurice that he had simply "tried, in all sorts of queer ways, to make children and grown folks understand that there is a quite miraculous and divine element underlying all physical nature . . ."[16]

As a story of the child archetype and the individuation process, *The Water Babies* has several features not present in *The King of the Golden River*. Jung says that the child often represents the potential of new life in death, or the whole birth-death-rebirth cycle. Such an idea would explain why people have been uncertain whether Tom and Elsie and Mr. Grimes actually died, or which world they inhabit from one part of the book to another. Again, Jung says that the child often has an androgynous character, symbolizing the potential unity of the opposites. Kingsley suggests this possibility by the pairing of Tom and Elsie. Such a pairing is found in many nineteenth century works. It does not strike us as realistic today and it probably was not realistic then, but is perhaps to be understood in this symbolic sense. Third, Jung says that a *group* of children or youths may be interpreted to indicate an intermediate stage in the vision of the new personality. Tom at first sees only the water "beasts," not the babies. Later he goes to school and plays with many water babies, and toward the end of the story he and Elsie separate from the rest.

The same change from multiplicity to unity takes place in Tom's experience of the magical women. Nineteenth century fantasy contained many magical women. Paired with the child, the magical woman represents the nurturant unconscious. Kingsley's spiritual receptivity, his love of nature, his frequently expressed attraction to death, his reliance on his wife and his fear that she would die before him—all suggest that his busy life was a strain and that he sought relationship to the maternal archetype.

Alice in Wonderland

Soon after *The Water Babies* came *Alice in Wonderland,* a revolutionary event because it brought the pursuit of pleasure for its own sake into children's books. Alice represents a reaction not so much against ego-defensive selfishness and greed as against the tyranny of the ego processes themselves—logic, reason, schooling, propriety, all the cultural purposiveness which gradually shuts off one's capacity to experience freshly and playfully, and to be aware of one's grotesque, incongruous "id" characteristics.[17] It is no accident that the Victorians produced not only the genre of children's fantasy but also that of nonsense. The two are combined in *Alice.*

Dodgson, of course, was a lecturer in mathematics at Christ's College. A stammerer in adult company, he tended to avoid adults, especially women, and to seek out children. From the content of poems written primarily in the early 1860's, there has been some speculation that he fell in love about this time. At any rate, his emotional life seems to have been in flux at the time of the creation of *Alice.* The famous boat trip with the Liddell children took place on July 4, 1862. He had entertained them on many previous occasions, but the stories he told that day were remembered by everyone as particularly good.

"I distinctly remember," wrote Dodgson, "how, in a desperate attempt to strike out some new line in fairy-lore, I had sent my heroine straight down a rabbit-hole, to begin with, without the least idea what was to happen afterwards."[18]

What did happen afterwards, and what made the day memorable, was that Alice became a child-hero who explored the underground of the unconscious and ultimately defied its threatening queen. When the Queen says, "Off with your head," Alice attains full size and shouts to the assemblage, "You're only a pack of cards!" The first part, in which Alice follows the nervous rabbit down the hole, falls for a long time, changes size unpredictably, almost drowns, meets an assortment of animals, etc., has a number of features in common with the beginning of *The Water Babies*. Indeed, it has been interpreted similarly, as symbolizing childhood sexual curiosity, sexual feeling, and return into the mother's body. Another interpretation is that Alice goes deep into the unconscious, and that her changes of size suggest Jung's description of the archetypal child as "smaller than small and bigger than big"—helpless and weak in some ways but also capable of great deeds, such as resisting the unconscious or revitalizing the personality. Although Alice meets some animals not so different from those in *The Water Babies*, most of them are rather perverse, touchy creatures, and she is also often threatening to them. These are indications that Carroll's attitude toward the unconscious was more ambivalent than Kingsley's.[19]

The marvelously strange country of Alice's world can be experienced only through Alice's childlike tolerance and receptivity. Much of the charm of Alice lies in the fact that her efforts to be quite sensible and rational rebound queerly in the strange underground world, seeming utterly to defeat rationality. Yet at critical moments reason does bring Alice mastery of the situation. Thus, she plays the role of the archetypal child who mediates between the ego and the unconscious.

Alice also represents a central part in the author's personality that was not easy to express in normal adult life. Absurdity and logic are, after all, closely related, and the lecturer in mathematics was in many respects removed from "real life." He never took on adult sexual and family roles and was rather rigid and perfunctory in his professional duties. His pleasure in little girls had unpleasant overtones of which he himself was sometimes partially aware. In other words, he was in many respects immature, "childish," and burdened with neurotic defenses. But in knowing and loving Alice Liddell, he was able to realize the positive aspects of the child in himself, and through this inner child, to experience and portray something of the confusing, frightening, fascinating world of his unconscious. That Alice's adventures culminated in a feeling of renewal on the part of the author is suggested by the rather odd epilogue. The older sister has a reverie in which she envisions Alice as a fine adult, though always simple and loving as a child, understanding little children and giving them pleasure with her stories. This grown-up Alice I would take to be Carroll's positive image of himself.

Jung said that the archetypal child sometimes has the character of a god and sometimes that of a hero. In other words, the nascent attitude may be one of complete harmony with nature, or the emphasis may be upon a mustering of ego forces to overcome obstacles to personality growth. Gluck, Tom, and Alice are described as neither gods nor heroes. They represent something intermediate: the adoption of childlike attitudes in the interests of expanding an imperfect, frustrated personality.

At the Back of the North Wind

The first divine child in children's fantasy was Diamond in George MacDonald's *At the Back of the North Wind,* which began to appear in serialized form in 1868. Appropriately, the diamond, or the shape of a diamond, is a common symbol of wholeness and unity. Diamond has loving parents and a trusting relationship with that magical woman of many aspects, the North Wind. Diamond's character and his accomplishments in the real world—he is the child as seed or creative agent—are described almost reportorially, as though the author wants to show us that such a personality can indeed exist. In the ordinary course of events, Jung says, the archetypal child grows up to be a hero, to carry out the mission of unifying the personality. However, the divine child cannot become a hero, because he represents the vision of a personality already perfect. Diamond dies, or is carried off by the North Wind, and one may note that a similar pattern is followed in other stories of the divine child, such as St. Exupéry's *Little Prince* or Maurice Druon's *Tistou of the Green Thumb.*

This story of the divine child is the only one in the group that seems not to have had special circumstances connected with its writing. MacDonald began his career as a Congregational minister, but he was a writer during most of his long life and is best known as a writer of serious fantasy. The composition of *At the Back of the North Wind* occurred during his most productive period and seems to reflect not an unusual psychological experience but a particularly smooth integration of his two worlds. Like Kingsley, MacDonald was not afraid of death. It seems likely that any special relationship to the magical woman was a psychic outgrowth of the death of his mother when he was eight years old.[20]

The child as hero is not a typical character in early children's fantasy, although there was considerable emphasis on mythic heroes and "great men" in contemporaneous adult literature. Giglio in *The Rose and the Ring* (1855) is certainly a comic hero, but this Twelfth Night story was written as much for the governess of Thackeray's children as for the children themselves, and has rather more to do with the masculine and the feminine than with the archetype of the child. MacDonald's *The Princess and Curdie* or the stories of Mowgli in *The Jungle Book* are better examples, but they appeared later, after mid-Victorian self-reliance began to give way to late-Victorian stagnation and rigidity, and as intellectuals began to separate from the "establishment."

Conclusions

These works of fantasy for children seem to support Jung's view that when conscious life becomes one-sided, archetypal images "rise to the surface in dreams and in the visions of artists to restore the psychic balance, whether of the individual or of the epoch."[21]

In "Sigmund Freud in his Historical Setting," Jung portrays Freud as a representative of his age, his concepts to be understood as reactions against nineteenth-century hypocrisy, shallow morality, and conventionality.[22] However, Jung was also a representative of the post-Victorian age, and one may suppose that his ability to abstract the concept of individuation was made possible by the conditions accentuating the need for it, first in England and later in Europe.

I do not mean to imply that the individuation process does not continue to find expression in works of fantasy for children. And yet, in contemporary works there is less emphasis upon the "archetypical child" and magical woman than there was in the nineteenth century. For the last generation the band of comrades and the wizard have been predominant figures in fantasy for children.[23] Today, perhaps, there is less need to "become a child again," more need for a sense of community and a sense of direction. It is begond the scope of this paper to document these changes; their significance for children's literature remains to be explored.

Footnotes

[1] See, for example, Edward A. Pohlman, "Childlessness, Intentional and Unintentional Psychological and Social Aspects," *Journal of Nervous and Mental Diseases,* 151 (1970), 2-12; N. M. Simon and A. G. Senturia, "Psychiatric Sequelae of Abortion," *Archives of General Psychiatry,* 15 (1966), 378-389; and Philippe Aries, *Centuries of Childhood, A Social History of Family Life* (New York: Random House, 1962).

[2] Ravenna Helson, "Sex-specific Patterns in Creative Literary Fantasy," *Journal of Personality,* 38 (1970), 344-363.

[3] This section is based primarily on the following books: Geoffrey Best, *Mid-Victorian Britain: 1851-1875* (New York: Schocken Books, 1972); W. L. Burn, *The Age of Equipoise* (New York: Norton, 1967); Walter E. Houghton, *The Victorian Frame of Mind, 1830-1870* (New Haven: Yale University Press, 1957).

[4] Sir John Clapham, as quoted by Best, p. 228.

[5] Mario Praz, "The Victorian Mood: A Reappraisal" in Richard A. Levine, ed., *Backgrounds to Victorian Literature* (San Francisco: Chandler, 1967), p. 72.

[6] Best, p. 74.

[7] Harold Perkin, *The Origins of Modern English Society, 1780-1880* (London: Routledge & Kegan Paul, 1969), p. 347.

[8] G. M. Trevelyan, *English Social History: A Survey of Six Centuries, Chaucer to Queen Victoria* (New York: Longmans, Green & Co., 1942), p. 545.

[9] C. G. Jung, "Conscious, Unconscious, and Individuation" and "The Psychology of the Child Archetype," *The Archetypes of the Collective Unconscious,* in *Collected Works* (Princeton, New Jersey: Princeton University Press, 1969), 9.

[10] W. G. Collingwood, *The Life and Work of John Ruskin* (Boston: Houghton Mifflin, 1893).

[11] Roger Lancelyn Green, *Tellers of Tales* (London: Ward, 1965), p. 28.

[12] M. Steig, "Dickens' Excremental Vision," *Victorian Studies,* 13 (1970), 339-354.

[13]C. G. Jung and Aniela Jaffe, *Memories, Dreams, Reflections* (New York: Random House, 1961).

[14] Guy Kendall, *Charles Kingsley and His Ideas* (London: Hutchinson & Co., 1947), p. 160.

[15]F. J. H. Darton, *Children's Books in England: Five Centuries of Social Life* (Cambridge: Cambridge University Press, 1932), p. 263.

[16]Kendall, pp. 117-118.

[17]Nina Auerbach, "Alice and Wonderland: A Curious Child," *Victorian Studies*, 17 (1973), 31-47.

[18]Roger Lancelyn Green, *Lewis Carroll* (London: Bodley Head, 1960), p. 33.

[19]Jung says that the fate of the child illustrates the kind of psychic events that occur in the entelechy or genesis of the self. For example, "The threat to one's inmost self from dragons and serpents points to the danger of the newly acquired consciousness being swallowed up again by the instinctive psyche, the unconsciousness" ("The Psychology of the Child Archetype," p. 166). Alice herself becomes serpent-like after ingestion of some of the contents of the unconscious.

[20]Robert Lee Wolff, *The Golden Key: A Study of the Fiction of George MacDonald* (New Haven: Yale University Press, 1961).

[21]"Psychology and Literature," in *The Spirit in Man, Art, and Literature; Collected Works*, 15. 104.

[22]In *The Spirit in Man, Art and Literature; Collected Works*, 15.

[23]Ravenna Helson, "From Magical Woman to Wizard: Changing Patterns in Fantasy for Children," *Proceedings of the XVIIth International Congress of Applied Psychology* (Brussels: Editest, 1972), pp. 1515-19. See also *Psychology Today*, 7 (1973), 107.

Family Conflicts and Emancipation in Fairy Tales*

Walter Scherf

Perhaps no other chapter dealing with children's literature is so burdened with misunderstandings as the one dealing with fairy tales. In most discussions even the initial preconceptions are wrong. Many misuse the term "fairy tale," treating everything alike, putting into one pot, as we say, whatever looks like folk tradition or originates from the influence of folk tradition.[1] But because the various kinds of folk tales have absolutely different functions and because they are accordingly absorbed in very different ways, we must study them separately.[2] As to their retelling and adaptation by modern authors, we must analyze the new versions in an additional dimension. They reflect their authors' regressive resumptions and psychical fixations, and often enough they demonstrate that these authors took the wrong vehicle for their intentions.[3]

Going back to the original narrative situation

To separate the various kinds of oral tradition is not so difficult as it seems to be if we ourselves are acquainted with story-telling and if we know the various expectations of our listeners. In other words, if we really will understand the texts, we must go back to the original situation of their telling. Only there the function becomes apparent. Looking only at the final fixed texts in print leads one astray.

Let us simplify story-telling to a model. There is on the one side the public, the expectation of the listeners, and on the other the narrator with his repertoire, his ability, and his sympathetic understanding of the listener's expectation. If we consider the results of current folktale recording in Europe, then we see that *Sage* and *Schwank* predominate: the "numinous" or the demonic tale on the one hand, the jest on the other. The function of the jest is to take aim at human instinct and the dependent inclinations: at avarice, jealousy, stupidity, folly, sexual addiction, voraciousness. The rigid patterns of comportment are depicted in a very realistic, in a drastic, way. Man is portrayed in his dependencies, in his subjugations—and these dependencies and subjugations are conveyed *ad absurdum* in releasing laughter. By realistic I mean that the dependencies are unmasked realistically, but he who is dependent is shown only as a type of one so inclined. He is led out on the scene only as a figure without any profile or depth, onto which every spectator is allowed to project his own image. If the spectator's personal conflicts were not so strong and similar, he would not listen to such tales; and, what is more, they would not have been handed down from generation to generation for millennia. These tales have changed only their circumstantial requisites.

It is remarkable that among all kinds of folktales the requisite change in the jests is most evident. The content has not changed and the type of the story is internationally spread over the world.[4] Only what is conditioned by the historically, sociologically, politically

---

*An address arranged by Professor Barbara Walker and delivered July 23, 1973, at the International Youth Library, Munich, Germany.

different settings has changed. Jests are realistical observers.[5]

Naturally a good jest narrator is not obliged to stick to traditional jests. He can adapt even actual happenings in the jest way, and he can even adapt a magical tale— substituting a jest figure for the hero in order to bring his listeners to laughter: e. g. , at a boaster, as in the case of the tale of the brave tailor, "Seven with one Stroke." [6] This is the way of the jest narrator. His listeners are expecting a magic tale of a dragon slayer, but he is cheating them: he switches to another wavelength and makes a jester from the originally expected hero. Bert Brecht called such an unexpected substitution a *Verfremdung*.

But let us continue our review of differing expectations. It is obvious that an animal fable or an example story replies to the listeners' desire to be instructed about the right patterns of behavior.[7] We all hurt ourselves when we behave in conflict with the rules and ways of life of our society. It depends on our positive or negative attitude how we intend to make our way in the given social environment. But in any case what we need, and just what children wish, is an unsentimental, objective instruction in how to adapt to current social patterns. This has nothing to do with individual psychical conflicts. It is practical introduction into social interdependencies; it is the unmasking of social relations and their influence on our own life. The fable is, seen from the society's side, naturally the traditional vehicle of social instruction. It secures patterns of behavior by tradition. To give an example, I quote a tale from Montenegro,[8] as it is transferred within a certain clan, so that all the kinsmen and particularly their rising generation become confirmed in an attitude, in their special way of life. Perhaps even now in the socialist Montenegrin republic the same "virtues" are valid and the same fables are retold.

The Husband's Test

When the mother of the famous hero, Pope Mile Jovović, got married for the first time, she placed herself the day after the wedding on the threshold of the house. When her husband returned home, she began to spin. There she sat, barring the way, and waited. When her husband tried to squeeze through between her and the wall, she packed her bundle and returned to her parents. "This is not the right husband," she stated.

After some time she married again and exactly the same thing happened. Returning home, she decided never again to marry. But her people pressed and she tried a third time. She repeated her old game; she placed herself on the threshhold, she spun, and she barred the way when her husband returned home. But this man took it amiss. In his temper he kicked her aside and cried, "Clear off, you impudent wench. Is there no other place where you can sit, and must you await me with the distaff?"

She did not lament. On the contrary. "All right," she said, proudly and gladly. And in this house she stayed until her death. In her own words she explained: "Who behaves like this is also a protector, if it proves to be necessary." And there we are: such a woman bore and such a man begot the famous hero, Pope Mile Jovović.

The meaning of fables is in their social function. Communism knew this from its beginnings. Thus the fable has become one of the most important kinds of children's literature—and if we study political education, one of the most significant kinds.[9] But what puzzles the critical observer is the usual compilation in anthologies. There you find fables from all periods and all societies from oral and from literary tradition, as a terrible and incomprehensible mixture. It is not the collected "wisdom of the world," but a haphazard gathering of texts which have lost their function. Artifacts are usually collected for studying history. But artifacts in disorder are good for nothing.

It is, as we are going to see, useful to stay some time with the fable. It gives us the opportunity to understand better the different functions of the various kinds of oral tradition, which have been alive during such an incredibly long time. But now we may ask the function of the so-called *Sage*, the folk tale with numinous kernel and demonic fascination.[10] I have during my life heard quite a lot of folktale narrators. They have not been only backwoodsmen. I have heard soldiers and industrial workers telling demonic tales, city people in hospitals, and miners. Every time I got a shock when I recognized the transition from the seemingly unconcerned "people say" to the suddenly revealing report of encounters with the unfathomable demonic world and to autobiographical confessions. It is necessary to be a good listener, to develop the sagacity for the right atmosphere, to switch to the right wavelength. Then pleasantry turns to earnestness. This is a convincing confirmation of our model, which is to show how different in quality the traditional forms of communication are—because of their different functions. I regret that we cannot continue now with a function analysis of the demonic tale, of the public's expectation and the narrator's aim. I must instead refer to the books of Max Lüthi from Switzerland and Lutz Röhrich from West Germany.[11] But the essence of these aims and expectations is the conviction that man is delivered up to the powers of the other side and that man is overcome by them.

This is the moment to note an unusual aspect of current children's literature. There is far reaching dependence upon the kinds, types, and motives of oral tradition, much more than we usually suppose. The demonic tale, for instance, which has been domesticated and handed down in very simplified versions for a hundred years in elementary readers, popular magazines, and children's books as a pleasant Rhineland or Alpine or Scottish romanticism, finally beats through the insulating layer and recovers its old function. I allude to the new role of occultism in American and British books,[12] to Alan Garner,[13] and to Otfried Preussler's masterpiece, *Krabat*.[14]

There are, naturally, more kinds of oral tradition we could deal with: the hero legend, the legendary lives of kings and saints, the family sagas, the wonder tales, and, as to children's literature in particular, the funny short tales and language games; and last but not least the very complex material of children's rhymes and children's games. I stress "very complex" because the material is as unequal as it could be. Nobody has really tried to distinguish the different origins of tradition, and, so far as I know, nobody has tried to separate the different functions. This is really a challenge. But our theme is the magic tales, the *Märchen* in their proper sense, which are originally told by adults for adults, but which are loved by children in a striking way—not only in our modern industrial society. From now on we shall exclude every other kind and type of oral tradition from our considerations.

Whoever will study the material will find open doors. Within the last seventy years Antti Aarne from Finland and Stith Thompson from America have worked out an international index of types.[15] It contains detailed annotations of the contents, enumerations of the motives, and a bibliography of versions and secondary literature. The following observations are based upon Aarne-Thompson's range of magic tales insofar as they take part in children's literature.

But already from the beginning arises the question, what is really the difference between adult tradition and children's tradition? Well, I believe that Linda Dégh's model is the key to understanding. Linda Dégh is a Hungarian scholar now working at Bloomington. She has completed, with her students, an excellent field study in a region of Hungary and has demonstrated how there are, in the same village, side by side, a primary and a secondary tradition.[16] The primary tradition always strives for optimum opportunities to unfold. The secondary tradition in turn hands down short, limited, rigid reports of the tales of the primary tradition. Before the war most people of the studied villages went to the large Rumanian farms in order to work there for the greater part of the year. After curfew the time of the story-tellers began. They had a fire before their hut, and the public could choose to whom they would like to go. Every story-teller had his repertoire and his personal style. Children were excluded, but they always slinked into the circle of the listeners.[17] The very great story-tellers achieved filling nearly a whole night with one tale—with only one tale. A Grimm fairy tale in comparison is read in about ten minutes.

After the war the border between Hungary and the Bukovina was closed. Another work organization began. The essential social structures changed. But the pressure to tell the old *Märchen* was not eliminated. It broke through in an unexpected place: the death-watch or wake proved to be the new opportunity. The mourning family invited the great story-tellers to sit beside the corpse, to watch together with the family and the close friends and to tell tales. It is remarkable that the good narrators made it a point of honor to extend one tale through a whole night of watching.

While the primary tradition thus flourished, at the same time—before the social shifting as well as thereafter—the much more limited public of house and family maintained a secondary tradition. The women tell their husbands' tales in a shortened, simplified, much more modest way. They narrate for children, their own and those of the neighborhood. A most striking fact is that when a narrator dies, it is usually the son who inherits his father's repertoire, and nobody else touches the treasure of tradition. It is taboo. But if there is no male heir, the widow jumps in. She is the same woman who previously related only the rigid versions of the secondary tradition. Suddenly she exhibits the same ability and resourcefulness as her husband had shown. She switches to the primary tradition, and the community does not discriminate in according her recognition and acceptance.

These experiences show our usual fairy tale collections in a new light. Up till now the French took it for granted that Perrault's tales would be the criteria for well told fairy tales, and the Germans thought the brothers Grimm were the *non plus ultra* of the fairy tale tellers. We suppose that Perrault knew very well the literature of colportage,[18] and from Jakob and Wilhelm Grimm we know exactly from whom they got their material.[19] Among them there was nobody who belonged to the primary tradition, and neither Perrault nor the brothers Grimm were inspired by the high literary style of two tales which they got from the North German painter Philipp Otto Runge. His naive and at the same time highly artificial adaptations of "The Juniper Tree"[20] and "The Fisher and His Wife"[21] became the basic pattern upon which Wilhelm Grimm rewrote and modeled all the material he got hold of. His authorities were a nurse and a peasant's wife who, by our model, did not even belong to the secondary tradition. Both women transferred and adapted what they had heard from unknown sources to the nursery of bourgeois families. What is especially interesting is that an extensive range of Grimm tales—Little Red Riding Hood, Sleeping Beauty, Cinderella, the first part of Hansel and Gretel, Cat-skin, and even the subsequently excluded Bluebeard and Puss-in-Boots—have been handed over from Perrault and his collection in French to German bourgeois families who liked to converse in French at home.[22] It has been proved that all these Grimm tales passed through French-speaking German families and Ludwig Tieck's romantic fairy theater. Jakob and Wilhelm Grimm's annotation, "widely spread and popular," has proved to be misleading.

What really is important for our subject is demonstrated by the model of primary and secondary tradition. It reflects the direct *Märchen* expectations of adults as well as of children. Once again we ask ourselves, what, really, is the cause of children's obvious predilection for magic tales? This predominating interest awakens as soon as the first sentences of the narrative begin. A determined expectation arises. What kind of determination? What are the motives? What causes the expectations?

Basic family conflicts

Some time ago I did a study based on 176 magic tales in order to investigate their introductory motives. The study included only those magic tales which play a part in children's literature.[23] Among the 176 texts, 169 reflected a typical family conflict in the first sentences: son-father, daughter-father, son-mother, daughter-mother. Representing 52% of the total, the *son-father conflict* places all the others in the shade. Sometimes various practical difficulties at home, for example the father's poverty, oblige the son to leave his family. Such conditions seem relatively harmless. More grave is the father's death, which, by the way, is interpreted by the listener not as the physical death of his own father, but as the factual end of their relationship. Most numerous are the tales beginning with the motive of the misjudged son.[24] It may be that the son is attracted by the adventure (and this is the reason why even Puritan Robinson left his father), but in most cases the father shows his son the door for any of a number of different reasons.

And just this experience responds to the conflicts over loosening of family ties which every child must go through. He is forced to cut off the old family relations and to enter a world which has been heretofore absolutely unknown. It is not the world before our door or beyond the quarter—every child already knows a big part of the outside world by car and by television. But psychologically he has not depended on it. And the necessity to establish our psychological relations with the not-yet-explored inner structure of the outside world changes things completely. The child is forced to leave the old support and to make his way in an inner condition, so that we might say he is a stranger to himself. Thus it is only another form of speaking if the story-teller says: "The father and mother are dead." He who is meant could still sit at his parents' table at home. But the supporting relations which he took for granted have gone, suddenly, without warning. They are dead. The son must develop his own new relations, supporting relations, and he does not know with whom.[25]

Let us stay with the facts given by the tales. In approximately half of all son-father tales it is the father who surrenders his son to unknown and dangerous powers, to sorcerers and demons. Or the father curses his son into his "dark shape."[26] He exposes him in an unknown country, or he condemns him expressly to death.

Max Lüthi points out the introductory isolation of the hero.[27] My analysis of children's magic tales proves that he is right in 98% of all cases. And the son-father tales demonstrate it most dramatically.

The isolating motives of the *daughter-father* tales look somewhat different. Let us sketch them in some detail. These motives isolate the girl, with whom the listener dramatically identifies. These isolating motives allow the listener to enter again the old individual conflict and to go through the old scenes anew. The listener is again confronted with the severed relation with the beloved father. It seems that before the story-teller says more than once upon a time there was a rich king; or once upon a time there was a merchant; or a miller, or a poor laborer, in the listener's imagination the never-surmounted conflict immediately appears and the empty outline of the king, merchant, miller, or laborer becomes filled by the picture of the listener's own father in happier days, when the inner relationship had not yet been disturbed. The story-teller continues, speaking of the father's death, the destitution, the tormenting misjudgment, and the cursing, which transforms the listener into a being strange to himself. He is exposed to insoluble tasks, thrown into despair, given over to demons, and suppressed by his father's frantic and cruel tyranny—confronting him with the alternative either to be rejected forever or to be addicted to him forever.

It sounds harmless and nice, does it not, when the brothers Grimm relate from "dark memories," as they say, that tale of the very poor little girl which was adapted in a rather childish and sentimental way,[28] but which was dear also to other romantic poets, as we read from their memoirs:

> Once upon a time there was a little girl whose father and mother had died. She was so poor that she did not have even the smallest chamber in which to live and no little bed in which to sleep, and finally she had really nothing but the clothes she wore on her body, and a little piece of bread in her hand that was given to her by some pitiful heart.

As adult listeners we naturally bar the reappearance of the old pictures, of the old despair, when everything that was dear to us had to be given up, and when we were obliged to set out hope upon utterly strange people, upon an unknown "pitiful heart." In another tale which projects the same conflict, we hear of a laborer who dies and leaves two children. The brother must take service and the girl remains alone. As a reflection of the lost happier childhood and at the same time as a remote and unconscious hope for a future establishment of an inner relation to a man not yet known, the brother takes his sister's picture with him abroad.[29]

To be misunderstood and misjudged—who did not end his childhood with this cruel experience? Who was not confronted as King Lear's youngest daughter was by her father?[30] And who has not been chased away after the test of his ability to say what is indispensable in this world? The elder sisters recite fulsome praises. But what is really indispensable is love which does not strive to possess.

Take note what a horror spreads among children when a puppet player is showing

"Rumpelstiltskin," when the miller, in order "to give himself reputation," sends his own daughter to the king and throws upon her a task which nobody can perform.[31] Or can one? Do not our forces develop when we are pushed into despair and destitution? They grow, surely, but they grow in a rather demonic way, and the puppet player's Kasperle and Punch must help and defeat them in the end.

Most tales in the daughter-father conflict group show the surrendering to a demonic being. Seemingly unwittingly the father promises his daughter to a person from the other world. It looks as if it would be expressly his task to loosen and even cut off the old psychological relations and to transfer them into a stranger, into a being which is imprisoned in his dark shape, in an iron oven, transformed into a wolf, a fox, a lion, or a bear. As to the father, his heart is heavy when he is obliged to execute the transference. Let us hark back to that tale in which the father takes off on a journey in order to fulfill the wishes of his three daughters.'[32] It was the youngest who asked for such strange things as a "klinkesklankes Lovesblatt," as a rose in mid-winter, as a singing and springing lion's "Eckerken"—the little sprite of the great lion. It is the father who insists, "promised is promised," that his daughter married King Frog.[33] This relation, too, was established in the same way as the relation to the lion. In an English version, which is more complete than the Grimm's tale, the three daughters are sent out by their father, one after the other, to go for water from the well at the world's end.[34] But the well belongs to the prince in the shape of a frog.

So we can easily continue. It is the father who after the advice of his intelligent daughter asks the king to get that fallow ground in which, as we find later, the golden mortar is hidden.[35] Or he sends his daughters, one after the other, to the enchanted house in the woods.[36] He surrenders "St. Mary's child" to the holy virgin, but it is not difficult to find out that behind the Grimm's version there was another in which not the holy virgin but a demonic being took the daughter.[37]

Countless are the tales, often enough told in broadside and chapbook style, in which the father promises his daughter to a stranger who seems to be proper and well-to-do, but in reality is nothing but a robber and a murderer.[38] The theme is widely spread from Perrault's "Bluebeard" and the Grimms' "Fichter's Bird" to the Dutch ballads from Halewijn and Ungerer.[39] The meaning is nothing but the fact that the relations between daughter and father have entered the most serious conflict. It is significant that the bride who got into this horrible situation partly because of her own fault delivers herself from the murder pit or cries for her brothers:

> Dear brother, heart's brother mine,
> Mercy upon your little sister!
> The brother was sitting at the cool wine.
> Her cry fell into his window.
> Dear comrades mine,
> I hear crying my only little sister!

The sister-brother relationship has substituted for the not-yet-surmounted daughter-father conflict. It will play its part until the true love relation to an outside man is developed.

Most tales of the daughter-father conflict group begin with the alienation and expulsion.

83

But there is also quite a number of tales belonging to the Cap o' rushes type. The father is not willing to let his daughter live her own life. He immures her in a big tower, he banishes her deep under the earth, he mounts guard before her sleeping room and he builds unsurmountable walls round the castle. When the virgin Maleen succeeds, after seven years of imprisonment, to loosen a stone of the tower, then the tale demonstrates how torturing the period is during which the father refuses to release his daughter.[40] There are enough autobiographies reflecting just this painful experience. But finally after seven years Maleen is free. She pushes the loosened stone out of the wall. But what she finds outside is a desert, abandoned country. The father is dead, her family is dead, the castle is burnt down, she is absolutely alone. Cap o' rushes, rescuing herself by flight, faces the same situation.[41] Her magic verse, when resolutely beginning her own way, is:

> Behind me dark, and before me bright.
> No one may see where'er I go.

Thus much about some details from that group of tales which begin with a daughter-father conflict. The group comprises 18% of the investigated magic children's tales. In this group the theme of surrendering to demons predominates. Some of these demonic beings can be disenchanted and redeemed, others cannot. Then our heroine's lover must liberate her. Relatively rare is the motif of expulsion by the father's death. More frequent is the motif that the father will bind his daughter fast forever. In this way we could continue and analyze the tales which begin with a *daughter-mother* conflict, a group also comprising about 18% of the total. It shows new centers of gravity: in some instances the girl must endure oppression and torture; in others she is simply chased abroad. To be sure, her adversary is her stepmother, and her secret helper in various shapes is her real mother, who has died.[42] However, what we need to do is to read the tale in the way it unfolds its effect between a narrator and his listeners. And the naive reader takes the tale in just the same unreflective way. The beloved mother is dead and the stepmother or a witch rules: it means only that our inner relations are cut off, that our mother is transformed. But the wonderful days of a lost childhood are undestroyable.[43]

We glimpse finally the smallest group—those tales which reflect a *son-mother* conflict. It comprises only 11% of the total. But it is not necessary to give all the material here now. I hope I can publish the complete investigation at a later date, saying for instance something about Lucky Hans, a tale which is only a joke, but which tells us the deplorable truth that there are mothers enough who effectively prevent their sons from acting independently, and sons so weak that in difficulties they always save themselves by flight home, as in the earliest childhood.[44]

Magic tales taken as an opportunity for psychodramatic projection

In any case I have tried to demonstrate, only considering the texts themselves, and keeping in mind that they are primarily unfolded between a narrator and his listeners, that children's so-called magic tales do nothing but reflect basic family conflicts, which push the child forward to emancipation. To be sure we have analyzed only the beginnings of the tales. We have not yet continued to study how the disposition of the conflict occurs. We have not yet followed our identification figures in order to see how they realize their emancipation. Nor have we examined the conclusions. But what I have done in addition to giving factual material about the conflicts, is to illustrate the likely reception by the child who is listening to these tales. The material is one thing; the reception is another. The material is accessible to everyone—but what can be affirmed about children's reception of fairy tales? The first point is the living existence of these tales during long periods in which the social patterns of behavior have changed often and essentially. The second point is that the introductory motives obviously stir up and fascinate the children. One can even break off and invite listeners to continue themselves—by telling, painting, or writing. The results show most strikingly that the children develop the conflict of the introductory disposition and fill it with their personal projection. The third point is the experiences of the story-tellers, puppet players included. For them it is easy, by the way. If among the spectators is a child who cannot bear the anguish,[45] he can always cry for Kasperle and Punch. And one or the other figure has to do nothing more than to peep around the stage curtain. He is a living guarantee of the good conclusion. The fourth point, finally, is in the case studies of the analysts.

In other words, I maintain that a magic tale is told only because the listeners' stowed-away family conflicts have need of it. The narration of the so-called magic tales is a traditional play of figures which are shaped to take the listeners' projections. Magic tales are psychodrama of family conflicts which claim to be worked through. And these family conflicts are the various departure situations of individual emancipation. A simple meaning of emancipation is to become adult. Naturally we should not interpret the four basic conflicts in a narrow way. The introductory motives of the misjudged youngest son by no means lead only little boys to spontaneous identification. What in the tales themselves is laid out as a son-father conflict is taken by some listeners surely also as a projective opportunity for a daughter-father conflict. I have often heard from adult men that when they were little boys an identification with Cinderella gave them great relief in playing out their own torments of being misunderstood and abandoned. Cinderella's longing for the dead good mother who helps secretly and mystically is not only a girl's longing.

We could be content with these statements and we could look for the *résumé*. Surely it would be very useful if somebody would systematically collect the case studies scattered in psychoanalytic publications,[46] and if others could hunt after more material about the reception of magic tales as a projective drama of family conflicts and emancipation. What is more, we could encourage children to tell projective stories. Every child is stirred up by these conflicts in a way that an adult usually refuses to understand. But the excited child is prepared to bring them out and to perform them. We then would have only to study the children's games. I wonder why until now no one has made a systematic study of the psychodramatic aspect. In any case, the work of the German psychiatrist Josephine Bilz, is an initial attempt.[47] But the professional collectors of children's rhymes and children's games have been obsessed for generations, in any case in Europe, by the mythological idea. They were quick to recognize Brunhilde in the wall of flames when city children in some courtyard were singing "Little Mary sat on a stone," while dancing around one of their playmates.

The parallel self-expression in games

I think everybody knows versions of those games in which children provoke the demonic beings. It is amazing how many games exist around the world. Either the children in chorus or a game leader provokes the demon in ritualized dialogue. Naturally, oral tradition is dialect tradition and every translation kills that strange atmosphere of suspension between horror and laughter. In any case I shall attempt to give an example from Cologne. One child, the designated witch, is hiding before the cellar door outside the house. It is late afternoon, the angelus bell is ringing:

> "Old wench, why are you sleeping such a long time?" cry the children down from the courtyard.
> The witch pretends to be awakening. "What time is it?" she asks.
> "Half goat's tail," is the impudent answer.
> "Why are the bells ringing so sweetly?" she asks.
> "Because your husband is dead," cry the children, with satisfaction.
> "Who has done this?" howls the witch.
> And the children, screaming "I!" "I!" rush away, the witch in hot pursuit.

One of them will become her victim and successor.

In one of the oldest German children's rhyme collections, done by Karl Simrock,[48] we find versions of the wolf game. The wolf is hidden behind a shrub. The goose-herd is crying for his geese, and the geese must pass the dangerous place. The ritual dialogue runs as follows:

> All my little geese, come home!
> We cannot.
> Why?
> Because of the wolf.
> Where is the wolf?
> Behind the bramble.
> What is he doing there?
> He is looking for a stone.
> What is he doing with the stone?
> Sharpening his knife.
> What is he doing with his knife?
> Cutting our throat!
> Why, little geese, come home!

The children are obliged to run for their lives, the wolf jumps from behind the shrub and tries to catch his prey. Sometimes the demon is a fox. If the playing ground offers a cave or hole or hut, so much the better. In such games the fox must limp.[49] In others the children assemble on a cart in the farmyard.[50] They make as much noise as possible because they provoke the demon who has crept under the cart. In a pause he suddenly knocks against the floor.

> "The roaring man is under the cart," he roars.
> "Who is there?" ask the children.
> "A man-eater."

"What do you want?"
"To eat a man."

It is significant that in some games children insert a joke. They ask the terrible roaring man with what he intends to eat a man, and he answers earnestly, "With a knife and fork." Thereupon the children, who try to suppress their laughter, ask:

"Do you have any?" And the foolish roaring man admits, "No." "Then," cry the children, "Try to fetch them!" And with an irresistible scream they dash away, the roaring man at their heels.

In Sweden it is a sleeping bear who is provoked by the children:

Björnen sover, björen sover,
i sitt lugna bo.
The bear is sleeping, the bear is sleeping,
in his quiet den.

Also, in Russia I have been told similar versions. In English game collections I found scattered material. Dutch children play the game in which one child has to hunt blindfolded after the other children, introducing it with a remarkable dialogue:

Look for a pin!
I do not find any.
Look for a needle!
I do not find any.
Look for man's flesh!

Whereupon the game begins with a horrible scream.[51]

We could easily continue.[52] There is no doubt that games in which a group of children provoke a demon are very widely spread. Being in a group, which gives the necessary support, the child provokes anguish and horror in order to stand the test, to master anxiety and the shudders of horror, and finally to wear them out. The psychological procedure is the same as that of the magic tale. But not only is the psychodrama itself the same, even the contents are the same—in any case in those tales where hero or heroine falls into the claws of demons. As to the form, there are relatively few dialogues with demonic beings to be found in magic tales. I have not yet looked systematically for them. Little Red Riding Hood's questions to the grandmother who is replaced by the wolf are popular enough.[53]

Our purpose has been to study the family conflicts and the trend to emancipation as they are represented in children's magic tales. Our conclusion is that children's magic tales have but one function: they help in breaking away from the old family relations and to lead to real emancipation and adulthood.[54] This in return is the real reason why countless modern children's books, which pretend to be realistic, depend in their roots upon the conflict and emancipation model of the magic folktale.[55]

I hope I have made clear that for millennia oral tradition has reflected two different human requirements: the physical and psychological disengagement of the child from his parents which cannot be executed without grave emotional shocks, and the adaptation to the society, which can be eased by unsentimental behavior instruction. In order to fulfill his social tasks, a person must first have become an autonomous individual. The modern preachers of enlightenment overlook this fact as wilfully as did the moral apostles of yesterday, who followed only one interest: to transfer mechanically their rigid patterns of behavior because they tried to prolong the society of their period. But from human terror and ruins one will never build a human and humane society. There we are. The so-called old magic tales, with their requisites which only literary academicians by their protests try to prevent from being changed, retain, side by side with fables and example stories their sense and their function as psychodramas of the necessary emancipation of the child and his transformation into an adult who is able to master his individual conflicts, who lives and works autonomously and self-responsibly.

Footnotes

[1]This is unfortunately the case. One typical and significant example is Julius E. Heuscher's book, *A Psychiatric Study of Fairy Tales* (Springfield, Illinois: Thomas, 1963).

[2]The best report of what has been done in the field of fairy tale research has been given by Max Lüthi: *Märchen* (Stuttgart: Metzpler, 1971). For distinguishing the various closely related forms of oral tradition, see pp. 7-16.

[3]Here we renounce studying the "Kunstmärchen" as well as the fantastic tale. See Göte Klingberg, *The Fantastic Tale for Children* (Gothenburg: School of Education, 1970); Anna Krüger, *Das Fantastische Buch*, in *Jugendliteratur* (München), 6 (1960), 341-363; Richard Bamberger, ed. *Das Irrationale in Jugendbuch* (Wien: Leinmüller, 1968); Mimi Ida Jehle, *Das Deutsche Kunstmärchen von der Romantik zum Naturalismus* (Urbana: University of Illinois, 1935); Gertrud Mudrak, *Das Kunstmärchen des 19. Jahrhunderts in seinen Beziehungen zur Volksüberlieferung* (Doctoral Thesis; Wien, 1953); Brigitte Ewe, *Das Kunstmärchen in der Jugendliteratur des 20. Jahrhunderts* (Doctoral Thesis, München, 1965). See also the analysis given by W. Scherf, note 47.

[4]The basic reference tool for all research work (although it does not include the demonic tale and the legend) is: Antti Aarne and Stith Thompson, *The Types of the Folktale: A Classification and Bibliography* (Helsinki: Suomalainen Tiedeakatemia, 1964). See also S. Thompson, *The Folktale* (New York, 1952).

[5]In the same series of research reports in which Max Lüthi's book on the fairy tales appeared, there is available also a useful report on jest research: Erich Strassner, *Schwank* (Stuttgart: Metzler, 1968).

[6]The Brave Little Tailor (AT 1640, Grimm No. 20, Bechstein No. 1), first published by Martin Montanus, 1557, in his "Wegkürzer."

[7]See Erwin Leibfried, *Fabel* (Stuttgart: Metzler, 1967); Klaus Doderer, *Fabeln* (Zürich, Freiburg i. Br.: Atlantis, 1970).

[8]The following, somewhat shortened tale is taken from Gerhard Gesemann, *Heroische Lebensform* (Berlin: Wiking Verlag, 1943), p. 152.

[9]See Walter Scherf, *Emanzipatorische und gesellschaftspolitische Tendenzen in der Kinder- und Jugendliteratur*. In *Bertelsmann Briefe*. (Gütersfoh, 1973), No. 79, pp. 9-18.

[10]A convincing analysis of the difference between Märchen and Sage has been given by Max Lüthi, for instance in, *Volksmärchen und Volkssage* (Bern, München: Francke, 1961), 22-48. One of the foremost experts of "the other world" is Lutz Röhrich. See his basic research report, *Sage* (Stuttgart: Metzler, 1966); and his book about the patterns of reality in magic tales, *Märchen und Wirklichkeit* (Wiesbaden: Steiner, 1964).

[11]Max Lüthi, *Das europäische Volksmärchen* (Bern, München: Francke, 1968). See also note 2. As for L. Röhrich, see note 10.

[12]Titles from the U.S.A. which touch upon the child's or young adult's preoccupation with the occult: Zilpha Snyder, *The Witches of Worm* (New York, 1972); *The Headless Cupid* (New York, 1970); *The Egypt Game* (New York, 1967)—child-play of Egyptian magic ceremonies; Dale Carlson, *The Mountain of Truth* (New York, 1972); F. E. Randall, *The Almost Year* (New York, 1972). All are publications of Atheneum.

[13]See e.g. Alan Garner, *Elidor* (London: Collins, 1965).

[14]Otfreid Preussler, *Krabat* (Wurzburg: Arena, 1971). The basis of Preussler's book is a Serbian tale of a sorcerer, Master Krabat. It has many motives common with the "Märchen" of the magician and his pupil, AT 325, Grimm, No. 68, Bechstein, No. 35. See Emmanuel Cosquin, *Les mongols et leur prétendu rôle dans la transmission des contes indiens vers l'occident européen: Étude de folklore comparé sur l'introd. du Siddhi-Kur et le conte du magicien et son apprenti*, in *Revue des traditions populaires*, 27 (1912), 337-373; 393-430; 497-526; 545-566. In many versions of this type the father is confronted with the task of recognizing his son after three years, in the form of an animal. If he fails, the son will belong to the magician forever.

[15]See note 3.

[16]Linda Dégh, *Märchen, Erzähler und Erzählgemeinschaft* (Berlin (Ost): Akademie-Verlag, 1962).

[17]Children themselves strive to become adult. They see an extraordinary opportunity to learn more about the secret wants and the disguised behavior of adults, and the adults basic psychological conflicts are the same as the children's conflicts.

[18]See the excellent study, following different methods of research, by Marc Soriano: *Les contes de Perrault* (Paris: Gallimard, 1968).

[19]A good survey has been given by Ruth Michaelis-Jena, *The Brothers Grimm* (London: Routledge & Kegan Paul, 1970). More historical details about the collection and its sources have been given by Wilhelm Schoof, *Zur Entstehungsgeschichte der Grimmschen Märchen* (Hamburg: Hauswedell, 1959).

[20]Because of its so called cruelty, "The Juniper Tree" (AT 720, Grimm No. 47, Bechstein No. 66) is in most cases not included in English editions for children. But Joseph Jacobs published as his No. 3 a parallel version from Henderson's *Folk-Lore of the Northern Countries* under the title "The Rose Tree."

[21]AT 555, Grimm No. 19, Bechstein No. 55. Aleksander Sergeevič Puškin's version from 1836 influenced the eastern oral tradition and became an important source for eastern children's literature. See also the doctoral theses of Margareta Rommel, *Von dem Fischer und syner Fru* (Karlsruhe, 1935). The best account of how this tale came despite hindrances into the Grimms' collection is given by Albert Wesselski in *Deutsche Märchen von Grimm* (Brünn, München, Wien: Rohrer, 1942), II, pp. 55-60.

[22]See the excellent doctoral thesis of Rolf Hagen, which is, unfortunately, only available in typescript: *Der Einfluss der Parraultschen Contes auf das volkstümliche deutsche Erzählgut und besenders auf die Kinder- und Hausmärchen der Brüder Grimm.* (Doctor Thesis, Göttingen, 1954).

[23]Paper given in March, 1968 at a congress of the European Folk Tale Society, "Das Märchen als Erlebnisraum des Kindes. Wie der kindliche Zuhörer durch die Eingangsmotive in das Märchenerlebnis geführt wird," 26 pp. (typescript).

[24]Father trusts only the two eldest boys. Everything they do is all right, they already belong to the establishment. But one day the unexpected breaks into the satisfied and settled world: every night somebody devastates father's orchard, stealing the golden apples. Father asks the eldest boy to watch. But he falls asleep. He asks the second boy, but also he proves to be a good-for-nothing fellow. Only after new hindrances is the misjudged youngest son, with whom the listener identifies himself, allowed to watch. These introductory motives belong in most cases to the type AT 550, Grimm No. 57, which has been developed in its classical way by Pëtr Pavlovic Eršov, in his 1834 "Kenck-Gorbunok" (The Hump-back Horse); or it introduces AT 551, Grimm No. 97, Jacobs No. 71, or Bechstein, No. 13.

[25]As to this point of view, which takes the emancipation conflicts as the real motivation for children's interest in fairy tales, compare J. Henscher (see note 1), Ottokar Graf Wittgenstein, *Märchen, Träume, Schicksale* (Düsseldorf, Köln: Diederichs, 1965), and Agnes Gutter, *Märchen und Märe* (Solothurn: Antonius-Verlag, 1968).

[26]The best analysis of the "Dark Shape" has been given by Edmund Mudrak, "Der Tierbräutigam," K. V. Spiess and E. Mudrak, *Deutsche Märchen, Deutsche Welt* (Berlin: Stubenrauch, 1939), p. 484-505. See also, E. Mudrak, "Das Volksmärchen," *Jugendliteratur* (München), 4 (1958), No. 7, 309-317, esp. p. 311.

[27]In his book, *Das europäische Volksmärchen* (see note 11).

[28]"Die Sternthaler," Grimm No. 153. There are references from Jean Paul as well as Achim von Arnim. A Swedish chapbook from 1846 is entitled "Stjern-Riksdalyarne."

[29]AT 403A: Zitterinchen, Bechstein No. 61. But compare also Grimm No. 135, "The White and the Black Bride."

[30]"Love Like Salt," AT 923, Grimm No. 179, Bechstein, second collection, No. 24. Compare also Karl Simrock, *Die Quellen des Shakespeare* (Bonn: Marcus, 1872), II, p. 215-235; and Emil Bode's Doctoral Thesis, *Die Learsage vor Shakespeare* (Halle: Niemeyer, 1904).

[31]At 500, Grimm No. 55. Compare Jacobs' excellent No. 1: "Tom Tit Tot." He took it from a contribution in Suffolk dialect by Mrs. Walter-Thomas in *Ipswich Journal*, 1877.

[32]AT 425, a type of tale usually called, after Apuleius, "Amor and Psyche." During the 18th century it

became widely known in Europe through Madame de Villeneuve (1740: *Histoire de la bête*) and Madame Leprince de Beaumont (1757: *La belle et la bête*). The Grimms published their version 1815 as what is now No. 88, following a narration of Wilhelm Grimm's wife, in English editions usually represented by an incomplete version with the title "The Lady and the Lion." Compare also Grimm No. 127 ("The Iron Oven"), Bechstein No. 16 (who follows the French tradition), and Jacobs No. 48: "Black Bull of Norroway," and No. 50: "Three Feathers."

[33]AT 440, Grimm No. 1, Bechstein No. 36.

[34]Published by Joseph Jacobs as No. 41. His source was Leyden, *The Complaynt of Scotland, with additional touches from Halliwell.* It could be that the children's song "Froggy Would a-Wooing Go" originated from this folk tale.

[35]AT 875: "The Clever Peasant Girl," Grimm No. 94. Carl Orff based his opera "Die Kluge" on this tale.

[36]AT 431; Grimm No. 169.

[37]AT 706, widespread in southern Europe; Grimm No. 3.

[38]AT 955, Grimm No. 40 and 73a, Bechstein No. 84a. AT 311, Grimm No. 46 and 66, Bechstein No. 23, 83a, and 90a. AT 312, Perrault No. 3, Grimm No. 62a, Bechstein No. 70. Jacobs published, as his No. 26, "Mr. Fox," a version which he took from Blakeway's contribution to Malone's *Variorum Shakespeare,* 1790. The professional literature on the Blue-Beard group is too large to be quoted here. See W. Scherf in the complete Bechstein edition (Munich: Winkler, 1963), p. 826-827. A most interesting analysis is given by Marc Soriano (see note 16), p. 211-212.

[39]See the rich annotations to the Swedish "Ballad of the Robber Rymer" in E. G. Geijer and A. A. Afzelius, *Svenska folkvisor* (Stockholm: Haeggstöm, 1880), II, p. 274-279. For English ballads see the Thomas Rymer versions.

[40]AT 870, Grimm No. 198. Compare also AT 884, Bechstein No. 39. Waldemar Liungman's doctoral thesis should be taken as a base for all further research in this field: *En traditions-studio över sagan om prinsessan i jordkulan* (Göteborg, 1925). Scandinavia is particularly rich with versions of the type "The Princess Confined in the Mound."

[41]See Anna Birgitta Rooth, *The Cinderella Cycle* (Lund: Gleerup, 1951). AT 510B, "Cap O'Rushes"; Perrault No. 10, Grimm No. 65 and 71a, Bechstein in his second collection No. 1, Jacobs Nos. 11, 56, 73, and 83.

[42]KHM 510A, Perrault No. 6, Grimm No. 21, and Bechstein No. 62. The first comprehensive study on this type has been made by Marian Roalfe Cox: *Cinderella* (London, 1893). A more important book now is the doctoral thesis of A. B. Rooth (see note 37). As to the Cinderella analysis see Soriano (note 16), p. 141-147.

[43]It is not only Cinderella who creeps weeping in the ashes of the still warm fireside, but it also for instance is that kind girl who is chased from home and pushed into a well. The most comprehensive study on the type AT 480 (Perrault No. 5, Grimm No. 24, Bechstein No. 11, 51a, and 66a, Jacobs No. 43 and 64) is Warren E. Roberts' *The Tale of the Kind and Unkind Girls* (Berlin: de Gruyter, 1958).

[44]The son-mother conflict is also reflected in tragic tales, which would better be classified as "Sage" rather than as "Märchen." They belong to AT 780 type, on which Lutz Mackensen wrote his study, *Der singende Knochen* (Helsinki, 1923). See also Leopold Schmidt, *Die Volkserzählung* (Berlin, 1963), p. 48-54. Most of these tales are mournful and dismal. See Grimm No. 28 and Jacobs No. 9, "Binnonie." W. Wackernagel published in 1843 as No. 3 of his tales from the Aargau, without title, a tale of a mother persuading her son to kill his sister—retold by Bechstein as No. 3 in his second collection. On the other hand, the foolish bargains of Lucky Hans (AT 1415, Grimm No. 83, Bechenstein No. 22) known worldwide in children's literature, are also not to be classified as "Märchen" but as jest. H. C. Andersen adapted the tale and gave it a somewhat different meaning: "Hvad fatter gjoer, det er altid det rigtige." See also the excellent analysis given by Wittgenstein (see note 25). Incidentally, good examples and analysis of the son-mother conflict are given by Erik H. Erikson in *Childhood and Society* (New York: Norton, 1964); Sigmund Freud, *Drei Abhandlungen zur Sexualtheorie* (Wien: Deuticke, 1947), always serves as a basic study. It is significant that not only Ludwig Bechstein, who was a natural child, not knowing his father (probably a French soldier), found his great opportunity to retell lucky Hans in his personal way, but also that Adelbert von Chamisso, the French refugee, who was a very lonely man and during his whole life, longed for the lost childhood in his parents' castle in the Champagne, was fascinated by the tale and set it in verse.

[45]The first serious research into the so-called cruelty in fairy tales has been done by Lutz Röhrich, "Die Grausamkeit in deutschen Märchen," in *Rheinisches Jahrbuch für Volkskunde*, 6 (1955), 176-224. See also, W. Scherf, "Was bedeutet dem Kind die Grausamkeit der Volksmärchen?" *Jugendliteratur* (München), 6 (1960), No. 11, 496-514.

[46]It is a pity that Julius E. Henscher (note 1) and Ottokar Graf Wittgenstein (note 22) did not do better research even on what had been published already from the Freudian point of view. Eric Fromm, *The Forgotten Language* (New York: Holt, Rinehart & Winston, 1951), is only speculative. The best survey of psychological contributions is given by Hans E. Giehrl, *Volksmärchen and Tiefenpsychologie* (München: Ehrenwirth, 1970).

[47]The first to stress the correspondence of fairy tale interest and children's games was Josephine Bilz, "Märchengeschehen und Reifungsvorgänge unter tiefenpsychologischem Gesichtepunkt," in C. Buhler and J. Bilz, *Das Märchen und die Phantasie des Kindes* (München: Barth, 1958), p. 73-111. See also W. Scherf "Kindermarchen in dieser Zeit?" (München: Don Bosco, 1961).

[48]Karl Simrock, *Das deutsche Kinderbuch* (Frankfurt a. M.: Bronner, 1848), See No. 854, p. 209.

[49]See e.g. Johann Lewalter, *Deutsches Kinderlied und Kinderspiel* (Kassell: Victor, 191) p. 240, "Fox, come out on one leg!"

[50]O. Runkel, "Volkstümliche Spiele Westerwälder Kinder," in *Zeitschrift des Vereins für rheinische und westfälische Volkskunde* (Wuppertal-Elberfeld.) 27, 1930. (No. 1/2) p. 67.

[51]J. van Vitn, *Nederlandsche baker—em Kinderrijmon* (Leiden: Sijthoff, 1874), p. 107.

[52]First of all, the very rich material in the English language should be collected systematically. Here only a very few examples can be given. Characteristic is the game of children playing in a ring around a blindfolded child in the middle. They are anxious not to become recognized and surely they feel deep horror when singing the old tune: "O do you know the Muffin Man, who lived in Drury Lane?" The blindfolded child, will touch one of them with his stick. And the touched child is obliged to hold the stick

and to sing the second verse, running the risk that the child who in fact represents a demon will guess who he is. To the same group belongs the pantomime game of Old Roger: "Old Roger is dead and he lies in his grave/ They planted an apple tree over his head/ the apples grew ripe and they all tumbled down/ There came an old woman a-picking them up/ Old Roger got up and he gave her a poke/ This made the old woman go hippety-hop!" See also William Wells Newell, *Games and Songs of American Children* (New York: Dover, 1963), pp. 153-167.

[53]The tale of Little Red Riding Hood is probably not a magic tale in its proper sense, but a warning example from the period of wolfman superstition. The tale is registered as AT 333. Perrault gave a version as his No. 2, Grimm as No. 26, and Bechstein as No. 9. Compare Marianne Rumof's doctoral thesis, *Rotkäppchen* (Göttingen, 1951). See also Soriano (note 16), pp. 148-160.

[54]Let us go back again and see the starting point: listening to introductory motives, children play over and over what life itself is asking of them. And it is the same with the different stations of adventure they pass following the tale itself—always in danger of perishing. They enter the castle of the enigmatic princess (AT 329, Grimm No. 191). On 99 stakes the severed heads of the suitors who could not answer the magic riddles already sneer at the listener, and the empty hundredth stake is waiting for him. But beyond all fear, the listener knows in his heart that he will not perish.

[55]See W. Scherf, "Das Kinderbuch, eine Visitenkarte der Gesellschaft," in Udo Dorbolowsky and Eberhart Stephan, *Die Wirklickeit und das Böse* (Hamburg, 1970), pp. 131-142. Also see W. Scherf, "What has our society to tell its rising generation?" 34pp. (Typescript).

Misunderstood: A Victorian Children's Book for Adults

Lynne Rosenthal

Florence Montgomery's *Misunderstood* (1869) is an unusual children's book in that it was not originally written for children but for their parents. Although on its publication it was read by both children and adults, the book, as Montgomery explains in the preface, was "intended for those who are willing to stoop to view life as it appears to a child, and to enter for a half-hour into the manifold small interests, hopes, joys and trials which make up its sum." Although much had been written about and for children throughout the century, children, Montgomery observed, had not previously been described from their "own point of view," and for that reason had often been "overlooked and misunderstood."[1] Montgomery wrote *Misunderstood* to point out and to correct misunderstandings between parents and children, which were, she believed, based on inaccurate and therefore confused assumptions about the nature and psychology of the child. If previous writings for and about children had been concerned with molding the child's character, Montgomery's book was one of the first to describe the child's behavior without attempting to direct it. In writing *Misunderstood* Montgomery hoped to change the behavior of parents rather than of children.

I

Misunderstood opens at Wareham Abbey, Sussex, where the two young protagonists, Humphrey and Miles Duncombe, ages seven and four, are awaiting the arrival of their father. Lady Duncombe has died two years before the story begins, and the boys are in the care of a French governess, Virginie. Sir Everard Duncombe, who is an M.P., visits his motherless children only on occasional weekends. During each of these "flying visits," Virginie, who suffers from "nerves," greets Sir Everard with accounts of Humphrey's misbehavior, of how "he would climb impossible trees and jump from impossible heights," endangering not only his own life, but that of his younger brother who invariably follows his example.

Humphrey is as healthy, active, and bold as Miles is sickly, passive, and mild. While Humphrey is "proof against colds, coughs and accidents of all kinds," Miles has a "tendency to a delicate chest." Inevitably, following each early morning mushroom hunt or visit to the pond instigated by Humphrey, Miles takes to bed with a fever. With his clinging and affectionate ways, Miles is his father's favorite. Lady Duncombe, on the other hand, had favored Humphrey, recognizing the loving nature beneath his rougher manner. After his wife's death, Sir Everard had interpreted Humphrey's restlessness as lack of feeling, and, when he sees Humphrey playing, concludes his son "has not much heart." On the contrary, Humphrey misses his mother, and, certain that neither his father nor Virginie care for him, spends much time in his mother's room, trying to "fancy he felt her arms around him and her shoulder against his head" (p. 169).

The greater part of the book describes Humphrey's adventures and their consequences. Humphrey's taste for the marvelous is nurtured by a sailor uncle Charlie, Lady

Duncombe's brother, whose exotic stories provide a model for imitation. Following a tree-climbing episode inspired by one of these tales, the boys are caught in a downpour and Miles becomes dangerously ill. When Miles recovers, Humphrey's buoyant spirits confirm his father's conviction that Humphrey lacks "heart." Forbidding him any further tree-climbing, Sir Everard returns to London, only to be handed a telegram informing him that "an accident has happend" at home. Certain that this time Miles is near death, Sir Everard decides that "no punishment could be severe enough for Humphrey." On his return home, however, he finds that it is Humphrey, not Miles, who has been hurt.

The lure of the tree has proven too strong and Humphrey has disobeyed his father's orders. His fall from the tree will, the doctors tell Sir Everard, leave Humphrey paralyzed. When Humphrey is told that he will never walk again, he wants to die, and asks his father to help him make out his will (he leaves his toys to Miles). Humphrey's wish is soon fulfilled. A lengthy scene displaying Humphrey's anxiety to join his mother in Heaven makes Sir Everard aware, for the first time, of the depth of his son's feelings for his mother, of his having "heart" after all. The book concludes with Humphrey's death.

II

The description of Humphrey's death set off a wave of Victorian sentimentalism equaled only by the deathbed scenes of Little Nell, Paul Dombey (on whose death Humphrey's is largely modeled), and Eric.[2] In *The Image of Childhood*, Peter Coveney explains the widespread interest in literary descriptions of the deaths of children during the second half of the nineteenth century as "the commercial expression of something detectably sick in the sensitive roots of English child fiction." Nostalgia for childhood, as Coveney demonstrates, often became "a means of escape from the pressures of adult adjustment, a means of regression towards the irresponsibility of youth, childhood, infancy, and ultimately nescience itself."[3] This nostalgia, Coveney asserts, could also be expressed through idealized pictures of children frozen into an innocence which growing up would inevitably corrupt. The view of childhood as innocent and passive is illustrated in Ruskin's observation in his preface to John Camden Hotten's edition of *German Popular Stories*. A child, he said,

> should not need to choose between right and wrong. It should not be capable of wrong. It should not conceive of wrong . . . Obedient as bark to helm, not by sudden strain or effort, but in the freedom of its bright course of constant life.

However, despite the book's obvious appeal to sentimentality, we cannot adequately explain either the great popularity of *Misunderstood,* or Montgomery's intention in writing it by referring to Victorian nostalgia for the innocence and stasis of childhood. In *Misunderstood,* childhood is as problematic for the child as adulthood is for the adult. Far from being an ideal child, Humphrey is always getting into trouble. Far from being exempted from the dilemmas of choice, he is tormented by "restless questions" and misunderstandings, which end only with his death.

That some readers recognized Montgomery's intention of providing a realistic rather than an idealized picture of the child is evidenced by the following observation in *The Saturday Review* (January, 1870):

> We were not prepared for so faithful and suggestive a picture of childish life as . . . *Misunderstood*. And such a picture is valuable, for the early stages of youth appear to be less and less comprehended as we drift further into the vortices of civilization . . . . Child-life itself does not sufficiently appeal to passion and sensation to claim strong interest from our hurried intelligence, yet its problems cannot be neglected. Mechanize the world as we may, we have not yet heard of any scheme by which children can be ignored without serious mischief to society.

As the reviewer's comment suggests, if children were sometimes idealized in theory, they were as frequently ignored in reality. With increasing affluence, it has become commonplace for upperclass parents to separate themselves physically from their children; mothers as well as fathers frequently led full social lives, leaving their offspring in the care of servants. Segregated from the adult world downstairs, the child lived in the nursery with Nurse and Governess, rarely seeing his parents.[4] With his decreasing visibility, the child's real nature was obscured. As *The Saturday Review* observed, Sir Everard, although not a bad father "as fathers go," is "an impersonation of the ignorance shown by parents who see little of their children," and must rely for insight into their children's characters on brief glimpses and second-hand accounts of their behavior, supplemented by assumptions about child psychology picked up from a wide variety of often conflicting sources.

<h2 style="text-align:center">III</h2>

We can best assess the significance of Montgomery's attempt to draw a realistic portrait of child-life by considering *Misunderstood* in the context of a group of nineteenty-century children's books which it superficially resembles. The contrast between spontaneous and restrained childhood behavior around which *Misunderstood* revolves was a convention of nineteenth-century didactic literature for children. As Gillian Avery observes, juvenile fiction, from its inception as a recognized genre in the latter years of the eighteenth century, for the most part represented a history of "adult taste in children,"[5] presenting the child with an image of himself to which he was expected to conform. As the technological achievements of the industrial revolution during the late eighteenth and early nineteenth centuries undermined tradition and quickened social change, children's books became one of the most important instruments in the socialization of the young. In order to shape the productive character structure required by a growing middle-class ethic, book after book offered the child useful facts along with advice on how to behave, stressing the value of utilitarian, rational action and moral behavior, but discouraging imagination and play.

In fashioning their image of the child, didactic writers drew on at least three basic and somewhat contradictory models of child development. They were influenced by Locke's picture of the mind as a "tabula rasa," a blank sheet to be inscribed by the educator with useful information, by Rouseeau's idea of the child as naturally good and of education as a process gradually unfolding innate capacities with a minimum of outside interference, and by the older religious concept of human nature according to which the child was originally sinful, and the goal of education was to reshape his wicked impulses. Although each of these models of childhood placed a different emphasis on the polarities of restraint and spontaneity, reason and imagination, work and play, the practice of didactic writers was to juxtapose one model on another, blurring the distinctions between them. Rousseau's principle of allowing the child to learn through the first-hand experience of things (object-lessons), for example, was frequently adopted by didactic writers in order to instill utilitarian knowledge or Christian morality.[6]

Thomas Day's *Sandford and Merton,* published in three volumes between 1783 and 1789, is a prototype of countless didactic works, published during the first half of the nineteenth century, and it remained one of the most well-read children's books until the latter decades of the century. Day's story contrasts the willful, impetuous behavior of Tommy Merton, the model of the Bad Boy, with the diligence, productivity and restraint of Harry Sandford, Day's ideally Good Child. By the end of the book the "natural vivacity" of Tommy's character has been cured, and Tommy transformed into a fair copy of Harry through the efforts of the clergyman tutor Mr. Barlow, whose goal in education is to give "good impressions." By means of pointed anecdote, object lesson and moral lecture, Mr. Barlow teaches Tommy that useful and virtuous behavior will invariably be rewarded, and impulsive, irrational behavior invariably punished.

A common procedure in didactic literature was to punish with sickness or even death the child who failed to make the rational or virtuous choice. Mrs. Sherwood's *The Fairchild Family,* published in four installments between 1818 and 1849, was "calculated to show the effects of a religious education." Little Augusta Noble, who insists on playing with candles, dies an agonizing death by fire, "a warning to all children who presume to disobey their parents"; in the most memorable incident in the book, Mr. Fairchild punishes his children by showing them a gibbet on which hang the remains of a man who first quarreled with and then murdered his brother. Although the technique of the Awful Example found its most common application in religious works such as *The Fairchild Family,* it was commonly used in secular books as well. *Dangerous Sports: a Tale Addressed to Children Warning Them against Wanton, Careless, or Mischievous Exposure to Situations from which Alarming Injuries so often Proceed* (1808), makes even the simplest childhood activities seem dangerous. It warns the child against tops and jumping, and advises him to "think before you taste, and taste before you swallow." When, despite his mother's warning, Alexander insists on going out for a ride, the chaise is overthrown and, although "every kind of assistance was lavished on him," he "died at the end of a few hours." Augustus, on the other hand, lives to be thankful that "he had escaped a similar fate only by his obedience to his mother."

The tension between freedom and restraint, imagination and reason, persists in children's books through the 1860's. It can be seen in the battle between Peter Parley and Felix Summerly, the respective pseudonyms of Samuel Goodrich and Henry Cole. The *Parley* books, which were published in great numbers beginning in the 1830's, were repositories of facts on every conceivably useful subject.[7] The *Summerly* books, on the other hand, were, as Cole announced in his first volume in 1841, "purposed to cultivate the Affections, Fancy, Imagination and Taste of Children." The appearance of Catherine Sinclair's *Holiday House* in 1839, of *Grimm's Fairy Tales* in translation in the 1840's, of Dickens' *Hard Times* in 1854, and of Lear's nonsense rhymes and Carroll's *Alice* in 1846 and 1865 respectively, represented important steps toward increased imaginative freedom for children. But for the most part, even the fairy tale was concerned with shaping the child's character in some direction. In Charles Kingsley's *Water-Babies* (1863), for example, the transformation of the young chimney sweep Tom into a Christian gentleman progresses as his actions become increasingly acceptable to the fairy Bedonebyasyoudid.

IV

Misunderstood is unique in that while it is deeply concerned with the problem of socialization, it refuses to deny the child his physical, imaginative, and emotional freedoms. In fact, it insists that these freedoms are essential to the well-being of children and adults alike. Although Montgomery's book clearly develops out of the pattern of traditional children's literature, it alters the conventions of this genre in several important ways. Like writers in the didactic tradition, Sir Everard favors his younger son because he is obedient. But while the didactic writers valued obedience and restraint as external signs of a rational, virtuous character, Sir Everard values these qualities as signs of an affectionate one. Sir Everard's failure to recognize the depth of Humphrey's feelings has its source in faulty logic. Associating Miles's submissiveness with affection, he incorrectly concludes that Humphrey's more active, restless nature signifies a lack of "heart." Montgomery attempts to correct this error by showing that the traditional mode of judging the child's character by his outward behavior is inadequate when feeling, rather than reason, is valued.

Children, Montgomery asserts, feel very deeply even when at play. Humphrey's apparently carefree play following a mushroom hunt that has put Miles in bed with a fever is not, as Sir Everard believes, proof of his callousness. Alone, Humphrey experiences an "overwhelming sense of the void in his life," a void caused by the death of his mother and the possible loss of Miles:

> This feeling must go, he could not bear it, and he fought with it with desperation; for it was an old enemy, one with whom he had often wrestled in desperate conflict before, and upon whose attacks he always looked back with horror. Deep down in his heart it had its being, but it was only every now and then that it rose up to trouble him. (pp. 165-166)

As the foregoing passage indicates, for Montgomery children were neither the unthinking creatures pictured by Ruskin or the rational beings described by the utilitarians. They are troubled by fears which they can neither understand nor communicate to adults, and which are, in consequence, all the more intense. It is these irrational feelings, Montgomery suggests, that children attempt to relieve in play. Humphrey tries to forget his fears by thinking "of his garden, of his games, and of all the things which constituted the joy of his young existence" (p. 166).

If for children play represents a safety valve for an unmanageable excess of feeling, social life serves the same purpose for adults. Montgomery addresses her adult readers as "Children of a larger growth, but children in understanding still," who "wrestle with this undefined feeling ... this mysterious thing, which we, with our maturer experience, call sorrow." If children seek escape from sorrow in games, adults of the middle and upper classes seek the same escape in "society, traveling or excitement," and working-class adults seek it in "the public house" (pp. 166-167). In her assertion that adult pastimes as well as childhood play are expressions of anxiety, Montgomery offers a far-reaching criticism of the quality of Victorian social life, which becomes all the more trenchant in the light of Humphrey's death. For if Montgomery views play as a necessary release for feelings not easily expressed in the ordinary business of life, Sir Everard is quite right in the belief he shares with the writers of didactic fiction—play is dangerous. Humphrey's tree-climbing eventuates in his fall.

The contradiction between the importance of emotional release and its apparent dangers constitutes the central dilemma of Montgomery's book and is symbolized by Humphrey's paralysis. The Victorian middle class had socialized children to accept the goals of social mobility and the gospel of industry. They had believed that it was possible to be happy living a useful but emotionally constricted life. In *Misunderstood,* however, the principle of utility no longer compensates for the sacrifice of personal impulse and feeling. If Humphrey's death is a direct consequence of his need for self-expression through play, it is not seen as a punishment for it; despite his half-hearted belief that Humphrey "must and should learn to obey," Sir Everard never punishes his son, and occasionally wonders whether restraint "was too much to expect of such a young creature." Unlike the didactic tradition where the parent was at fault if the child persisted in heedlessness, *Misunderstood* offers no rationale for Humphrey's death. Sir Everard blames neither Humphrey or himself.

At the heart of Montgomery's book is a profound uncertainty about the ends for which children were to be socialized. It is significant that Sir Everard is an M.P. For although he has himself achieved worldly success, there are suggestions that he is frequently depressed and frustrated by the demands of his professional life. Montgomery describes the colleagues who come to dinner at Wareham Abbey as a group of "rusty old gentlemen," and Sir Everard himself ironically refers to them as "aboriginies." Uncle Charlie, the romantic spokesman of the book, more bluntly calls them "wild men." Describing his life in Parliament to his children, Sir Everard pictures himself "fast asleep" and suggests that "the queen is generally asleep herself" (p. 185). Sir Everard does not blame himself for his frequent absences from home—"That is what a man of the world must do,"—but neither does he regret that a crippled Humphrey will be "debarred from every path of usefulness or honour which man delights to tread—alike shut out from active service, and learned profession" (p. 218).

But if Sir Everard does not seem to care whether his children lead useful lives, he does not think it likely that they will be able to follow their inclinations either. When Humphrey expresses a wish earlier in the book to become a sailor like his Uncle Charlie, Sir Everard ruefully replies, "I don't think that will exactly be your vocation" (p. 59). Were he to survive to adulthood, Humphrey would almost certainly live a life much like that of his father. That Humphrey is being prepared for politics is suggested by his impressive knowledge of history and by his ability to recite long lists of facts from the *Peter Parley* books. Virginie believes that it is necessary to "remember all the battles of the War of the Roses" in order to "go into Parliament" (p. 112), but Montgomery suggests the uselessness of this endeavor by pointing out that Sir Everard cannot remember the dates of any of the battles he must himself have arduously memorized as a child. Humphrey's non-utilitarian preference in literature is suggested by the fact that when he makes out his will, it is *The*

Boy's Adventures, rather than *Peter Parley,* that he bequeathes to Miles among his most treasured possessions.

But Miles, timid and in poor health, is unlikely to derive any benefit from this legacy. It is a bleak comment on Victorian society that the sickly and passive Miles, rather than the energetic Humphrey, will probably survive into adulthood. In his much read essay *On Education* Herbert Spencer had made the startling observation that among the educated classes children and younger adults appeared to be neither as physically developed nor strong as their seniors. Spencer balmed this apparent depletion in youthful vigor on the increasing pressures of social life, which, in wrecking the parental constitution, had through "hereditary transmission" taken its toll on the progeny as well. Advising the parent that the preservation of his child's health was a moral duty, Spencer prescribed a program of exercise and play in order to make the child physically fit for the "wear and tear" of a social life in which bodily endurance was essential to the contests of commerce and the preservation of national prosperity.[8]

Although Miles can be seen as an example of the devitalized children Spencer describes, there is no suggestion in *Misunderstood* that his condition can be cured by gymnastics, or that any physical therapy would be intended to create a useful social being. Montgomery's criticism of the stresses created by life in society appear to be more far-reaching than Spencer's and aimed in quite a different direction. In *Misunderstood* children and parents alike suffer from an emotional as well as a physical debility. According to Spencer's utilitarianism, play was useful because it stimulated happiness, which was itself useful because it facilitated the individual's productivity. For Montgomery, as has been remarked, play functions rather as an outlet for a dammed-up reservoir of feeling. The child who feels more, Montgomery suggests, will play more. The unvoiced question underlying *Misunderstood* seems to be one about the nature of feeling itself. Montgomery observes that the feelings most common to adults and children are anxiety, depression, and a sense of loss. That these feelings are socially created, rather than natural, however, is suggested by Humphrey's happy memories of his mother. Humphrey's ability to remember Lady Duncombe, a memory his younger brother does not share, gives him his special emotional identity and explains his willingness to die in order to rejoin her.

The feeling appropriate to childhood, Montgomery asserts, is "joy," the "boundless faith" and "vivid imagination" that "all things are possible" (pp. 252-4). This feeling has its source in the loving care of children by their parents, particularly the mother. In making the mother aware of her importance to the child, Montgomery hoped to spark the maternal feelings that would enable her to nurture feeling in her children. In this emphasis on the mother's role in the development of the child, Montgomery would appear to have been most directly influenced by Wordsworth, who in *The Prelude* had recognized an "active principle" running through all of nature and had traced the child's ability to feel himself part of "this active universe" to the animating power of the mother's love:

> blest the Babe,
> Nursed in his Mother's arms, who sinks to sleep
> Rocked on his Mother's breast; who with his soul
> Drinks in the feelings of his Mother's eye!
> For him, in one dear Presence, there exists

A virtue which irradiates and exalts
Objects through widest intercourse of sense.
No outcast he, bewildered and depressed.
Along his infant veins are interfused
The gravitation and the filial bond
Of nature that connect him with the world.[9]

It is to Wordsworth that Montgomery refers Sir Everard when in chapter xvi he is "baffled" by Humphrey's readiness to die. Children, Montgomery explains, paraphrasing the poet, see the entire universe as alive, "partly at their feet, and part from them." Since to the child "all things are possible," to Humphrey, death—"the land which is very far off"—seems more active than life itself because it is animated by his mother's presence (p. 252). It seems clear that despite the religious overtones in which Humphrey's death is couched—Miles cheers him on with a hymn: "Around the throne of God in Heaven/Thousands of children stand," (p. 286), Humphrey's thoughts about Heaven center solely on his wish to rejoin his mother and regain the life of feeling she represents.

Humphrey's determination to die forces Sir Everard to examine the meaning of life from his son's perspective: "What," he asks himself, "did life mean to Humphrey?" Lord Duncombe's answer is quintessentially romantic: to be alive is to experience "the blessing of movement." For children, happiness lies in the "mere sense of being and moving" (pp. 219-20). Sir Everard now becomes aware of "the endless motion of nature," and his new definition of happiness as "being" leads him to place new value on the life of the imagination as well. The utilitarian knowledge and skills of "two of the greatest surgeons of the day" are unable to cure Humphrey. The objective language of the medical men inadequately communicates the subjective horror of the calamity. Sir Everard wrestles with the words "cripple" and "paralysis," unable to "grasp the idea" of how one can be "paralyzed for life" when life is defined by movement (pp. 215-7). As even the simplest words lose their rational significance for Sir Everard, only the nonsense rhyme that Miles recites seems to have meaning:

All the king's horses and all the king's men
Will never set Humpty-Dumpty up again.   (p. 229)

In Book V of *The Prelude*, Wordsworth had described a similar impasse in growth in contrasting the Boy of Winander, who is described as one of the "race of real children; not too wise,/Too learned, or too good," with the model child, the product of utilitarian education (pp. 365-425).[10] The Boy, who spends his time in play, at one with nature, dies before he reaches the age of twelve. Although this child's death is unexplained, it like Humphrey's seems to be a symbolic one. Wordsworth's hope in writing *The Prelude* was that the active principle which had nourished his own childhood would continue to create generations of "real children," that spontaneity and natural feeling would not, as he feared, disappear in the face of mechanization. *Misunderstood* may be seen as one judgement that by 1869 Wordsworth's fears had become realities. Montgomery's book is a very late romantic statement of the Wordsworthian theme. In explaining children to their parents, Montgomery hoped to shock her adult readers into an awareness of the paralysis

101

of their own lives; to make them conscious of the degree to which they had become alienated, not only from their children, but from the sources of their own inner vitality. *Misunderstood* was significant not only in what it told parents about their children, but in what it implied about themselves.

Footnotes

[1] Florence Montgomery, *Misunderstood* (Leipzig: Tauchnitz, 1972), p. 7. Subsequent references, indicated by parenthetical page numbers in the essay, are from this edition. Montgomery's many stories for children include *A Very Simple Story* (1867) and *Seaforth* (1878).

[2] Frederick Farrar's *Eric; or Little by Little* (1858), a book about school life in which a remarkable number of children die. Amy Cruse classes *Eric* and *Misunderstood* together and thinks Professor Conington's remark that certain children's books of the day set him off crying "in a London club or no matter where" refers to these two works and to a typical response on the part of adult readers. See Amy Cruse, *The Victorians and their Books* (London: George Allen & Unwin, 1935), p. 301.

[3] Peter Coveney, *The Image of Childhood* (London: Richard Clay and Co., 1957), p. 240.

[4] For a detailed description of the Victorian nursery see Marion Lochhead, *Their First Ten Years* (London: John Murray, 1956).

[5] Gillian Avery, *Nineteenth Century Children* (London: Hodder and Stoughton, 1965), p. 170.

[6] Although for the most part the Rousseauesque idea tended to be distorted through its assimilation into the utilitarian and religious modes of child-rearing, it underlay all systems which emphasized the child's need for freedom, such as that of the Swiss educator Heinrich Pestalozzi and that of Pestalozzi's disciple, Friedrich Froebel, under whose influence the kindergarten movement, with its emphasis on play as a means of education began in England in the 'fifties. By 1869, however, the influence of these systems in England was minimal.

[7] The original impulse for the *Parley* books came from America. When Goodrich published his *Tales of America* (1827), his series of informative books proved so successful in England as well as in America (over seven million copies were sold in England between 1830 and 1869, the year of Goodrich's death), that a host of English imitators began to write under the same pseudonym.

[8] Herbert Spencer, *Education: Intellectual, Moral and Physical* (Paterson: Littlefield, Adams and Co., 1963), pp. 222, 260.

[9] William Wordsworth, *The Prelude*, ed. Ernest de Selincourt and Helen Darbishire (Oxford: Clarendon, 1959), 1850, II, 234-44.

[10] The model child is described in V, 293-364.

Sacrifice and Mercy in Wilde's "The Happy Prince"

Jerome Griswold

In a recent issue of *Ladies' Home Journal* (October 1973) Bruno Bettelheim suggests that the virtue of children's literature lies in the lessons it teaches about sacrifice. Bettelheim endorses Aesop's "Ant and the Grasshopper," "The Three Little Pigs," and "Cinderella" because these tales advocate the repression of impulsive desires and show a child that pragmatic intelligence can plan for compensatory rewards.

A clear understanding of the idea of sacrifice as a kind of self-discipline that provides for future rewards is essential to a critical reading of Oscar Wilde's "The Happy Prince" because the tale deliberately advocates mercy as an alternative to sacrifice. The compassion of the characters of the story radically juxtaposes the selflessness of mercy against the kind of utilitarianism that Bettleheim subscribes to where every sacrifice wins some personal benefit. In one sense, Wilde's tale is an elucidation of Christ's most frequent comment to the Pharisees: "Go learn the meaning of the words—*What I want is mercy, not sacrifice*"; and the similarities between the Happy Prince and Christ, we shall see, are abundant and specific.

Wilde's theme of "mercy, not sacrifice" appears at several levels in the story and we can see it best if we divide the characters into three groups. The townspeople from the opening of the tale to its conclusion remain unchanged and reveal the shortcomings of the idea of sacrifice. The Swallow occupies the center of attention of the story and his metamorphosis seems to represent most clearly the transition from sacrifice to mercy that Wilde advocates. The Happy Prince himself, though he has undergone a change of heart before the story opens, remains throughout the tale an unchanged exemplar of the lesson and value of mercy.

I. The Townspeople. Sacrifice, as Bettleheim noted, is the pragmatic conclusion of common sense. It has two fundamental elements: repression (of impulsive desires for immediate pleasure) and compensation (the reward promised for this kind of behavior). These two elements are most clearly associated with the townspeople throughout the story. In many ways the poignant symbolism of "The Happy Prince" escapes them, and they stare as dumbly at the statue in the end of the tale as they did at its beginning.

As the tale opens the statue of the Happy Prince is for the Town's adults, most clearly a symbol of repression. When he sees the statue, the Town Councilor, for example, experiences a delight which he feels is immoderate for a man like himself who must be concerned with the pragmatic, and so represses that delight rather than appear unpractical to others. A mother whose child is crying uses the statue for a remonstration since "The Happy Prince never dreams of crying for anything." And for the disappointed man the statue is an occasion for speech full of the secret misery and falseness that comes from repression and envy: "I am glad there is someone in the world who is quite happy."

Only for the Charity Children is the statue a symbol, not of eliminative repression, but of inclusive identification: it reminds them of the angels they have seen in their dreams.

103

Their visionary innocence is far different from the stern repression required of them by the Mathematical Master who, like Blake's Beadle in *Songs of Experience,* has charge over them.

This difference in vision at the tale's opening is not unlike that at its close where the question is not one of repression but compensation. After the Happy Prince has given away all his gold leaf and jewels and the Swallow's corpse lies at the statue's feet consumed by their tireless exercises in mercy, the statue itself is naked and shabby. "In fact," the townspeople observe, "he is little better than a beggar."

The compensation the Happy Prince and the Swallow deserve is far different from what they receive at the hands of the townspeople. The Art Professor, by a pragmatic aesthetic, concludes: "As he is no longer beautiful, he is no longer useful." The Town Corporation, agreeing, discusses new uses for the metal. The townspeople are blind to the lesson of selflessness and instead argue selfishly about which of them will be portrayed in the next statue.

The true compensation that the Prince and the Swallow deserve is seen by God and his angels, who see as clearly as the Charity Children. This compensation, however, is not a reward that has been planned for by the Prince and the Swallow as if all their actions had an eye on the future and were pragmatic sacrifices; instead, the recognition by God and the Angels seems gratuitous (since unasked for), the gift of divine mercy.

In fact, the idea that selfishness is attached to sacrifice and selflessness to mercy is illustrated throughout the tale in the lives of the townspeople. The small sacrifices of the palace girl who waits for the seamstress to finish her dress for the ball show a girl who thinks of the world in terms of utility, and her impatience is shown to be selfishness. On the other hand, the seamstress' care for her sick son at her own expense is a commendable act of mercy. The Professor of Ornithology who pompously writes what is accessible only to a few can be compared with the playwright who writes for all but without the deserts of compensation that the Professor undeservingly receives. The abstemiousness of old Jews who count their coins in the Ghetto shows selfish repression by way of a Semitic stereotype that is far different from the selfless actions of the matchgirl who earns money for her tyrannical father.

Above all, it is through the unmerciful righteousness of the good burghers and townspeople that Wilde spells out quite clearly his rejection of sacrifice and his endorsement of mercy. Their righteousness is the vain result of lives where pragmatic sacrifices have played a great part both by ways of self-repression and by way of undeserved compensation that has been confused with moral worth. The result is that the rich make merry at the expense of the beggars and the Watchman scolds the two hungry boys of the tale as if poverty and reprobation were the same.

II. The Swallow. This same note of righteousness and practicality is found in the Swallow at the beginning of the tale, but it modulates as the Swallow undergoes a metamorphosis through the lessons of mercy he receives from the Happy Prince. His attachment to the Reed, for example, was selfishly imperious: "Shall *I* love you?" he has asked her. His friends have counseled that love for a Reed would be impractical, since he loves to travel, and the Swallow agrees, somewhat proud of his ability to sacrifice her, never thinking of sacrificing his desire for travel. His criticisms of the town ("I hope [it] has made preparations" for my stay) and the statue of the Happy Prince ("What is the use of a statue if it cannot keep the rain off?") repeat the selfish pragmatic considerations shown in the townspeople.

The minor sacrifices the Swallow has to make in the "dreadful" Northern European clime of the town, however, will be abundantly repaid in the fantastical compensations he expects to find in Egypt. Europe and Egypt are wholly different places: one the land of dreary Puritanical sacrifices and repression of immediate pleasures and the other a fairy tale realm of jewels, lotuses, mythical kings, scented heavens—in short, the compensatory world of unalloyed pleasure so often insinuated and promised, as Bettelheim has observed, in children's literature.

Each time the Happy Prince asks the Swallow to delay his migratory trip just a day longer to perform some small task, the Swallow must choose between the fabulous Egypt of compensation or another day of sacrifice in the repressive clime of Europe. Each time he reluctantly concedes one more day: to take the ruby from the Statue's sword to the seamstress with the sick son, to take one of the sapphire eyes to the starving playwright, and finally to take the last sapphire to the matchgirl who has lost her matches.

The beginning of the Swallow's metamorphosis can be marked after this series of trials from his decision to stay with the Happy Prince now that he is blind. Perched on the statue's shoulder he tries to console the Happy Prince with tales of fabled Egypt as if it were a heavenly compensation the Prince could expect for his actions. The Prince listens politely to the stories of the Nile, red ibises and golden fish, the Sphinx, camels and merchants with amber beads, the ebony King of the Mountain of the moon who worships crystal, pygmies who war with butterflies, and more before he objects: "Dear little swallow, you tell me of marvelous things, but more marvelous than anything is the suffering of men and of women. There is no mystery as great as Misery." This substitution of the mystery of misery for the fantasies of compensation has, in a way, been prepared for in the Swallow's discovery that the Happy Prince is not pure gold but alloyed gold and lead. The coincidence of happiness and misery is the mystery the Happy Prince shares with the Swallow. The Prince in effect asks him to see Egypt and Europe as one.

Sent on a mission over the city and experiencing this unific vision of the mystery, the Swallow now feels compassion instead of righteous repulsion for the beggars and children who are hungry. He returns to the Prince and they make a compact to strip the gold leaf off the statue which the Swallow will, not sacrificially and reluctantly, but freely and willingly give to the hungry. The approaching winter brings death for the migratory bird and the naked Prince, and the tableau of their dying creates the memorial to mercy that the townspeople judge unattractive.

III. *The Happy Prince.* The townspeople never come to see beyond the sacrifice, and the Swallow only begins to understand that his separation of Europe and Egypt, of repression and compensation, must give way to the unific mystery of misery and the gift of mercy. The Happy Prince, however, preaches for the duration of the story Christ's message to the Pharisees: "Go and learn the meaning of the words—*What I want is mercy, not sacrifice.*" But it was not always so with him. In his account of his personal history and how he came by his name, the Prince tells the Swallow that as a child he used to live in the land of Sans Souci. It was a world not unlike the Swallow's Egypt where infantile and absolute (if not autistic) pleasure was assured by a gardenwall boundary that excluded (as effectively as repression) whatever was painful. The Prince reports he was "happy" there "if," he most pointedly adds, "pleasure is indeed happiness." Now, in his second life as a statue, the Prince descries the misery and pain of the world in the alloyed mystery he speaks of to the Swallow.

If the fact that the Prince is "dead" to the land of Sans Souci (which implicitly and symbolically is maintained by repression) does not clearly imply that he is unconcerned with sacrifice, then his treatment of his jewels makes this fact far more obvious. Jewels have always been associated with those compensatory heavens of children's literature and, more particularly in this tale, they play an important part in the Swallow's Egypt: jade, beryls, amber, crystal, etc. The Prince's merciful liberality with his jewels is not the result of a Puritanical asceticism but of commiseration for the poor, and not the result of pragmatic planning for compensation but of guileless selflessness.

There are a number of resemblances between the Prince and Christ which give the theme of "mercy, not sacrifice" a particularly religious ring: as a statue the Prince is a representative, he shows us the way to be happy, he is a "prince of peace," he is twice-born, his death is a merciful gift to others. But perhaps less obvious is the Prince's role as the "bread of life." The gift of his jewels provides food for the seamstress and her son and for the playwright; and when the hungry children receive the statue's gold leaf they pointedly rejoice: "We have bread now." The Prince in effect says, "Take, eat, this is my body, which I have given up for you."

In terms of this mythic interpretation the Swallow's gift is a "partial" one. The Prince who surrenders his body to be eaten makes the "total" gift; the Swallow plays the role of an assistant, a disciple. His sacrifices are reluctant and the Prince must constantly ask him, "will you not stay with me for one night," as Christ at Gethsemane asked his disciples to watch the night with him. Since the Swallow's death is that of a disciple and is "partial" compared to the "total" gift of the body as food, he participates in the ritualistic eating of the Prince's body only through partial and symbolic mitigation: he eats only bread.

The Prince's sacrifice is total. He makes of himself not only a gift of food but a gift of fire. As the tale concludes he has been consumed by the hungry and his metal is consumed in a fire. And as he has been the gift of food for some, he has also been the loving gift of fire to others: to the unappreciated playwright who can afford no fire, to the unloved matchgirl who has lost her matches.

Pragmatic sacrifices depend upon repression and compensation. While Bettelheim is perfectly correct in his endorsement of children's literature that teaches sacrifice as means of providing "armor" against adversities (as in "The Ant and The Grasshopper" or "The Three Little Pigs") or insinuates the promised "jewels" of well-being to the ungrudging (in "Cinderella") he fails to see that sacrifice produces the righteous "armor" of the townspeople and the selfish orientation of the Swallow's Egyptian "jewels." Mercy is selfless. The Prince surrenders both the "jewels" and the gold plate that constitute the "armor" of the self. He ceases to exist as "he" but through mercy exists everywhere, diffuse, as food for others.

Jane Eyre's Childhood and Popular Children's Literature

J. Sloman

In her description of Jane Eyre's childhood with the Reed family at Gateshead, Charlotte Bronte evokes an intense quality in Jane's experience. Jane's fears and indefinable longings transform her surroundings into something larger and more threatening than real life. It is possible that this section of the book is also transformed by Jane's memory, for she is recalling it as an adult, and certainly Jane's precocious accusations of Mrs. Reed (if not her resentment itself) are less like what a child might have said than what an adult, remembering an oppressed childhood, might wish too late that she had been able to say. This mixture of a child's feelings with an adult's ability to express them contributes to Jane's effectiveness as a character. But her significance as a child character becomes more evident when she is compared to the characters in some children's books popular in the generation or two before Bronte wrote, many of which presented a sanctimonious and unduly optimistic view of the child's capacity to adjust to the adult's need for family harmony and order. Judging from *Jane Eyre*, these books did not do justice to the child's feelings. However, the characters of the Reed children and some aspects of Jane's experiences at Gateshead are partly based upon these other works. Bronte seems to have recognized their influence on a child's fantasy life and used them as a source of material, while rejecting their simplifications about the child's nature. Some of the power of Bronte's novel comes from qualities it shares with these children's books, inadequate as they usually are.

Bronte, unlike most contemporary children's writers, imagined at least some children as having intense and complicated inner feelings which could not be expressed within the genteel environment. Such a child, like Jane, having to exist without love and without understanding or acceptance in a place like Gateshead, might naturally have hostile feelings. Too timid and powerless to try to express them, except under immense pressure, this child might well appear nasty and withdrawn, unloving instead of unloved. The contrast between Jane's usual sullen appearance and her unexpectedly violent outburst causes her to be thought of as evil; the Reed family and their servants connect her general unresponsiveness with some kind of intrinsic moral flaw, although they give her nothing to respond to positively. This lack of insight into reasons for a child's failure to express affection is shared by the Reed family and the majority of children's writers of the late eighteenth and early nineteenth centuries. All too often, these writers treat the child's loving behavior as a commodity which he can exchange for parental approval; certainly, the visible appearance of this behavior seems more important than whether it is truly felt, because such writers assume that a normal, virtuous child will feel (and ought to feel) love for his or her guardians. Bronte's sympathetic analysis of Jane's character implies a rejection of this attitude towards the child, held by many of her contemporaries who wrote for children.

However, there are a few works, then as now seeming highly ambiguous in their intentions (*Gulliver's Travels,* for example), which Bronte also uses, for the specific purpose of evoking the heroine's ambiguous ideas about herself. One might consider these works also to be "children's literature," but perhaps in the sense that they articulate problems or feelings about human nature that children, even more than adults, could not verbalize, although children might experience these problems with greater immediacy. Bronte uses these works as symbols, to give concrete expression to Jane's feelings at times when these feelings are so confused as to be beyond description. One effect of Bronte's insight into this relationship between literature and inarticulate feeling is that *Jane Eyre* itself becomes a book of this type.[1]

Generally children's books of that time taught their readers that they had a role in society *as children*, distinct from whatever their future roles as adults might be (needless to say, this was not expressed in so many words). Children were expected to be "agreeable," and in that attitude had definite functions: to be a source of diversion and entertainment, to create an atmosphere of relaxation and delight, and thus to soften the lives of the careworn adults who were supporting them. Children were expected to prattle, and it helped for them to be attractive. These expectations are present even when the writer shows genuine fondness for children. In Sarah Fielding's *The Governess* (1749), the oldest child at an idyllic girls' school, Jenny Peace, repeats what her mother told her when she grieved too long over a dead cat:

> If, therefore, you give way to this Melancholy, how will you be able to perform your Duty towards me, in chearfully obeying my Commands, and endeavouring, by your lively Prattle, and innocent gaiety of Heart, to be my Companion and Delight?...I expect, therefore, *Jenny*, that you now dry up your Tears, and resume your usual Chearfulness. I do not doubt but your Obedience to me will make you at least put on the Appearance of Chearfulness in my Sight: But you will deceive yourself, if you think that is performing your Duty; for if you would obey me as you ought, you must try heartily to root from your Mind all Sorrow and Gloominess.[2]

Fielding does stress that the child will benefit when she is no longer torn apart by intense passions, and all the girls in her story are, or quickly learn to be, happy. The demand made on the child is validated by the affection made available to her if she obeys—a reward which is not offered to Jane. Similarly, in John Newbery's affectionate work, *A Little Pretty Pocket-Book*, a description of a good boy is followed by the statement, "This character, my Dear, has made every body love you; and, while you continue so good, you may depend on my obliging you with every thing I can."[3] The adult's love for a child is a reward for the child's proper behavior; fortunately, the love expressed in the writer's tone undercuts the potential threat in his words.

Other writers seem to demand more of the child without any obvious worldly reward. Mrs. Sherwood, in *Stories Explanatory of the Church Catechism*, tells the story of Margaret Green, the youngest of three sisters, who spent her infancy with a nurse and on her return to her family began to demonstrate a compulsively mischievous sort of behavior; in contrast to her older sisters, "she was a little, rude, romping girl, and would climb up the trees, and scramble over the wall of her papa's garden; and if she had a clean frock put on, it was so dirty in half an hour, that it was not fit to be seen."[4] This is disorderly behavior, indicative of a sick or sinful nature. Mrs. Sherwood feels that Margaret has a naturally "giddy" temper, and has her mother punish her by locking her up, refusing her dinner, and tying her hands behind her back. These methods fail and Margaret remains uncontrollable for years, until she falls ill and is returned to her nurse to recover her health. The nurse talks to Margaret about her feelings and manages to convince her that God will help her to control herself: but Mrs. Sherwood does not draw the obvious conclusion that the nurse's affection had more impact than Mrs. Green's rational punishments. The material of this story is at odds with the author's message, and the possibility that the child suffered from being taken from her nurse in the first place is not discussed.

Interestingly, Mrs. Sherwood revised *The Governess* (1820), keeping Fielding's situation—nine students at a "little female academy" take turns describing their childhoods and then telling stories—but transforming its message to illustrate her own Evangelicalism. Fielding treated envy, cunning, and so on, as the results of education and individual character, which made it possible for the girls to reform themselves, with the guidance of older students and the governess herself. However, Mrs. Sherwood considers these qualities to be "sinfulness," which makes it impossible—even impious—to think of being helped by anyone but God. Sherwood's governess cannot reason with her students; she can only convince them to pray. Now discontent and envy have become irrational attitudes whose origin and cure are beyond human comprehension.[5] The child who experiences discontent is at once more evil and more helpless than she was in Fielding's book, frighteningly isolated in the sight of God and unable (because of her evil nature) to resolve to help herself. Mrs. Sherwood's revision is instructive in showing how a concept of the ideal child that stressed his or her happiness in the context of the well-being of society could become an unattainable ideal once the primary reality outside the child became a distant and critical God.

Mrs. Trimmer's *History of the Robins* shows that the author values love and family harmony, but she treats these spontaneous emotions as if children and parents could turn them on at will, and she explicitly attributes a deep social significance to the feelings displayed by the members of a family for each other. The robin family is a "model" in the sense that it epitomizes the qualities of a nuclear family, and this kind of family, embodying qualities of industry, self-control, and self-sacrifice, is treated as the fundamental unit of society. On one occasion, when the robin children quarrel with each other, their mother reproves them in terms which are close to political:

> "Are these the sentiments ... that subsist in a family which ought to be bound together by love and kindness? Which of you has cause to reproach either your father or me with partiality? Do we not, with the exactest equality, distribute the fruits of our labours among you? And in what respect has poor Pecksy the preference, but in that praise which is justly her due, and which you do not strive to deserve? Has she ever yet uttered a complaint against you, though, from the dejection of her countenance, which she in vain attempted to conceal, it is evident that she has suffered your reproaches for some days past? I positively command you to treat her otherwise, for it is a mother's duty to succour a persecuted nestling; and I will certainly admit her next my heart, and banish you all from the place you have hitherto possessed in it, if you suffer envy and jealousy to occupy your bosoms, instead of that tender love which she, as the kindest of sisters, has a right to expect

of you."[6]

Mrs. Trimmer refuses to analyze the children's hostilities in emotional terms, but is very concerned with their larger impact on the social organism. The children are made to see that they have a function in this organism. Although too helpless to contribute to its support, they can at least refrain from impeding their parents' contributions, and their good behavior can make their parents feel that their industry is appreciated. These attitudes make heavy demands on a child who is part of a nuclear family, a possibility which Mrs. Trimmer does not raise, and should be irrelevant to a child like Jane, who is not part of one.

In lesser works, whose authors do not have so coherent a vision of the child's role as the two previous writers, the reader is left to draw his own inferences about the seriousness of discontent in a child; one concludes that it is serious because of the severity of its effects. In a poem called "The Disappointment," a girl who is discontented because it is raining outside is taken to see a beggar weeping in the cold; "pretty little Fanny" sees the point and calms down.[7] One discontented child is thrown from a horse and another is punished, as Jane is at Lowood, by having to wear a cap and bells at school.[8] There is such disproportion between the child's misbehavior and its consequences, that quirks of temperament or behavior seem tantamount to sin, and that disturbing the peace within the family seems capable of disturbing the social fabric itself. Even in the comic poem *Jack Jingle and Sucky Shingle* the sulky girl seems to be a frustrating irritant to those around her:

> Here's sulky Sue,
>   What shall we do?
> Turn her face to the wall,
>   Until she comes to:
> If that should fail,
>   A smart touch with the cane,
> Will soon make her good,
>   When she feels the pain.[9]

But Sue is cured by the influence of Jack, a cheerful boy. Ann Taylor wrote two poems contrasting Jane, an open girl who shows her feelings because she has nothing to hide, with Eliza, who puts on a facade of good nature in order to win approval. However, she finds it too difficult to conceal her true fretfulness, and she is forced to uproot her "bad habits" in order to gain love.[10] Taylor states "My sweet little girl should be cheerful and mild." However, some aspects of the Taylor volume may have appealed to Charlotte Bronte. Like the Bronte sisters' book of poems, *Poems for Infant Minds* was a joint publication of Ann, Jane, and Adelaide Taylor. The names Jane and Eliza are repeated in *Jane Eyre* for girls whose characters recall Taylor's Jane and Eliza. Most interesting, though, is the resemblance between a poem by Ann Taylor written in ballad style and the ballad which Bessie sings to Jane:

> But how many wretches without house or home,
>   Are wand'ring naked and pale:

> Oblig'd on the snow cover'd common to roam,
>> And pierc'd by the pitiless gale.　　　　　　　　　　　　　　(p. 24)

Nevertheless the moralistic attitude towards children in a genteel setting and the sympathy expressed towards the archetypal orphan are unresolved. The reader may want to force a connection, to perceive the conventional child and the orphan as two aspects of "the child" which are artificially separated in two kinds of poetry; Charlotte Bronte's accomplishment is to have seen the orphan child "out there" as the personification of the ordinary child's inner life.

Unresolved tensions exist in both trivial and more accomplished works. In *The Careless Little Boy,* Horace throws stones and accidentally hurts his grandfather. His punishment—for disobedience even more than for throwing stones—is to be left alone while his family goes for a drive. In solitude, he meditates on what he has done and prays for forgiveness. Then his brother returns to ask him to rejoin the family. There is no indication that Horace might resent the punishment instead of being grateful for the delayed pleasure.[11] A rare exception to this magnification of discontent is Maria Edgeworth's character Rosamond in "A Day of Misfortunes"; her irritability is realistically caused by physical discomforts, like a cold room, and is cured on the same level. But even Edgeworth does not try to deal sympathetically with a child who refuses to be consoled, or who persists in demonstrating some form of disturbing behavior.

In effect, a refusal to be agreeable implies a refusal on the child's part to be socialized. Jane, who hides in a window-seat to escape from her Reed cousins, or to read, or just to look at the weather, is indeed a threat to the Reeds' sense of their own worth. Jane eventually learns from the servant, Bessie, who later becomes her friend, how her behavior has turned other people against her:

> "Bessie, you must promise not to scold me any more till I go."
> "Well, I will: but mind you are a very good girl, and don't be afraid of me. Don't start when I chance to speak rather sharply: it's so provoking."
> "I don't think I shall ever be afraid of you again, Bessie, because I have got used to you; and I shall soon have another set of people to dread."
> "If you dread them, they'll dislike you."
>> (pp. 33-34)[12]

Jane learns to manipulate difficult situations by maintaining the appearance of self-control and she learns to speak wittily or ironically to the powerful figures who try to control her. Much later, at a dangerous moment with Rochester, she even says, "a weapon of defence must be prepared—I whetted my tongue" (p. 240).

What Jane's terryifying aunt, Mrs. Reed, has done in her attempt to control Jane is to confuse her niece's individualistic character with the conventional image of the discontented genteel child, who in so many children's stories was presumed to be sinful and thus to deserve severe punishment. In actual fact, Mrs. Reed's own children (Georgiana, Eliza, and John) follow this stereotype very closely. A story called *The Glutton* describes a spoiled and wealthy boy with nothing to do, whose behavior mingles unhappiness, which he himself doesn't recognize, with compulsive overindulgence and indifference to the feelings of others:

> Constantly engaged in self-gratification he paid no attention to others, and knew
> not the rules of common civility. If spoken to by strangers, he would hang down his
> head in stupid silence or mutter some unintelligible answer. At table he would be
> sulky to see others helped before him, and if requested by his mother to wait for his
> favorite dish till the company were ready to partake of it, he would express his
> discontent so audibly that some lady present would not refuse the request of her
> kind visitor. As soon as his own greedy meal was finished, without waiting for others,
> he would push away his chair and leave the room to seek some new gratification.[13]

Sullenness and the impulse to gratification are surely John Reed's characteristic qualities, though he also demonstrates the more sophisticated pleasure of terrorizing another human being when he attacks Jane. In *Emily Ascott, or the First Theft,* Emily is a basically good girl, whose greed for sweets gets her in the power of a dishonest servant. Guilt and anxiety destroy her health, and Emily's misdeeds are revealed to the world when the servant is caught and tried; the event causes her mother's death and Emily lives on as a murderess.[14] Emily's decline is comparable to John's, although John commits suicide. In Mrs. Fenwick's "The Bad Family" (1809), the six children include a boy who always picks fights, a boy who eats all the time, and one who is too indolent to bother learning. Significantly, the author imagines these children punished by social ostracism and friendlessness; the doors of genteel society are shut to them because of their unpleasant behavior.[15] John Reed combines the qualities of these three boys; though Bronte goes beyond schoolroom sins like stealing food, she introduces John as one who "gorged himself habitually at table," whose mother does not require him to study, and whose appearance is generally "unwholesome" (p. 7). References to such personal traits connect John to the stereotyped sinful child, which a reader might use to place him.

Georgiana Reed, who looks like a china doll, is an equally conventional figure. Her beauty is enough to make her agreeable (p. 12); it substitutes for virtue and goodness, and, according to Bessie and the governess Mrs. Abbot, it would arouse compassion were Georgiana ever to require it. Bessie says, ". . . a beauty like Miss Georgiana would be more moving in the same condition." "Yes, I doat on Miss Georgiana!" cries the fervent Abbot. "Little darling! — with her long curls and her blue eyes, and such a sweet colour she has; just as if she were painted!" (pp. 21-22). Both Eliza and Georgiana are allowed to dress up in expensive clothes. Eliza is distinguished by possessiveness and avarice (p. 24) and by an uncontrolled temper (p. 12); her self-assurance enables her to manipulate the adults in her family although she lacks conventional beauty. As self-willed little aristocrats, the Reed sisters resemble such girls as Augusta Noble in Mrs. Sherwood's *The Fairchild Family* and Rosamond's cousin, Bell, in Edgeworth's "The Birthday Present" in *The Parent's Assistant,* in which Rosamond labors over a fragile gift that Bell contemptuously allows to be ruined. Both Mrs. Sherwood and Maria Edgeworth bring out the selfishness of the rich little girl by demonstrating its painful effects on her less wealthy relatives. This is only a partial parallel to *Jane Eyre,* however; Rosamond and the Fairchild children are not wealthy, but they are definitely genteel and they belong to loving families, unlike Jane. These writers do not deal with the poor child's sense of being an outcast; truly poor children in their books are treated sympathetically, but are introduced primarily to provide test situations which will determine whether the genteel child is selfish or benevolent.

The spoiled child of these children's books is characteristically self-destructive; he or she degenerates morally and physically, and does not always live to grow up. A recurrent sign of this inner disintegration is a susceptibility to irrational fears (of the dark, of common people, of animals). By being made to confront situations that arouse these fears, children are at once punished and taught to perceive their own irrationality. Similarly, Jane is punished for hitting her cousin by being locked up alone in the room where her uncle died some years before. This treatment is supposed to get her to pray and thus to confront her sinfulness, yet Mrs. Abbot stimulates Jane's fears by warning her, ". . . if you don't repent, something bad might be permitted to come down the chimney, and fetch you away" (p. 10). What Jane actually thinks about in the locked room is the injustice of her situation, which reinforces her feelings of rebellion, perhaps even creates them.[16] Though she has not feared ghosts before, she now learns to fear them and ultimately has a fit, stimulated by a strange gleam of light. Her "violence" in this fit confirms Mrs. Reed's feeling that Jane is an alien being. Mrs. Reed has been punishing a child who was not spoiled as if she were, and has thus contributed to turning Jane into an outsider.

Perhaps Bronte would have approved of John Reed's being punished in this way. However, that would have been superfluous, since the spoiled child is in the long run self-punishing. John and his sisters eventually meet stereotyped fates: John dissipates himself and his family's property in a life of sensuality, and then kills himself - which in turn causes his mother to die. Georgiana grows fat and dull, and marries for money. Eliza becomes a nun, a less conventional ending, but surely a variation on the loveless existence that the selfish child was generally expected to bring upon himself or herself. Jane, on the other hand, makes a series of intense friendships with women, including Bessie, who remain loyal to her; she wins Rochester's love and she refuses to marry St. John Rivers, who does not love her, for that reason alone. Jane's emotional sensitivity and her adherence to it as an absolute value bring the reward of an emotionally satisfying life.

II

Bronte also makes use of children's literature of a more complex and problematic type—that sort which often leads one to ask whether children can truly understand what they are reading, or even whether children ought to read it. Not only do such works avoid stereotypes, but they frequently question the philosophical and moral bases of society and not just the society in which these books first appeared. Often they yield multiple interpretations, sometimes conflicting with each other, while still being able to evoke an intense response on the level of narrative or of emotional suggestiveness. Perhaps it is the adult reader's recognition that such books are more complex than he once thought that makes him feel that children cannot understand them; still, the possibility of two or more levels of understanding allows these books to provide continuity for the child as his responses to life approach those of the adult. They appear to work this way in *Jane Eyre*. Bronte uses these more profound works to show how they answer to and provide expression for Jane's complex mental states; they do justice to her developing feelings, whereas the sort of literature discussed above only seems to mock them. It is fascinating to noticie how often Jane's identity is defined in terms of literature.

One example of the second kind of children's literature is *Gulliver's Travels,* which Jane had enjoyed as a fantasy before her experience in the red room, but which arouses a characteristically adult reaction afterwards:

> Yet when this cherished volume was now placed in my hand—when I turned over its leaves, and sought in its marvellous pictures the charm I had, till now, never failed to find—all was eerie and dreary; the giants were gaunt goblins, the pigmies malevolent and fearful imps, Gulliver a most desolate wanderer in most dread and dangerous regions. I closed the book, which I dared no longer peruse, and put it on the table, beside the untasted tart.   (p. 17)

Though Jane rejects *Gulliver's Travels,* her response to it is a genuine one, for she sees her own experience projected in Gulliver's isolation and fear. After *Gulliver's Travels* fails her, though, Jane turns to Bessie, who sings a ballad which Jane has heard before; but she now finds "in its melody an indescribable sadness" (p. 18). Then, a ballad about a "poor orphan child" moves Jane to tears, which are a kind of catharsis. Bronte evidently feels that ballads (associated with common people, like Bessie) can articulate deep feelings which are conventionally inexpressible. Though one would not now consider ballads as being on the same literary plane as *Gulliver's Travels,* many readers of the eighteenth and nineteenth centuries read them as expressions of universal human feelings which were disguised or ignored in more polished verse, and even made serious comparisons between ballads and epic poetry or tragedy. Later in *Jane Eyre,* Rochester sings a ballad which affects Jane so deeply that he almost manages to seduce her (the occasion when she has to whet her tongue). Ballads are thus associated with two points in the novel when Jane's feelings are deeply touched and when she consciously feels her own identity clarifying itself.

A final example is the satiric description of the uniformed girls at Lowood School, who are reminiscent of the charity school children in the "Holy Thursday" poem in Blake's *Songs of Innocence.* Bronte's description is satiric because she so clearly brings out the conflict between the attitudes of the girls, who realize that they are being made to look ugly, and the attitudes of the Brocklehurst women, who think that the girls are attractive because they approach uniformity and are dressed in a manner appropriate to their poverty. Though Jane does not think of Blake consciously, to the reader the parallel is very clear, and Blake's irony, based on the condescension of the genteel observer, is the same as Bronte's. Blake's lyrics, like *Gulliver* and like the ballads, are hardly "intended for children," or only for children, yet they do express feelings that a child might conceivably have.

Bronte, then, makes plentiful use of the stereotypes of contemporary children's literature in defining Jane's situation as a child, in communicating Jane's complex feelings, and in defining the conflict between her view of life and that of the unsympathetic people who surround her. Children's literature relying on stereotypes is used negatively, to show what Jane is not, while great literary works are used positively, to give universal significance to certain points when Jane's identity undergoes some critical change. Many significant aspects of Jane's childhood experience have parallels in the children's books, or types of children's books, that were popular in the early nineteenth century. The major impression that one derives from Bronte's use of these books is that she had a concern with representing a child's feelings and in doing justice to their intensity; the conventional images of the "good" child and the "bad" child failed to provide insights into the child's sense of himself as an individual. Bronte does not ascribe a political significance to Jane's feelings because Jane as a child had no way to see herself as a political being, and Bronte does not consider Jane sinful because the personal causes of Jane's unhappiness are so much more obvious and immediate. The very concept of the sinful child is treated as pathetically irrelevant; it is associated with adults who are incapable of recognizing the child's inner life and who know of no other way to explain forms of misbehavior that do not fit into their organized world. Indeed, these adults have a persistent and disturbing need to organize that leads them to overreact against even the slightest evidence of deviation in the child (such as the girls' curly hair, at Lowood).

An ideal norm for social relationships, that included the agreeable child as an integral part, appears to have been formulated in the popular children's literature of the eighteenth century. At first the value of this norm in holding society together was emphasized and it was not dissociated from a normal desire for reciprocated love within the family. However, by Bronte's time, the social form appears to have been detached from the desire for love and deviations from it acquired the dimensions of sinfulness. Moreover, characterizations of children assumed too readily that most children belonged to a nuclear family; outcasts like Jane could not be dealt with under the usual conceptions of the good and bad child. Jane is instead considered as an essential child, whose nature is explored without reference to inadequate, class oriented notions of "the child," while at the same time the acceptance of these ideas by other figures in the novel is a device that emphasizes Jane's isolation from her childhood guardians.

Footnotes

[1] I have not included the Brontes' juvenalia in this study, because I was primarily interested in an analysis of *Jane Eyre*, and not in a study of Charlotte Bronte's development.

[2] Sarah Fielding, *The Governess* (London, 1749), pp. 33-35.

[3] John Newbery, *A Little Pretty Pocket-Book* (facsimile edition), ed. M.F. Thwaite (New York, 1966), p. 64.

[4] Mrs. Sherwood, *Stories Explanatory of the Church Catechism*, 6th ed. (London, 1819), p. 156.

[5] Because they are so mysterious, they become suitable material for fairy tales, although Mrs. Sherwood disapproves of them. Fielding and Sherwood both use the device of having Mrs. Teachum state that some aspects of fantasy are dangerous, after Jenny has just finished telling a story based on the *Odyssey* (in Fielding) and a fairy tale (in Sherwood). The fairy tale is less violent than the *Odyssey*.

[6] Mrs. Trimmer, *The History of the Robins* (London, 1869), pp. 19-20. The original publication date is 1786. Jane Eyre's interest in a robin at the start of the book may be designed to show that she has something in common with Mrs. Trimmer's ideal child.

[7] Ed. Andrew Tuer, *Stories from Old-Fashioned Children's Books* (New York, 1899-1900), pp. 129-30.

[8] *Ibid.*, pp. 119-22.

[9]*Jack Jingle and Sucky Shingle* (York, n.d.).

[10]*Poems for Infant Minds* (London, 1808), pp. 69-72.

[11]*The Careless Little Boy,* 4th edition (1822).

[12]References to *Jane Eyre* are taken from the Norton Critical Edition, ed. Richard J. Dunn (New York, 1971). Page numbers appear parenthetically in the text.

[13]Tuer, p. 254.

[14]*Emily Ascott, or the First Theft* (Birmingham, n.d.).

[15]Tuer, pp. 149-50.

[16]This treatment and Jane's reaction to it suggest an interesting parallel to Dr. Itard's treatment of Victor in Truffaut's movie, *The Wild Child.* The action of *Jane Eyre* and the action of *The Wild Child* are contemporary (the 1790's, a period of revolution).

Front View of the Astrolabe

From *The Complete Works of Geoffrey Chaucer,* ed. W. W. Skeat (Oxford: Clarendon Press, 1894), III, following p. lxxx.

116

Chaucer's *Treatise on the Astrolabe*: A Handbook for the Medieval Child

Thomas J. Jambeck and Karen K. Jambeck

Chaucer's *Treatise on the Astrolabe* is seldom read nowadays except by the most conscientious student, then reluctantly; and for good reason: forbiddingly technical, the *Treatise* reflects little of the doctrinal "ernest" or winsome "game" for which Chaucer is admired. But, however ominous its subject matter, the *Astrolabe* is significant in the literary canon of the Middle Ages, for it is one of the few extant works written specifically for a child. This "litel tretys," the author tells us, was undertaken at the "besy praier" of his ten year old son Lewis. The child's eager opportuning and Chaucer's evident pride in his son's "abilite to lerne sciences touching nombres and proporciouns" allow the reader a rather uncharacteristic glimpse of the poet in a domestic moment. While historical records and his own poetry have familiarized us with Chaucer as a man of civil affairs, diplomatic confidant to the court, and literary entrepreneur, the *Astrolabe* discovers Chaucer the parent, one whose desire to instruct his son in the skills of the adult world warrants our attention in a very special way. Traditionally, social historians have rejected the notion that there existed in the Middle Ages either a concept of the child or a concomitant theory of his education. In his *Centuries of Childhood,* Philippe Aries, for example, notes that not until the fifteenth century does there appear an awareness of the special nature of the child and an educative process suitable to his condition. We have then, according to Professor Aries, "a change corresponding to a desire, new as yet, to adapt the master's teaching to the student's level. The desire to bring education within the pupil's understanding was in direct opposition not only to the medieval methods . . . but also to humanist pedagogy which made no distinction between child and man. . . ."[1] The *Treatise on the Astrolabe* belies both the date and the attitude, for within its brief compass there emerges a consistent, thoughtfully conceived, and humanely executed principle of instruction which attests not only Chaucer's awareness of his son as a child but also his concern for an appropriate pedagogical discipline.

Because the formal study of astronomy or its undifferentiated medieval synonym "astrology" was reserved for older students, Chaucer was wary that complicated equipment or murky abstractions might well dampen his son's fledgling interest. He consequently scales his program of instruction to the abilities and desires of young Lewis. Like the astrolabe Chaucer provides his son—one "so small" as to be "portatif aboute," this "litel tretys" is similarly manageable: its conclusions, drawn "under full light reules" in "light Englissh," are not "to harde to thy tendir age of ten yeer to conceyve." But, for all the diminutives, there is no hint of condescension. The astrolabe is, after all, "noble," "suffisant" for "oure orizonte." So, too, the manual, "rude" though it may be, rehearses problems which are nonetheless "trewe," their inferences "subtile" enough to explore the outer limits of Lewis' intellectual horizon. With characteristic modesty, indeed the kind of self-effacing diffidence which recalls the poet-narrator of the *Canterbury Tales,* the father assures young Lewis that this treatise is not of his own making: "I n'am but a lewd compilator of the labour of olde astrologiens, and have it translatid in myn Englissh oonly for thy doctrine."[2] That Chaucer translated his treatise in large part from the extant *Compositio et Operatio Astrolabii* of Messahala, an Egyptian astronomer of the eighth century, has been well established. In fact, as has been frequently noted, Chaucer follows Messahala's organizational scheme rather closely, beginning, like the Latin original, with a description of the astrolabe, its workings and capabilities, and concluding with a series of practical problems of graduated difficulty in its operation. But Chaucer's treatise is by no means a slavish rendering. Therein lies its importance. On the one hand, the collation of the two texts serves to illustrate Chaucer's mode of adapting his source to the needs of a ten year old; on the other, while Chaucer never explicitly defines his concept of childhood, implicit in his adaptation are certain fundamental attitudes about children, their formative experience, and the literature which underpins that experience.

Since Lewis' Latin is "yit but small," the primary modification Chaucer makes for his young pupil is to render Messahala into the boy's native language. What is particularly striking in this regard is that Chaucer's translation seldom betrays its Latin source. Couching his language in the "light Englissh" of his son's idiom, Chaucer rarely lapses into easy cognates and, as the following examples testify, painstakingly avoids Latinity in favor of the "naked words" of Lewis' vernacular:[3]

halve circles (554:16)	semicirculos (175:13)
loke (557:30)	considerare (185:35)
heyghte (561:41)	altitudinis (190:46)
in the same wise (558:33)	similiter (176:17)
which day is lik to which day (553:15)	equalis (175:15)
stremes of the sonne (550:2)	radius solis (218:27)
shine thorugh bothe holes of thi rewle (550:2)	transeat (170:2)
wote (550:3)	computato (225:29)

Similarly, where Messahala's penchant for abstraction might well tax Lewis' elementary scientific background, Chaucer replaces the abstruse with a visual specificity befitting his son's level of comprehension: Messahala's rather hazy "rei accessibilis" is made concrete in Chaucer's version as "the tower"; "solsticium hyemale" becomes "the lowest point where the sonne goth in wynter"; "altitudinem medie," the "highest of the sonne in the mydde of the day." In fact, Lewis' native experience controls Chaucer's exposition: the father domesticates the fussy erudition of the expert to the child's homelier vocabulary. Thus, the "reet" of the astrolabe, a perforated plate which represents the heavens, is described as "shaped in manere of a nett or of a webbe of a loppe [spider]" (546:3). The pin which joins the several plates of the instrument is in "manere of an extre [axeltree]" (548:14). So, too, the network of coordinates radiating out from the center of the astrolabe are "croked strikes [flax sheaves] like to the clawes of a loppe, or elles like the werk of a wommans calle [hair net]" (548:19).

But Chaucer's adaptation goes well beyond the concerns of an intelligible vocabulary, for his syntax as well manifests his intention to spare Lewis the necessity of having to ravel the convolutions of Messahala's periodic style. Excusing himself for the "rude endityng" and "superfluite of wordes" which characterize his translation, Chaucer explains that both are necessary because "curious endityng and hard sentence is ful hevy at onys for such a child to lerne." Thus, at every turn, Chaucer naturalizes the Latinate periods of Messahala into a syntactical collocation which is at once more colloquial and homespun. A few brief examples should suffice. In his description of the computation of the sun's altitude, Messahala characteristically organizes his material around a series of subordinating conjunctions:

> When you want to know the altitude of the sun, hang the astrolabe by its ring from your right hand, and with your left side turned towards the sun, raise or lower the rule, until a ray of the sun traverses the holes of both sight vanes. . . . But if you want to know the exact time and also the ascendant, set the degree of the sun upon the almucantherath of its altitude, on the side of the east, if the altitude was taken before noon; or on the side of the west, if the altitude was taken after midday; then the hour upon which the nadir of the degree of the sun will have fallen will be the present hour, and the Sign which was on the east side of the horizon is rising, that is ascending; and that which is on the western side is setting.   (Gunther, p. 170)

Recognizing the difficulty for a child to trace the intricate causal and temporal relationships which subordination entails, Chaucer structures his version around a compressed succession of independent members, each introduced by the simple coordinate *and,* each describing a discrete step in the welter of requisite manipulations: "Put the ryng of thyn Astrelabie upon thy right thombe, and turne thi lift side ageyn the light of the sonne; and remewe thy rewle up and doun til that the stremes of the sonne shine thorugh bothe holes of thi rewle. Loke than how many degrees thy rule is areised fro the litel crois upon thin est lyne, and tak there the altitude of thi sonne" (550:2).

That is not to say, of course, that Chaucer's treatise is entirely devoid of complex syntactical structures, for some fifty percent of his sentences contain dependent clauses (as compared to eighty percent in Messahala). However, where Chaucer does subordinate material which is of secondary importance, he relies largely upon the natural junctures of sentence order rather than semantic or even morphemic cues. For example, as Chaucer describes the pin which joins the several plates of the astrolabe, he abuts idea to idea in a compact series of relative clauses. What emerges, however, is not so much a precisely delineated construct of interdependent syntactical parts, but a progression of coordinate elements, curiously independent, which are linked together in almost paratactic fashion: "Than is there a large pyn in manere of an extre, that goth thorugh the hole that halt the tables of the clymates and the riet in the wombe of the moder; thorugh which pyn ther goth a litel wegge, which that is clepid the hors, that streynith all these parties to-hepe" (547:14). Similarly, in his description of the "moder," the main informational plate of the astrolabe, Chaucer avoids the periodicity which inheres in a succession of relative clauses by arranging them as parallel independent statements: "This moder is dividid on the bakhalf with a lyne that cometh descending fro the ring doun to the netherist bordure. The whiche lyne, fro the forseide ring unto the centre of the large hool amidde, is clepid the south lyne, or ellis the lyne meridional. . . . Overthwart this forseide longe lyne ther crossith him another lyne of the same lengthe from eest to west. Of the whiche lyne, from a litel cross in the bordure unto the centre of the large hool, is clepid the est lyne, or ellis the lyne orientale" (546:4-5). The stylistic effect is apparent. Chaucer's preference for parataxes, the relative absence of causal and temporal connectives, indeed his insistence upon a sequential arrangement which focuses upon each detail in turn by a kind of incremental delineation, reinforce the impression of the writer's forbearance, his humane desire to clear away the tangle of Messahala's "curious endityng" and "hard sentence."

As might be expected, Messahala's treatise, intended as it is for older students, reflects little concern for pedagogical technique. Dense with the minutiae suitable to advanced study, Messahala's tract is marked by a method of presentation which is terse if not downright perfunctory. Once given, a general principle is assumed to be mastered, its implications readily inferred, and its practical applications obvious. Chaucer makes no such assumptions. His is not the expert's enthusiasm for comprehensiveness. Rather, as he points out in his introduction, this treatise proposes to "teche" only a "certein nombre of conclusiouns." He pares away those problems which are either inappropriate to Lewis' portable instrument or too advanced for his "tendir" comprehension. Thus, of the forty-seven sections which comprise the *Compositio et Operatio Astrolabii,* only twenty-six correspond to the Englished version. Moreover, within the sections adopted from Messahala, Chaucer focuses solely upon details that are relevant to the novice's level of understanding. For example, in his discussion of the computation of the "Motion of the Sun and the Day and the Month," Messahala includes a welter of tangential information: "When you wish to know the degree of the sun, set the alidade upon the day of the present month; then the degree touched by its tip will be the degree of the sun. Look to see of what Sign it is, and note it on the zodiac of the rete on the other side. Also note its nadir, which is likewise the degree of the 7th Sign. And you may also find the day of the month from the degree of the sun; for the alidade, when once set upon the degree of the sun, will point out the desired day" (Gunther, pp. 169ff). Chaucer, on the other hand, deletes the unnecessary technical terminology and supplementary propositions to concentrate upon a single, elementary process: "Rekne and knowe which is the day of thy month, and ley thy rewle up that same day, and than wol the verrey poynt of thy rewle sitten in the bordure upon the degre of thy sonne" (550:1). Having separated out the core of information suitable to his pupil, Chaucer takes special care to define and redefine its salient features, to underscore crucial functions, and to make troublesome abstractions palpably graphic. With the general principle before him, Lewis is provided a series of practical exercises, evidently of Chaucer's own computation and happily "compowned" for the child's benefit "after the latitude" of Oxford: "Ensample as thus:—The yeer of oure Lord 1391, the 12 day of March at midday, I wolde know the degre of the sonne. I soughte in the bakhalf of myn Astrelabie and fond the cercle of the daies, the whiche I knowe by the names of the monthes writen under the same cercle. Tho leyde I my reule in the bordure upon the firste degre of Aries, a litel within the degre. And thus knowe I this conclusioun" (550:1). Lest Lewis miss the point of the demonstration or his attention momentarily flag, Chaucer gently tugs his pupil back to the lesson with the indulgent admonition to "understond wel" a second, at times a third, example of the principle's workings.

Neither remote nor pedantic, Chaucer's pedagogy conveys the familiarity and warmth of a father's standing beside his son, looking intently over his shoulder as he guides the child through a maze of intricate operations.

A corollary to Chaucer's mode of amplifying Messahala's text is his proclivity for repetition. Adhering to his own dictum—"Me semith better to writen unto a child twys a god sentence, than he fogete it onys"— Chaucer avails himself of the traditional rhetorical conventions of *repetitio* (repetition) designed not only to embellish but also to emphasize the significance of one's material. Unlike Messahala whose treatise is notably free of any dilation, Chaucer's *Astrolabe* is replete with the schoolmaster's *topoi* (commonplaces) and schema designed to anticipate and thereby catch the student's puzzlement short of confusion. As Chaucer introduces the astrolabe to Lewis, for instance, he employs the figure *conduplicatio,* the repetition of a word or phrase of words in successive clauses, apparently to serve as a mnemonic device: "The est syde of thyn Astrolabie is clepid the right syde, and the west syde is clepid the left syde. Forget not thys, litel Lowys. Put the ryng of thyn Astrolabie upon the thombe of thi right hond, and than wol his right side be toward thi lift side, and his left side wol be toward thy right side. Tak this rewle generall, as well on the bak as of the wombe syde" (547:6). Similarly, as Chaucer approaches a crucial point, particularly a general principle upon which subsequent discussion is based, his inclination is to make almost extravagent use of anaphoric cues such as "understond wel" or "forget not thys" to call attention to the "conclusioun" and its purport: "Understond wel that these houres inequales ben clepid houres of planetes. And understond wel that some tyme ben thei lenger by day than by night, and som tyme the contrarie. But understond wel that evermo generaly the hours inequal of the day with the hours inequal of the night contenen 30 degrees of the bordure. . . ." (552:10). But the most prevelant device is the elementary scheme of *interpretatio* or *synonymia,* used largely to rename technical nomenclature in homelier terms and signalled invariably by the catch-phrases "that is to seyen" ("But sothly the hous of the ascendent, that is to seyn, the first hous of the est angle, is a thing more brod and large" [551:4]), "or ellis" ("The whiche lyne is clepid the south lyne or ellis the lyne meridional" [547:4]), or the simple coordinate "or" ("the foure principales plages or quarters of the firmament" [547:5]). An adjunct to *synonymia* is Chaucer's penchant for recapitulating a concluding principle, underscoring its significance by a succinct restatement of its primary functions (*conclusio*): "tak there thin altitude meridian, this is to seyn, the highest of the sonne as for that day. So maist thou knowe in the same lyne the heighest cours that eny sterre fix clymbeth by night. This is to seyn that when eny sterre fix is passid the lyne meridional, than begynneth it to descende; and so doth the sonne" (553:13).

Although medieval pedagogy relied heavily upon repetition (with the chilling result that a student may have been subjected to the same exercises in his Donat for five or more years), Chaucer's use of repetition is strikingly modern in its conception. For Chaucer, mere duplication of effort neither aids nor insures comprehension. Rather, at the center of his technique is the abiding principle that the child, however untutored, is able to grasp the most elusive abstraction if it is assimilated to the constructs of his own experience. Thus, Chaucer's repetition is invariably purposive: the reiteration of detail and the restatement of idea never lapse into witless tautologies, but serve to connect, through a series of intelligible equivalences, the native categories of Lewis' perceptions with the operations of a more theoretical system.

In some extant manuscripts, the *Treatise on the Astrolabe* is titled *Bread and Milk for Children.* Whether the alternative title is Chaucer's own or that of a scribe is, on textual grounds, a moot point. On the more precarious grounds of tone, style, and authorial attitude toward both his material and his audience, the *Astrolabe* can hardly be characterized as a sop to a childish whim, for here there is no stooping to demeaning play. This is earnest work for both father and son. Indeed, the historical significance of the *Astrolabe* as the oldest treatise in English upon a scientific instrument confirms the popular assessment of its author as "learned Chaucer" (Gunther, 2 [1923], 202). But, his apparent technical craft aside, the measure of Chaucer's seriousness can be taken more clearly from his keen interest in his pupil's cognitive ability which, in turn, informs the treatise with a conception of the child striking in its modernity. Philippe Aries notes, for example, that the notion of childhood, "that particular nature which distinguishes the child from the adult," is a rather recent formulation. "In medieval society this awareness was lacking" (p. 128). Whether Chaucer's *Astrolabe* is the lone harbinger of the modern attitude toward the child is difficult to appraise; nevertheless, its very existence invites a re-evaluation of the medieval idea of childhood. And Chaucer himself provides the premise for such a study. At the outset of his treatise, Chaucer defines what is to become the index of his attitude toward young Lewis as pupil and his "besy praier" to learn the operation of the astrolabe: "he wrappith him in his frend, that condescendith to the rightfulle praier of his frend" (545). For Chaucer, the landscape of Lewis' experience is the requisite starting place to investigate the heavens.

Footnotes

[1] Philippe Ariès, *Centuries of Childhood,* trans. Robert Baldick(New York: Vintage Books, 1962), p. 187.

[2] *The Works of Geoffrey Chaucer,* ed. F. N. Roninson, 2nd ed. (Boston: Houghton Mifflin, 1957), p. 546. Hereafter, citations will appear in the body of the text with page and paragraph numbers noted.

[3] The Latin text is from *Early Science in Oxford,* ed. R. T. Gunther, 5 (Oxford: Oxford University Press, 1929).

"Queeney" and "Scottie": The Value of Paternal Letters

Richard Reynolds

The penny-post, said Saintsbury, was thought to have killed serious letter-writing, but did not finish the job.[1] Long-distance phone calls and easy high-speed travel now further diminish the epistolary art, and a basic form of children's literature, the parental letter, survives only under special conditions. Writer and receiver must be separated by substantial space and time before there is a prospect of meaningful correspondence; even then, the affluence incident to travel or distant schooling, and the convenience of Ma Bell, argue for the weekly call. The genre has, however, merits distinctly its own. The informal parental letter is easily read and understood not only by the recipient but by any teenager. When a series of such letters is available, and the author a professional writer, there are the further advantages of effective style, a dramatic context and an introduction to the reader of an author who probably reveals himself more readily than in his formal works. The letters of Samuel Johnson to "Queeney" Thrale and of Scott Fitzgerald to his daughter "Scottie" provide these benefits and give us special light on the attitudes and personality of each man.[2]

Johnson's thirty-two letters to Hester Maria Thrale are one of the major literary recoveries of the twentieth century, found as they were in 1932 among the family papers of her collateral descendants. She was the Thrales' eldest child, born on September 17, 1764, one day before Johnson's birthday anniversary (the Thrales customarily held a joint celebration). Johnson met the Thrales in January 1765 and lived with them for substantial periods from June 1766 until October 1782. Although Johnson could remark to Boswell that he would not have been fond of his own child had he one, and could write of a projected visit to Langtons' that "eight children in a small house will probably make a chorus not very diverting," he seems to have had a powerful affection for children. James Clifford remarks:

> Johnson's love for young people was an element in his character which Boswell almost completely ignored, and it is in his relations with the Thrale children that we see the old man in his kindliest role. He aided in their education, watched their growth with affectionate concern, and grieved over their ill health. He almost looked upon them as his own. First place in his heart was always held by the eldest—"Miss Hetty" as he referred to her, then "Queen Hester," which was shortened to "Queeney." Although her mother had other pet names which she used continually, such as "Hetty" and "Niggy," it is as "Queeney" that the child moves serenely across the pages of Johnson's letters and her mother's diaries.[3]

George Sherburn calls Johnson's prose style "perhaps the greatest of his achievements," and cites its balance, structure, rhythm, and precise choice of abstract nouns. His example of this balanced elaboration is drawn from the famous letter to Chesterfield:

123

```
The notice which you have been pleased to take of my labors
        had it been early,                had been kind;
    but it has been delayed
        till I am indifferent,            and cannot enjoy it;
        till I am solitary                and cannot impart it;
        till I am known,                  and do not want it.⁴
```

The first letter to Queeney, written when she was six and Johnson was sixty-one, and when Mrs. Thrale had just given birth to her seventh child, Sophia, has a similar schematic simplicity:

```
        tell little Mama          that I am glad to hear she is well
                                  and that I am going to Litchfield
                                  and shall come soon to London.
        Desire her                to make haste and be quite well
        Tell dear Grandmama       that I am very sorry for her pain
        Tell Papa                 that I wish him joy of his new Girl
    and tell Harry                that you have got my heart
                                  and will keep it.
                                  and that I am,
                                  Dearest Miss,
                                  Your most obedient servant
                                  Sam: Johnson          (p. 5)
```

A rhythmic structure appears many places in the letters, as in this, written in 1780: "If Ideas are to us the measure of time, he that thinks most, lives longest. Berkley says that one man lives more life in an hour, than another in a week; that you, my dearest, may in every sense live long, and in every sense live well is the desire of Your humble servant Sam: Johnson" (p. 19).

An equally familar, more substantive device of Johnson's style appears in the letters early and often—the interweaving of facts and reflection, usually accompanied by literary allusion: "Miss Porter has buried her fine black cat. So things come and go. Generations, as Homer says, are but like leaves; and you now see faded leaves falling about you" (p. 6). As if to set an example for Queeney of the way in which the observer should moralize upon his subject, Johnson writes her, at fourteen, that her letter to him about a military camp has been too sparse.

> If you are struck with the inconveniences of the military in a camp where there is no danger, where all the materials of pleasure are supplied, and where there is little but jollity and festivity, reflect what a camp must be surrounded by enemies in a wasted or a hostile country, where provisions can scarcely be had, and what can be had must be snatched by men who when they put the bread into their mouths, are uncertain whether they shall swallow it.   (p. 13)

Obviously Johnson compliments Queeney by not condescending to her; Mrs. Thrale appreciated that in her letter to Johnson a few days after the military camp message, saying "You have done Hester no small honour in writing such a letter to her as would be fit for the Prince of Wales" (p. 14). Other letters to Queeney by this time are similarly adult, speaking of landscaping, music, animals and Johnson's favorite subjects for correspondence, books and company. He is recurrently aware that Queeney is growing up and urges her to fulfill her potential.

> The greatest pleasure of life is the influx of novelty, and probably for that reason only our earliest years are commonly our happiest, for though they are past under restraint, and often in a very unpleasing course of involuntary labour, yet while every hour produces something new, there is no deep impression of discontent. Therefore, my charming Queeney, keep your eyes open, and enjoy as much of the world as you can...
>
> You, dear Madam, I suppose wander philosophically by the seaside, and survey the vast expanse of the world of waters, comparing as your predecessors in contemplation have done its ebb and flow, its turbulence and tranquility to the vicissitudes of human life. You, my love, are now in the time of flood, your powers are hourly encreasing, do not lose the time. When you are alone read diligently, they who do not read can have nothing to think, and little to say. When you can get proper company talk freely and cheerfully, it is often by talking that we come to know the value of what we have read, to separate it with distinctness, and fix it in the memory. (p. 19, 20)

The paragraph with which Johnson consoles Queeney, then sixteen, on the death of her father, equals in economy, directness, and eloquence, the well-known letter to Dr. Dodd, the day before that clergyman was hanged for forgery,[5] and the letter of condolence to Mrs. Edmund Burke on her father's death.[6] As in the message to Dodd, the essential elements are a quiet call to hope, mutuality of feeling, and a simple awareness of the writer's own frailty, so that the consolation seems neither formal nor pontifical:

> We are now soon to meet, our meeting will be melancholy, but we will not give way too long to unprofitable grief. The world is all before us—and Providence our guide. Life has other duties, and for you, my dearest, it has yet, I hope, much happiness. The Friendship which has begun between us, may perhaps by its continuance give us opportunities of supplying the deficiencies of each other .... The loss of such a Friend as has been taken from us encreases our need of one another, and ought to unite us more closely. (p. 25)

This attitude of reciprocal assistance was not used by Johnson only on such occasions. Later that year he writes Queeney that he has had a "poor, sickly, comfortless journey, much gloom and little sunshine. But I hope to find you gay and easy, and kind, and I will endeavour to copy you, for what can come of discontent and dolour? Let us keep ourselves easy and do what good we can to one another" (p. 28). Johnson was constantly alert to possibilities for happiness. When Queeney, at fifteen, debated whether she should wear a special new hat to a dinner party, he said "*do* my darling":

> Wear the gown and wear the Hat
> Snatch your pleasures while they last;
> Hadst thou nine Lives like a Cat,
> Soon those nine lives would be past.

Three major themes stand out in the letters of 1782-1784, the last three years of Johnson's life. He writes often of his failing health, but he explicitly realizes this is a tedious subject. He urges Queeney to study arithmetic, "a species of knowledge perpetually useful," and to read habitually, always guarding against the arch-enemy "total vacuity." Mrs. Thrale has recorded Johnson's view of much literature for children as being "too trifling to engage their attention":

> "Babies do not want (said he) to hear about babies; they like to be told of giants and castles, and of somewhat which can stretch and stimulate their little minds". When in answer I would urge the numerous editions and quick sale of Tommy Prudent or Goody Two Shoes: "Remember always (said he) that the parents *buy* the books, and that the children never read them."[8]

Johnson's measures against idleness, and his expression of them to Queeney, are as vivid here as elsewhere. In *Rasselas,* the astronomer is admonished, in times of solitude, to "fly to business or to Pekuah." When challenged by Mrs. Thrale for being repeatedly the last one to appear for breakfast Johnson replied "I would not come down to vacuity." And to Queeney, "If ever therefore you catch yourself contentedly and placidly doing nothing, *sors de l'enchantement,*[9] break away from the snare, find your book or your needle, or snatch the broom from the maid" (p. 35). The third theme of these years, heard throughout the series, is reproof of Queeney for the brevity and infrequency of her letters.

Johnson's last four letters are concerned with the crisis of Mrs. Thrale's marriage to Gabriel Piozzi, and her departure to Europe with him, leaving behind, until her return two years later, her four daughters, Queeney (twenty), Susy (fourteen), Sophia (thirteen), and Cecilia (seven). Three months earlier, in Mrs. Thrale's absence, Henrietta had died of whooping cough at age five. However deeply Johnson was affected by the rupture of his own close association with Mrs. Thrale, much of the displeasure evinced in his angry letter to her of July 2, 1784, is based on her abandonment of her daughters, as appears in the letter he wrote to Queeney one day earlier.

> I read your letter with anguish and astonishment, such as I never felt before. . . . I can only give you this consolation that, in my opinion, you have hitherto done rightly. You have not left your Mother, but your Mother has left you.
> You must now be to your sisters what your Mother ought to have been, and if I can give you any help, I hope never to desert you. I will write to the other Guardians.
> (p. 48)

When the anger of July had cooled slightly, Johnson, with a sense of his own rapid decline and Queeney's impending majority, distilled his advice to her into "these two maxims, which I trust you will never dismiss from your mind":

> In every purpose, and every action, let it be your first care to please God, that awful and just God before whom you must at last appear, and by whose sentence all Eternity will be determined. Think frequently on that state which shall never have an end.
>
> In matters of human judgement, and prudential consideration, consider the publick

voice of general opinion as always worthy of great attention; remember that such practices can very seldom be right, which all the world has concluded to be wrong.

Obey God.   Reverence Fame.

Thus will you go safely through this life, and pass happily to the next.   (p. 51)

In his final letter, September 2, 1784, three months before Johnson's death, he is "glad that after your storm you have found a port at [your guardian] Mr. Cator's." Johnson hopes that Queeney will remember him in her prayers. He had, in effect, seen her through to the end of her childhood and his life. His concern for the growth of her mind and the tranquility of her spirit is evidence of the love for her he so often professed.

Queeney seems to have assumed responsibility readily, as the eldest child in a large family so often does (Mrs. Thrale gave birth to twelve). But Scottie Fitzgerald, an only child, preferred fun, by her own statement. Her father thought she was pretty, vain, and romantic, much like himself, and never needed to urge her pleasure. "I feel very strongly about you doing [your] duty," Fitzgerald writes in his first letter to Scottie, then eleven and at camp. "Would you give me a little more documentation about your reading in French?" (p. 3). He then lists "things to worry about: courage, cleanliness, efficiency, horsemanship," and sixteen things not to worry about, among them popular opinion, dolls, insects, and parents. This call to duty is sounded repeatedly during the following seven years, from 1933 to Fitzgerald's death in 1940, as he struggled with finances, bad health, and the condition of Zelda, and as Scottie barely passed at Ethel Walker's School and Vassar. Like Johnson, Fitzgerald argues for the values of self-examination and expression to be achieved by keeping a diary, and he urges his daughter to pursue exacting studies:

> I want you to take mathematics up to the limit of what the school offers. I want you to take physics and I want you to take chemistry. I don't care about your English courses or your French courses at present.   (p. 18)

When she was older, he saw that her talents were exclusively literary, and though he no longer insisted on science, he recommended economics as useful. She intended to pursue only what was easy for her, he feared. He considered her Ogden Nash imitations careless and warned her that Nash had a meticulous knowledge of meter, while she had none. Later, at Vassar:

> This job has given me part of the money for your tuition and it's come so hard that I hate to see you spend it on a course like "English Prose since 1800." Anybody that can't read modern English prose by themselves is subnormal—and you know it.... The only sensible course for you at this moment is the one on English poetry—Blake to Keats (English 241). I don't care how clever the other professor is, one can't raise a discussion of modern prose to anything above tea-table level. I'll tell you everything she knows about it in three hours and guarantee that what each of us tells you will be largely wrong, for it will be almost entirely conditioned by our responses to the subject matter. It is a course for clubwomen who want to continue on from *Rebecca* and Scarlett O'Hara.   (p. 140)

Fitzgerald had written to Scottie about style when she was sixteen, in terms which

127

indicate his own predilections and talents:

> About *adjectives:* all fine prose is based on the verbs carrying the sentences. They make sentences move. Probably the finest technical poem in English is Keats' "Eve of St. Agnes." A line like "The hare limped trembling through the frozen grass," is so alive that you race through it, scarcely noticing it, yet it has colored the whole poem with movement—the limping, trembling and freezing is going on before your own eyes. Would you read that poem for me, and report? (p. 46)

The letters themselves do not approach, however, the style of Fitzgerald's best prose. He valued imagery highly (as did Johnson) and thought of himself as a poetic writer, but often his letters are as colloquial, casual, and hurried as those of most people, whereas Johnson seems always to have composed for posterity. Johnson's letters, deliberate, reflective, and careful, give the reader the sense of a forceful presence. Fitzgerald often takes positions similar to those of Johnson, but even when the phrases are good, there is a suggestion of uncertainty:

> I am sorry I wrote you that letter. Again let me repeat that if you start any kind of a career following the footsteps of Cole Porter and Rodgers and Hart, it might be an excellent try. Sometimes I wish I had gone along with that gang, but I guess I am too much a moralist at heart and really want to preach at people in some acceptable form rather than to entertain them. (p. 102)

> I rather hate to think of you out here [Hollywood] unless you were going right out for money by displaying your person in celluloid. It is a half-tropical and listless atmosphere. (p. 115)

> Most girls of your generation and your mother's and your grandmother's have had to decide difficult things at your age and it is silly to think that it is any strain peculiar to yourself. The young men are just as bad—some of them talk about having nervous breakdowns if they are conscripted. But *you* didn't cut your milk teeth on an aspirin tablet and I hate that raspberry sundae diction. Face what you've got to face and keep your chin where it belongs. (p. 149) . . . the wise and tragic sense of life. . . . By this I mean . . . the sense that life is essentially a cheat and its conditions are those of defeat, and that the redeeming things are not "happiness and pleasure" but the deeper satisfactions that come out of struggle. (p. 156)

These reflections are set in a context of news and advice about boys, parties, vacations, grades, spending, getting into Vassar, staying in Vassar, and reviews of Fitzgerald's college days and past and present difficulties. He gives a fuller description of his own hopes and disappointments, successes and triumphs, and of the world he has inhabited than Johnson does. Lonely and nostalgic, he imagines Scottie in a milieu similar to that he knew: "Listening to the Harvard-Princeton game on the radio with the old songs reminds me of the past that I lived a quarter of a century ago and that you are living now" (p. 157). Johnson, on the other hand, knew Queeney's youth was more sheltered and comfortable than his own had been. A more important distinction is that, whereas Fitzgerald was fearful his advice would not be taken, Johnson frequently accompanied his with explicit awareness of its futility. And, in fact, Scottie paid little attention to her father's wisdom.

128

At the last, Johnson shared common cause with Queeney in the event of her mother's marriage and abandonment of her children, and his letters end with approval of Queeney's conduct. The denouement of the Fitzgerald series is similar: Scott wrote Scottie that a sense of partnership arose for them out of Zelda's illness, and this adds to the tone of concern which pervades his letters. Toward the end, his attitude to Scottie is unusually pleased; he is delighted at the success of her play and her *New Yorker* story, and gratified that she does seem to be getting through Vassar, thus winning for him that feeling of achievement and release he described when she was sixteen: "Either you accept responsibilities and let me graduate from this unwelcome role of stern father or you stay another year in jail with the children" (p. 41). The final letter, written the month Fitzgerald died, contains familiar advice on how Scottie should conduct herself socially, and repeats the complaint that she does not write him frequently or fully enough. There is a foreboding that he was writing her for the last time, with thoughtfullness, ironic reflection and a finely conceived metaphor:

> I am still in bed—this time the result of twenty-five years of cigarettes. You have got two beautiful bad examples for parents. Just do everything we didn't do and you will be perfectly safe. But be sweet to your mother at Christmas despite her early Chaldean rune-worship which she will undoubtedly inflict on you at Christmas. Her letters are tragically brilliant on all matters except those of central importance. How strange to have failed as a social creature—even criminals do not fail that way—they are the law's "Loyal Opposition," so to speak. But the insane are always mere guests on earth, eternal strangers carrying around broken decalogues that they cannot read.
> (p. 163)

For twenty-four years after Johnson's death, Queeney lived quietly and independently. At forty-four she married a man he would almost certainly have approved for her, the naval hero George Keith Elphinstone. Scottie's attitude to her father's advice appears in her introduction: "these gorgeous letters, these absolute pearls of wisdom and literary style, would arrive at Vassar and I'd simply examine them for checks and news, then stick them in my lower right-hand drawer" (p. xiii). On the whole then, and in general terms, it may be said that Queeney listened and Scottie did not. But as Scottie realized later (p. xv), advice is more often appreciated when it does not come from parents.

Footnotes

[1] George Saintsbury, *A Letter Book* (New York: Harcourt, Brace & Co., 1922), p. 1.

[2] They appear in chronological context in the editions of Johnson's letters by R.W. Chapman, 3 vols. (Oxford, 1952) and of Fitzgerald's letters by Andrew Turnbull (New York: Scribner, 1963), but are also available seriatim in the editions by the Marquis of Lansdowne, *Johnson and Queeney* (London: Cassell & Co.; New York: Random House, 1932), with plates, and *The Queeney Letters* (New York: Farrar & Rinehart, 1934) and in *Scott Fitzgerald: Letters to his Daughter*, ed. Andrew Turnbull, with an introduction by Frances Fitzgerald Lanahan (New York: Scribner, 1965). My quotations are from the latter two editions.

[3] *Hester Lynch Piozzi (Mrs. Thrale)* (Oxford, 1941), p. 69-70.

[4]Albert C. Baugh, et al., eds., *A Literary History of England*, 2nd ed. (1948; rpt. New York: Appleton-Century-Crofts, 1967), p. 1003.

[5]*Letters of Samuel Johnson*, ed. Chapman, No. 523, II, 179.

[6]*Letters*, No. 437.1, II 88.

[7]Katharine C. Balderston, ed., *Thraliana* (Oxford, 1942; rpt. 1952), I, 416.

[8]S. C. Roberts, ed., *Anecdotes of the Late Samuel Johnson* (Cambridge University Press, 1925), p. 14.

[9]The beginning of Resnel's translation into French of Pope's *Essay on Man* ("Awake, my St. John!").

Jean George's Arctic Pastoral: A Reading of
Julie of the Wolves

Jon C. Stott

Although literary critics are surprised that they can effectively apply the techniques of their discipline to works for children which are thought of as simple, the reasons for their successes should be clear: good children's fiction, while it does not generally contain the social, economic, political, and sexual complexities found in adult novels, does operate according to principles inherent in all good writing. It differs from adult literature in degree rather than in kind.

One way of seeing the truth of this statement is to examine Jean Craighead George's *Julie of the Wolves,* 1973 Newbery Award winner, in terms of the pastoral tradition. To apply the term pastoral to a novel dealing with an Eskimo girl who early in the 1970's confronts a pack of arctic wolves may appear inappropriate to anyone who thinks of pastoral in terms of shepherds, Arcadia, and the Golden Age. Yet when we remember that the great Greek, Latin, Renaissance, and nineteenth-century American pastorals were written by sophisticated city dwellers, and that Jean George writes from the highly developed civilization of twentieth-century America, we are in a better position to understand the applicability of the term. As John Lynen has shown in his study of Robert Frost, the traditional elements mentioned above are not the essence of pastoralism, but tropes used to embody a basic literary structure: pastoralism "is always the product of a very highly developed society and arises from the impulse to look back with yearning and a degree of nostalgia toward the simpler, purer life which such a society has left behind."[1] Such is the case in *Julie of the Wolves,* in which the simpler, purer life of Eskimo society is regarded from the perspective of the American civilization which is encroaching upon and destroying it.

Pastoral literature is generally structured around a series of contrasts between a sullied, artificial, complex, urban world which represents turmoil, and in which are found all the more evil aspects of progress, especially greed, anxiety, and ambition; and a rural world which is natural, pure, and calm. In this setting, truth, tranquility, contentment, and innocence predominate. The pastoral world is seen as an ideal one in which the characters come closer to achieving a fundamental goodness of being than is possible in the actual world. This utopian land represents a way of life not realizable in ordinary existence, but only in a distant land, such as Arcadia, or in a distant time, such as the Golden Age. Thus, it represents what ought to be, and what once may have been, a golden past created in the minds of wistful men. Often, therefore, pastoral literature is ironic; for, written as it is from the perspective of a deficient actual world, it is a literature of the defeat of the ideal. It may at best express beliefs like those of Miles Coverdale, narrator of Hawthorne's *Blithedale Romance,* who thinks of his communitarian experiment as follows: "Let it be reckoned neither among my sins nor follies that I once had faith and force enough to form generous hopes of the world's destiny."[2]

131

Within this structure of contrasted worlds, the central action of the pastoral takes place: the withdrawal of the central character from the urban world to the rural one, and his inevitable return to the urban world. It might be said that if the author intends his characters to stay in the Arcadian world and does not view their end ironically, he is writing romance rather than pastoral, a form seen in Book I of *The Faerie Queene,* in many folk tales in which the hero and heroine are married and live happily ever after, and in even Doris Gates' *Blue Willow.* In these works, a land of the heart's desire is achieved and the normal vicissitudes of life are over; the characters live happily ever after. The writer of the romance is more interested in the qualities that enable the characters to get to the ideal land, whereas the writer of the pastoral is concerned with how the experiences in the ideal land influence the character on his return to the actual world. Chief among the motives for the character's withdrawal is his sense of dissatisfaction with the actual world. And no matter what may be his expectations of Arcadia, his experiences there and his reactions to them are crucial in the formation of attitudes he will take back with him.

Walter Davis, speaking of Shakespearian comedy, has argued that, in the calm of Arcady, the central character is able to engage in self-analysis and to return to the outer world in harmony with himself.[3] In a life close to the unity and harmony of nature, he learns, as Hallet Smith has shown, that the essence of the good life is the making of wise choices in which moral responsibility to others outside the self is of utmost importance. The shepherd must protect his flock.[4] Often, however, the growth of self-knowledge is painful and ironic. "The hero," Eleanor Terry Lincoln states, "faces the crossroads of choice, when the battle appears in cosmic perspective, or when the sky opens to permit a revelation."[5] As Erwin Panofsky has noted, the resultant awareness gives an elegiac tone to the pastoral process, for even in Arcadia there is death: the ideal fades even while one is experiencing it.[6] Nonetheless, the acceptance of the lessons to be learned enables one to return to and face the human condition as it is.

Scholars, most notably Leo Marx,[7] have shown how the basic structure and themes of pastoralism have been used by American writers to represent the clashes between the view of America as a new Eden and the forces of progressivism. The defeat of a pastoral America is seen throughout the literature from the closing pages of Crèvecoeur's *Letters from an American Farmer* to Norman Mailer's *Why Are We in Vietnam?* Natty Bumpo's idyllic past is destroyed by the civilized world in *The Pioneers,* while the joyous world of Tom Sawyer is replaced by the terrors experienced by Huckleberry Finn. Hawthorne, who had no sense of a golden past, perhaps best expressed the nature of the American pastoral vision in the opening pages of *The Scarlet Letter* when he stated that "the founders of a new colony, whatever Utopia of human virtue and happiness they might originally project, have invariably recognized it among their earliest practical necessities to allot a portion of the virgin soil as a cemetery, and another portion as the site of a prison."[8]   In addition to original sin, the main threat to the American pastoral ideal is, as Marx has shown, the counterforce, symbolically represented by the machine entering the garden. This counterforce is emblematic of the progressive drive of American civilization, a force which has, for two centuries, broken up the more settled ways of life, in which man had lived in greater harmony with nature.

Although *Julie of the Wolves* is Jean George's first fully developed pastoral novel, pastoral elements are implicit in her earlier works. For instance, *My Side of the Mountain*, published in 1959, while centering on the self-sufficient life spent by young Sam Gribley wintering in a hollow tree in the Catskills, has as its background the New York congestion from which the boy has escaped. The young lad must come to the painful realization that he cannot maintain his solitude and self-sufficiency. As Professor Bando, who significantly calls him Thoreau after the "pastoralist" who returned to civilization, tells him:

> Let's face it Thoreau: you can't live in America today and be quietly different. If you are going to be different, you are going to stand out, and people are going to hear about you; and in your case, if they hear about you, they will remove you to the city or move to you and you won't be different any more.[9]

While the main theme of the book is that Sam Gribley must learn self-sufficiency *and* interdependence, one detects in Bando's words the elegiac note so often found in pastoralism: civilization destroys Arcadia.

In *Gull Number 737* the pastoral note is more specifically psychological than geographical. Luke River's father, who has spent his summers on an island engaged in pure research on seagulls, must now become a practical scientist:

> "I'm more useful putting my knowledge to work right now." Luke detected a sadness in his father's voice. He felt pain, too, as he realized that the long hard hours of work, the lonely assignments, were over. There had been much that was beautiful about it. But now the Rivers family had to join the stream of humanity.[10]

But only in *Julie of the Wolves* do we see Jean George's pastoral vision fully developed.

First, the book is organized around the series of contrasts we have discussed above. Basically, the two opposites are the gussak or twentieth-century civilized world of the white man and the ages old, but fast disappearing, Eskimo world. The gussak world is most clearly seen in the central section of the book, in which Julie thinks back on her life in Barrow.[11] It is foremost a place where the evils of civilization, represented more than once by empty oil cans, are most obvious. We are told that in the Arctic:

> The frigid winter and the dry desert-like conditions . . . prevent metals, papers, garbage, and refuse from deteriorating as it does in warmer zones. In the Arctic, all artifacts are preserved for ages. Even throwing them into the oceans does not work a change, for the water freezes around them, and as icebergs, they come back on the shores. The summer sun unveils them again.[12] (p. 143)

Just as the work of civilization on the Arctic cannot be destroyed, so too the psychological marks it makes on the Eskimo society cannot be changed. TV dinners and cokes, quonset huts and electric stoves have replaced a life lived close to the land. Naka, Julie's father-in-law, has become a drunkard; other Eskimos lead airplane hunters on meaningless bounty hunts; and the old and honorable trade of hunting for furs has been turned into a tourist industry in which pelts are shipped to Seattle to be processed into souvenirs.

Set against this world is the life Julie and her father enjoyed in the seal camp while she was a young girl, and, more significant, the life of the wolf pack on the tundra. The dominant aspect of this world is the harmony among all of nature's creations, including man. As Kapagen, Julie's father, had told her: "We live as no other people can, for we truly understand the earth" (p. 81). This relationship is seen in the ritual ceremony in which the bladders of seals are thrown into the sea. As the old Eskimo woman tells Julie: "Bladders hold the spirits of the animals . . . . Now the spirits can enter the bodies of the newborn seals and keep them safe until we harvest them again" (p. 77). The harmony is most fully seen in the interdependence of the various life cycles on the tundra and particularly in the life of the wolf pack. With the exception of Jello, whose name suggests the weakness of the gussaks, each member works for the benefit of the others. Julie comes to understand the goodness of this pastoral world:

> She had her ulo and needles, her sled and her tent, and the world of her ancestors. And she liked the simplicity of that world. It was easy to understand. Out here she understood how she fitted into the scheme of the moon and stars and the constant rise and fall of life on the earth. Even the snow was part of her, she melted it and drank it.
>
> (p. 130)

In her Newbery acceptance speech, Jean George commented explicitly on the harmony of this world, referring to it as a Chinese puzzle in which the total interrelationship between the parts was crucial to its stability. She quoted Charles Edwardson, a biologist, who stated that "to survive in the Arctic you have to be innocent and respect nature."[13] She explained that in the wolves and their harmonious relationships and later in their harmony with Julie she found a symbol of the continuity between all forms of nature which is necessary for the survival of the Earth.

However, the contrasts in the book are not stark and absolute, for each of the novel's settings can be arranged on a spectrum varying from the purely pastoral to the totally civilized. The heroine's tundra camp near the wolves' den represents the life lived in complete innocence and in harmony with nature, while the camp in which she entertains the young hunter and his family marks a step away from this world. In the seal camp, the old Eskimo ways are still celebrated, but Eskimos from Mekoryuk "spoke English almost all the time. They called her father Charlie Edwards and Miyax was Julie" (p. 80). The towns of Mikoryuk, Kangik, Barrow, and Point Hope, from where Julie had hoped to board a boat for San Francisco, are progressively more civilized, while San Francisco, itself is the representative of the totally civilized world of the twentieth century. The presentation of carefully graded mixtures of the pastoral and civilized elements of the two worlds is deliberate, for it implies that the inevitable advance of civilization through the Arctic will destroy the pastoral world. As the novel nears its conclusion, we notice that oil drums dot the tundra and that airplanes fly over the ideal landscape, bringing the destructive forces of civilization.

Early in her life, her father had told Julie of the dangers of destroying the harmony of nature:

> Kapugen considered the bounty the gussak's way of deciding the amaroqs could not live on this earth any more. "And no men have that right," he would say. "When the wolves are gone there will be too many caribou grazing the grass and the lemmings will starve. Without the lemmings the foxes and birds and weasels will die. Their passing will end

smaller lives upon which even man depends, whether he knows it or not, and the top of the world will pass into silence." (p. 134)

The inevitable end of the pastoral world of the Arctic tundra is seen more forcefully in the fate of Julie's father, who, in terms of names, comes to resemble more his gussak appelation, Charlie, than his Eskimo name, Kapugen. Long a person who held nature in reverence and respect, he had been a man of true Eskimo wealth, a quality measured by intelligence, love, and fearlessness, rather than by material objects. But when Julie rediscovers him, he has married a gussak wife, purchased modern appliances, and bought an airplane which white hunters hire to shoot wolves. If so good a man as Kapugen has fallen to the worst ways of civilization, is there any hope for the others?

More important than the contrast between the two worlds of pastoral literature is the movement of the major character between these worlds and his reactions to his experiences, for his reactions will influence his future. Thus the growth of Julie's character is the center of the book's meaning. In examining this aspect of the novel, it could be said that *Julie of the Wolves* begins as a romance and ends as a pastoral. Julie, in leaving Barrow, believes herself to be setting out on a long journey to a specific end, San Francisco, to her a promised land which offers an escape from her unhappy life as an Eskimo child-bride. However, as her attitudes to the Arctic change, her journey becomes one of withdrawal and return into an ideal world and then, a sadder and wiser person, back to a reality which cannot be escaped.

The golden age of Julie's childhood was spent at the seal camp. Now remembered by her as hazy recollections of different colors, it was a time in which she and her father lived happily with their companions and in harmony with nature. It was then, too, that she first learned of wolves, her father telling her that "Wolves are brotherly. . . . They love each other, and if you learn to speak to them, they will love you too" (p. 78). However, this time passes and gussak law requires that the young girl be sent to school. "With that," Jean George writes, "Miyax became Julie" (p. 83). So begins her life in the world of civilized America. But as her existence with her Aunt Martha becomes unbearable, Julie has an escape: marriage according to the old Eskimo custom to twelve-year-old Daniel. Her husband is retarded, and when he attempts to force consummation of their marriage, she flees Barrow, hoping to hike overland to Point Hope, there to catch a steamer to San Francisco, the home of her pen pal, Amy Pollack.

At this point, San Francisco represents to Julie all that she feels is wonderful about civilization. When she had first come from the seal camp and met Americanized Eskimos, she had felt insecure. In an attempt to become one with them, she had secretly thrown away her *i'noGo tied,* the totem gift from the old woman of the seal camp. This act, along with her acceptance of the report that her father has drowned, signals her turning her back on her Eskimo past. As she receives letters from Amy describing her apparently wonderful life in California, the Arctic seems very dull to her:

The letters from Amy became the most important thing in Julie's life and the house in San Francisco grew more real than the house in Barrow. She knew each flower on the hill where Amy's house stood, each brick in the wall around the garden, and each tall blowing tree. . . . The second floor was always fun to dream about. . . . [And the pink room was] the one that would be hers when she got to San Francisco. (pp. 97-98)

But as she prepares to commence her journey, to reject the old Eskimo ways for the gussak life, she engages in a significant act that foreshadows her failure to reach the city. She asks her friend Pearl for bread, cheese, dried fruits, meats, and a bag of oats and sugar. These are gussak foods and are soon exhausted; she must then rely on her Eskimo tools and the wolves—through remembering lore taught her by her father—to survive; civilization proves to be inadequate. Yet, even though she grows in understanding and appreciation of the ways of the old Eskimos and of the wolves during the early weeks of her time on the tundra, she still has as her goal getting to Barrow so that she can go to Amy's home. Part One, "Amaroq the Wolf," ends with Julie hoping the wolves will support her on this journey.

It is significant that as she studies the wolves, Julie is constantly linking them to her father and the old Eskimo ways, a fact most strikingly seen in her naming the leader of the cubs, Kapugen, after him. She compares the playing pups to Eskimo children, and sees that the leader, Amaroq, has the qualities of Eskimo wealth—intelligence, love, and fearlessness. She comes to see the pack as her family and Amaroq as her adopted father. Moreover, her survival is due not only to her acceptance by the pack, whose habits she has carefully studied, but also to her remembering the old Eskimo customs taught her by her father. She builds a sod house and carefully wraps her clothes in a whale bladder to keep them from becoming damp while she sleeps. "This she had learned in childhood, and it was one of the old Eskimo ways that she liked, perhaps the only one" (p. 26). She remembers her father's warning about over-eating, hunts patiently as he had taught her to, and sings in celebration his song to Tornait, the spirit of the birds. But she feels awkward about her acceptance of her cultural heritage, scoffs "at herself for being such an old-fashioned Eskimo" (p. 59), and, at one point, prides herself that "she looked almost like the gussak girls in the magazines and movies—thin and gaunt, not moon-faced like an Eskimo" (p. 28).

Although as Julie breaks camp to follow the now nomadic pack she waves jauntily to an owl that she will see it in San Francisco, it is while she follows her wolves that her attitudes toward the old and new ways undergo significant changes. These changes are those we noticed earlier as being the ones generally experienced by the central character of pastoral literature. From the time she had discovered herself lost, Julie has felt a growing harmony between herself and the environment, and she now recognizes the goodness of the old Eskimo ways which are so closely related to her present wilderness existence:

> She began to think about seal camp. The old Eskimos were scientists too. By using the plants, animals, and temperature, they had changed the harsh Artic into a home, a feat as incredible as sending rockets to the moon. She smiled. The people at seal camp had not been as outdated and old-fashioned as she had been led to believe. No, on the contrary, they had been wise. They had adjusted to nature instead of to man-made gadgets. . . . Reaching Point Hope seemed less important, now that she had come to truly understand the value of her ulo and needles. (pp. 121-122)

To this point, the only discordant elements of the tundra world had been her attitudes toward the past, and Jello, who as a dissident lone wolf had been killed because he could not live in harmony with his kind and environment. Spiritually and physically, Julie has now entered the pastoral world and is at one with it.

> When it [the house in San Francisco] seemed almost real enough to touch, and very beautiful, it vanished abruptly; for the tundra was even more beautiful—a glistening gold, and its shadows were purple and blue. Lemon-yellow clouds sailed a green sky and every windtossed sedge was a silver thread. (p. 123)

Celebrating what Hallet Smith would refer to as the sense of the otium or contentment, she performs a traditional Eskimo dance.

But the pastoral world cannot last in this life, and, even as Julie achieves it, it begins to fade. First, the seal camp of her memory is no more for, as Kapugen is later to tell her and as she sings in the verses which conclude the novel, "the seals are scarce and the whales are almost gone" (p. 170). More important, she soon stumbles upon old oil drums, a sign that she is nearing civilization and that the gussak civilization is encroaching upon the tundra. Whereas earlier she would have been pleased to see these signs, her emotions are now mixed, for she has come to understand and take joy in her new life. Her complete understanding of the evils of civilization comes as the plane of bounty hunters shoots her adopted father, the wolf Amaroq. The opening of the sky mentioned by Eleanor Lincoln as central in the pastoral, literally occurs:

> The air exploded and she stared up into the belly of the plane. Bolts, doors, wheels, red, white, silver, and black, the plane flashed before her eyes. In that instant she saw great cities, bridges, radios, school books. She saw the pink room, long highways, TV sets, telephones, and electric lights. Black exhaust enveloped her, and civilization became this monster that snarled across the sky. (p. 141)

This is the counterforce which Leo Marx sees as the main destructive force in pastoral literature.

Julie accepts the moral responsibility so necessary to the development of the pastoral character, grieving over the death of the leader, and assuming temporary command while she nurses the injured Kapu back to health. Nevertheless, she still believes she can, in some way, maintain her pastoral existence, failing to understand that the death of Amaroq is a symbol of the death of the tundra. The wolves are an endangered species, being destroyed by civilization, and with their passing will come the passing of a way of life. At first, she decides that she will live alone in the old ways, building an igloo, hunting, carving, and preserving the Eskimo language. Later, when she learns that her father lives, she determines that she will return to him, to relive the old days of the seal camp, to teach the children of his village the old ways, and to save the wolves.

As she enters the village—which, incidentally, contains snowmobiles, machines Jean George feels are inferior to dog sleds—[14]and goes to her father's house, Julie experiences her final epiphany, the ironic revelation which John Stevenson argues is of major importance in pastoral literature.[15] At first, the house seems to approximate the seal camp. But, as she meets her father's gussak wife, sees the modern appliances, and watches Kapugen zip up the American-made arctic field jacket in preparation for a bounty hunt with tourists in his plane, she realizes the "Kapugen, after all, was dead to her" (p. 169).

Not only has he been destroyed by the modern, civilized world, he is now helping to destroy the pastoral tundra he and his daughter had so loved.

Julie's first thought is to escape. Rushing to the bench above the village she thinks she can still live as an old-fashioned Eskimo:

> She was an Eskimo, and as an Eskimo she must live. . . . And someday there would be a boy like herself. They would raise children, who would live with the rhythm of the beasts and the land. (p. 169)

However, Julie's pet plover dies. It had been chilled by exposure to the cold after the unnatural warmth of Kapugen's home. Symbolically, the bird, who had been called Tornait, spirit of the birds, a name the girl had learned from her father, has been killed by civilization, and Kapugen has been the agent. At this point Julie makes the crucial choice of the novel: she realizes that she cannot escape and faces the grim future of life in civilization, returning to her father. As she does so, she abandons the Eskimo language she has cherished, and, "in her best English" (p. 170), sings an elegy on the death of the old ways. The pastoral world of the Arctic tundra is past.

Is the conclusion of *Julie of the Wolves* one of total defeat and despair, or can the reader salvage any hope from it? To find an answer, we must remember that the dominant tone of the pastoral is elegiac, a lament for the passing of a purer, simpler, more harmonious way of life, and that, as noted by John Lynen in the passage quoted at the beginning of this essay, it is written from within and for a more advanced, sophisticated, urban culture. In all of Jean George's works, this point of view has been taken. Writing juvenile books, she has examined the difficult and painful transition from the golden age of childhood to the fallen and complex world of adulthood. Such a passage is disillusioning and there are many ironies; such is the nature of adolescence. Yet in each of these books, and especially in *Julie of the Wolves,* the greatest courage is found in the characters' ability to learn from the past and to accept the reality of the present, unpleasant though it may be. There is loss as well as gain, but to attempt to remain in a dead pastoral world would be unhealthy escapism. Julie's return to her father, filled with sorrow and disillusionment though it is, is her greatest act of courage. Faced with a choice, she has made the only acceptable one. Perhaps the lessons she has learned from the wolves will aid her in the difficult life ahead.

This analysis indicates how the techniques of literary analysis used in "adult" literature may be applied to illuminate children's fiction. Whether or not Jean George has deliberately and consciously imitated or drawn on specific pastorals is not important. The pastoral form has been and still is a viable structure for examining the contrasting state of simpler and more complex ways of living and for examining the growth of characters as they face these two ways. Irony, as we have seen, is inherent in the nature of the pastoral genre, and one aspect of irony, the disillusionment of the individual when faced with the discrepancy between the real and the ideal, can be used by the writer of novels for adolescents, who presents the growing and often painful awareness within his characters. For the literary analyst to apply these and other critical insights to specific classics of children's literature is for him to find in them a far greater richness, depth, and complexity.

Footnotes

[1] John F. Lynen, *The Pastoral Art of Robert Frost* (New Haven: Yale University Press, 1960), p. 12.

[2] Nathaniel Hawthorne, *The Blithedale Romance* (New York: Norton, 1958), pp. 38-39.

[3] Walter R. Davis, "Masking in Arden," *Studies in English Literature*, 5 (1965), 151-63; reprinted in Eleanor Terry Lincoln, *Pastoral and Romance* (Englewood Cliffs, N.J.: Prentice-Hall, 1969), pp. 71-82.

[4] Hallett Smith, "Elizabethan Pastoral," *Elizabethan Poetry* (Cambridge, Mass.: Harvard University Press, 1952); reprinted in Lincoln, pp. 12-144.

[5] Lincoln, "Introduction," p. 3.

[6] Erwin Panofsky, "Et in Arcadia Ego," *Philosophy and History Essays Presented to Ernst Cassirer* (Oxford: Clarendon Press, 1963), pp. 295-320; reprinted in Lincoln, pp. 25-46.

[7] Leo Marx, *The Machine in the Garden: Technology and the Pastoral Ideal in America* (New York: Oxford, 1964).

[8] Nathaniel Hawthorne, *The Scarlet Letter,* ed. Sculley Bradley, *et al.* (New York: Norton, 1961), p. 38.

[9] Jean Craighead George, *My Side of the Mountain* (New York: E.P. Dutton, 1959), p. 170.

[10] Jean Craighead George, *Gull Number 737* (New York: Crowell, 1964), p. 174.

[11] In the novel, Jean George carefully distinguishes between the use of the names Julie, applied when her heroine is a part of the white world, and Miyax, applied when she is in the old Eskimo world or alone with the wolves. To avoid confusion, I shall simply use the name Julie.

[12] All quotations from *Julie of the Wolves* are taken from the 1972 edition published by Harper and Row; page numbers are cited parenthetically.

[13] Jean Craighead George, "Newbery Award Acceptance," *The Horn Book Magazine*, 49 (1973), 342.

[14] George, "Newbery Award Acceptance," p. 340.

[15] John W. Stevenson, "The Pastoral Setting in the Poetry of A.E. Housman," *South Atlantic Quarterly*, 55 (1956), 487-500; reprinted in Lincoln, pp. 170-80.

139

Some Remarks on Raggedy Ann and Johnny Gruelle*

Martin Williams

Raggedy Ann is found everywhere: in card shops, doll shops, dime stores, bookstores. There are some twenty books in print, from the original Raggedy Ann series. Yet, if you look in any standard reference volume, you will find no entry on her or her author, Johnny Gruelle, dead since 1938. He was not even in *Who's Who*.

Johnny Gruelle was a hack. Or, to put it more politely, he was a prolific author and illustrator. He turned out a mound of children's stories, illustrated books, comic strips, drawings. He even illustrated an ambitious edition of the Grimm Brothers, very handsome stuff considering it was done by a self-taught illustrator.

Now if a man is that prolific, if he writes so many books in a series, and other material as well, one is apt to view his work with suspicion. His writing couldn't be very good if there's that much of it. And generally speaking, much of Gruelle's writing isn't good. But the interesting thing to me is that the best of Gruelle is very good indeed, and unique, as far as I know, in children's literature.

Probably I do not need to say that some hacks write well on occasion. Robert Greene, the Elizabethan playwright, might be considered a hack, but he is still read, and some of his plays are very good. Daniel Defoe is the standard example of a hack whose best work is still read. Here in America, we have the example of another children's author, the man who wrote *The Wizard of Oz*. L. Frank Baum wrote an incredible amount of material, under various pseudonyms, some male and some female, in addition to some fourteen books about Oz. We are only beginning to acknowledge that Baum was a very good writer and that some of his books are really excellent—say, *The Patchwork Girl of Oz,* or *Tik Tok of Oz,* or even better, a non-Oz book called *Queen Zixi of Ix,* which I sometimes think is the best American children's story ever written.

The problem with people who are prolific is that one has to read all in order to find any real good works. One has to sift, examine, and look at all, and that's not necessarily easy. I don't mean to say that I've done something terribly hard in reading Gruelle, but I have read a great deal of him, including all the Raggedy Ann books, and I have come to certain conclusions about him.

Biographically, from what I can discover from talking to a few people, and from looking Gruelle up in the few places where one can look him up, this very talented, very prolific man was a born innocent. It seems that he went through most of his life, almost until the end, without a moral problem to his name. He was kind to everybody simply because it didn't occur to him to be any other way. He was never tempted to be rude or mean. And it is that kind of moral innocence which is both the virtue and the limitation of his writing.

Johnny Gruelle was born in Arcalo, Illinois, in 1880, but he was raised in Indianapolis.

*An edited transcription of a tape recorded talk delivered at the University of Connecticut, October 25, 1973.

His father, Richard B. Gruelle, was a self-taught painter, well-known in the Middlewest for his landscapes. I think the American Middlewest, its ways, and its language are very much present in the Raggedy Ann books. If you want to find out attitudes and speech patterns of people of that time, I think you'll discover a lot of them in Raggedy Ann.

Gruelle and his brother Justin and sister Prudence apparently had healthy, somewhat casual upbringings. The father seemed to have let his children come and go pretty much as they wanted to, within reason. But they were all brought up with the idea of the importance of art with a little "a," rather than of a refined, somewhat snobbish thing called Art, with a capital "A." If one drew and painted, one produced art—whether it was editorial cartoons, comic strips, portraits of the wealthy or landscapes or whatever. Quality wasn't what made it art or not art. One did his best and didn't worry about Art.

While still in his late teens, Johnny Gruelle had become the cartoonist on *The Indianapolis Star,* and then a few years later, on *The Cleveland Press.* He did every kind of drawing that a newspaper might require of a staff cartoonist. He drew weather cartoons, political cartoons, and he illustrated stories for which there weren't photographs. He got through his work so fast and so well that he had time on his hands. He used that time writing and illustrating original children's tales. It turned out that the editor liked these, so he published them in the paper too.

Then in 1910, Johnny went to visit his father, who had by then moved to Norwalk, Connecticut. While he was there, the New York paper which was then called the *Herald* held a contest to see who could come up with the best idea for a Sunday comic feature. Johnny Gruelle entered the contest twice, under two different names, and he won the first prize and the second prize. The first prize went to the adventures of an imaginary little elf named Mr. Twee Deedle, which continued for several years in the *Tribune* and the *Herald Tribune,* and was syndicated to other papers as well.

Johnny, married by then, had moved his family up to a town in Connecticut near Norwalk, called Silvermine, an artists' colony. In Silvermine, he began turning out an incredible quantity of material for everything from *Physical Culture* magazine to joke magazines like *Judge,* and he wrote and illustrated children's stories for *Good Housekeeping,* and *Woman's World.*

Gruelle was a not uncommon combination of laziness and industry. Behind a man like that there is often a driving woman. Gruelle's wife Myrtle was apparently just that. She used to stop him if he felt like going fishing or like playing with the neighborhood children. She might drag him in to his studio and sit him down and say, "You've got some drawing to finish for *Life* magazine." And while he drew—this man-child Johnny Gruelle—she would sit and read him fairy tales.

The Gruelles had a daughter named Marcella whom they loved much. (At that point they had no other children; there were subsequently two sons, Worth and John Junior). Marcella died unexpectedly when she was fourteen years old. She had had a rag doll that had belonged to Prudence, Johnny's sister, her aunt. It was called Raggedy Ann, and in memory of Marcella, Gruelle wrote and illustrated a series of stories about the doll, and Marcella's other dolls, little short tales of imaginary about-the-house adventures. These became *Raggedy Ann Stories,* published in 1914. They were so popular that they were followed by sequels. Indeed, there was a sequel almost every year, and sometimes two a year, until 1937, the year before Gruelle died.

In the meantime, of course, the popularity of the Raggedy Ann books had meant other uses of the character. In the mid-1930's, for instance, Gruelle used to do a single newspaper panel drawing each day for a small distributing syndicate. Daily, there was a little drawing of Raggedy Ann with a verse, or a bit of advice, always very cheerful and happy and sun-shiny, as the stories usually are. Also in the '30's, partly for reasons of health and perhaps other reasons that I'm not quite sure of yet, Gruelle moved his family (the two small boys by then) to Miami. There this adult innocent met his first real temptations and, it seems, succumbed to them. Unexpectedly, he evidently gave up his former way of life. People in Silvermine tell me that when he would return north for a visit, he would be overweight, bloated, puffy-eyed, and talking away about the fact that he was busy every afternoon attending cocktail parties. Within a few years, Gruelle was dead. It was a combination of his illness plus the suddenly fast life he had begun to live in Florida, it seems. And as I have said, there was very little attention paid to his death, although his books were still selling then, as they still are now.

The first group of *Raggedy Ann Stories* is based on the idea, not a new one, that dolls have a secret life. They come to life when people are asleep or when people go away on a trip. They can walk and talk and have all kinds of adventures on their own. The dolls find a puppy and adopt it and have to make arrangements for the puppy when "the real-for-sure folks," as Gruelle calls them return. Or, Raggedy Ann falls in a bucket of paint and has to be scraped and washed and have another face painted on. There one gets a double perspective of the way the real people are thinking about all this—the way Marcella particularly is thinking about it—and the way Raggedy Ann (without ever admitting it to the real people, of course) is thinking about it herself.

These first stories were followed almost immediately by a collection of *Raggedy Andy Stories.* Raggedy Andy is of course the brother doll to Raggedy Ann. Some of these tales, I think, are charming. One of them tells how all the dolls sneak down into the kitchen one evening while the real-for-sure people are away and have a wild taffy pull. There's a last minute escape, when the dolls get everything cleaned up and everything exactly the way it was. Before the adults come through the front door, they all scatter up to the nursery and back into bed and get back in the same position as they were when they had been left.

Many of the stories in these early books are trivial. But children often like them. They like the premise of the secret life of the dolls and they don't mind the repetitiousness. There are other, later, collections of short Raggedy Ann tales. One is called *Marcella Stories,* and another is called *Beloved Belindy.* Now, Beloved Belindy was a black "Mammy" doll of a kind that would never be written about now. I don't think she's really patronized. I think she's just a nice matriarchal being in the midst of the other dolls, who happens to be black. I do think that some of the black servants in Gruelle's books are patronized but I don't think Belindy was. Anyway, *Beloved Belindy* was the fourth collection of short domestic tales about the dolls.

To go back a little bit, however, the third Raggedy Ann book, meanwhile, had been of a different sort. It is not a collection of short stories but a long tale called *Raggedy Ann and Andy and the Camel with the Wrinkled Knees.* (Long titles, and long phrases like that, charmed Johnny Gruelle, and he used them all the time.) In this story, Gruelle took us into his own version of fairyland, which he called the Deep Deep Woods.

It is supposedly a wooded area behind Marcella's backyard. But Gruelle's Deep Deep Woods is a very American enchanted place, by which I mean it is a singular combination of European elements and ones that he made up himself, using a very American imagination. There are witches but they aren't really very evil; they're unkind maybe, but that's the worst you could say about them. And there are wizards and magicians, some of whom are a little mean, and some of whom put spells on you but they aren't really very bad spells. And sometimes they hide people away. But that's about it.

Then there are princesses and princes: they are all very handsome or beautiful and sometimes they're disguised as other people or other things, and reveal themselves in the end. And there are kings, some of whom are grouches of course. Along with this there are little magical beings with names like Sniznoddle, Snarleyboddle, Little Weekie the Goblin, the Bollivar, the Snopwiggy, and his friend, the Wiggysnoop, and Mr. Hokus, who of course is a magician. And there are magic spells that can be broken with riddles like "why does a snickersnaper snap snikers?" That's not very European, is it?

The Deep Deep Woods is—again like Gruelle himself—an innocent kind of world, mostly full of niceness and kindliness and some naughtiness. Raggedy Ann herself early acquires a heart that is sewn inside her, a candy heart on which is written, "I love you." Well, if you've got "I love you" written all over your heart, you don't have many moral decisions to make. They come easy.

There is one device in these stories that comes up over and over again, one which is typical of the popular children's writing of the time—it also shows up in British children's literature—and that is the almost endless feast of sweets: donuts, creampuffs, ice cream sodas, ice cream. Book after book has mud puddles which turn out to be chocolate ice cream rather than mud, or fountains in the middle of the woods, enchanged fountains, which put out sodas, or bushes on which grow cookies or cream puffs or donuts. Everyone stops and eats his head off. It's enough to make a diet-conscious adult sick to his stomach.

There's another aspect of Raggedy Ann's kindliness that I find a little disturbing. On occasion, Raggedy Ann behaves like a real busybody in the Deep Deep Woods. She finds out that owls eat mice and she doesn't like that, so she converts the owls to cream puffs. You know, she has a wonderfully uncomplicated idea of what's best for everybody else. (Sometimes it reminds me of American foreign policy.)

But then there are marvelous small touches. For instance, in the book called *Raggedy Ann in the Deep Deep Woods,* the two dolls are wandering along, looking at the sights and saying hello to the animals, and they run into two old owls who live in a tree top. Mama Owl, who's old, and Papa Owl, who's also old and tired from having worked for years in a buttonhole factory. It's typical of Gruelle's inventiveness to make up that kind of thing.

But in reading these books, one may decide that this man is just pouring out words, and pouring out plots and ideas and incidents, and one may wonder: does he have any writing *style?* Does he have any sense of how to put words together gracefully? Or is he just pushing the plot along?

I think he did have a writing style, and I think it too was distinctly American. The hint comes from those words like the Snarlyboodle, and the Snoopwiggy, and Little Weekie. That's the kind of word-making that little children indulge in, making words and names out of bits and pieces of other words and sounds they've heard adults use. And I think Johnny Gruelle succeeded in several ways in writing stories by using the methods of a child, not an adult. For another example, there are the little repetitions he uses. Hookey the Goblin is always Hookey the Goblin. He's never the Goblin and he's almost never Hookey. That's his name, the whole thing:

"Mary Jane Adams lives down the street."
"Oh, Mary Jane?"
"No! Mary Jane Adams."

We've all heard children do this kind of thing, particularly small children. They're just learning to talk, perhaps, and just learning names, just learning the fact that most of us have three names, (and some of us four and five) and they like to say it all. It's a verbal game with them, and Gruelle used it in his books.

In *Raggedy Ann and Andy and the Camel and the Wrinkled Knees,* there's a character named the Tired Old Horse, but sometimes he's the Old Tired Horse, sometimes he might be the Tired Horse and sometimes he might be the Old Horse but usually he's the tired Old Horse or the Old Tired Horse, and he is never, never just the Horse. Elves and gnomes and fairies, or fairies and gnomes and elves, or gnomes and elves and fairies, and so forth—any order in which you can put the three together will show up eventually, but hardly every two of the three and certainly never just one of the three.

In *The Camel with the Wrinkled Knees* there are princesses and princes, and there is a Loony King and there is a witch, and there is the Old Tired Horse. But soon we meet a group of pirates who have a ship, a great big pirate ship that navigates on the land by virtue of the fact that it has four wooden legs which walk the ship along like a great horse. These pirates run around doing pirate things to the dolls and the people. But very early, Gruelle's charming drawings begin to reveal something to us: the great big red nose on the pirate leader is a false nose, and the bandanna on the mean looking pirate covers up the curly hair of a little girl. Gruelle's drawings reveal to us that this assemblage is really a group of Marcella's friends who are playing a game, pretending they are pirates. Soon we realize that the whole story is a game being played by the children about the dolls, and that they're making it up as they go along. We have all done that as children, surely. We start making up a story and acting it out with a group of our playmates. And it rambles and rambles; it goes in this direction and that. It goes in every direction it can go in until mother calls us for lunch or supper.

Johnny Gruelle put these tales together with the same kind of easy whimsy, the same kind of casualness, which children use when improvising a story-game for themselves. and he's the only writer that I've ever read (I may be ignorant of others) who consciously uses an imitation of the way children make up stories in writing a book for children.

Raggedy Ann and the Camel with the Wrinkled Knees is a very good example of it, and there are several other very good ones. For instance, *Raggedy Ann and the Magic Wishing Pebble.* (Now a magic wishing pebble is a wonderful thing if you find one. Look for one: it is absolutely white and absolutely round. If you find an absolute white and absolutely round pebble, it will give you all the magic wishes that you want.) As I say, it's a good book, but the characters do spend some time in the opening pages sitting around a cookie bush, gorging on soda and donuts.

Did Gruelle write any *great* books? I think he did write one great book: the book which was originally called *The Paper Dragon: A Raggedy Ann Adventure,* and is now published as *Raggedy Ann and the Paper Dragon.* It's about a little girl named Marggy who has lost her father. Well, he's sort of misplaced actually; it isn't a very bad situation. Nobody is anguished about the old boy. He's probably all right, but, you know, somebody's sort of misplaced him somewhere so we ought to find him. There's a naughty magician involved, and there's Marggy's mother in the story. And Raggedy Ann and Raggedy Andy are typically helping them in finding Marggy's father, or Marggy's Daddy as Gruelle would put it, in the Deep Deep Woods. The dragon of the title is a very Oriental dragon until it gets a hole punched in his side and is patched with a Sunday comic section stuck on with some filling from a cream puff. That Americanizes him.

The dragon is completely hollow inside and at one point the bad guy of the story props his mouth open with a stick because he wants to use him for a chicken coop. But that doesn't work very well because if the chickens can run in easily, they can also run out easily. The dragon is also full of dry leaves; it seems that a lot of fallen leaves blew in while he was yawning. Raggedy Andy gets put inside him at one point. He wanders around for a little while, and, as I remember, he can't find anything or anybody. All he finds are these dry leaves which have the dragon coughing from time to time, and eventually have him coughing Raggedy Andy out. It's that kind of rambling, meandering narrative which Gruelle does very charmingly, and particularly in this book.

The book also has good characterizations. Of course they are brief, almost blunt. Characterizations generally are brief and blunt in children's books, and very much so in this book, particularly of Raggedy Andy. He loves to get into boxing and wrestling matches. They never really amount to much, but he likes to box and wrestle. The villains and the bad magicians are always irrascible and usually rather foolish—propping the dragon's mouth open so that the chicken's could get in, but also get out. At one point, the villain says something like, "If you want to find Marggy's Daddy, you must do something for me first. That's the way it always is in fairy tales." And Raggedy Ann says, "But this isn't a fairy tale." "Of course it's a fairy tale!" he answers. "How else could you two rag dolls be walking around and talking if it wasn't a fairy tale?" That's blunt, and that's probably a child's way of looking at it.

There is one other Gruelle book which I'd like to recommend especially. As I said earlier, there's a whole collection of dolls in Marcella's doll nursery, and one of them is Uncle Clem the Scotch Doll. There's a book built around him called *Wooden Willie,* in which the Scotch Doll and the doll called Beloved Belindy have an adventure. Incidentally, this story originally appeared as a newspaper serial in 1922, and in that version it is a Raggedy Ann and Andy adventure.

I haven't said very much about Gruelle's illustrations, but anyone who has ever seen Gruelle's drawings, in that soft line of his, knows he has seen something special. To know how good they are, simply compare them to those in the books published after Johnny's death that have illustrations done by others, chiefly by Justin Gruelle, his brother, or by Worth Gruelle, his son.

I think there's no question that Johnny Gruelle's reputation would be much higher, and that he would be in the histories of children's literature, if he hadn't written so much. But he did write some very good books. And he had his own way of depicting a child's mind and a child's outlook. So I would like to think that before my life is over, we can read about Johnny Gruelle in volumes on American writers and in volumes on American artists.

E. Nesbit's Well Hall, 1915-1921: A Memoir

Joan Evans de Alonso

God gives us memory so that we may have roses in December.
—Sir James Barrie

More than fifty years have elapsed since we lived at Well Hall, Eltham, with E. Nesbit, in the unforgettable atmosphere of that household and its surroundings. It had already seen its heyday, and since the death of her husband, Hubert Bland, the financial pinch had been acutely felt. Old friends found it more difficult to visit, and it was war time. My mother, separated from my father, went to Well Hall to help E. Nesbit (Mrs. Bland to all of us, and later Mrs. Tucker when she remarried) run an elaborate and very modern poultry farm. My mother had had some training in the latest techniques. The old stables and back yard at Well Hall were duly set up for that purpose. To help the household finances, E. Nesbit was already selling garden produce to munitions workers at the nearby Woolwich Arsenal and to the Government as provisions for the two local hospitals.

It was arranged that my mother would join the enterprise as soon as my sister and I went away to boarding school in Huntingdonshire in the fall of 1915. During our school vacations, we children, my two brothers, Geoffrey and Ronald, my sister, Margrey, and I were to be P.G.'s (Paying Guests) at Well Hall. Hopefully we would be good companions (and we were) for E. Nesbit's adopted son, John, and for her granddaughter, Pandora.

John was the natural son of her husband, Hubert Bland, and his secretary, Miss Hoatson, commonly known as Mouse. Mouse was still living at Well Hall when we first went there, and remained I think until E. Nesbit remarried in 1917. This dimimutive, vivacious, and competent little woman, with her big brown eyes and mop of grey hair, was, when we arrived, the pivot of all the functional and complicated household finances at Well Hall.

The poultry farm, despite modern know-how, failed almost before it began. There was a shortage and rationing of chicken feed, and the hens, oblivious to the artificial lighting, refused to produce the projected two eggs every twenty-four hours. Futhermore, the water rats living in the moat killed off the hens at an alarming rate, and this soon ended the ill-fated enterprise. After that, mother did wartime work at a local munitions factory and we all made our home at Well Hall.

As I write, many long-forgotten incidents come to mind. In moments of psychological insecurity, childhood memories often bring unsuspected resources of personality. Many are the times I have savored the recollection of our first arrival at Well Hall.

It was at the beginning of the Christmas holiday in December, 1915. Mother met us girls at Liverpool Street Station and shuttled us across London to take a train down to Blackheath where we had to change for the Well Hall station. My brothers, each at a different Public School in the south of England, made it on their own. We all arrived without luggage and therefore with no ration coupons, an occurrence whose continued repetition was to become an endless annoyance. On the way, mother told us something about Well Hall and E. Nesbit. We had read some of her books. She also spoke to us about other people who were living at Well Hall, and especially about John Bland. In 1915 John was a day boy at St. Paul's School in London. He was a real loner and often very sullen, but for us he became another brother. He and Geoffrey grew to be the most intimate of friends. In the early years John would often carry my little sister on his shoulders, give his hand to his niece, Pandora, and tell me to hang on to his coat tails while he took us all over London to see the sights. We were indeed a strange foursome.

That first night we assembled for supper in the dining room, the old Hall, where a long oval table was placed lengthwise in front of a roaring fire. The table looked gay; there was the smell of food and the chatter of voices; everything radiated warmth. But we were bewildered. Grown-ups gathered; there were other P.G.s beside ourselves, and we children, seven to nine strong, as always, congregated at the far end of the table. And then E. Nesbit appeared on the stairway. She was fifty-seven at this time, rather stout, and dressed in flowing sort of dress not unlike today's Caftan, with a kind of longish oriental coat. She wore Turkish slippers and quantities of jangling bangles—she always wore those—reaching almost up to her elbows. Her face was small, her voice warm and soft. Her wispy hair was parted in the middle and knotted in a kind of bun at the back. She wore large spectacles and carried under her arm a box—she was seldom without it—in which was a tin of tobacco, cigarette paper, and a long quill cigarette holder.

She seemed to take us for granted, although she had never seen us before. I don't remember any introductions, but when the meal was served we most certainly were not ignored. One of the great things about life at Well Hall was that we were so much a part of it. We listened to real, palpitating conversations, and we gave our opinions as definitely as the rest. What a contrast to the very strict and conventional boarding school where we spent nine months of the year! Looking back, it seems to me that we lived far, far ahead of our time.

After dinner that night, as she was so often wont to do, Mrs. Bland suggested to John that he carry up some logs and light a fire in the drawing room, which was on the second floor. As he somewhat sulkily carried the basket of logs up the stairs, he dropped one. So far he hadn't said a word to any of us. He had just glared at us. I picked up the log and threw it at him. Furiously, he dumped down the basket and proceeded to chase me. We all became involved in the scuffle, and the ice was broken forever.

I don't remember what we played that night, but nearly always there was something exciting after dinner, in which all ages participated on equal terms, no matter who was visiting. For many old friends, Fabianists and budding poets and playwrights and other writers still came to visit Mrs. Bland. Bernard Shaw and H.G. Wells made frequent appearances at first, but as the war drew on and the old Fabian Group became less closely knit we saw them and the others less often. Whoever came, in any case, might join us in charades (very complicated, often, and inspired by our hostess), dumb-crambo, or rhyming games. Nouns and Adjectives was a great favorite to get everybody started. "The pot was beginning with G: the pot was Golden," Mrs. Bland would say, throwing a little ball to somebody, and then the person to whom the ball was thrown had to add another G-adjective, and so it went on. She excelled at rhyming games, patience, and chess, and she loved to play whist. A game that we played too often to suit me was "Devil in the Dark," a glorified form of hide and seek, in which one of the hiders had been marked in some way different from the others. One had to touch the person being found and feel his head to find out if he were the Devil. I was always terrified and hated it.

The time we spent at Well Hall had extraordinary impact on our lives. Here it was that we learned about the world, grew up, saw our boys become men and go to war, come home on leave, sometimes wounded, or not return at all. Around us we witnessed the destruction of the air-raids, and from the garden wall we watched the arrival of hospital trains at the little local station. We visited and entertained the wounded; we experienced the horrors, destruction, and deprivations of war. We saw the old house gradually become more decrepit, but we also watched a melancholy Mrs. Bland emerge from the shadow of her three years of widowhood into the security and support of her courtship and marriage with the Blands' old socialist friend, Mr. T.T. Tucker, the Skipper. We participated in good adult conversation at meals and in the imaginative activities that pervaded the household. We ran wild in what appeared to be limitless space on the very ourskirts of London.

What a training ground for life! What wonderful times we had there, where the order of the day—of our daily life—was shadowed, prodded, and shared by E. Nesbit's warm, enveloping personality. We grew up feeling the financial pinch, which was everywhere, but somehow the lack of money didn't really matter. Thrift and ingenuity were a cult: meanness was abhorred. People, laughter, games, fun, good conversation—there was plenty of all these. And however small and unimportant one was, if he had something worthwhile to say, he was always listened to and encouraged to express himself. Wartime food and rationing, the chanciness of meals, the emphasis on enjoyment, and the challenge of the unexpected: what better preparation for life in the twentieth century?

The spacious old eighteenth-century house we lived in, built over some much older flagstones, has been long since demolished. The site is now a park with a bandstand; when I last saw it the plans were for a children's library to be built upon the grounds, in memory of E. Nesbit. The flagstones, some dated 1586, are still there where the Hall stood in front of the little arched bridge—in earlier times undoubtedly a drawbridge—that joins the Moat Garden to the main grounds. In the sixteenth century this property belonged to the Roper Estate. Margaret Roper was Sir Thomas More's daughter, and legend has it that when he was beheaded in the Tower and his head placed on a spike by the river, Margaret rowed up the Thames, stole her father's head, brought it home, and buried it in the Moat Garden.

Well Hall as we knew it was said to have been built by George III. His watchmaker had lived in the lower part and one of the monarch's ex-mistresses was kept in seclusion on the top floor, where E. Nesbit was later to have her study and bedroom. The poor lady whiled away the time by playing the spinet. It was she who haunted the house, who sighed so loudly on the stairway. I heard her once and shivered.

Wings had been added to the main house, so that the ground floor sprawled out on both sides of the central Hall, the dining room in our day. This Hall had five doors. The main front entrance was seldom opened—the cold blast from outside was too much. A sign read, "The Front Door Is The Back Door," that is, the rear entrance from the Moat Garden side. This entrance gave onto a long passageway, flanked on each side by the bedrooms, that ran into the Hall. Besides the five doors, the Hall had the enormous well of the stairway, and the stairway which ended in the Hall. The walls were well over three feet thick, and there was but one large paned-glass window. During the air raids, we gathered in the Hall to play the most exciting games of "Demon"—a sort of group patience—by light of a flickering candle.

We were absolutely forbidden to go down to the moat level alone, unless of course we were in the punt. Beyond the crescent in front of the house ran the Eltham-Woolwich road, and a cottage stood at each side of the entrance. At first my mother lived in the cottage on the right, but as the war continued, she moved into the main house. All this has been demolished, but on the far side of the moat the old Tudor barn still stands, with a perfect example of an original Tudor fireplace.

Our life during the summer was mostly spent on the moat. The boys, some years older than we girls, would tie us up and shove us off in the old punt with no paddle. But Pandora, my sister, and I soon became experts at rocking ourselves to places of help. On ropes knotted to the old trees that shaded the moat we would swing out and try to kick the far barn wall. We read under the shade of these trees, argued, and played badminton and other games.

Few restrictions were placed on us, but many a warning or reminder was posted in rhyme and signed by Mrs. Bland with her initials, E.B., formed into a fourleaved clover. A good example is the poem, "The Order of the Bath":

> We know Hygeia's votary refrains
> From throwing matches down the drain,
> Yet some there be who must be better taught,
> Don't use Hygeia's temple as they ought.
> They leave the fountains dripping, bang the door,
> And pour libations on the temple floor,
> Not in the vessel which her Grace provides
> For votaries to scour their foul outsides.
> Who, in the madness of life's low pursuits,
> Invades the temple in his muddy boots?
> And, with the impiety the gods abhor,
> Rubs off the mud upon the temple floor
> (And even on the temple's mat once whiter
> Than snow—the impious, sacrilegious blighter!)
> Who shuts the windows, that the steam may fall

In tears and slowly sap the temple wall?
Who strews old shoes about the bather's path?
Who leaves the soapy water in the bath?
    Miscreants, repent! And sin this year no more!
    With reverent heart approach the bathroom door;
    Thus shall Hygeia's blessing still attend
    Upon you till one-nine-two-one shall end.

And though we were left free and wild to amuse and fend for ourselves, we were expected to appear for meals. The sound of the first gong meant "Wash-up." At the clang of the second, five minutes later, we were looked for at the table, neat, clean, and civil, at the evening meal in clean clothes, and no squabbling allowed!

Food rationing required that we each have our own colored jar with our ration of sugar, and the same for butter or margarine. A certain amount was taken from each ration every week for cooking purposes. No swapping was allowed until Thursday; then the bargaining began. Cooking, whenever possible, was done in a hay-box cooker. This was a large insulated box with two round, deep holes. The food, after having been brought to a boil in special long, round casseroles, went into the box between preheated iron discs; the lid was sealed tightly, and the casseroles left to cook for hours.

How the whole domestic running of the household was managed, I just don't know. Help came and left; the maids' sitting room became another bedroom, occupied by another P.G. I do remember a boy of about eleven, a cook's son, called Pelham, walking backwards and falling into a large crock of hot marmalade. His knickers were scraped and the marmalade, made with everybody's precious sugar, was reboiled and served. After that, when the marmalade was passed around at breakfast, one said politely, "Have some Pelham!"

In spite of the wartime shortages, E. Nesbit, who loved to prepare delightful surprises, would organize fancy dress dances for us, always using what was on hand. That was half the fun. She would spend hours on the most minute detail, showing more enthusiasm than any youngster. Some evenings she would sit down at the piano and play songs. "Rolling down the Medway" was a great favorite, and we would all sing lustily. Often the carpet would be rolled back for dancing. At other times she would play old sailor ditties to please Mr. Tucker.

Sometimes days would pass without our seeing her. She would be up all night writing, trying to meet some deadline. It was then that she could be ill-humored, though not for long. John would say, "Look out, Mother is casting a gloom." And was she ever! She could be as cantankerous as her own cantankerous Psammead, but in all fairness it was seldom. When *we* started to quarrel, she would produce this magnificent advice: "Try to say nothing. Once you begin you don't know how to stop."

E. Nesbit had many whims. She adored flattery and loved to shock people. But though we often regarded her with awe and bewilderment, she inspired our love and affection. She liked to be embraced, and embraced us often and called us "dear," which I relished, since it was something my own family never did. She smoked like a trooper. She suffered from bronchitis and asthma and so did I. Many times when we were both ill I would be invited to sit in her room and listen to her stories, help in making a dress

151

or mending a sheet, or I would be handed a large magnifying glass and told to see if I could find a pig in some old engraving or print of Shakespeare. She was an enthusiastic Baconian.

Many memories surge up: the hours I spent playing with pieces of the Magic City, scattered and abandoned in the attic; the ritual of washing up the teacups with Mrs. Bland in the dining room in a wooden bowl—a very feminine undertaking and a high privilege—; weeping with her as we saw the first Zeppelin that came down in flames and watched the black human shapes fall from the buring wreck; the unexploded bomb the boys found in the garden that had to be detonated; the piece of shrapnel she found on the pillow beside my sister's head when she came to wake us up because there was an air raid, and my sister in her blue bloomers walking along the high Moat-Garden wall, picking up the red bricks and throwing them down angrily at my brothers in the punt on the moat below. The wall still stands; the bricks are still missing. So much living surrounded us, and so much destruction and death: the comings and goings of so many people long since forgotten.

E. Nesbit's greatest gift to us children was that she, this very talented and busy woman, was generous—generous with herself, her time, her pleasures, her friends, her flowers, her fun. She seemed to have time for us all, to need us, to enjoy us. This little poem, written to console us three young girls when the boys went back up to college—the war was over then—may help to give some idea of the freshness with which she handled and charmed many situations:

Jan. 19th, 1920. The Boys Go Up to Cambridge.

Darlings, Margery, Avril and Joan!
Now the boys have left us alone
We will not grieve and make rainy weather
But put on our hats and go out together.

We will not grieve about Fortune's malice
But hurry away to the picture Palace
Where the jolliest pictures are shown
Darlings, Avril, Margery, and Joan.

We will not cry for our lost boy Cambs
But go and return by Electric Trams.
That tram conductor shall not hear a groan
Darlings Margery, Avril and Joan.

And then perhaps—I don't know—we'll see—
We *might* go down to the Ferry for tea.
A jollier idea could hardly be known
Darlings, Avril, Margery and Joan.

And we did go down to the Ferry for tea, where the Skipper, dear Mr. Tucker, served his Mate, as he often called her, and the three of us with a wonderful tea.

The Expression Of Social Values In The Writing Of E. Nesbit

Barbara Smith

Edith Nesbit Bland would no doubt have been considered an unconventional personality regardless of the era into which she happened to be born. She reached adulthood during the late Victorian age, however, and in that age she appeared remarkably advanced in her personal behavior and values. The most comprehensive biography—by Doris Langley Moore—traces Nesbit's strong individualism from her childhood to her death. Moore spices her chapter about the Blands' involvement in the early Fabian Society with details about E. Nesbit's personal appearance and habits which might lead one to believe that she was indeed the prototype of today's liberated woman. E. Nesbit cut her hair short in the 1880's, wore "aesthetic" loose-fitting dresses, and smoked in public. Moore further promotes the image of the Blands' Bohemianism by stressing the radical nature of their socialist politics:

> These views were then regarded as little less than seditious: one needed as much moral courage to confess to them as one might need today to confess to an out-and-out belief in the most extreme form of Communism. The outrageous young Blands were Socialists.[1]

Socialism in the general sense was perhaps an "outrageous" idea in comparison with the more conservative and staid beliefs of Englishmen of the same social stratum as the Blands, yet the Fabian Society itself was by no means a group of political firebrands.

In *The History of the Fabian Society* by one of its original founders, Edward Pease, the types who were initially attracted to Fabian ideals are described as being comfortably middle-class intellectuals:

> the seed sown by Henry George took root, not in the slums and alleys of our cities—no intellectual seed of any sort can germinate in the sickly, sunless atmosphere of slums—but in the minds of people who had sufficient leisure and education to think of other things than breadwinning.[2]

In the introduction to the 1963 reprinting of Pease's history, Margaret Cole points out the exclusiveness of the early Society membership, despite the fact that its primary goal was to "abolish poverty." And in the political spectrum of that period the Fabians were comparatively moderate in their radicalism.

The words "gradualist," "evolutionary," and "practical" attached to Fabian doctrines indicate the non-revolutionary methods of which the Society generally approved. There were, nevertheless, left-wing and right-wing factions within the society itself. In a letter to a friend E. Nesbitt explains these divisions:

> There are two distinct elements in the F.S. . . . . The practical and the visionary—the first being much the strongest—but a perpetual warfare goes on between the parties which gives to the Fabian an excitement which it might otherwise lack. We belong—needless to say—to the practical party, and so do most of our intimate friends . . . (Moore, p. 107)

153

Hubert Bland was in fact one of the most conservative members of the Society and seemed to have had much influence on his wife's political commitments. H. G. Wells, who was at one time a member of the Society and a frequent visitor to the Bland household, makes a case for an innate difference in the couple's political natures. In his *Experiment in Autobiography* he writes:

> It was, I am convinced, because she, in her general drift, was radical and anarchistic, that the pose of Bland's self-protection hardened into this form of gentlemanly conservatism. He presented himself as a Tory in grain.

> She acquiesced in these posturings. If she had not, I suppose he would have argued with her until she did.

> But a gay holiday spirit bubbled beneath her verbal orthodoxies and escaped into her work. The Bastables are an anarchistic lot. Her soul was against the government all the time.[3]

All of this must be remembered in considering the political and social views in E. Nesbit's works. As a member of the Fabian Society, she was by association more politically unorthodox than most people in her social and historical context. Yet the organization was itself middle-class and moderate, and her background was middle-class. Her husband's powerful personality may have had the effect of diluting her commitments, and the domestic conflicts between them may also have tempered these enforced beliefs with an undercurrent of resentment.

The families in the three Bastable books and in the magic series are unmistakably middle-class, although their parents' financial statuses have the tendency to fluctuate. The family in *The Railway Children* is also only temporarily poor, because of their father's absence. All of these children often come into contact with persons whom they consider poor, however, and a frequent result of these encounters is initial if not long-term misunderstanding.

One character, Oswald, is the principle mouthpiece for E. Nesbit's satire of existing conditions. As a part of the program of their newly formed society for doing good deeds the children in *The Wouldbegoods* try to befriend a Mrs. Simpkins, who has a son in the war. Oswald in his humorously embellished style explains the children's fascination with soldiers as the partial reason " . . . why we sought to aid and abet the poor widow at the white cottage in her desolate and oppressedness."[4] They finally arrive at weeding her garden as a means of helping her, but by mistake pull up turnips and cabbages which her son had planted before he left. Mrs. Simpkins reaction to their good deed is quite emotional:

> "You wicked, meddlesome, nasty children!" she said, "ain't yo got enough of your own good ground to runch up and spoil, but you must come into *my* little lot? . . . Dratted little busybodies . . ." (p. 57)

Although everything turns out well in this episode, the children are often the victims of antagonisms which are tinged with class-resentment, perhaps because they so often put themselves into the position of trying to be charitable to those they consider less fortunate than themselves.

In another episode in *The Wouldbegoods* the children get the idea of providing lemonade for "poor and thirsty" travelers at a roadside "Benevolent Bar." The Bar has mixed success since some of the people who pass by seem not to think too much of the youngsters' philanthropy. One mutters: "Bloomin' Sunday-school treat." And Oswald recalls that:

> One man told us he could pay for his own liquor when he was dry, which praise be, he wasn't over and above at present; and others asked if we hadn't any beer, and when we said "No," they said it showed what sort we were—as if the sort was not a good one, which it is.

> And another man said, "Slops again! You never get nothing for nothing, not this side of heaven you don't. Look at the bloomin' blue ribbon on em! Oh Lord'!" (p. 214)

Finally the children get into a row with three "big disagreeable men" and some rough boys from the village, but they are rescued by two previously made friends. Oswald sums up the failed venture by deciding:

> I really think we shall never try to be benevolent to the poor and needy again. At any rate not unless we know them very well first. (p. 220)

By making these encounters fail, E. Nesbit shows the tensions and inequalities which exist in a class-ridden society.

The children's own perspective about what it means to be poor is forgivably naive, yet E. Nesbit herself makes invidious distinctions between them and the lower-class characters they meet. The really poor people and inevitably the villainous ones speak broken or Cockney English. In *The Story of The Treasure Seekers* a robber and a burglar invade the Bastable home during the space of one evening. Oswald says of the robber (who is really a friend of their father). "I did feel so sorry for him. He used such nice words, and he had a gentleman's voice."[5] The real burglar speaks in a slangy dialect:

> "All right, governor! Stow that scent sprinkler. I'll give in. Blowed if I ain't pretty well sick of the job, anyway." (p. 166)

Oswald notices, " . . . his face was red and his voice was thick. How different from our own robber!"

Another characteristic of certain poor people is that they are not as quick as the Bastables, who are of course very bright and inventive. Oswald suspects that the poor widow Mrs. Simpkins "would not understand poetry," so they decide not to make her a gift of one of Noel's poems (*Wouldbegooods,* p. 55). Mrs. Pettigrew, the cook at Moat House, lacks the most rudimentary literary understanding. Oswald remarks:

> She thinks Albert's uncle copies things out of printed books, when he is really writing new ones. I wonder how she thinks printed books get made first of all. Many servants are like this. (p. 69)

In *The New Treasure Seekers* the Bastables meet some poor children while they are on a picnic with some adult friends. Oswald notes "they did not seem to be very clever children, or just the sort you would choose for your friends, but I suppose you like to play, however little you are other people's sort."[6] At first the children wonder why the village children have not been taught to play rounders, but they soon realize it is "because it is most awfully difficult to make them understand the very simplest thing" (p. 283).

Joan Evans de Alonso lived at Well Hall, Eltham, in the E. Nesbit household from 1916-1920. The Evans family spent all their school vacation there and knew the author and her family very well. Mrs. Alonso pointed out in a conversation with me that an English upbringing was a class-conscious matter, and that the E. Nesbit children are true to the English upbringing of that period. She added, "Children were very sure of their standards in behavior and taste."[7] It is problematic, then, whether E. Nesbit unwittingly stereotypes the poor or points out differences that did in fact exist.

In the last book of the series the Bastables continue their efforts to aid the poor with the usual unsuccessful results. They make a disgustingly soapy "conscience pudding" for Christmas and do not seem to realize that they are not really performing a service by trying to give it away to someone who is needy. The Cockney accented ire they inspire in the strangers they insult by trying to give away their gift is, by this time, familiar. An incident in which they play a trick on a porter with a fake gift basket of food again points up the difficulty of interacting beneficially and without misunderstanding with one's social inferiors.

At the end of *The Wouldbegoods* Oswald remarks:

> "If anything in these chronicles of the Wouldbegoods should make you try to be good yourself, the author will be very glad, of course. But take my advice and don't make a society for trying in. It is much easier without." (p. 282f)

Perhaps E. Nesbit herself would agree with this advice after her experiments with social work and giving mammoth Christmas parties for one thousand poor children at a time.[8] Certainly the Wouldbegood Society is generally unsuccessful and merely serves to get the children into more trouble rather than to keep them—or get others—out of it. With their mischief the children also antagonize adults who are not poor, but the fact that English poor people are also proud makes it difficult for the Bastables to "help" them without prompting resentment.

An exploration of adults' involvement in activities of social uplift occurs in *The New Treasure Seekers*. Eustace Sandal and his sisters Miss Sandal and Mrs. Bax have interests very much like some of E. Nesbit's own friends. It is amusing to see the Bastables' childish interpretations of this family's social ideals and to speculate whether E. Nesbit is having some fun with the dedicated types she was familiar with in the Fabian Society. Oswald's descriptions of the Sandals are certainly tinged with a kind of humorous misunderstanding and skepticism:

> Father knows a man called Eustace Sandal. I do not know how to express his inside soul, but I have heard father say he means well. He is a vegetarian and a Primitive Social Something, and an all-wooler, and things like that, and he is really as good as he can

stick, only most awfully dull. I believe he eats bread and milk from choice. Well, he has great magnificent dreams about all the things you can do for other people, and he wants to distill cultivatedness into the sort of people who live in Model Workmen's Dwellings, and teach them to live up to better things. This is what he says. (p. 193)

When the youngsters visit Mr. Sandal's sister, who lives by the sea, they discover that she is much like her brother. Miss Sandal lives in a very bare white house and she tells the children upon their arrival that "The motto of our little household is 'plain living and high thinking'" (p. 188). She is also a vegetarian and does not keep a servant. Oswald observes pointedly, "She was kind, but rather like her house—there was something bare and bald about her inside mind" (p. 190).

When Mr. Sandal has an accident, Miss Sandal leaves them in the care of a cook and the children hatch several plans to earn some money for their absent hostess. To their young minds the only reason for enduring such a "cold rice pudding" existence is that one is poor and does not have the resources to do better. Mr. Sandal's accident, incidentally, is the result of climbing up on some scaffolding to give a workman a tract on temperance. He manages to make both of them fall off, and it is only a dust cart passing underneath that saves their lives. The workman, it turns out, is a teetotaler. Mr. Sandal's benevolent efforts are in this case just as ineffectual as the children's. Fortunately the Sandal family is redeemed by a third member, Mrs. Bax, who smokes cigarettes and has short hair. The Bastables like her very much after they discover that she does not particularly appreciate them acting like "Sunday School children" just for the sake of maintaining quiet in the house. Oswald asserts, "Mrs. Bax, now that her true nature was revealed, proved to be A1" (p. 275). Obviously this "advanced woman" and the Bastables are kindred spirits.

Although some older women win the admiration of Oswald and the others, Oswald as narrator is a remarkable, if juvenile, "male chauvinist" in the comments he makes about his sisters and about girls in general. His criticisms are perhaps more grating to the sensibilities of a contemporary woman reader than they might have been to a young reader of past decades. However, it is still curious to consider why a woman writer would be so consistently anti-female unless her motive was to be subtly satirical of sex-role stereotypes. If Oswald is E. Nesbit's vehicle for expressing dissatisfaction with women's position in late Victorian society, his anti-female declarations are so similar in tone to those made by actual male supremacists that few readers would realize that she was not supporting the *status quo*. Certainly the intended satire would completely escape her young audience. There are so many references of this type that only a few of them can be included here as examples.

In *The Story of the Treasure Seekers,* after capturing the "robber," Oswald shares a celebration feast with his father and his robber-friend. Oswald remarks:

We sat up till past twelve o'clock, and I never felt so pleased to think I was not born a girl. (p. 172)

During one of the children's councils they smoke the pipe of peace using an old bubble pipe:

We put tea-leaves in it . . . but the girls are not allowed to have any. It is not right to let girls smoke. They get to think too much of themselves if you let them do everything the same as men. (p. 141)

Since E. Nesbit herself smoked, one can assume she intended to satirize sex role stereotypes.

In *The Wouldbegoods* Oswald's attitude is that of pained and superior benevolence towards the weaker sex. He tolerates girls at the same time that he criticizes them, always mindful that his duty as a brother is to be patient with the stupid feminity of his sisters. It is the girls who arrive at the idea of a society for doing good deeds, and Oswald and Dicky immediately realize its potential for inhibiting their plans for having fun (p. 43). Oswald subscribes to the theory that there are particular roles which males and females are best fitted for and that each sex has its particular nature. When girls cry about killing rats, Oswald reasons:

> Girls cannot help this; we must not be waxy with them on account of it, they have their nature, the same as bull-dogs have, and it is this that makes them so useful in smoothing the pillows of the sickbed and tending wounded heroes. (p. 109)

When Alice, the more tomboyish of the two sisters and therefore Oswald's favorite, balks at baiting her fishing hook, Oswald observes in the same vein:

> Girls are strange, mysterious, silly things. Alice always enjoys a rat hunt until the rat is caught, but she hates fishing from beginning to end. We boys have got to like it. (p. 151)

Oswald undoubtedly feels some pressure as the eldest boy in the family to set a manly example for the others, and his view of girls is no doubt typical of a preadolscent in the early 1900's. Girls faint, are naturally inclined towards giggling, and even the best of them have the habit of crying, but boys must transcend these failings even if it means hiding their feelings.

At least one adult agrees with Oswald's opinions about the position of women. In *The New Treasure Seekers* an old sailor tells the children a story about a man who is arrested for smuggling on his wedding day. Alice asks what his wife did about this and the sailor explains, "*She* didn't do nothing, . . . It's a woman's place not to do nothing till she's told to . . . " (p. 212).

The old man's values are also properly Victorian, but E. Nesbit herself knew that there were alternative and less passive ways for women to conduct their own lives. Moore points out that E. Nesbit was always a tomboy and that this influenced her attitudes as well as her actions:

> She was not a masculine woman, but neither was she, in the full sense of the term, a feminine one. Strange paradoxes were everywhere apparent in her. she gloried in material independence, but spiritually, as her relations with Hubert Bland must show, she exemplified dependent womanhood. She loved children, but was not . . . maternal. (p. 219f)

In analyzing the general weaknesses of E. Nesbit's adult poetry, Moore points out that she made an effort not to reveal her inner feelings in what she wrote:

> No one can suspect that she had any marked partiality for her own sex; she seldom attempted to conceal her preference for the other; yet, again and again, she wrote love

poems as if addressed by a man to a woman. Her motives, it may be assumed, were connected with the shrinking from reality which she has described; she wanted to write love poetry, but not to expose her heart. (p. 225)

Perhaps she adopted Oswald's perspective in the children's books for the same reason.

Noel Streatfeild in his semi-critical work about E. Nesbit, *Magic and the Magician*, attributes her preference for her male characters and the accuracy with which they are depicted to the pleasure she derived from the companionship of her own two brothers as a child.[9] Whether her motivations for preferring male characters were simple or complex, only in one work, *The Railway Children*, does she allow a female character to take decided precedence over her brother. Roberta, the oldest of the three children, is obviously the author's favorite. Nesbit writes:

I hope you don't mind my telling you a good deal about Roberta. The fact is I am growing very fond of her. The more I observe her the more I love her. And I notice all sorts of things about her that I like.[10]

Streatfeild believes that Roberta is really a kind of emotional surrogate for E. Nesbit's son, Fabian, who died suddenly at the age of fifteen, several years before the writing of this work. Although Bobbie has many qualities which E. Nesbit admires, she protects herself from too painful an involvement with her character by making her a girl (Streatfeild, p. 122).

Paradoxically, despite E. Nesbit's obvious bias in favor of men in her own group of acquaintances and in her literary creations, she did not support the movement for women's suffrage. Moore indicates that her stance against women's rights was greatly influenced by her husband:

The behavior of certain feminine agitators was exciting derision at that time all over the country, and E. Nesbit showed no greater sympathy towards them than was felt by women whose political views were less advanced than hers. Nevertheless, two or three of her friends were of the opinion that she was by no means opposed to the breaking down of sex barriers on principle, and might have taken part in the movement herself had it not been for Hubert Bland's influence. (p. 266)

Something of Bland's influence must be indicated by the painful domestic situation which he imposed upon her. Not only did he carry on a series of affairs throughout their marriage, he also required that she accept as her own the children of her companion-housekeeper—children of whom he was the father. H.G. Wells emphasizes the subterfuge that pervaded life at Well Hall during the time that he visited the Blands:

Then gradually something else came into the *ensemble*. It came first to the visitor at Well Hall as chance whispering, as flashes of conflict and fierce resentment, as raised voices in another room, a rush of feet down a passage and the banging of a door. . . . You found after a time that Well Hall was not so much an atmosphere as a web. (p. 516)

The ambivalences which these arrangements aroused in E. Nesbit's psyche must have been great. Perhaps the pro-masculine attitudes in her fiction served as an escape from the constrictions of her own situation. An early poem must reflect her real attitude; in "The Wife of All Ages" Nesbit writes:

> Suppose I yearned, and longed, and dreamed, and fluttered,
>   What would you say or think, or further, do?
> Why should one rule be fit for me to follow,
>   While there exists a different law for you?[11]

At the end of the poem the wife admits that she will still willingly accept whatever part of his affection her husband allots to her. In her children's books this serious issue is only indirectly present: E. Nesbit usually insures free reign for the children's adventures by eliminating one or both parents from their midst.

The most obvious stereotypes in E. Nesbit's writing are not of poor people or of women, but of minority groups. Jews, Indians, "savages," and Blacks all merit a derogatory phrase or two. In *The Story of the Treasure Seekers* the children visit a moneylender, Z. Rosenbaum, whom they believe to be a generous benefactor. Mr. Rosenbaum has "a very long white beard and a hookey nose—like a falcon" and he says that he can lend the children a pound at sixty per cent interest, payable when they are twenty-one (p. 105). Oswald remarks, "And all the time he was stroking the sovereign and looking at it as if he thought it very beautiful." Whatever the author's opinion, the children believe in Mr. Rosenbaum's kindness and Alice asks why he is not invited to the party at their Uncle's mansion after the family's fortunes have changed:

> But everybody laughed, and Uncle said—"Your father has paid him the sovereign he lent you. I don't think he could have borne another pleasant surprise."   (p. 206)

Of course Jewish moneylenders are not appropriate party guests.

In *The Story of the Amulet,* which makes the most positive statement of any of the works about the need for social reforms, there is nevertheless an adventure in the financial district in which Old Levinstein and another Mr. Rosenbaum are portrayed as being selfish, usorious, and incapable of speaking "decent" English.[12]

The expression "nigger" is used indiscriminately in several of the works. In *The Story of the Treasure Seekers* the Indian uncle compliments Oswald by saying " . . . he's a man! If he's not a man, I'm a nigger! Eh!—what?" (p. 198). In a recent edition of *The Conscience Pudding,* excerpted from *The New Treasure Seekers,* the word nigger is deleted. Obviously it had little negative significance to white people at the time that E. Nesbit was writing, but merely expressed the attitudes that she and her audience shared about the negligibility of dark-skinned people.

In *The Phoenix and the Carpet,* one of the children suggests that they can escape from a band of savages by going into the water, because, as he explains, "I've—heard—savages always—dirty."[13] In this case the children have been negatively indoctrinated, whereas in the case of the first Mr. Rosenbaum, they were innocent about the attitude they were expected to hold.

These incidents and phrases are hardly essential to the total conceptions of the works as a whole, yet they do indirectly reflect the attitudes of the society in which

Nesbit did her writing, if not her personal opinions. Indeed, it is very difficult to pin down E. Nesbit's attitudes on any of these matters. Is she serious or satirical in her statements about the role of women? Is she in fact more sympathetic toward her bungling wouldbegoods' efforts to alleviate the sufferings of the poor than she is toward the poor themselves? To what degree are her attitudes affected by her own experience of social reform movements and by her husband's encouragement of her commitment to certain causes? Do any of these matters bear consideration when it is known that E. Nesbit usually wrote under the constraint to earn money and therefore to please her publishers and the public, if not always herself?

These questions are partly answered in her later works, in which, as Moore points out, she is much less subtle in expressing her personal views, often to the detriment of her story (p. 266). In *The Story of the Amulet* (1906) there is, however, a skillful blending of a children's magical adventure and a clear-cut statement of E. Nesbit's social concerns. This is the most philosophical of the three magic books about the children Cyril, Anthea, Robert, and Jane, and it is also the most fascinating on an adult level. Her magical plot device, the idea of travel through time, enables her to explore themes which go beyond a mere fantasy for children. The amulet, which transports the children to different civilizations of the past, is much more complex in its magic than the Psammead or the Phoenix and the carpet, because it requires a highly abstract understanding of the dimension of time. The children gradually learn to think of time in unconventional ways, following the advice of the Psammead that "Time and space are only forms of thought" (p. 61). Not only does their understanding of the particular concept grow, but in all the three magic books they seem to increase in wisdom as a result of their magical adventures.

In the first of the series, *The Five Children and It,* the children are quite thoughtless in the wishes they ask the Psammead to grant them and they usually suffer more than they benefit from the magic they have at their disposal. In *The Phoenix and the Carpet* the children get into just as much trouble, although there is the added excitement of being instantly transported in space to a new setting. The Phoenix has the role of a semi-adult figure and provides both instruction and entertainment for the children. In both these works they learn to take into account the feelings of others, since the Psammead as well as the Phoenix are demanding and self-centered. In *The Story of the Amulet* the children have reached the stage at which they can appreciate the lessons of "history" and carefully follow the directions which safe use of the amulet requires.

At the beginning of the novel the children are walking in a district where there are several pet shops. They feel sympathy for the animals who are in cages, because they had once been trapped in a besieged castle themselves. There is the implication that their magical adventures provide experiences which help them to mature and become better persons.

Two of the things which E. Nesbit emphasizes in her depictions of the ancient civilizations the children visit are the dispensation of justice and the condition of the working or slave classes. She also compares the level of past civilizations with the state of affairs in England, and often the present is seen as being little better than the past. When the Babylonian Queen visits the children, she is amazed at the state of the working classes. E. Nesbit provides biting social commentary in this scene:

> "But how badly you keep your slaves. How wretched and poor and neglected they seem," she said, as the cab rattled along the Mile End Road.
> "They aren't slaves; they're working people," said Jane.
> "Of course they're working. That's what slaves are. Don't you tell me. Do you suppose I don't know a slave's face when I see it? Why don't their masters see that they're better fed and better clothed? Tell me in three words."
> No one answered. The wage system of modern England is a little difficult to explain in three words even if you understand it—which the children didn't.
> "You'll have a revolt of your slaves if you're not careful," said the Queen.
> "Oh, no," said Cyril; "you see they have votes—that makes them safe not to revolt. It makes all the difference. Father told me so."
> "What is this vote?" asked the Queen. "Is it a charm? What do they do with it?"
> I don't know," said the harassed Cyril; "it's just a vote, that's all! They don't do anything particular with it."
> "I see," said the Queen; "a sort of a plaything . . . "   (pp. 168, 170)

Through her fantasy E. Nesbit expresses criticism about real social wrongs. The children have social consciences themselves. In Egypt they hear the workers protesting their wretched conditions and when they are able to confront the Pharoah, Anthea takes the opportunity to ask him to grant the workers' demands as a condition of their continuing with their magic exhibition (p. 238).

In the chapter entitled "The Sorry-Present and the Expelled Boy" E. Nesbit makes her most serious indictment of the present by having the children travel into the future. In its details E. Nesbit's picture of what is to come is very much influenced by the Fabians' social ideals. Everything is clean and beautiful. Littering is a major offense. The little boy the children meet is named Wells, after the "great reformer" and he actually likes school, where he is able to pursue an independent project each year. The people dress in soft clothes and although the little boy's house is bare of ornaments, it is to these children very beautiful. From their comments the little boy's mother assumes that the children come from a very backward country and she is miserably upset when she is whisked into the present and sees the horrible conditions which the children take for granted.

This may seem heavy-handed for a child's book, but the clear statement of E. Nesbit's views on serious matters does not detract from the adventure, and at least one gets the satisfaction of seeing that indeed E. Nesbit's political commitment did extend to her fiction. The magic books are altogether more sophisticated because a third-person adult narrator is used. Although these children are less well-defined and less real than the Bastables or the Railway Children, there are more ideas to get hold of in the fantasies. In the last work in the magic series there is sincere concern for the poor, and even the issue of male superiority is finally counterattacked. At a lecture which the children attend with the Psammead the speaker wishes that the boys in the audience will grow up to be "noble, brave and unselfish," and the wish comes true because it is said in the presence of the magic creature, who grants all wishes. Anthea remarks that it is too bad that the lecturer did not include girls, because she and Jane will have to try to attain these qualities on their own. Jane replies that the girls no doubt have these traits already "because of our beautiful natures. It's only boys that have to be made brave by magic" (p. 295). *The Story of the Amulet* ends on a note of reconciliation between the past and the present with the joining of the souls of the Egyptian priest and the learned gentleman, and hope for the future has already been provided, as seen through the children's own eyes when they visit it themselves. How such an ideal world is to be made reality is not specifically explained, but E. Nesbit has at least stated ideals in which she believes. In a letter to H.G. Wells, E. Nesbit admits that she wishes that she could write books like his *Modern Utopia*.[14] *The Story of the Amulet,* which was perhaps influenced by Wells' *Time Machine,* is undoubtedly E. Nesbit's attempt to write a highly idealistic work for children. It corroborates Joan Evans de Alonso's summary assertion about her commitments:

> She foresaw an ideal future. In spirit she was definitely a social thinker.

In conclusion, the question should be raised whether the matters which have been discussed here are important to the children who read the E. Nesbit books now. If E. Nesbit's purpose was to satirize the attitudes of her contemporaries toward women and the poor, she does it so subtly that few children would be able to see through the stereotyped images she presents to the protest underneath. It is likely that the very delicacy with which she pokes fun at establishment values is the result of her own ambivalence about these values and also of her doubts about using writing for children as a platform for adult ideas. E. Nesbit's magic books are less dated and also less negative in the social images which they promote than the works in the Bastable series and have much to offer contemporary readers. *The Railway Children* is the best of the non-magic books because of its successful depiction of real children, both female and male. All the novels, however, have elements in them which are entertaining both to children and to an adult reader who enjoys travelling back through time to the consciousness of childhood.

Footnotes

[1]Doris Langley Moore, *E. Nesbit, A Biography,* rev. ed. (1933; rpt. London: Ernest Benn, 1967), p. 102.

[2]Edward R. Pease, *The History of the Fabian Society,* 3rd ed. intro. Margaret Cole (1918; rpt. Liverpool: Frank Cass & Co., 1963), p. 19.

[3]H. G. Wells, *Experiment in Autobiography* (1934; rpt. Philadelphia: J. B. Lippincott, 1967), p. 515.

[4]E. Nesbit, *The Wouldbegoods* (1901; rpt. London: Penguin,1971), p. 54.

[5]E. Nesbit, *The Story of the Treasure Seekers* (1899; rpt. London: Penguin, 1971), p. 163.

[6]E. Nesbit, *The New Treasure Seekers* (1904; rpt. New York: Coward McCann, n. d.), p. 283.

[7]From an interview, May 31, 1972, in Cambridge, Massachusetts.

[8]Moore, p. 141.

[9]Noel Streatfeild, *Magic and the Magician, E. Nesbit and Her Children's Books* (London: Abelard Schuman, 1958), p. 66.

[10]E. Nesbit, *The Railway Children* (1906; rpt. London: Penguin, 1971), p. 114.

[11]E. Nesbit, *Lays and Legends* (London: Longmans, Green & Co., 1886), p. 82.

[12]E. Nesbit, *The Story of the Amulet* (1906; rpt. Clinton, Mass.; Colonial Press, n.d.), pp. 172-174.

[13]E. Nesbit, *The Phoenix and the Carpet* (1904; rpt. London: Penguin, n.d.), p. 70.

[14]Moore, p. 228

In Quest of Ms. Mouse

Helen Kay

The story of the mouse in search of a husband has been told many times in many lands over the last several thousand years. While the mutations of the story provide interesting material for the folklorist, there is particular fascination in tracing the varying social attitudes towards a marriageable woman, as they are represented in the fable.

One of the earliest versions is found in a folk tale from Greece, called *The Mouse and His Daughter.*[1] In this telling, the mouse father, proud of his possession, a beautiful daughter, wishes to find her "a worthy suitor . . . but not a mouse . . . " The father can find no one fit for "my little girl" until he approaches the sun, suggesting "I could not give her to anyone else, but someone like you"—that is, the strongest.

The sun confesses that he can be hidden by a cloud; the cloud claims that he can be scattered by the wind; the wind asserts that he is not really the strongest either because "he cannot blow a Tower down." As to the Tower, "to cut a long story short," he has digging within his walls a suitable husband for the beautiful mouse daughter—another mouse.

The Japanese also claim this tale under two titles: *The Beautiful Mouse Girl,*[2] and *The Mouse's Wedding.*[3] Here both parents worry about a husband for their daughter "Lovely." None of her many suitors pleases them. The father says: "I am going to search for the most powerful being in the world" as a fit husband for Lovely. The father ends up before a blank wall, but within the wall lives a most powerful mouse, and a very obliging Lovely is happy to marry the mouse her father has found for her.

In these early versions, the socializing purpose seems subordinate to the wit and dry humor of the animal fable. This balance changes over the centuries, as we may see when the Greek fables ascribed to Aesop (500 B.C.) spread to India, where they became part of the *Panchatantra* or *Five Books,* written in Sanskrit about 200 B.C.[4] The *Five Books* are a compilation of moral tales written by a holy man to educate a rajah and his three sons, and among them we find the tale of the marrying mouse.

There is an interesting difference between the Indian animal tales and the Greek fables on which they are based. In the Greek animal stories, the animals always act in accordance with what is believed to be their "natural behavior." As G. K. Chesterton defined it: in "Aesop or Babrius or whatever his name, a wolf is always wolfish; a fox always foxy." The Indian fable has a style of its own; here animals "are treated without regard to their special nature, as if merely men masked in animal form."[5]

In *The Mouse Maiden,* the heroine is at first a mouse dropped by a falcon into the lap of a childless guru as he meditates on the shore of the Ganges. In time she grows into a beautiful maiden; and when she is twelve years old, of marriageable age, her guru-father begins an unsuccessful search for "the strongest" as a bridegroom.

He looks only among the most powerful forces of nature—the sun, the cloud, the wind, and a mountain (which replaces the original wall or tower). All the powerful

165

elements confess their own weakness and refuse the match. "Only between two persons who are well-matched in means and in blood should there be a marriage or friendship, but not between high or low."[6] The caste system of like-to-like is maintained. Within the mountain is a strong, tunnelling mouse, and the maiden begs to be metamorphosed back into a mouse so she can enter his little hole in the mountain and join him in marriage.

The stories from *The Five Books* travelled by various routes into the oral and written traditions of all the countries of the world; and every country in its own way adopted the tale of the marriageable mouse, "The Mouse Maid Made Mouse." In the mid-twelfth century Marie de France wrote a series of fables in French.[7] She tells us in her prologue that the poems are based on an English version of the Fables translated from the Latin by King Alfred.

While scholars state that she was wrong in her ascription, her fables are certainly based on ancient traditions; some seem to derive from Aesop and some from Oriental versions. Her handling of *The Mouse Maiden* is interesting because there is a supportive psychological point of view as well as a unique reversal of sex roles. She tells the story of a male *mulet* (a kind of mouse which she says resembles a *suriz* or ordinary mouse) who sets out to ask for the daughter of the "most unique" in marriage. "In olden days, there was a mouse so proud, that he only wanted the daughter of the highest for a wife." Obviously a soldier king would seek such uniqueness in his queen. "If I could not have the daughter of the most powerful, I do not want a wife at all," says the proud mouse.[8]

In a seventeenth-century version of the tale, La Fontaine with wit and sarcasm challenged the Brahmin-guru with "La Souris Metamorphosée en Fille."[9] If he could make magic to turn a mouse into a girl, why did he then have to ask who was the strongest, and why did he finally let the girl down? La Fontaine continues to play with the *ronde* in his characteristic fashion; the rat (strong mouse?) should have sent the girl to the cat; the cat to the dog; the dog to the wolf .... But finally, "what spouse is not better than the sunshine?" he asks.

Marianne Moore turns to fable to deeper poetic ends in her idiosyncratic version of La Fontaine. The mouse poem exists in two texts which differ considerably: I quote from the later.

> A mouse fell from a screech owl's beak—a thing I cannot pretend
>   To be Hindoo enough to have cared
> To pick up. But a Brahmin, as I can well believe, straightened
>   The fur which the beak had marred.
>   . . . . .
>   the Brahmin sought a sorcerer,
> Eager to right what had been unfair, and procured the key
> To restore the mouse to her true identity.
>   Well, there she was, a girl and real,
> Of say fifteen, who was so irresistible
> Priam's son would have toiled harder still to reward her
> Than for Helen who threw the wholé world in disorder.
> The Brahmin said to her, marveling at the miracle—
>   Charm so great that it scarcely seemed true—

> "You have but to choose. Any suitor I know
>   Contends for the honor of marrying you."
>   —"In that case," she said, "the most powerful;
>   I would choose the strongest I knew."
> Kneeling, the Brahmin pled, "Sun, it shall be you.
>   Be my heir; share my inheritance."
>   . . . . .

The girl is refused by all but the rat, whom she accepts; the poet says:

> Explain how a lass so fair, incomparably made,
>   Could not earn for herself redress
> And have married the sun. Fur tempted her caress.[10]

Here the fable reveals implications beyond those of the sexual roles and a philosophical comment on humanity at large.

Of other twentieth-century versions, only a post-suffragette version in 1921 shows awareness of the social implications.[11] The author tells the tale direct from the *Panchatantra*, yet "protects the right of every young girl to choose her husband" by a simple addition. The father qualifies all his questions to the most powerful natural forces with the phrase "If she will choose you."

The girl begs off. The sun is too ardent; the cloud too cold; the wind too variable; and the mountain too harsh. But "like almost to like" wins out. True to the Indian version, she is changed back to a mouse and accepts the rat, choosing "more or less her own kind" for a husband.

Two modern re-tellings of the same version for children show no such sensitivity and retain all the assumptions of the original. *Ushaa, the Mouse Maiden*[12] is reassured that "Father will find you a husband" and in *Tales from India*[13] a very timid maiden who cannot bear to look at the sun explains when she finds a mouse; "He is my kind." Changed back into a mouse, she saves her own modest happiness and the caste structure as well.

The Constant Little Mouse[14] must have been—rather dismally—inspired by the Japanese fairy tale. Here "Lovely" becomes the saccharine "Sweetie Pie" who really loves a mouse called Count Nutcracker to begin with. Her parents want better things for her and drag her around a bit, until—still faithful—she discovers her own true love in a wall.

In the latest story, *The Mouse's Wedding*,[15] female autonomy vanishes even further into the distance, for the author returns to the version of Marie de France. The male mouse sets out to find for himself the daughter of the strongest, the daughter of the most powerful thing in the world; he asks in marriage the daughter of the sun.

And so it goes; the marriageable mouse through the ages, eternally docile, eternally humble, forever shoring up the customs of her day. Ms. Mouse, Ms. Mouse with a mind of your own—where are you now we need you?

Footnotes

[1]"The Mouse and His Daughter," *Folk Tales of Ancient Greece*, ed. Georgios A. Megas (Chicago, 1970), p. 18.

[2] James E. O'Donnell, "The Beautiful Mouse Girl," *Japanese Folk Tales* (Caldwell, Idaho, 1958), p. 33.

[3] Tokyo Kobunsha, "The Mouse's Wedding," *Japanese Fairy Tales* (1885).

[4] Arthur W. Ryder, "Tales from the Panchatantra," *Gold's Gloom* (Chicago, 1925), p. 132.

[5] Franklin Edgerton, *The Panchatantra* (London, 1965), p. 127.

[6] Stith Thompson, *The Folk Tale* (New York, 1951), p. 376.

[7] *Marie de France: Fables*, ed. A. Ewert and R.C. Johnston (Oxford, 1966).

[8] Henriette d'Arlin Lubart, trans., "Del Mulet ki quist femme," in Ewert and Johnston, pp. 48-51.

[9] *Les Fables de la Fontaine* (Paris, 1964), Poem VII, Book 9.

[10] Marianne Moore, *Fables of La Fontaine* (New York, 1964), pp. 215-217.

[11] F. T. Cooper, *Argosy of Fables* (New York, 1921), p. 209.

[12] Mehiel Gobhar, *Usha, The Mouse Maiden* (New York, 1969).

[13] Asha Upadhuau, *In Tales from India* (New York, 1971).

[14] William Weisner, *The Constant Little Mouse* (New York, 1971).

[15] Ruth Belov Gross, *The Mouse's Wedding* (New York, 1972).

Discerning the Animal of a Thousand Faces

Deirdre Dwen Pitts

In the marketplace of modern children's literature, children wait in well-behaved wonder for the coming of the latest unnatural hero, their imaginative world dominated by continental cats, tiresome intellectual bears, prankish monkeys, hysterical birds, priggish stuffed toys, and domesticated, slavering brutes, all wound up and talking cocktail morality with thick, ungifted tongues. What relief an older child must feel when he is finally able to cut through all the decadent silliness with a clean piece of naturalism by Jack London or Jean George or a skillfully integrated fantasy by Kipling. Then, at last, he can judge that while fiction is not true, good fiction should be, at least, equal in magnitude to the truth.

Heroes of all kinds are popular with children, who are indiscriminate as to the race, creed, or species of their candidates. Long before adults began to produce literature especially for them, children took their pleasure from folk narratives, whose special contribution to literature was the evolution of the hero. The animal hero, especially popular with younger children, appears frequently in folk tales, but the majority of his roles in the tales and in the myths are supporting ones. It is generally felt that the animal motif in religion and art of all times usually symbolizes man's primitive and instinctual nature (which could account for its popularity with younger children), and fables, folk tales and myths are full of supporting evidence.[1] Although the animal motif is now part of our literary tradition, we do not generally interpret identically its use in folklore and literature. It would be a troublesome task to prove, for instance, that the animal silliness in much current children's fiction is symbolic of our failure to integrate the instinctual psyche into our lives. The really troubling question is whether we may be pushing a traditional folk motif too far in modern children's fiction, and whether overuse of the motif reveals a basic weakness in our orientation toward the natural world. In other words, as a result of some preconscious and traditionally reinforced acceptance of the animal as a kind of anthropomorphic extension of ourselves, are we historically and finally unable to accept the animal as a separate and independently evolving species?

An enormous lore of half-truth and ignorance about nature and about animals and their behavior comes to us through folk tradition, which always minimized the differences between man and animal. In folktales, for instance, the two are never far apart: traditional tales date from the time when the world was not yet man-oriented and man and animal struggled together against uncontrollable natural forces. Animals are rarely the antagonists in these tales; enemies are usually undefined monsters, ogres, witches, giants, devils, demons, with only an occasional wolf. The tales are full of faithful and helpful animals, mostly in supporting roles. Of the tales current in western oral tradition in which the animal is the hero, most have their sources in literary fable collections from India, Aesop, and medieval cycles such as Reynard the Fox.[2] In these tales, the animal is permitted speech and is frequently dominated by some universally human moral trait which can be successfully integrated with animal behavior. The trickster fox or rabbit and the stupid bear are common, but the variety of animal actors in these tales is at least as great as that of the fables.

In the myths, of course, animals are not the heroes. They are allied with the gods in sharing the burden of natural and supernatural threat in an uncontrolled world. Although the differences between man and animal are minimal in myth, since both are subject to manipulation by the gods, their friendly relationship is less apparent than in the tales. The animal is given the role of pet or tool of the gods, who occasionally assume his shapes to carry out romantic or political intrigues. As if to further illustrate the easy come and go between the species, mortals are often punished with animal transformations. Animal nature balances delicately with man's in the ambiguous Pan, god of the natural world, who is sometimes friendly, sometimes not. As though overweighted by supernatural pressure, the balance tips toward hostility to produce marvelous but rarely friendly creatures like the minotaur, centaurs, satyrs, harpies and troubled monsters like Cerberus.

Ambiguity seems to dominate the treatment of animals throughout folklore. Following patterns set by early literary fable collections, folktales employ animals in ways which make it hard to decide whether the hero is really an animal or a human being after all. Enchantments throughout European *märchen* involve transformations of humans into animal forms with few interruptions of their affective powers. The enchanted prince, for instance, nearly always talks the heroine into negotiating his release. The ambiguities extend even farther in the myths, where, with the gods in control, anything can happen. How could a maiden afford to be kind to animals when the next one could be Zeus? About these comings and goings Stith Thompson says: "For people accustomed to such an equivocal conception of the main actors in their fiction, it is no wonder that a multitude of tales, many of them less serious in import than the mythologies, should show animal actors in all sorts of distinctly human situations" (p. 217). Although the remark was made in relation to folktales, it could apply as well to modern children's fiction, where the tradition of ambiguity seems to be at work on a purely literary level. On the psychological level, however, the tradition may be at least partly responsible for reinforcing a certain cultural ambivalence toward the animal, easily detectible in popular stories, love of the animal rising naturally from our traditional acceptance of him as an extension of ourselves, hatred of the animal resulting from his traditional symbolic association with our instinctual or (pejoratively) bestial nature.

We began in the last century to understand the meaning, and in this century the consequences, of the hostility between man and animals, and our guilt provoked a surge of literature intended for children but actually serving the adult need for expiation. Prototypical of such guilt-ridden literature is Anna Sewell's *Black Beauty* (1877), whose sentimentality need no longer be described. It is worthwhile to note, however, that the novel is still regarded as a classic by some critics in spite of its flaws, which are both conceptual and technical. As an attempt at realistic fiction, it is flawed technically by the fabulous device of the talking animal. Conceptually, Beauty is an extension of man, condescendingly raised to a level of sensitivity and reasoning, which allows him no existence independent of man's will. Refinements of the formula have evolved since, but in these stories animals are only titular heroes: since they are victims in the man-oriented world, they are either tools or pets of man and achieve stature only as his limping counterparts. *Lassie* is a fair exception. Burnford's *Incredible Journey* is more typical: an otherwise passable narrative is marred by the constant *deus ex machina* human attention required for the animals' survival.

Some evidence of our inability to separate the animal from his traditionally symbolic role can be found in those gently (for children) ironic stories in which the curious monkey (George) plays his irresponsible pranks, the small brown bear (Paddington) outwits humans, and the French cat (Fredou) babysits an inferior human child. These cannot be defended for their pedagogical value as fables because their localization and complex subplotting deny them that generic label. Under these circumstances, the fabulous animal becomes simply a trickster without a purpose. As cleverly disguised superior beings, these tricksters ordinarily throw a rather sickly cast of stereotyped human beings into confusion by the end of the narratives, whose main charm, in retrospect, becomes a kind of cynical degradation of both human and animal states.

We are beginning to learn that there are powerful forces and loyalties at work in the animal world, and even the elementary school child knows that the dignity of that ordered world is beyond question and that its natural balance is precarious. The traditional literary view of the animal as a kind of court jester or comic figure is always pleasureable. Finding in children's literature, however, an historical and finally disproportionate emphasis on the animal as imperfect human or impotent tool of man or simply victim of our current taste for literary irony and put-on seems to point toward some unresolved conflict or ambivalence that is resistant to change. Children's literature and criticism are simply not moving fast enough to keep up. Critically speaking, we adults, easily frightened and confused about our fictional images, set up all kinds of metaphorical categories to protect the "true" human image from the fantastic shapes arising out of the modern literary vogue for unconscious levels of expression. In the interests of truth, why are we not equally as sensitive about the fictional image of the animal? We seem unable to make the most basic formal distinctions between stories about fantastic and realistic animals. The editors of an authoritative critical volume on children's literature (Arbuthnot's *Children and Books*), whose format is set up according to literary types, simply admit the confusion and gather all children's books dealing in any way with animals into one chapter, dividing them among three arbitrarily labelled categories: "Ourselves in Fur," "Animals as Animals But Talking," and "Animals as Animals." This chapter is flanked on one side by the chapter, "Modern Fantasy," on the other by "Realistic Fiction." No formal distinctions are made, for instance, between *Black Beauty* and *The Jungle Books,* which coexist side by side as "Animals as Animals But Talking." The effect is a kind of unintentional critical barbarism perhaps unavoidable in our present state of confusion. The obvious division here, providing some differentiation at least, is that if it talks or behaves like a human, it is fantastic. Clearly, a change is needed.

A number of animal stories have transcended the traditional ambivalence in one way or another. Two world-views evolving from fantasy and realism have made it possible to deal seriously with animals of relatively heroic proportions that are at least equal to the truth. In 1894, Kipling's fantasy, *The Jungle Books,* gave the animal a world apart from the man-oriented one, unified with laws, language, etiquette, even class distinctions among the species. In a literary sense, this work was a prototype for the later Potter books, *Wind in the Willows*, and all specifically animal worlds to come. In these fantastic worlds, animal needs and satisfactions are paramount, and laws, language and etiquette follow prototypical lines: they are worlds from which man is excluded or in which he is ancillary to the action, or into which he enters at his own risk and to whose social orders he must eventually conform, or quit forever as Mowgli did.

The second world-view in which the animal achieves a truthfully heroic stature was probably a minor result of evolutionary theory in the mid-nineteenth century, and treats the animal as different from man in degree only, not in kind. In Jack London's *Call of the Wild* (1903), man and animal alike struggle against the hostile natural world, oriented toward neither man nor animal, in which all animal species are at once prey and predator, yet are forced to seek symbiotic relationship against frontier desolation. *Call of the Wild* is the prototype of this world-view and, certainly, Jean George's *Julie of the Wolves* is, so far, the culmination of the form in literature intended for young readers. In the novel, both Julie and the young wolf come to their relationship as unskilled dependents. Later, having reached their fullest development in the relationship, human and animal move on, apart, in absolute equality as mature members of the species. Since no such human development takes place in London's *Call of the Wild, Julie of the Wolves* outstrips the prototype in further evolution and refinement of the formula.

With either of these world-views it is possible to avoid the traditional ambiguities and ambivalence in so much of our animal fiction. Scuttling nervously down New York streets, the talking animal is a pathetic mechanism; released in a carefully structured and unified fantastic world of his own, the same talking animal evolves in the dignity of territorial jurisdiction. In literary worlds where mutual survival is the central and perhaps only real issue, all species are equal and free of human condescension.

Our ambivalence has implications for children, who are born realists. Anyone, watching a child turn from television or the printed page to ask, "Is it real?" knows that the confusion arises from contact with the arts. Children, now more than ever, need early education in the experience of art, whose media are more than ever part of their lives. For the literary experience, they need preparation—basic genre work in early elementary school. They need to be taught that no literature is the truth, that different kinds of stories (tales, myths, romances, fantasies, and realistic fiction, for examples) mean different things only relative to the truth, and that what literature means is often at variance with changing cultural attitudes. And, certainly, we need to become aware of the critical problems in animal fiction in order to explain to children the disparity which seems to exist between the animal that we know through science and domestic relationships and the hero of a thousand brutish faces in the arts.

Footnotes

[1] For a pleasantly popular discussion of the topic, well-supported with illustrations and examples from literature as well as art and religion, see Carl G. Jung, *Man and His Symbols* (New York: Doubleday, 1964).

[2] The interrelation of these sources is so complicated that even tracing the history of a single tale is difficult. See Stith Thompson, *The Folktale* (New York: Holt, 1946), pp. 217ff.

The Concept of Oz

David L. Greene

The Land of Oz, setting for L. Frank Baum's fourteen Oz books (published from 1900 through 1920), is for most readers a complete and believable fantasy world. In this respect, it ranks with J.R.R. Tolkien's Middle-Earth, C.S. Lewis's Narnia, Lloyd Alexander's Prydain, and most recently Ursula K. Le Guin's Earthsea. Most scholarly discussions of Baum's creation have reached a relatively simple conclusion: Oz is a Utopia, reflecting an optimistic view of man's potentialities or at least an optimistic answer to the complexities of our own primary world and to the flaws in man's character.[1] I believe that Baum's secondary world is more complex than this view indicates. His basic themes necessitate a world which is quite other than Utopian.[2] These themes are the acquisition of self-knowledge and the importance of reality in the face of deception and self-delusion.

To be successful, a secondary world must be detailed and relatively consistent, and it must bear some resemblance to our own world, so that we will be able to suspend our disbelief toward it. In this sense, Lewis Carroll's worlds are unsatisfactory, which paradoxically is one reason for the greatness of the Alice books, since they are based on logical impossibilities. It is particularly difficult to use a sub-creation as a satisfactory literary device—as is all too apparent from many of the "sword-and-sorcery" paperbacks on the newsstands. Either the secondary world becomes central, and character and theme become subordinate; or the fantasy land seems unrelated to character and theme, or even competes with them. A sense of place is important in most fantasies, but too many writers seem to believe that all that is necessary for a good fantasy is a believable secondary world. A sub-creation must not only bring about a sense of wonder, it must also accomplish the difficult trick of being important to the events and characters without dominating them. On the whole, Baum's world is successful in both regards.

Baum's conception of his fairyland is frequently, though not always, technological. Several of Baum's best-known creations, for example, are mechanical men, including the Tin Woodman, who first appeared in *The Wonderful Wizard of Oz* (1900), and Tik-Tok, a clockwork robot introduced in *Ozma of Oz* (1907). Oz magic is not so much an art as it is a science, arrived at through experimentation and often dependent on special equipment. Of the major authors of fantasy, Baum is the most willing to accept technology as basically beneficial; many other writers (Tolkien most strikingly) are either indifferent to technology or frightened by it.[3]

Geographically, the world of Oz is created with care. The four major divisions of Oz (the countries of the Winkies, Gillikins, Quadlings, and Munchkins) are delineated with a fair degree of precision, as is the Emerald City, situated in the middle of Oz (somewhat like the District of Columbia, the capital of Oz and its immediate environs are not part of any other political division). Oz is surrounded by the Deadly Desert, which has magical destructive properties. Outside the desert are various fantasy kingdoms—Ev, Ix,

Mo, Merryland, and others—and surrounding the entire continent is the great Nonestic Ocean. The Ozian world is mappable and, indeed, has been mapped several times.

Oz is peopled by an astonishing variety of grotesques, magical and otherwise, including a man whose body is made of wood and whose head is a pumpkin, a living scarecrow, a woodchopper made of tin, a living sawhorse, creatures who are blown up like balloons, people who eat thistles, and many others. This strange melange is ruled by the Princess Ozma, who ascended the throne of Oz at the end of *The Marvelous Land of Oz* (1904).

The egotistical isolation of many groups and individuals throughout the Oz books produces a distorted perception of reality. Many inhabitants of Oz are unwilling to attempt to understand those outside their own small groups. They create their own views of others and hold to these views rigidly; their insularity makes them incapable of seeing reality. Ozma, whose rule of Oz is never complete, is not only unable to end such isolation, she is also unaware of the existence of many of the different peoples in her realm. Not surprisingly, conflicts abound in such a situation. The battles between the Horners and the Hoppers in *The Patchwork Girl of Oz* (1913) occur because each group is convinced of its own superiority, and each group is equally ridiculous. A similar situation on a larger scale occurs in *Tik-Tok of Oz* (1914); in this book, the people of the small Oz kingdom of Oogaboo know so little about the world outside their mountains that the queen thinks she can conquer the world with an army consisting of sixteen officers and one private. Sometimes individuals have the same impervious sense of their own superiority. In *The Lost Princess of Oz* (1917), for example, when the various animals of the Emerald City argue about which is superior, each argues for himself.

Neither the characters in Baum's fantasies, nor the dangers they go through, nor the Land of Oz itself is what one would expect of a Utopia. Most of Baum's books have loosely organized quest plots, with a young boy or (more often) girl as a protagonist for children to identify with. During the quests, the participants face imprisonment, transformation, or other dangers, and in facing these threats successfully, they gain self-knowledge. Usually the main characters learn that they must place their confidence in themselves, for other supports might be humbug, like the Wizard of Oz. In *Rinkitink in Oz* (1916), for instance, Prince Inga loses the support of wealth and position. His kingdom is destroyed and his people enslaved, but with the intermittent help of three magic pearls, a fat poetic king, and a talking goat, he rescues his people and very nearly saves his parents. (Because Baum turned a non-Oz manuscript written about 1905 into this 1916 Oz book, he does not allow Inga to rescue the king and queen but delegates this task to an unconvincing *dea ex machina*, in the person of Princess Dorothy.)

Unlike the minor characters who have a false view of others, several important figures in the adventures promote a false view of themselves. Baum often depicts pretenders to wisdom, as he does with the three wise men of Gotham in his version of the nursery rhyme in *Mother Goose in Prose* (1897); in this early work, the three Gothamites are trapped by their own pretensions into going to sea in the ill-fated bowl. Professor H.M. Woggle-Bug, T.E., of *The Marvelous Land of Oz* and many later books is a satire on pompous pedantry ("T.E." stands for "Thoroughly Educated"); he seldom causes problems because his advice is usually ignored. The Frogman of *The Lost Princess of Oz* (1917) is particularly interesting, for he gives up his pretense to wisdom early in the book; he is therefore able to become an important member of the party which rescues the kidnapped ruler of Oz.

Baum's deepest depiction of hypocrisy is in the title character of *Queen Zixi of Ix* (1905), a fantasy which takes place in a kingdom bordering Oz. Queen Zixi is a witch, six hundred and eighty-three years old, who has remained alive through magic. She appears young and beautiful but is unable to fool a mirror: "her reflection . . . showed to her an ugly old hag, bald of head, wrinkled, with toothless gums and withered, sunken cheeks." In order to appear as beautiful to herself as she does to all around her, she manages to steal a magic wishing cloak owned by the sister of the boy king of Noland. She soon discovers that the cloak will not work for anyone who steals it, and realizing her own foolishness, she resolves to be contented with her lot. Later she renders great assistance to Noland when it is invaded. But when she appeals in the last scene to the fairy queen whose band had made the cloak, she is rejected: "Plead not to me, Queen of Ix! . . . You know that we fairies do not approve of witchcraft. However long your arts may permit you to live, you must always beware a mirror!" Even one who has become admirable cannot have appearance changed into reality.

In Baum's sub-creation, transformations must be broken because they are false. For example, Bilbil, the talking goat of *Rinkitink in Oz,* is returned to his true form as Prince Bobo of Boboland, and he is ashamed of what he has been (even though many readers find him more interesting as a goat). Mombi, the witch in *The Marvelous Land of Oz,* is unable to escape justice even when she takes the form of a griffin. The many transformations in *The Magic of Oz* (1919) and *Glinda of Oz* (1920) nearly lead to disaster in both books. Transformations into inanimate objects are feared most of all. The purpose of Ojo's quest in *The Patchwork Girl of Oz* (1913) is to disenchant the marble statue that was once his uncle; when the rescuers in *The Lost Princess of Oz* finally discover Princess Ozma, she is imprisoned in a peach pit. Both transformations are frightening rather than ludicrous. Transformation from one form of life to another raises complex questions of personal identity; transformation from life to non-life is terrifying. As a child, I was not so much frightened by Medusa's severed head as I was by what Perseus did with it.

Oz is surely not Utopian in a visionary sense. Rather it is a proving ground for various personages who learn through dangers and conflicts. Frequently these adventures raise complex philosophical and psychological questions centering around reality and pretense. Oz can be heady fare for young readers.

Footnotes

[1] Four important discussions of Oz argue a Utopian view: Edward Wagenknecht, *Utopia Americana,* University of Washington Chapbooks No. 28 (Seattle, 1929); S.J. Sackett, "The Utopia of Oz," *The Georgia Review,* 14 (Fall, 1960), 275-291; Fred Erisman, "L. Frank Baum and the Progressive Dilemma," *American Quarterly,* 20 (Fall, 1968), 616-623; and Michael Patrick Hearn, *The Annotated Wizard of Oz* (New York, 1973), pp. 74-75. See also Ben Indick's discussion of Baum criticism in the Spring, 1974, issue of *The Baum Bugle,* the journal of The International Wizard of Oz Club, 220 North Eleventh Street, Escanaba, Michigan 49829.

[2]Baum tries consciously to make Oz Utopian in chapter three of *The Emerald City of Oz* (1910), which describes social, political, and economic life in Oz, and in chapter fifteen of *The Patchwork Girl of Oz* (1913), which describes the Ozian penal system. The little we see otherwise of the actual governing system is not Utopian, and these few references have little effect on the stories themselves.

[3]Douglas G. Greene and I discuss Baum's attitudes toward technology at greater length in our introduction to his 1901 "electrical fairy tale," *The Master Key*, scheduled for publication in February, 1974, by Hyperion Press.

Artistic Awareness in Early Children's Books*

Justin G. Schiller

When Lewis Carroll first composed his search for the White Rabbit, he did so not merely as a whimsical bit of nonsense prepared by an Oxford mathematics lecturer but with an apparent understanding of the type of books needed by children and with a sharp eye toward criticizing works then currently available. The story opens:

> Alice was beginning to get very tired of sitting by her sister on the bank, and of having nothing to do: once or twice she had peeped into the book her sister was reading, but it had no pictures or conversations in it, "and what is the use of a book," thought Alice, "without pictures or conversations?"

And although there have been many illustrators who have since attempted to interpret the characters of *Alice in Wonderland,* the original designs by John Tenniel are as much a part of the story's enjoyment today as they were more than one hundred years ago. How many other nursery classics have made text and artistry inseparable to the minds of generations of readers? L. Frank Baum's, *Wonderful Wizard of Oz* has never had better illustrations than the originals of W.W. Denslow; and how many thousands upon thousands of people have enjoyed the drawings of George Cruikshank to the *Household Stories* of the Brothers Grimm? To deny their majesty of design as a rationale for publishing a more up-dated version (as some might call it) would be like depriving the adventures of Peter Rabbit and Mrs. Tiggy-Winkle of Beatrix Potter's watercolors. They have merged and become so essentially part of the story that we could never fully accept any new set of illustrations.

Thus we accept the reliance upon art in children's books, and note that the dependency encourages the child's imaginative faculty and at the same time commits the reader to the story. But there are other ways to attract interest in a book. What about the placement of pictures in relation to the printed text? Or a particular typography, whether novel or simply legible? The material and design of the binding might even suggest what treats are in store behind the covers, this being especially important in the days when books were not issued with printed paper wrappers or dust-jackets as we know them today.

The overall production and concept of design in children's books are matters of great importance, and the Children's Book Council of New York must be praised for bringing this awareness to public attention. This is one of the chief motives for the annual Children's Book Showcase, and it seems so natural a concern that we can easily lose sight of its difficult evolution during the past three centuries. There were many social attitudes which greatly inhibited the maturation of juvenile literature, but a number of pioneer authors and publishers constantly challenged obstacles to produce a better product. In the survey that follows, I shall examine several forms of design and

*A paper read at the Second Children's Book Showcase, sponsored by the Children's Book Council, at Drexel University, Philadelphia, March 19, 1973.

trace their development to the late nineteenth century when specific improvements crystalized in the artistry of Walter Crane.

We can trace the origin of books designed specifically for children roughly to the second half of the seventeenth century, when numerous works on the need for "Youthful Piety" were published, generally bound in dark brown or black leather to convey an added authority and sternness. These books, modelled after John Foxe's *Acts And Monuments* (commonly known even in Elizabethan times as "The Book of Martyrs"), recorded in endless procession the pious lives—and even more pious deaths—of young children. Despite the serious subject-matter of these martyrologies, most of the early volumes have very soft and unpresuming titles—like James Janeway's *Token for Children* (1671), or the small collection of emblematic and biblical verses written by the author of *Pilgrim's Progress* and originally published in 1686 as *A Book For Boys And Girls: Or, Country Rhymes For Children.* The text pages were very crowded with warnings against damnation, the type-size was quite small. These books rarely had illustrations; when they did carry pictures, scenes of various physical or spiritual torments were usually portrayed.

It has been traditional to take the *Orbis Pictus* of Johann Amos Comenius as the first picture-book for children. Published in 1658 as an illustrated book of objects to instruct German students in proper Latin vocabulary and word-lists, it was immediately translated into several languages, and about 225 separate editions were printed before the end of the nineteenth century. But we must wait for another generation before we find books designed for the amusement as well as the education of children.

It was not until 1690, in his famous essay concerning attitudes of education, that the English philosopher John Locke proposed a revolutionary thought: as soon as a child knows the alphabet, he should begin reading for pleasure:

> To this purpose I think Aesop's Fables the best which, being stories apt to delight and entertain the child, may yet afford useful reflections to a grown man . . . . and if his Aesop has pictures in it, it will entertain him much the better and encourage him to read.

What few people know, however, is that Locke produced an anonymous edition of Aesop in 1703—prepared as an entertaining text as well as providing fables in both English and Latin for young scholars—and for this very rare volume he included seventy-four illustrations engraved on five copperplates (Fig. 1). The book is regular octavo size, printed in a variety of type-styles to designate the emphasis of syntax, and with sufficient margins on each page, unlike Comenius with its tightly filled columns; the one copy I have seen was bound in contemporary brown leather with gilt spine label, not unpleasant as a binding but still rather awesome for younger readers. A visit to the fable collections at the Library of Congress or the Metropolitan Museum of Art in New York would strengthen this impression that editions of Aesop published prior to 1703 were either too academic for children or printed as an illustrated folio and much too large for them to handle; editions published after John Locke, in particular Samuel Croxall's translation of 1722 and the beautifully produced Baskerville version translated 1761 by Robert Dodsley, were chiefly printed in octavo or dodecimo size and filled with delicate engravings.

It is generally thought that John Newbery was the first to specialize in books for the nursery, and of course his name was borrowed by the American Library Association for

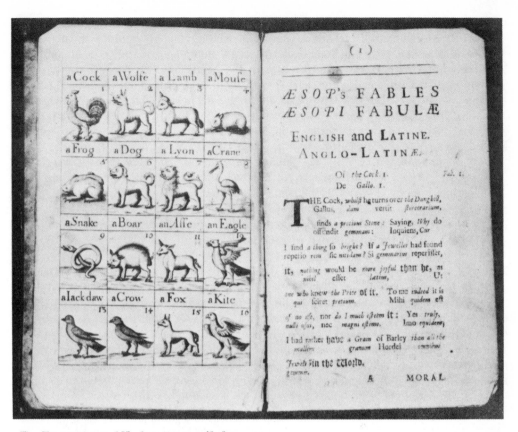

Fig. 1. ESOP'S FABLES, In English
& Latin, Interlineary [by John
Locke]. London: A. & J. Churchil,
1703. First edition. Authorship
acknowledged in the second edition
(London: A. Bettesworth, 1723).

The Trumpeter Gad-Fly has summon'd the crew,
And the Revels are now only waiting for you.

Fig. 2. [Roscoe, William]. The
Butterfly's Ball, And The
Grasshopper's Feast. London: J.
Harris, 1 Janry 1807.

their annual children's literary award. But Newbery was preceded, if only by two years, by another London bookseller—Thomas Boreman—who set up his outdoor stand near the statues of the two giants in Guildhall. By 1740 Boreman had the idea of publishing children's books that could easily be held in the hands of their young owners, still to contain pretty pictures and with readable type. In all he produced ten volumes which have become known as "Gigantick Histories," although each measured less than 2½ inches high and were printed in very limited quantity during a four year period. The books typically described various London landmarks, in Boreman's rather light style with interpolated verses: the *Gigantick History of the two famous Giants in Guildhall; Curiosities in the Tower of London; History of the famous Cathedral of St. Paul's; A Description of Westminster Abbey*; and a biography of Cajanus, the Swedish giant—actually the story of a person born in Finland 1709, and filled with anecdotes of foreign travel ending with his present residence in London 1742.

But besides providing an entertaining text, good woodcut illustrations, and an innovative dwarfed format, Boreman included in each book a list of juvenile subscribers. While in works of literature and science this practice was well-established, Thomas Boreman was the first to employ it in books for children. What a thrill for a youngster to find his name in print in his own reading-book, and how proudly he must have exhibited it to all the household and even more proudly to his playmates—which, in turn, would probably fill them with envy and have them plague their own parents for sufficient money to subscribe for copies next time. The books were well bound in a decorative blind-stamped paper over boards, and it is regretful that so few copies of these delightful miniatures have survived.

As mentioned before, John Newbery's name has become synonymous with the history of children's book publishing—and well it should, for during the period between 1742 and 1802 he and members of his family published over four hundred titles intended strictly for children, many of which ran into ten or more editions. Most of Newbery's books are educational in design, or at the least morally instructive, and his success in the field may be due to his "plum-cake" philosophy—that is, adding just enough sugar and sweetness to his stories to disguise the moralizing sermons demanded by parents and so popular in the late eighteenth century.

To Newbery must go credit for the invention of a new format in children's books—taking the basic principle from Boreman's "Gigantick Histories" with its compact size to fit comfortably in a child's hand but now enlarging the book to an average four inches, thus making it more substantial to wear and handling. He also adapted Boreman's use of decorative paper, but rather than having only one color John Newbery imported from the continent various multi-color floral designs on paper overlaid with gilt ornaments. This made his little volumes glisten and shine like gold on the bookshelves, and he quickly secured the following of everyone interested in buying nursery literature. Inside these covers Newbery had to create a series of books that would be nearly as impressive as their bindings, and this he did quite well, so that many of the titles reflected their charm and appeal: *The Renowned History of Little Goody Two-Shoes, A Little Pretty Pocket Book, Juvenile Trials for Robbing Orchards*, etc. Take for example his *Entertaining Traveller*, published about 1780 and known to exist only in four copies. This chapbook attempts to combine the tradition of a Robinson Crusoe adventure with a juvenile allegory somewhat akin to *Pilgrim's Progress,* and so it is extensively sub-titled:

> A Brief Account of the Voyages and Travels of Master Tommy Columbus, in Search of the Island of Wisdom; with a description of that island: as also of the Rock of Curiosity, the Court of Ambition, the Field of Luxury, and the Desert of Famine.

Another chief concern to Newbery was the need for illustrations in children's books, not just a few sparse woodcuts but many pictures to amuse the child and get him to select these pretty books over any volumes issued by competitors. Let us examine *A Pretty Book Of Pictures: For Little Masters And Misses: or, Tommy Trip's History of Beasts and Birds;* first advertised to be published in 1753, the earliest copy to have survived is the fifth edition (circa 1764), preserved in the rare books collection at the Free Library of Philadelphia. This and later printings contain a woodcut frontispiece and 59 text illustrations of the various creatures, with descriptive verses under each design:

> Of the Bison, or Wild Ox
> The Bison, though neither / Engaging or Young,
> Like a Flatt'rer, can lick you / to Death with his Tongue.

And in his concern for illustrations, Newbery must also be credited with having introduced the pictorial binding—a preview of such pictures which might occur inside as part of the text or simply illustrations used only as decorations. Up until this time books were issued in plain wrappers or colored paper boards, and infrequently they might have a small paper label with an abbreviated title pasted to the upper cover; now, just as other publishers had tried to duplicate Newbery's gold bindings, a gradual trend toward pictorial wrappers developed between 1790 and 1820—after which time it would be difficult to locate any English juvenile in original condition that did not have some form of illustrated binding.

With the advent of the nineteenth century I can begin referring to typographical consideration in books for children, since up until 1805 most juvenile productions might be described as not particularly well-printed. Then, just after the start of the new century, the former manager of Elizabeth Newbery's bookshop—John Harris by name—took over his employer's business, changing the imprint, and began to explore new methods of dealing with the rapidly grown competition. After re-issuing a number of old Newbery titles, and publishing a few new ones written by Newbery authors still under contract, Harris planned and produced in 1805 the first in a new series of chapbooks—with ¾-page copper illustrations and engraved text verses on each of its sixteen pages. His first title was *The Comic Adventures of Old Mother Hubbard And Her Dog*—the earliest known or surviving printed text of this popular nursery rhyme. This is one of the first juveniles ever written solely to amuse, with the illustrations done in an attractive fashion, its neat bold text well-spaced and totally legible. Needless to say, the success of the publication was instantaneous. Harris said that "upwards of ten thousand copies" were distributed in a few months, although less than one dozen apparently survive today. He reprinted it the following year, and also brought out a continuation and a sequel. Pirated editions of the chapbook were to be found everywhere, and it rapidly established itself as one of the chapman's stock productions. Old Mother Hubbard has taken a leading place among nursery rhyme characters, and the British Museum catalogue records twenty-six different titles under her name.

In a true sense this may be described as the "Golden Age of Chapbook Publishing." No longer was cheaply printed and folded paper flogged for sale in the market-place. A stream of these finely engraved nursery verse-books had now taken their place. Most distinctive among them was the very popular *Butterfly's Ball and Grasshopper's Feast* written by Sir William Roscoe, a member of Parliament from Liverpool, reprinted from the *Gentlemen's Magazine* in 1807 by John Harris as part of his nursery series (Fig. 2). The poem was newly illustrated by William Mulready, later a member of the Royal Academy and designer of Britain's first postage stamp. Later this same year Mulready also designed twenty page engravings for the first edition of *Tales From Shakespeare* by Charles and Mary Lamb, and these designs are so accomplished that many authorities had been of the opinion that they were done by William Blake.

It was at the beginning of the fifth decade in the nineteenth century that the designing of children's books took a more professional, if not scientific, turn under the instigation of Sir Henry Cole (1808-1882). In 1841 he looked around for books to entertain his own children and was distressed at the volumes that were available. Nursery rhymes popular during the past thirty-five years were now printed only in the cheapest and most unpleasant editions, while many of the fairy tales had become debased in literacy and illustrated with the oldest and crudest woodcuts. He decided to supply the need himself, using the pseudonym of "Felix Summerly," and for this project he received the enthusiastic support of a young publisher named Joseph Cundall. Together they devised the "Home Treasury Series of Books, Pictures and Toys"—a collection of traditional children's stories written in literate fashion, attractively designed by William Pickering and finely printed by Charles Whittingham at his Chiswick Press. Selections were taken from art masterpieces by Raphael, Titian, and Hans Holbein, along with commissions given to the best modern book illustrators; these included William Mulready, Harrison Weir, John Absolon, and J. C. Horsley (the latter being credited with drawing the first Christmas greeting card, originated 1846 by Cundall and Cole). It was an attempt to put representations of the best art into the hands of children for their early appreciation, and there is every indication that they succeeded.

We might briefly examine the basic production formula of these "Home Treasury" books. The texts were carefully selected, well-written and adapted to children but never at a sacrifice of or substitute for imagination. The illustrations were appealing and the arrangement fitted comfortably with the text. And, finally, a colorful paper board binding was used, partially inspired by Newbery's use of Dutch floral wrappers, but here in a more determined geometrical pattern of bright yellows, blues, reds or greens. One aspect of the book never dominated or detracted from another: the type-design (generally Caslon Old-face) blended well with the large, bold illustrations on adjacent pages, and for the more expensive productions the binding was often a gilt pictorial cloth—quite an early use for this type of binding style during the 1840's. In the original announcement of 1843 Sir Henry Cole described his specific intention for this new series: to restore to the tales a sense of tradition without deterioration or added impurities. It was an attempt to preserve historic origins within a folk-lore framework.

In keeping with the nineteenth-century spirit of change and invention, many people sought new approaches to old problems. The quest for design and decoration in books went beyond decorative borders and page illustrations to the text itself. There are several instances where typography has produced amusing effects in the presentation of popular children's literature. Perhaps best known is the "Tale of a Mouse" from *Alice's Adventures In Wonderland.*

> Fury said to a mouse, That he met in the house,
> 'Let us both go to law: I will prosecute you.—
> Come, I'll take no denial; We must have a trial:
> For really this morning I've nothing to do.'
> Said the mouse to the cur, 'Such a trial, dear sir,
> With no jury or judge, would be wasting our breath.'
> 'I'll be judge, I'll be jury,' said cunning old Fury;
> 'I'll try the whole cause, and condemn you to death.'

This form of word-arrangement is called emblematic or "figured verse," where the poem is printed in such a way that it resembles something related to the subject-matter—in this case, a play on the word "tail." Words forming visual analogues is a practice quite common today, for the technique is frequently employed in the lettering of advertisements (especially for head colds) or in the design of book jackets.

Another innovative use of typography occurred in the first printed appearance of "The Story of the Three Bears," as written by Robert Southey and published 1837 in his literary magazine *The Doctor.* Here type styles were used to transcribe voice patterns of the titled characters as all enquired who had eaten their respective bowl of hot porridge, sat in their separate chair, or lay in their own bed: black letter gothic was used for the Great, Huge Pappa Bear; a medium form of Caslon Old-face was adopted as the voice of Mama Bear; and small italics were employed for the squeal of Wee Baby Bear. The visual distinction between each of the three speakers is retained in most nineteenth century reprints of the story, but none portrays the difference so dramatically as Southey's first use of it. Curiously, the protagonist of this original version is not the familiar Goldilocks we all know but a mischievous old woman who enters the home of the three bears after she has ascertained they were not inside; she goes about the familiar porridge-tasting, chair-sitting, and bed-warming, until at last she is discovered by the returning residents and quickly makes her secape through an open window. The first use of a little girl in the story occurs in a volume of collected tales published and edited by Joseph Cundall in 1850. The girl is named Silver-Hair, which was later altered to Golden-Locks probably to conform better to the illustrations, and again changed sometime later in the century to its present contraction. Cundall's reason for changing the character of the intruder is given in his prefatory remarks: there are simply too many stories already told about old women, and childhood curiosity seemed a natural (if not improved) substitute for mischievousness.

English picture-books reached their highest level in the final thirty-five years of the nineteenth century. The person mostly responsible for the achievement is Walter Crane. While for many years he has been overshadowed by the popularity of Kate Greenaway and Randolph Caldecott, time has shown him to be the true master of his craft and he is undergoing an enormous revaluation in connection with revived interest in Art Nouveau. Crane's picture toy-books are the perfect marriage of color and design, while the

He perceived the beans had sprouted,—grown so very tall and high,
That the topmost of their branches
  seemed to lose itself in sky.
"I must climb," cried Jack, delighted,
  "it seems strong enough to bear;"
When his mother would prevent him,
  no remonstrance would he hear.
Up he goes among the branches,
  easy as a winding stair;
Climbing on for hours, he reaches
  desert lands and bleaker air.
Was no sight or sound to cheer him,
  and he very hungry grew;
As he wandered, sick and weary, an
  old woman came in view:
She was old, her garments tattered,
  and half blind she seemed, and
  lame.

Fig. 3. Walter Crane's Toy Books. New Series. Jack And The Beanstalk. London: George Routledge, circa 1874.

decoration of text and arrangement are full witness to his imaginative fantasy. In his own version of *Jack And The Beanstalk,* we see three chronological sequences taking place in one picture, without disturbing the aesthetic unity of the whole (Fig. 3). Jack's mother, furious that her son traded their cow for a handful of beans, throws them about the house and garden; Jack awakes the next morning, looks out of his bedroom window, and sees the beanstalk fully sprouted reaching into the sky; and then, the chief action in the foreground, Jack climbs the grown stalk in hopes of finding adventure and his fortune. The movement carries the viewer from one picture to the next, each in turn not being static like a tableau but full of activity, so he can readily imagine Jack climbing hand-over-hand, up the branches and through the clouds. Most of Crane's other nursery art is of this same detailed calibre, and in a way it is testimony to his greatness that so many of his books have today become so rare—not because the number of copies originally printed were small, but because of frequent handling in their fragile bindings most of them were read to pieces.

Involved on a daily basis with growing collections of early children's books, I am constantly reminded of the rich heritage of this field during the past three hundred years. But this has not blinded me to the exciting things happening this moment in publishing modern juvenile literature. New talents have come to make their own mark on history, and we should fully recognize the combined efforts of writers, artists, editors, designers, and production staffs who have blended their skills to produce truly beautiful books for children. It is this continued incentive for greatness in the production of children's books that the masters of the first three hundred years would consider their finest legacy.

"Over the Garden Wall / I Let the Baby Fall": The Poetry of Rope-skipping

Francelia Butler

One wouldn't suppose that so scholarly an activity as the collection of rope-skipping rhymes could be a life-endangering occupation, but on a recent trip to Belfast, in a predominantly I.R.A. section, I learned that even children's chants can become a matter of life and death.

Going with an Irish driver into a sector where there has been considerable trouble, I started to pull a skipping-rope from my purse. "You fool! Do you want to get us killed?" the driver hissed as he crushed the rope down in my pocketbook. "It has red, white and green handles. Anybody at a window is liable to think it's red, white and blue and you're asking their children to jump to the colors of the British flag. They'll pick us off." He told the children I had no rope and asked them to fetch a length of clothesline.

If the incident reflected the unusual stress experienced by the people of Belfast, it also said something about the importance of skipping rope and the rhymes that accompany it as a form of expression. I am convinced that through the act of skipping, of overcoming the demonic power of the rope, the child achieves a bodily and psychic loosening of emotional strictures. The rhymes, ancient in origin, durable and widely distributed, are a way for unconscious elements in the personality to surface. This is apparent in Belfast and in less explosive places as well, for skipping rope is practiced in widely diverse countries and cultures.

In Belfast, for example, children in large families are often forced to tend younger brothers and sisters, and their frustration may come out in rope-skipping rhymes. One child commented that her mother didn't like her to skip too much, since it wore out her shoes. Then she began:

> My wee brother is no good.
> Chop him up for firewood.
> When he's dead
> Cut off his head,
> Make it into gingerbread.

Another skipper in Belfast added this one:

> Eni eni mino mo
> Set the baby on the po [pot]
> When it's done
> Clean its bum
> And give it a lump
> Of sugar plum.

However, babies can be a nuisance to skippers everywhere. In England and New Zealand children chant:

186

Over the garden wall
I let the baby fall.
My mother came out
And gave me a clout
Over the garden wall.

And in the United States, baby care is a problem, too:

I had a little brother,
His name was Tiny Tim.
I put him in the washtub
To teach him how to swim.
He drank up all the water,
He ate up all the soap.
He died last night
With a bubble in his throat.

Most rope-skipping rhymes about family relations have to do with a skipper's relationship to his or her mother. Often the mother appears as disciplinarian, as in this rhyme I heard in Belfast in two versions, the first from a girl's, the second from a boy's point of view:

My mother said
I never should
Play with gypsies
In the wood.
If I should
She would say,
"Naughty girl to disobey
"Disobey disobey,
"Naughty girl to disobey."
I wish my mother would
Hold her tongue.
She had a boy
When she was young.
I wish my father would
Do the same.
He had a girl
with an awful name.

The boy's variant
of this rhyme:

My mother said
I never should
Play with gypsies
In the wood.
The wood was dark,
The grass was green,
In came Sally
With a tambourine.
I went to the sea—

Jacob Cats (Dutch, 1618).
Courtesy Folger Shakespeare Library.

No ship to get across.
I paid 10 shillings
For a blind white horse,
I was up on his back
And was off in a crack,
Sally told my mother
I would never come back.

The girl with the "awful name" that father had in the first version sounds like Sally "with a tambourine" in the second—the kind of girl who causes sons to repudiate motherly advice about sex outside marriage. Once that taboo is broken, the youth may be "at sea" for a while until he sets up his own code of conduct. The Platonic rider, reason, must ride the horse, the emotions. He may not see his way at first, but some Sally will get the message back to his mother that he will never return to the old emotional dependency.

As disciplinarians, mothers can be monsters. This Scottish rhyme was given to me by Reginald Oakes:

Kilty kilty Calder
Couldn't play his drum;
His mother took the bellows
And blew him up the lum.

"Lum" is Scottish for chimney. A mother, presumably, scolds her daughters in this rhyme, which I heard in the Slovenian section of Yugoslavia:

Katarina, Barbara,
Look how you've cared for the house!
A chicken's been stolen
The feathers all plucked—
Eaten no doubt in Ljubljana.

Everywhere, mothers and food are closely associated. In this French rope-skipping rhyme a mother is calling to her children:

Soup's on, on, on!
Come and get it, get it, get it!
Never leave the rope empty,
The one who does get punished.

And a succession of children keep the rope warm and turning—just as their mothers have kept the pot of soup warm for generations at the back of an old French stove.

Another French rhyme tracked to the 16th century and associated with the image of Rabelais's Gargantua goes:

Pan, pan, pan.
Mama is at Caen.
I've eaten 10 eggs,
The heads of two cows,
A hundred pounds of bread,
And still I am hungry!

188

The mother figure, food and religion are combined in this rhyme jumped in Italy:

Jump, Pilate!
The Holy Mother takes you in her arms—
Gives you a spoon of rice—
Leap into Paradise!

By this leap of faith, any naughty child who identifies with Pilate is forgiven, and in passing through the ordeal of the rope, symbolically reaches a better world on the other side of it.

In a Greek school rhyme, a child expresses guilt for ingratitude over a mother's goodness:

How can I hurt my mother
To make her upset?
Sings all day and night
For my own good she tries.

I heard this skipped recently in Athens by Victoria Antoniou, a visitor to Athens from Volos, Greece. She was jumping in one of the numerous parks in Athens called "Joy of Children," this particular one having been planned about 15 years ago by Demetrios Pikionis, a famous architect. Small in size, it gave the impression of being much larger because of the varied levels of woods and water. It was a hot day, but children were comfortable either in the wooded parts or in two play areas covered with thatched roofs. In another "Joy of Children" park, boys, too, were doing a kind of rope-skipping—vigorous jumping over a ring of elastic held taut around the legs of two other children facing each other. Not so common in America, this game is very popular in Greece, India, Afghanistan, Turkey and Argentina.

Mother is not always regarded respectfully. Here's an American look at her:

My mama and your mama live across the way.
Every night they have a fight and this is what they say:
Acka backa soda cracker
Acka backa boo
Acka backa soda cracker
Out goes you!

In a Belgian rhyme, there are suggestions that the mother may not be all she might be:

My mother bought a herring,
A herring without a head.
She put it in front of the window.
Two policemen came and took my mother along.
My mother began to yell,
And did my mother yell!
Did my mother yell!
Still another one, that makes two.

189

As for father, he sometimes appears as disciplinarian, as in this French rhyme:

"Papa, give me some tea!"
"No my daughter, after dinner."
Daughter in a tantrum
Breaks the teapot
Father, furious,
Pulls her hair.

The father as disciplinarian also appears in this extinct Frisian rhyme, used for swinging and possibly skipping in Germany in the area of Norden in 1875. It was given to me by Heinz Kurth, an author of children's books.

Jan Plojet's son fell through the floor,
Fell on his nose
In the peppernuts vat.
Come out, you thief! Come out, you scamp!
He has been too long in the swing [or rope].
One last push
Another shove
And let the swing [rope] come to rest.

Like many rope-skipping rhymes that have a rhythmic quality, displaying their ballad origin, this rhyme was originally sung.

Grandmothers come in for attention in the rhymes, as in this one from Belfast:

Granny in the kitchen doing a bit of stichin'
In comes a bogeyman and chases Granny out.
"Oh!" says Granny. "That's not fair!"
"Oh!" says the bogeyman. "I don't care."

A French rhyme considers grandmothers and death:

A.B.C.D.
My grandmother is buried
In a field of chicory.
When the chicory begins to sprout,
My grandmother will come out.

There are variants of this rhyme, all reflecting the idea that life does go in a cycle from death to rebirth, that it is part of nature's plan—an idea accepted matter-of-factly by many children.

The position of sisters and aunts is sometimes ambiguous, as in these two Belfast rhymes:

My Aunt Nellie had a bile [boil] on her belly.
She rubbed it up and down.
She sold pigs' feet at the bottom of the street,
And a policeman knocked her down.

My sister Fanny walks very canny.
For she isn't very steady on her feet,
She spends all her money
Drinking with her honey
In the pub at the corner of the street.

Unlike Aunt Nellie, Aunt Jane is well thought of by Belfast skippers. The following rhyme is included in a prize-winning rope-skipping program produced by David Hammond for the B.B.C. in 1971. It is old, but I have heard it several times in Belfast:

My Aunt Jane she called me in.
She gave me tea out of her wee tin.
Half a bap and sugar on the top,
Three black lumps out of her wee shop.
My Aunt Jane she's awful smart.
She bakes wee rings in an apple tart.
And when Halloween comes round,
Fornenst that tart I'm always found.
My Aunt Jane, she's a bell on the door,
A white stone step and a clean swept floor.
Candy apples, hard green pears,
Conversation lozengers.

A "bap" is a large round bun, like a hamburger bun. "Fornenst" means "beside," and "conversation lozengers" are little round candies in a tube with love messages on each candy wrapper, such as "I love you," "Be mine," "Take me home."

In the rhymes that refer to siblings, jealousy of a new brother is a common theme, as as illustrated by this well-known American rhyme:

Fudge, fudge,
Call the judge.
Mama's got a baby.
Ain't no girl
Ain't no boy,
Just a plain old baby.
Wrap it up in tissue paper.
Put it on the elevator.
First floor, miss!
Second floor, miss!
Third floor, miss!
Fourth floor—
Kick it out the door.

The same theme appears in this one, also frequently skipped in America:

Johnny over the ocean.
Johnny over the sea.
Johnny broke a milk bottle
And blamed it on me.
I told Ma.

191

Ma told Pa.
Johnny got a lickin'—
Ha! Ha! Ha!

Occasionally, the rhymes suggest incest, as in this one from Belfast:

Two little girls in blue, lad,
Two little girls in blue.
They were sisters; we were brothers,
And learned to love the two.
One little girl in blue, lad,
Who won your father's heart,
Became our mother.
I married the other,
But now we have drifted apart.

Skipping is done at a period when sex roles are not yet clearly differentiated. Children prefer the company of their own sex and in general girls do more rope-skipping than boys. There is rivalry between the sexes, as in this rhyme from Belfast:

Georgie and Jack are dressed in black,
Silver buckles behind their backs.
Foot for foot
Knee for knee
"Turn back Georgie and come with me."
"I have a leg for a stocking,
"I have a foot for a shoe,
"I have a kiss for a bonnie wee lass,
"But I have none for you."

Jack has his answer. Georgie is growing up. Such buried meanings in the rhymes are often sexual, and represent a catharsis for the child who acts out his or her fantasies through the chants.

The act of skipping itself is a discharge of tension. For this act, the prop, the rope, is a cheap and readily available toy. I have seen children use clothesline, a leather strap (Spain), a rope made on a string loom (France), plaited straw (Hungary), elastic (Greece) or a stiff wicker (Sweden). I have seen Cherokee Indian children using honeysuckle vines, and I am told that in India ropes of roses are sometimes used.

Often, rhymes are concerned with the process of growing up, of self-mastery. One interesting rhyme I have heard in England, Ireland and America consists of a series of questions:

What are you doing here, Sir?
Drinking up the beer, Sir.
Where'd you get the beer, Sir?
It wasn't far nor near, Sir.
Why do you speak so bold, Sir?
Because I've got a cold, Sir.
Where'd you get the cold, Sir?

Up at the North Pole, Sir.
Pray, what is your name, Sir?
My name is—[and the child jumps to the letters of his name.]

One wonders if these questions reinforce the magic of the rope, the demon, and the primitive association, as Neal Raisman, U. of Massachusetts, reminds me, of the moving rope with the magical protection of the circle. If the right answers are given and stumbling on the rope is avoided, the child can loosen himself from family relationships and begin to enter the adult world. The final line is concerned with name magic, with personal identity.

A French rhyme is about lettuce, whose fate is to be eaten in a salad once it reaches maturity. This rhyme is popular not only in France but also in Vietnam, where it no doubt arrived during the French occupation.

O, the salad!
When it grows up,
People will eat it
With oil—
And with vinegar!

At the word, "vinegar," the rope is turned very fast—a custom common in several countries, where "pepper" and "vinegar" denote speed.

The "Teddy Bear" rhyme seems to be universal. In his quest for self-mastery, the little hero, the rope-skipper, goes through certain motions:

Teddy Bear, Teddy Bear,
Turn around.
Teddy Bear, Teddy Bear,
Touch the ground.
Teddy Bear, Teddy Bear,
Show your shoe.
Teddy Bear, Teddy Bear,
That will do.

Many Americans consider this rhyme a purely American product of the Teddy Roosevelt period, but I have found it in South Africa, Luxembourg, Ecuador and the Niigata prefecture in central Japan, where the rhyme is regarded as old. Teddy Bear is generally referred to as "Mr. Bear."

The hazy, ambiguous quality of many rope-skipping rhymes relates them to dreams as a way of expressing the inexpressible. Scraps of material from the unconscious seem to emerge in the following rhyme given to me by Litizia Maroni Lumbroso of Rome:

There were three children on the seashore.
Turnips, onions, five cents a bunch!
The prettiest and tiniest began to sail.
While she sailed, her ring fell in the sea.
She raised her eyes to the wave,
Turnips, onions, five cents a bunch!
She saw a fisherman.

"O, fisherman of the wave,
"Come and fish over here."
"When I have caught turnips, onions, five cents a bunch,
"What will you give me?"
"Ten pieces of gold, an embroidered purse,
"Onions, turnips, five cents a bunch."

A child has lost a ring, a symbol, perhaps, of psychic wholeness. She seeks help from the fisherman, who draws on the source of all life, the sea.

The rhymes are sometimes concerned with a child and his comrades. One rhyme I heard in Belfast was:

All in together, girls.
No mind the weather, girls.
I spy a lark, sitting in the dark.

This rhyme, which has been traced to Roman sources, must have entered Roman Britain, where, in due time, it was transported to our own South. Thirty years ago, I heard it chanted in Virginia on the playgrounds of black schools. There is an element of fear in the rhyme, perhaps a warning against strangers, which is frequently suggested in rhymes, as in this one from the Dominican Republic:

A little coach driver
Asked me last night
If I would like
To have a ride.

And I told him,
With lots of thanks,
That I get seasick
Riding in coaches.

Erotic rhymes are found almost everywhere. In this one, which I heard in Belfast, the child tries to foresee his own emotional future, possibly with premonitions arising from his family life:

The wind, the wind, the wind blows high,
The rain comes tumbling from the sky.
[Child's name] says she'll die
If she doesn't get a man with a rosy eye.
She is handsome, she is pretty
She is a lass from Belfast City.
A knock at the door and a ring at the bell—
Ah, my true love, are you well?

Though speech seldom accompanies the rope-skipping ritual in Greece, see-sawing is a different matter there. No test of skill is involved—only the erotic back-and-forth movement of a father's leg—or, for older children, the seesaw board. For this game there are rhymes, some of which have sexual overtones. A psychic castration is suggested by some rhymes, perhaps a displaced hurt to compensate for entering the taboo area of incest:

> See-saw, I see-saw myself.
> I fall and I hurt myself badly.
> And I hurt my knee,
> And my Pagona weeps for me.
> And I hurt my nail,
> And my sister-in-law weeps for me.

Another expresses romantic interest:

> Come up, apple,
> Come down, pomegranate, for me to ask you:
>
> "What's the girl doing?"
> "She's knitting a string to give to Ramandam
> "And he will give her a glass and a comb and a little stool for her to sit and talk
>   to the earth."

One is reminded of the Delphic Oracle on her little tripod as she breathes in knowledge of the future through a crevice in a rock on Parnassus.

In her book "Picasso's World of Children," Helen Kay describes a painting and a statue by Picasso that portray his daughter Paloma skipping rope:

"In the canvas, Paloma's eyes are concentrating on her feet; the rear foot is held high in the air as she soars, while the front foot just toes over the rope—the hands clutch the skip rope as tightly as a lifeline. Her torso is made up of angles and cubes, showing the body's movement. The whole is held together and framed by the loop of the rope itself. Paloma seems to hang in the air. Yet she is grounded by the rope that whirls underfoot.

"The sculpture is humorous, a parody of Paloma at play. It is made up of two old wicker wine baskets and a hemp of rope. Her hair is corrugated paper, cast in plaster, topped by a bow that resembles a small airplane, ready to take off. On the child's feet is an actual pair of oversized, discarded shoes. Here, too, the leaping child is anchored in the air by a rope underfoot—and suspended by it. . . . These are twin documents of a child's uninhibited play."

So Picasso captured for Spain and for the universe the freedom expressed by the child in the ritual of skipping rope, a freedom expressed most directly in a final rhyme, chanted by a lonely child in Luxembourg:

> Little rope, little rope, oh my little rope,
> Unwind yourself from the round ball:
> Twirl round and round and high.
> Take me outdoors to the air and the sun.
> Out of the room, out of the house, the narrow house;
> Nobody can catch us!
> Little rope, little rope, oh my little rope,
> Unwind yourself from the ball. *

Remarks

It may be a mistake to think that reading has anything to do with literature, especially in childhood. Reading for grown-ups is conditioned by many non-literary kinds of appeal— snob appeal; pornographic appeal; the appeal of isolation and withdrawal in a crowded place; a tic-like pleasure in killing time by following print (about on a level with biting one's nails); the relief of distraction from unpleasant thoughts by the unravelling of a mental puzzle. Children are obviously susceptible to all these appeals, and to others, more specialized, as well.

Series and comic books appeal to the collecting instinct. It is highly satisfying to the young to have a complete set of anything; it is even better, in a world of difficult lessons, to have mastered an entire area of knowledge and experience chosen by oneself. ("Bet you haven't read all the Fives books; *I* have!")

The Nancy Drew series—revised to remove its more overt racism—continues to act as a rite of passage for many sub-teen girls. (*Biggles,* in England, used to capture both boys and girls.) There is a competition between friends to see who can read all the titles first—rather like the older marathon of reading all the way through the Bible, a chapter a night, without skipping any of the begats. The books are formulaic in construction, incorporating the same basic elements every time—a mystery, a clue, a chase, an attack, a capture, an escape, some classy social events, and triumph, accompanied by rich gifts.

One eleven-year-old, after reading twenty-seven Nancy Drew adventures, suddenly said, "You know, I always know what's going to happen in these books now; they're *all the same*": after which disillusion she read them only occasionally, as a kind of duty.

Yet the same child at age twelve still alternates the *Ring* trilogy, *Jane Eyre, Go Ask Alice* and Paul Zindel with her younger sister's Enid Blyton. Enid Blyton, imported from England, has achieved enormous popularity locally, for all its differences of language and culture; and, despite the modish revulsion of parents, children by the million in England and America go right on reading her.

Another appeal of the series is that it provides material for an in-group; all Enid Blyton fans or Nancy Drew followers read the same things and have endless opportunities for conversing about the books or challenging each other about them. Connected with this is the sense of support and confidence which a simple, formulaic plot inspires. Really exciting and original stories are often almost more painful than pleasant till they have been read or told often enough for a child to be able to surrender to the suspense in comfort, knowing that *really* everything is going to be all right.

When young children want to know at the beginning of a story if it will end happily, we are reminded that reading is an emotionally risky business, and self-protection demands that the risks be reduced to an acceptable level. A pattern repeated often enough, yet varied in each book or story with just enough skill for the basic similarities to be veiled gives the best of both worlds—the best of the expected and the best of the unexpected.

Perhaps the strongest pull of many books which seem to adults to be naive, ill-written, or clumsy may lie in their closeness to some fantasy essential to a certain stage of development. Yet that closeness must not be so great that it leaves no room for expansion.

I remember going back to *Heidi* after a lapse of many years and realizing with surprise that what I remembered with such pleasure simply was not in the book. I had, so to speak, done more than half of it myself. Across the skeletal plot and the sparse sentences, my imagination had grown a great vine of feeling, conjecture, and event; the fantasy evoked constituted the deepest level of appeal.

Is it not true that many of the perennial favorites are of this kind? that somehow they have the power of leaving spaces, of attracting a child's attention into themselves so that the story becomes personalized?

This means, perhaps, that they outline in some subliminally recognizable way one of the myths through which the growing mind organizes itself against the chaos of experience. In our growing we are all like Proteus—we slip from lion to tree, from fish to fire, and there are times when only the grasp of story can help us recognize and hold our form.

Barbara Rosen

Eight Current Children's Books: A Mixed Bag

A Book of Animal Poems. Selected by William Cole. Illustrated by Robert Andrew Parker.(Viking, $8.95).

What a Wonderful Bird the Frog Are. Edited by Myra Cohn Livingston. (Harcourt Brace Jovanovich, $5.25).

Peep Show. Selected and illustrated by Pamela Blake.(Macmillan, $3.95).

Storm and other Old English Riddles. Translated by Kevin Crossley-Holland. (Farrar, Straus & Giroux, $3.95).

Whizz, by Edward Lear. Illustrated by Janina Domanska.(Macmillan, $4.95).

The Raucous Auk, by Mary Ann Hoberman. Illustrated by Joseph Low. (Viking, $4.95).

I Hear You Smiling and other Poems, by Felice Holman. Illustrated by Laszlo Kubinyi.(Scribner's, $4.95).

Song of the Seasons, by Robert Welber. Illustrated by Deborah Ray. (Pantheon Books, $1.95).

William Cole is a well-known and widely respected anthologist, and he lives up to his reputation in his *A Book of Animal Poems.* One might quibble about the omission of Blake's tiger or Burns' mouse, but it would be an ungrateful response to a collection which tries to avoid the over-anthologized poem and which gathers so many remarkable poems that are not easily accessible elsewhere. Mr. Cole is obviously a voracious reader of poetry and completely *au courant.* He includes excellent animal poems by Edward Field, John Haines, James Harrison, Sandra Hochman, Marge Piercy, and W. D. Snodgrass. What was most fascinating about the anthology for me, however, was coming across gems by little known writers such as Thomas W. Shapcott and Russell Hoban.

THE FINCHES

A tiny spill of bird-things in a swirl
and crest and tide that splashed the garden's edge—
a chatterful of finches filled the hedge
and came upon us with a rush and curl
and scattering of wings. They were so small
I laughed to see them ludicrously gay
among the thorny stalks, and all that day
they teased me with their tiny-throated call.

They were a jest, a scampering of neat
brisk sweets, they were all such frivolities
I did not think to call them real, I was
too merry with their flight to see the heat
that angered their few days, to recognize
my own stern hungers in their fragile cries.
                                        —Thomas W. Shapcott

MAINE SEA GULLS

Two gray-winged farmers of the sea, they ride
The drowsing summer wind to reap the tide,

And as they go they slowly squawk together,
Chatting as farmers do about the crops and weather.
"I look for rain," says one. "Wind's in the east."
"Clamming's been poor," his friend says, "but at least
The herring's coming in across the bay."
"Ayeh," they both agree, and flap away.

—Russell Hoban

Cole's collection offers a pleasing variety, from the strong lyrical pieces of D. H. Lawrence to the lively humor of Hilaire Belloc, and the poems are well complemented by the superb drawings of Robert Andrew Parker.

In his Editor's Note, Mr. Cole comments: "This isn't a book to gulp down at one sitting. Pick it up now and then, and if you get to thinking about a certain animal, let's hope you'll find a poem about it here." More than that, *A Book of Animal Poems* is a book that can be read over the years, one that would be enjoyable and satisfying to a person from his early youth to his old age.

Myra Cohn Livingston's *What a Wonderful Bird the Frog Are* is a delightful collection of witty and zany poems, as the title suggests. The anthology ranges from first century B. C. Greek satirists (all of them from Dudley Fitts' translation of *The Greek Anthology*) to recent comic poems by Richard Wilbur and William Jay Smith. Although the anthology does not reflect the scope of an anthologist like Mr. Cole, the many favorites gathered here make for lively reading. *What a Wonderful Bird the Frog Are* would be an excellent anthology to use on a junior high level, where so many students are conditioned to think of poetry as mysterious or dull.

Peep Show by Pamela Blake is by far the most handsome book in terms of typography, art work, and design. A small collection of short poems and songs of Eighteenth Century origin, it is colorfully illustrated by Ms. Blake's own linoleum cuts, which themselves skillfully capture the flavor of Eighteenth Century England. The twelve point type not only adds to the elegance of design, but provides a text easily read by younger people. *Peep Show* would serve as an excellent introduction to poetry for primary school-age children. It would be a worthy addition to any library, simply for its art work and design, a reminder to us in this age of cost-cutting and efficiency that the physical appearance of a book can create a pleasure of its own.

Kevin Crossley-Holland has translated thirty-six Anglo-Saxon riddles from the *Exeter Book* for his fine collection *Storm*. These are excellent translations. Mr. Crossley-Holland keeps the flavor of the four stress alliterative Anglo-Saxon line, but does not become a slave to it. Thus the poems read as poems, rather than translations.

I saw a strange creature,
a bright ship of the air beautifully adorned,
bearing away plunder between her horns,
fetching it home from a foray.
She was minded to build a bower in her stronghold,
and construct it with cunning if she could do so.
But then a mighty creature appeared over the mountain
whose face is familiar to all dwellers on earth;
he seized on his treasure and sent home the wanderer

much against her will; she went westward
harbouring hostility, hastening forth.
Dust lifted to heaven; dew fell on the earth,
night fled hence; and no man knew
thereafter, where that strange creature went.

The delight in riddles is ageless. Mr. Crossley-Holland's introduction to the book is lucid and interesting and provides teen-age readers just enough background for understanding and enjoying the form and content of Anglo-Saxon poetry. A "Solutions and Comments" section at the end of the book is a fine example of intelligent literary and historical scholarship which should be made more available in texts for young people. The excellent illustrations by Miles Thistlethwaite give clues to the riddles—aids but not answers. One might say that they themselves are pictorial riddles, and as such they are a fitting complement to the text.

Whizz is essentially a book for young children which illustrates six limericks by Edward Lear. Janina Domanska's drawings are colorful and imaginative. The device of having characters march across a bridge, a new character coming on stage (or should one say, on bridge?) with each new picture is as fanciful and pleasing as the limericks. The cumulative effect and the final comic surprise are sure to make young people laugh.

Mary Ann Hoberman's lyrics about animals in *The Raucous Auk* are witty and well-executed. Two samples should suffice to give the flavor of her work.

RHINOCEROS

I often wonder whether
The rhinoceros's leather
Is as bumpy on the inside
As it is upon the skinside.

PENGUIN

O Penguin, do you ever try
To flap your flipper wings and fly?
How do you feel, a bird by birth
And yet for life tied down to earth?
A feathered creature, born with wings
Yet never wingborne. All your kings
And emperors must wonder why
Their realm is sea instead of sky.

Ms. Hoberman uses a variety of verse forms in *The Raucous Auk*—rhymed couplets, haiku, the limerick, ballad forms, and others. This book should have a wide appeal for young children. Joseph Low's distinctive illustrations are an added attraction. His gazelle is as graceful as the one described by Ms. Hoberman, and his artistic wit matches hers in his illustrations of the rhinoceros and the hippopotamus.

In reading *Song of the Seasons* and *I Hear You Smiling*, I was reminded of Kenneth Koch's comments in his *New York Review of Books* article, "Teaching Great Poetry to Children":

—*NYR*, Sept. 20, 1973, p. 25

Koch's perception is all too recognizable and distressing for those of us who have spent time teaching in the public schools. Too many adults think of children as a pre-human species or as delicate creatures to be protected from the cruel world. Consequently, individuals in America probably take longer to grow up than almost anywhere else in the world. Plus growing up with the resentment of being *condescended to.* This condescension can best be illustrated by giving the complete text of Robert Welber's *Song of the Seasons*:

> Sing a song of spring
> Rain on the tree
> Rain on the flowers
> Rain on me
> Sing a song of summer
> Sun on the tree
> Sun on the flowers
> Sun on me
> Sing a song of autumn
> Wind on the tree
> Wind on the flowers
> Wind on me
> Sing a song of winter
> Snow on the tree
> Snow on the flowers
> Snow on me

The fact that each line shares a two-page spread with a smudgy pastel, everything soft and cute, does not help very much. I much prefer the poem by the sixth grade student which Koch quotes in his article:

> Giraffe! Giraffe!
> What kicky, sticky legs you've got.
> What a long neck you've got. It
> looks like a stick of fire . . . .

How much more imagination, how much more poetry in the sense that Frost once defined it: "Saying one thing in terms of another"!

Felice Holman in *I Hear You Smiling* is also a victim of the idea of preparing a cute pie for "little tots", as well as not taking very much trouble with rhythm and technique, apparently under the illusion that anything set in line form is good enough for children's poetry. Many of her poems have an arbitrary, overly-casual rhyming. Others lack a sense of rhythm, as in the first lines of "The Flower Trap" which read like prose:

I'm trapped
among the flowers
in the middle of my rug.
They hold my feet and
try to plant me with them.

Some of her poems, such as "Elevation" and "Sulk," succeed quite well, but generally the book is marred by a lack of craftsmanship and imagination.

On the whole this has been a good year for children's books. However, it seems some book editors need to develop better taste and gain a higher respect for children. Until this happens, we will continue to see the publication of children's books which display less imagination and seriousness than children themselves.

Alexander Taylor

Poems, Prayers, Pets, and a Princess

A Birthday for the Princess, by Anita Lobel. Illustrated by the author. Ages 4-8. (Harper and Row, $5.95).

The Brownstone, by Paula Scher. Illustrated by Stan Mack. Ages 3-8. (Pantheon Books, $4.50).

Games (and how to play them), by Anne Rockwell. Illustrated by the author. Ages 5 and up. (Thomas Y. Crowell Co., $5.95).

He Was There from the Day We Moved In, by Rhoda Levine. Illustrated by Edward Gorey. Ages 5 and up. (Harlin Quist, Inc., $1.50).

The Knee-Baby, by Mary Jarrell. Illustrated by Symeon Shimin. Ages 2-5. (Farrar, Strauss and Giroux, $4.95).

Morris Brookside, a Dog, by Marjorie Weinman Sharmat. Illustrated by Ronald Himler. Ages 3-8. (Holiday House, $3.95).

Nana Upstairs and Nana Downstairs, by Tomie de Paola. Illustrated by the author. Ages 3-6. (G. P. Putnam's Sons, $3.95).

A Nutty Business, by Ida Chittum. Illustrated by Stephen Gammell. Ages 3-8. (G. P. Putnam's Sons, $4.29).

Pippa Mouse, by Betty Boegehold. Illustrated by Cyndy Szekeres. Ages 2-6. (Alfred A. Knopf, $2.95).

Poems and Prayers for the Very Young, selected and illustrated by Martha Alexander. Ages 2-5. (Random House, $.95).

Riff, Remember, by Lynn Hall. Illustrated by Joseph Cellini. Ages 9-12. (Follett Publishing Co., $4.95).

To Catch a Tartar, by Lynn Hall. Illustrated by Joseph Cellini. Ages 8-12. (Follett Publishing Co., $4.95).

It is both a strength and a weakness of picture books that they must always be a collaborative effort. Even when author and illustrator are one and the same person, the eye and the ear must collaborate. When the team effort is successful, we readers receive the best of two worlds plus a whole even more pleasurable than its parts. Failure, in most cases, means failure to be published, which doesn't concern us here. But, we do often see cases in which one collaborator falters and the other carries the crippled work across the line to publication. Of the twelve books to be discussed now, I consider only six totally successful collaborations. The remaining six vary widely in degree of artistic shortcomings and/or narrative weakness, but the artists are more often in the role of team booster.

To begin, an example of fine teamwork bent on slapstick comedy, *The Brownstone,* written by Paula Scher and illustrated by Stan Mack. The situation is inherently funny: the six apartments of a little brownstone house hold six animal tenants of drastically different needs and habits. Miss Cat needs to practice her singing. The Mice need a decent meal. And the Bears need to take their winter nap. Landlord Owl tries various ways of rearranging his household, with resultant disasters in the stairwell and between ill-matched floor-mates. With polite dialogue in the face of ridiculous situations, the zany characters strive to prove to each other—and to us—that they are civilized people, after all, and the goings-on could hardly be their fault. Add illustrations, and this little tale of getting-along-together-despite-our-differences takes wing. Clashing day-glo greens, pinks and oranges accent the nonsense while the cut-away view of the brownstone, showing all six apartments at once, not only increases the fun but helps small children visualize the chaos.

More slapstick, teamed with an ecology message and an unusual look at life in Appalachia, forms the basis of *A Nutty Business* by Ida Chittum. This book attempts more than *The Brownstone* and almost brings it off. When Farmer Flint's wife and daughter require new calicoes, he decides to gather nuts to sell to city folks. A band of squirrels nut-nap, bombard and picket ("Nuts to Us!") in protest. Finally, an agreement is reached between people and squirrels.

The characterization of the hill people is done more by the author than the illustrator and it is done well, especially their unique sense of humor. Unhappily, I cannot say the same for the avenging squirrels, who are inexplicably portrayed by Stephen Gammell as a rather urbane street gang of repulsive half-rat, half-human creatures dressed in nothing but green tennis shoes. His drawings of the Flint family and the frenetic action are far more suitable.

The narrative itself is not without fault. In spots, the action skips confusingly. For example, at one point, Farmer Flint announces he must take the nuts from the granary and store them in the house. "This is a nutty business," Madam Flint exclaims, presumably in response—but she is already slipping about on nuts we never knew were moved. Further on, the pronoun "they" is used twice in rapid succession, first to mean Madam Flint and her daughter, Glory Ann, and next to mean those nasty squirrels. Night falls and the scene abruptly shifts while we ponder the referents.

There is also an irritating habit of rarely having characters "say" anything to each other. They cry, reply, sputter, bid, retort and advise, all of that accomplished in two pages.

To her great credit, Ms. Chittum gives us many fine flashes of wit in the strange hill dialect, often nicely played off against physical comedy:

> "There are nuts other places besides the woods," cried Madam Flint, whizzing past on a dozen rolling nuts. Glory Ann toppled to the floor. "Some wear straw hats by day and chase squirrels by night."
> "That's a sight I would like to see," cried Farmer Flint.
> "You have only to look into the mirror, sir," called Madam Flint. There was an explosion of crockery as she smashed into the china cupboard front on.

Moving from the ridiculous to the sublime, we meet two books dealing with the relationship between small boys and the important women in their lives: mother, grandmother and, in one case, great-grandmother. Mary Jarrell's *Knee-Baby* is a dethroned king. Alan's mother's lap is busy with a new lap-baby and he is relegated to the far less desirable roll of hanger-on at the knee. This is a very private world we are privileged to visit. The intimacy of pet-names and secret games makes the reader feel almost an eavesdropper. Symeon Shimin's pastel illustrations, throbbing with movement, warmth and emotion, carry on the illusion of a reality that we glimpse for just a moment and that exists somewhere without us after the book is closed. This is a very special, tender, loving work that shows deep understanding of an especially difficult time in a small child's life.

Much the same can be said for *Nana Upstairs and Nana Downstairs*, written and illustrated by Tomie de Paola. Here we meet a small boy on his weekly visits to his grandmother, whom he calls Nana Downstairs, and his bedridden great-grandmother, Nana Upstairs. With a child's logic, Tommy bridges the ninety-year gap between himself and Nana Upstairs and enjoys her company immensely. What joy he must give her we can only guess from the illustrations, pastels and line drawings at once warm and comical, as befits the very young and the very old. When death comes to Nana Upstairs, Tommy makes a child's peace with his grief.

Not all children enjoy the kind of families Alan and Tommy are blessed with. Anita Lobel deals with an entirely different situation in her *A Birthday for the Princess*. Ms. Lobel is a good writer and a wonderful illustrator, but this latest effort is disappointing, not because it is bad, but because it could have been much better.

The story begins with great promise. No one listens to the Princess. No one cares what she thinks. Even her birthday party is planned for her while "The princess sits straight in her chair and writes neatly in her copy book." It's a situation with which the reader can identify and one we'd all like to know how to get out of. This is where the narrative fails us. The way out, it seems, is to run away with an organ grinder and his monkey and live an idyllic life of dancing, kissing and eating strawberries.

Where is the big confrontation scene in which the King and Queen pay for their cruelty, or Come-to-Realize or, at the very least, shut up and listen for once? Simply quitting the scene seems unfair, unsatisfying and maybe even unethical. Has our Princess no wit, no courage, no character? If not, perhaps her parents are right. Maybe she's not worth listening to!

One could cry "artistic license." The illustrations of the Arcadian scenes are nearly enough to earn Ms. Lobel the right to write any way she pleases. But only nearly enough, for she could have given us a strong climax and then gone on to the same denouement. The weak story line is regrettable in so beautifully produced a book, one worth having for the pictures alone, which are lovely tapestries filled with fanciful detail, humor and color. It is doubly regrettable when the premise of the story was so promising.

The problems of tension and climax are important also in *He Was There from the Day We Moved In* by Rhoda Levine. This is a most uncommon dog story, a shaggy dog story with metaphysical implications. The dog in question is found on the day the family moves into a new house. It is sitting in the garden and seems to be waiting for something or someone. It accepts food and patting, but neither responds nor moves closer. Four-year-old Ogden tries the physical approach, hugging, jumping up and down, turning somersaults. Nothing. His older brother, the narrator, takes a more intellectual tack. He believes the dog is waiting for a name. But what name? It must be the right name . . .

Tension mounts at a steady rate, but the story ends before it is dispelled. An important lesson is learned in the process. Our nameless narrator concludes, "I, myself, am still working on the whole thing. (The dog) is waiting: I am thinking. We're both trying. And, like my mother always says, that's about the best anyone can do . . ."

An ending like that might be hard to take at bedtime, but for stimulating creative thought, this book is worth triple its weight in teaching manuals. The allegorical possibilities are intriguing. Who or what is that dog? Happiness? Success? Meaning? Or an elusive quality of life we seek without ever naming it correctly? The illustrations further compound the mystery, with sparse detail and characters who wander in vast grey space and often seem about to vanish from the page. Only the dog and his spot in the garden receive full-page treatment and appear substantial. Is the dog perhaps reality?

Lest I give the impression that this book is too relentlessly symbolical for very young minds, I hasten to add there is wit and fun for all in both narration and illustrations. A compelling, haunting book that works across a large age span.

Note must be made, however, of the print arrangement. Its large, clear typeface becomes muddled because of margins so tiny that sentences on facing pages run into each other.

A steady diet of metaphysical dogs would be hard to take. Marjorie Weinman Sharmat gives us a more conventional dog story, but one with fine, quiet humor. *Morris Brookside, a Dog* receives his name easily. He invites himself to join the Victorian household of Mr. and Mrs. Humphrey Brookside and his smile resembles that of a friend of theirs named Morris. The Brooksides, a genteel elderly couple, are charming in print and picture as they dust family portraits on the piano, putter in the garden and mount their giant tricycles. Their problem with Morris begins with his refusal to associate with other canines and ends with his final peculiar choice of feminine companion. In all, this is a droll, quiet tale, as comfortable and calm as the very likeable Brooksides . . . and Morris. Ronald Himler's line drawings complement the text perfectly.

The love of dog stories evident among the picture book set grows to an obsession by the third or fourth grade. It's a lucky thing for avid readers of this genre that their favorite authors are as tireless in production as they are in consumption.

Two dog stories by Lynn Hall, who has penned horse and dog sagas aplenty, appear in tandem and make me wonder if one was written with the right hand while the other was done simultaneously with the left. Tacked between twin typewriters, perhaps, is The Formula: Dog loses master—Dog finds new master—Dog loses second master—Dog finds third master. Insert one boy with offbeat, difficult personality, one picturesque setting, one noble cover portrait of noble dog by Joseph Cellini. Toss gently and season with a genuine love of animals and the desire to project oneself into the brain of a borzoi (*Riff, Remember*) and a mutt (*To Catch a Tartar*).

What can one say about this kind of book? I know from experience young readers love them. Even reluctant readers will go for them, and that's no small accomplishment. What they lack, it seems to me, is creative energy, the kind of excitement generated when idea and human mind struggle to stretch and mold one another. What these books offer instead is the assurance that the reader will get exactly what he or she came for, one dog story with just enough humanity to be interesting but not terribly important. And certainly not disturbing.

Three diverse books of specialized appeal worth mentioning:

Poems and Prayers for the Very Young assumes that the very young feel a need (or *should* feel a need) to thank God from sun-up to bedtime. I disagree, but many would not. For those in the latter category, you can't go wrong with Emerson, Coleridge and Unknown at $.95.

Pippa Mouse is billed as "six read-aloud, read-alone stories," but would do better as read-to-me for the preschool set. I fear the modern first grader is too sophisticated for such cuteness, but the tales are short, sweet and simple and the illustrations are downright cuddly.

Finally, *Games (and how to play them)* might also be called (and how to illustrate them). Anne Rockwell's pictures are delightfully silly. Bulldogs dressed as toreadors playing Bull in the Ring to the amusement of a bulldog senorita peering coyly from behind her fan. Fish in party clothes huddle beneath an elegant loveseat to play Sardines. A goofy gang of frogs demonstrate—what else?—Leapfrog. And so on, for a total of 43 games that look as good as the illustrations. While directions are simple, few children can organize a group in an unfamiliar activity. A teacher or parent plus the book, however, would make for great fun and nonsense.

Sandra Fenichel Asher

Poems for and by Children, and How to Pass Them Around

Pass the Poetry, Please, by Lee Bennett Hopkins. (Citation Press, New York, $2.65).
Eggs Amen!, verses by John Goldthwaite, 10 illustrators. Ages 7 and up. (Harlin Quist, Inc., $1.50).
Here's Looking at You!, verses by Ed Leander, 13 illustrators. Ages 5 and up. (Harlin Quist, Inc., $1.50).
From Bad to Worse, verses by Geraldine Richelson, illustrated by Claude Lapointe. Ages 7 and up. (Harlin Quist, Inc., $1.50).
The Geranium on the Windowsill Just Died but Teacher You Went Right On, verses by Albert Cullum, 29 illustrators. Ages 7 and up. (Harlin Quist, Inc., $1.50).
My Own Rhythm, by Ann Atwood, photographs by the author. Ages 8 and up. (Charles Scribner's Sons, New York, $5.95).
The Ballad of the Burglar of Babylon, by Elizabeth Bishop. Illustrated by Ann Grifalconi. (Farrar, Straus and Giroux, New York. $4.50).
Visions of America by the Poets of Our Time, edited by David Kherdian. Illustrated by Nonny Hogrogian. (Macmillan Publishing Co., Inc., New York. $5.95).
Relax, edited by W. F. McDowell. (Hopefield Publications, Whitehouse Newtownabbey, County Antrim, Ireland).

Children and poetry—of course they go together. We have all jump-roped and limericked and cursed and, yes, even graffitied our way through childhood in rhyme. The mystery is, why do children and poetry come apart? Who, indeed, killed Cock Robin? Current blame points at the schools; we have many true traumas from the songless to prove how they were "turned off" by six classes of analysis on William Cullen Bryant's "Thanatopsis" or Alfred Noyes' "The Highwayman." (Insert here a small voice pleading that she *liked* "The Highwayman," and at age 40 can still recite it. But then, she even liked "Invictus," the dope, so don't listen to her.)

The problem seems to lie not only in the chestnuts and choices, but also in the feeling among many young people in school that poetry is something that is done unto you, rather than something you do, or conjure with. But how does the hard-pressed, textbook-ridden teacher who would like to find new poems and ways of playing with poetry, start? In *Pass the Poetry, Please,* Lee Bennett Hopkins of Scholastic Magazine has just the thing, a gift to all teachers of lower and middle grades. A resource book, a bibliography, a happy, personal plea, the book offers classroom-tested ideas for getting poems out of the box of a "poetry unit" and into all areas of learning, as well as brief reviews of poems children like and biographies of those who write them. His taste is excellent, and, unlike most "how to" books, this one is a pleasure to read. Here you can find out what a Japanese Senryu is, how kids can write one; you can find listed the anthology that has the most poems about dogs, or how to build a "poetry cube" with beginners. There are thoughts on the effects of Dr. Seuss and Bobby Dylan, and a list of good filmstrips and records available. It is an open-handed, passionately considered accumulation. I'm passing it on to my son's second grade teacher.

But must the schools be responsible for everything? Once kids are confirmed readers, they will simply read what is lying around. And what is lying around is up to parents. Here for consideration are books of poems that look and taste nothing at all like the grim anthologies of my youth, designed to present a gilt-edged tradition to young minds. (And succeeding, mostly.) In general they are colorful, easy to nibble at and handsomely designed.

Eggs Amen!, with verses by John Goldthwaite, is one in an attractive, experimental series put out by Harlin Quist, Inc. In this book, as in others of the series, well-known contemporary artists have contributed individual illustrations, so that one book may have as many as twenty-nine different artists. It is true that the pictures intend to illustrate the verses, and mostly do, but these are primarily picture books whose startling, often surrealistic designs are the greater part of the books' impact. Example: the cover of *Eggs Amen!* features a purple-suited gentleman out of whose collar emerges, not a head, but a fluffy, two-headed chicken. The variation in techniques from page to page is bracing, but does not, I feel, destroy the book's unity of design. Children's verses have always been at home with wild absurdity; why shouldn't the illustrations be too? Mr. Goldthwaite strains his nonsense at moments but most of the verses are delightfully varied, pert and able. I particularly liked "Black Bird's Blues," an environmentalist lament about the bluebird turned into a blackbird by a "rain of fine debris."

Here's Looking at You, with verses by Ed Leander, published in the same series, is a riddle book with a difference. The question posed at the start is, how do *you* look to the animals you look at? The rhymes are lucid but awfully easy, printed in satisfactorily huge letters. If you don't guess right away which beast is addressing you, there's always the vivid pictures to give it away. Here we are shown the mouse's point of view when a huge boy peers into his mousehole, or, funniest of all, an upside down boy in an upside down room, seen flywise. What nicer way to discover that your own point of view isn't the only one?

In *From Bad to Worse, Silly Tales in Silly Verse,* Geraldine Richelson has written some whopping good cautionary tales for wicked children, a genre instantly recognizable to fans of Hillaire Belloc. She even has a pyromaniac almost (almost) as dearly distasteful as Belloc's famous "Matilda." Her verse is crisp, emphatic and witty. She is not above using colloquialisms to good effect.

> "The kittens ran to get some help
> But they could only mew and yelp,
> So no one ever got the point
> That you were burning up the joint."

The crucial wallop of a cautionary verse is that wicked children do, and must, come to disaster. They are not rescued by kindly firemen, nor do they merely lose a week's TV for their sins. More often, if they don't eat they starve—literally, as does Ms. Richelson's "Awful Augustus." I am always disturbed by the cruelty of these tales, but then, parents have to express their feelings too! This genre insists that children as well as adults belong to society. But still, must we have both the thumbs of Conrad, the thumb-sucker, cut off by the "Scissors Man?" Spock and I fail to get the joke. It is hoped that the very extremity of the solution will spare children from believing it all for one minute.

Claude Lapointe's illustrations are wonderfully cartoonish and detailed, rather traditional, as befits the traditional nature of these tales. The print has a wobbly, hand-set look that is most pleasing.

In the determined effort to avoid the sweetsy and the tame in children's literature, there seems to be a new rash of books aimed at expressing children's real anxieties and conflicts. Some have been very successful. *The Geranium on the Windowsill Just Died but Teacher You Went Right On,* another in the Harlin Quist series, purports to express in short verses and nightmarish surrealism of design the terrible anxieties little children feel in school. The verses, by Albert Collum, are written *as if* by children themselves, and that's a big as if: it adds up to bad poetry and bad therapy. The verses are infected with feelings of guilt, shame (mostly bodily shame), invisibility, impotence and incompetence. The child-teacher relationship is *always* that between hypocrite-tyrant and victim.

I find the emphasis of the collection thoroughly distasteful. My own children shivered over the bright, weird pictures, but could not concentrate on the verses. They just tuned out. No wonder.

> "Sometimes I don't pee straight.
> And Jimmy next in line always reports me.
> I guess Jimmy pees straight all the time.
> Is that why he's your favorite?"

What teacher with an average of twenty-two kids has the time, much less the interest, to care who pees straight? The picture that accompanies this bit of verse shows a huge orange lady (the teachers are all of inordinate size) holding a little purple boy in each hand. And guess what! The boys are actually peeing. Only one of them has wobbly purple pee, and the other has what my pediatrician calls "a nice, straight stream." This type of imagination does not alleviate or even release anxiety—it creates it.

It is a pleasure to turn to Margaret Atwood's book of nature photographs accompanied by her own haiku, *My Own Rhythm*. Since the haiku were expressly written to go with the pictures, there is a lovely collusion of feeling between them. Some of the haiku are vivid and some are ordinary; none of the photographs, however, is ordinary in the least. There is clear intimacy of detail in her pictures as well as romantic sweep. The first eleven pages are Ms. Atwood's introduction to haiku as a mode of perceiving, and to this end she offers warm comments on Basho, Issa and Buson. This is all admirable but a bit deadening. Anyone over eight would probably enjoy looking at this book; anyone under fifteen would probably skip the introduction.

Elizabeth Bishop's *The Ballad of the Burglar of Babylon* has been brought out in a splendid children's edition featuring woodcuts by Ann Grifalconi. The woodcuts are dramatic and moving, full of the windy isolation and long perspectives that Micuçú, the doomed criminal, experiences as he hides out from the police in the hilltop slums above Rio. The story is true, Ms. Bishop tells us; she was one of the "Rich people in apartments/ [who] Watched through binoculars." Micuçú is treated unsentimentally; we are told at the beginning how many people he has killed ("though they say he never raped."). But his determination to live ninety hours free rather than ninety years in jail, and his intensified awareness of the two levels of life in Rio, both the "fearful stain" of slum life above, and the glittering city below, give the tale a rigor that goes far beyond the basic drama of the chase. We know in the end that he has indeed lived his hours, and that it was poverty, "of the poor who come to Rio/ And can't go home again" that has doomed him. Elizabeth Bishop's consummate reserve and painterly clarity of style make this a classic for any age.

The poems in *Visions of America*, the only real anthology reviewed here, were not written "for children" any more than the ballad of Micuçú was. Just for people. David Kherdian has put together a tasteful selection of some contemporary poets who trace their lineage through Williams and Olsen back to Whitman. Most appeared in Donald Allen's *The New American Poetry*. Well-known pieces are included: James Wright's "The Blessing," Ginsberg's "A Supermarket in California," Williams' "This is Just to Say." But there are many fine surprises as well. What these various talents have in common is the supple, colloquial voice, a penchant for making direct statements with oblique humor, and the presence in their poems of America's tin can Eden, a place of gaseous rivers, hydrant summers and back lot baseball. These poems lie open to the reader. They go a long way toward presenting the new movement in American poetry, as well as suggesting how immediate and unfussy a poem can be. They are poems not to analyze, but to emulate.

It is amazing how much more mature and passionate are the poems written by children than the poems written for children. From what must be an extraordinary school in Ireland come annual publications of children's art and writing that demonstrate the power of young people to feel, to question their world, and to write well. Of course there are verses on spring, girlfriends, and giving up fairies, but these young people are forced to live with war too, and their fury and uncertainty find vivid form in poems. Many successfully feel their way into the lives of others. What is it like to be insane, to care for the insane, to be crippled, to be an old field worker or a busman in Belfast? What does it feel like to come home and find your family missing? It's of the wounded world they ask, where did you get that red?

Stunning student photographs and artwork set off the writing. Respect is the keynote, respect for children's abilities and feelings, and these books, a tribute to the teachers as well, put to shame any school literary magazine I have seen. I don't know where one can buy them. The publications, cheerfully entitled "RELAX," are put out by the Hopefield Secondary School, Whitehouse Newtownabbey, County Antrim, Ireland. Perhaps next best to being part of such a school would be to send for some copies. And then pass them around.

Kim Kurt Waller

The Tiger's Bones and Other Plays for Children, by Ted Hughes. Illustrated by Alan E. Cober (Viking Press, $5.95).

A poet can look at an urn and draw conclusions about the universe; but, a playwright, even a children's playwright, must examine a human being. The playwright has no choice at all. Human flesh and blood, human bones and foibles are the subject matter. The poet can roam the world and write about skylarks, pleasure domes, daffodils, wrecked statues. At bottom, of course, both playwright and poet are concerned with the existence of a very naked ape, but the poet can use other objects, other forms of life, to learn about this creature. The playwright must use the creature itself, one specific creature, a creature which, at the end of the play, might well be seen to stand for all creatures of its kind, but during the play, stands only for itself.

Because of the very special demands involved in constructing a play (one is a playwright, but not a poemwright or novelwright, etc.), it is simply not enough to be a good writer, not enough to be a sensitive and thoughtful poet, not enough to have a "significant" message handed down to an audience from a mountaintop upstage center. One must know how to put a play together. And Ted Hughes does not. His words are often lovely; but, with rare exception, his characters show little growth; and, with no exception, his plots are gratuitous.

Something happens, not because the events worked out that way, but because it seemed like a good idea at the time, as if one were free to develop a children's play by tossing in whatever the fancy pumps up. Even in children's theatre, where fantasy can have a different kind of run, the work needs to develop organically from end to end, one step following the next, not one step left out.

But, in this collection of ex-radio plays, there are tremendous gaps. The plays begin and end, but lack a middle. Sometimes, as in *The Tiger's Bones,* there seem to be two different plays. We know much more about the peripheral characters in *Beauty and the*

Beast than the central ones, so love and transformation become a mere change of costume. A wonderfully bizarre devil enters mid-way through *Sean, the Fool, the Devil, and the Cats* for a three-page monologue, then we never see him again. It's no wonder. The monologue is, essentially, narrative. In three pages, we never see this devil act on anything or with anyone. His being there affects nothing. He simply talks himself out of the play.

Hughes' promiscuous use of a narrator, in one guise or another, in every single play, is like hunting hummingbirds with a howitzer. It might be fine for radio; but, on stage, the play is blown away. It would be so simple to convert just about every narrative passage into a real scene. In Story Theatre, the narrator is actually a part of the drama, weaving in and out of every scene, totally and actively involved (somewhat like Tevye in *Fiddler on the Roof,* to choose another style). Language is dialogue, a part of the dramatic process, but never used for its own sake. One of the ironies of theatre is that beautiful words, unless they are an integral part of the entire theatrical package, can ground a play as surely as pig-iron.

Mr. Hughes makes the mistake of telling us practically everything, including the message; and, in case the slower children don't get it, he'll often tell it again. His words do all the work. Either he doesn't trust the machinery of the stage, or he doesn't know how to use it, for theatre becomes poetry only when every one of its elements actively combines to form the image, not otherwise. Pure poetry is filet mignon; theatre is poetry on the hoof.

Ted Hughes must be given credit for attempting to create intelligent, imaginative and gutsy plays for children. Though he often mistakes bald ideology for dramatic substance, compared to Clutch Cargo and all the other kiddie garbage oozing out of our culture, his work is a relief. Unfortunately, that isn't enough. Only one play is more: *Orpheus.* There is mystery in this work, transcendence. It grows beyond the earth; and, for all its flaws, it moves us within whispering distance of the life-song. Death, distant as a sunset, close as a dawn, sings, too. It is a play to make a child wonder. Orpheus' music becomes the music of the universe, and that is an exquisite thing.

Stephen Howard Foreman

Suppose You Met a Witch, by Ian Serraillier. Illustrated by Ed Emberley. Ages 4 to 8. (Little, Brown, and Company, $5.95). Poem first published in **Belinda and the Swans** (Jonathan Cape, Ltd., 1952).

> "Suppose *you* met a witch. . . .
> . . . Suppose
> She pounced from out a bush,
> She touched you, she clutched you,
> What would you do? . . . ."

Ian Serraillier's deliciously scary poem poses a timeless fairy-tale question and answers it by way of Miranda and Roland's hair-curling adventures with Grimblegrum, a terrifying twist of witchy, warty willow-root. Lucky for Miranda that she is the proud possessor of a magic wand that—eventually—enables her to outwit Grimblegrum's evil plans.

This read-aloud story in verse is loosely based on *Sweetheart Roland* by the Brothers Grimm. Happily, it leaves at least some of the gorier violence behind. And, ecstatically, it transforms Miranda from a passive, long-suffering, love-lorn maiden into a vital, no-nonsense female, "quick in all she did, a nimble wit, her brain / busy as a hive of bees at honey time." Roland, too escapes the familiar male chauvinist piglet model, being a "mild and dreamy boy / musical as a lark" who bravely strikes up a song even as the two children are clapped in Grimblegrum's sack and borne away to be dinner.

Miranda quickly proves herself the real heroine of the tale. It is she who takes on the lion's share of thwarting the witch's hearty appetite for nice, plump children. She transforms herself and Roland into great white swans that fly away to freedom. But Grimblegrum's art nouveau seven-league boots soon put her just a few steps behind her prey. As she chants, "Gobble you yet, I'll gobble you yet," Miranda once again wields her wand. On one of the more spectacular double-page spreads in the book, Emberley captures the swans just at the point of their magical transmutation—Miranda into filagree rosebush, and Roland into piper. And just in the nick of time! As Grimblegrum reaches out her yellow-clawed hand to pluck the rose, Roland's magic flute dances her into a convenient thornbush:

> "One note one,
> She spun like a top.
>
> Two notes two,
> She hopped and couldn't stop.
>
> Three notes three,
> and into that thorny, thistle-y tree
> with a hop, skip, and jump went she."

The children make their final escape, and a cowherd finishes the job by burning all that wickedness into a quiet, dark cinder. . . . But, as we've been warned at the beginning, that may not be the end of the tale. After all, the whole poem is a warning: the days and dangers of witchcraft are still not over; if YOU met a witch, you'd better have a W-A-N-D handy.

This book is an excellent marriage of verbal and visual arts for children. It avoids the familiar trap of condescending. Despite the lush illustrations, it doesn't supply *everything*. The language is somewhat difficult and sophisticated. Serraillier's poetry is roughly-textured, full of slant rhymes, uneven lines, and a beguiling sense of word play which is so often missing from the watered-down, easy-reading, patronizing pages of juvenile literature. Listen as Grimblegrum dances to her doom:

> "Hi!
> Ho!
> shrieked she,

and "Tickle-me-thistle!" and "Prickle-de-dee!"
And battered she was as she trotted and tripped,
And her clothes were torn and tattered and ripped,
till at last,
all mingled and mangled,
her right leg entangled,
her left leg right-angled,
firm as a prisoner pinned to the mast,
she
   stuck
      fast."

Kids will probably miss the literal meaning of some of the words in the poem—did *you* ever hear of a "tantivy" (headlong, galloping) rhyme? I didn't. But that's okay. In fact, it's great. Too many books give children no room for mental stretch. This one gives young listeners the fun of puzzling out the meaning of new words from their context, or from their relationship with the pictures. Or they can simply sit back to enjoy the story, and the syncopated pattern of words.

Serraillier's bumpy, jumpy verses are handsomely integrated into the bubbling flow of Ed Emberley's vivid illustrations, which take the eyes galloping away on a visual adventure all their own. In fact, the illustrations all but steal the show. They dive through a full spectrum of color, changing from cool, midafternoon blues to hot sunset oranges to spooky midnight purples with the mood of the tale. Emberley interweaves the plant and animal symbols of English witchcraft into his energetic pictures—owls, bats, spiders, and unnameable creepycrawlies leer out of the busy pages. Trees and ferns, willows and thorntrees dance eerily into shadowy spirit-shapes. The longer—or more often—you look at these pictures, the more you're likely to see. *Suppose You Met A Witch* is a wonderful book to wander through again and again, even once the story is familiar, helping a youngster find what s/he missed the first, second, or even third time through. For the action is as much visual as verbal. The flame-filled endpapers take you on the last lap of the story even though the words are done. As your eye wanders across the pages, you can almost catch a glimpse of Grimblegrum dancing behind the fire in optical-illusion motion. It makes you want to flip back through the pages just one more time. How refreshing it is to find a picture book that doesn't wear out the first time around.

Ellen Schecter

On Texts and Illustrators: Eight Books

The Juniper Tree and Other Tales from Grimm, edited and translated by Lore Segal. Illustrated by Maurice Sendak. Ages 9 and up. (Farrar, Straus and Giroux, $12.95).

King Grisley-Beard, by the Brothers Grimm. Translated by Edgar Taylor. Illustrated by Maurice Sendak. (Farrar, Straus and Giroux, $3.95).

The Damp and Daffy Doings of a Daring Pirate Ship, by Guillermo Modillo. All ages. (Harlin Quist, $4.95).

Number 24, by Guy Billout. Ages 5 and up. (Harlin Quist, $1.50).

Millicent the Monster, by Mary Lystad. Ages 5 and up. Illustrated by Victoria Chess. (Harlin Quist, $1.50).

The Supreme, Superb, Exalted and Delightful, One and Only Magic Building, by William Kotzwinkle. Woodcuts by Joe Servello. Ages 5-8. (Farrar, Straus and Giroux, $5.95).

The Nicest Gift, by Leo Politi. Ages 5-8. (Charles Scribner's Sons, $5.95).

King Stork, by Howard Pyle. Illustrated by Trina Schart Hyman. All ages. (Little, Brown and Company, $5.95).

Maurice Sendak has become a powerful force in eradicating the false notion of children as blank slates of innocence easily marked by violence and bloodshed. His portrayal of the inner anger of Max in *Where the Wild Things Are,* and his use of nudity and camp art allusions in *The Night Kitchen* (where the Oliver Hardy bakers try to force Mickey into a loaf of social conformity before his escape in a Hap Harrigan plane to assert his individuality) contradict those frequent child-book stereotypes of kiddies with fluffy kitties surrounded by wise and loving adults.

Such critical reactions as the insistence of Bruno Bettelheim that the portrayal of Max's rebellion against adult authority is psychologically harmful, or the fatuous desire of some librarians to put a diaper on Mickey in later editions of *The Night Kitchen,* have been swept aside by public acceptance and admiration of these books, making them best sellers and earning Sendak the Caldecott award for *Where the Wild Things Are* in 1964. A major benefit of Sendak's work has been a new survey of older boundaries of children's literature, resulting in a healthy sense that children's literature is not really separate from adult literature after all.

In *The Juniper Tree,* a collection of tales from the brothers Grimm selected by Sendak and Lore Segal, yet another milestone has been reached. Common reactions to the Grimm tales deny them status as children's literature because they are too filled with violence, mutilation, cruelty and sexual motifs (described by Freudians in the *Imago* and, later, the *American Imago*); we may instance the themes of castration and Oedipal complexes in "The Juniper Tree," puberty rituals and menstruation in "Little Red Riding Hood," and necrophilia in "Snow White." Hence many editors either suppress the stories altogether, bowdlerize them, or publish the tales in a mistranslation, politely called "a retelling for children."

In the present collection of twenty-seven tales, twenty-three translated by Lore Segal and four by the late Randall Jarrell, we have a different and praiseworthy endeavor. The stories are translated with close accuracy to the German original, at the same time achieving a smooth flow in English. The editors confront the heavy use of grand guignol devices in the Grimm tales by selecting "The Story of One who Set Out to Study Fear," in which the main character embraces a corpse that threatens to strangle him when warmed into life; "Fitcher's Feathered Birds" with its hacking off of heads; and "The Master Thief" where a hanged man from the gallows is used to distract the Count from his bedroom while the sheet is taken from his bed. All these stories bear faint resemblences in theme and motif to other, more well known Grimm tales, and give us an excellent opportunity to read Grimm tales which have not become hackneyed through retelling. But not all the tales in the collection are obscure or exotic. "The Devil's Three Golden Hairs," "The Fisherman and his Wife," "The Golden Bird," "Rapunzel," "Hansel and Gretel," and the greatest of all the stories, "Snow White and the Seven Dwarfs," are all presented in completely accurate translations.

That "Snow White" is the finest of the stories stands almost without challenge. The first paragraph of this tale is a model of perfection of the storyteller's art: compression of detail; introduction of mood, theme, and problem of plot through narrative and archetype; and advancement of action in one brief passage:

> Once it was the middle of winter, and the snowflakes fell from the sky like feathers. At a window with a frame of ebony a queen sat and sewed. And as she sewed and looked out at the snow, she pricked her finger with the needle, and three drops of blood fell in the snow. And in the white snow the red looked so beautiful that she thought to herself: "If only I had a child as white as snow, as red as blood, and as black as the wood in the window frame!" And after a while she had a little daughter as white as snow, as red as blood, and with hair as black as ebony, and because of that she was called Snow-White. And when the child was born, the queen died.

And in the ending of the story, the justice that comes to the evil Queen is given in explicit detail with none of the squeamish omissions seen in other versions:

> And as she went in she recognized Snow-White and, what with rage and terror, she stood there and couldn't move. But they had already put iron slippers over a fire of coals, and they brought them in with tongs and set them before her. Then she had to put on the red-hot slippers and dance till she dropped down dead.

It is obvious, then, that in *The Juniper Tree* there is none of the too prevalent desire to shield "tender" minds from portrayal of violence. Attempts to protect and to shield have in the past turned children away from literature, because television among other sources offers violence in steady fare, and expurgated, bowdlerized books by comparison seem pallid and uninteresting. But, fortunately, the folk tradition, from which the Grimms derive their tales, has never made the distinction between literature for children and literature for adults. *The Juniper Tree* is a healthy and laudable example of a collection book which does not present children's literature as a separate and anemic entity written in a different style and on a separate subject from adult literature.

My only regret as to the choice of stories is that the excellent "Aschenputtel," the Grimm version of "Cinderella," long neglected because of its portrayal of the two stepsisters' cutting off of toes and heels to make the glass slipper fit, has been omitted. Teachers and librarians have always seemed to prefer the more "polite" version by Perrault which omits these details but lacks the well integrated plot of "Ascheputtel." A small quibble.

As to the illustrations themselves, there is one drawing per story, and the moments illustrated are perceptively selected. Sendak's particular talent for the grotesque and especially his ability to create much movement in a small black and white drawing are everywhere in evidence. The illustration for "The Master Thief," in which the corpse of the hanged man, propped up in the window of the bedroom, has drawn the master of the house out of bed with a pistol in his hand to fire at the intruder, while the mistress of the house, breasts akimbo, shrieks in fear, is a masterpiece of dramatic movement, suggesting the prior action of the story and that to come. The others show a similar genius in capturing the main action of the tale in one moment.

My only objection to Sendak's illustrations is his inability to evoke either evil or brooding malevolence. When a mood of the sinister is needed, he does not achieve it. The most obvious example of this is the illustration to "Hansel and Gretel." Although the moon is portentously cloud-covered, other details belie the ominous setting of Hansel in a cage and Gretel kneeling before the witch. A great dog sits on top of the cage; the dog in Germanic lore is often associated with the devil, as in Goethe's *Faust*. But Sendak's dog is more of a watch dog, benevolent instead of satanic. The witch is herself too much of a pussycat in the June Darwell mode to create the necessary tinge of evil and danger needed to evoke the plight of Hansel and Gretel in the forest of evil. Sendak comes nearer to a sense of brooding peril in his illustration to "Rapunzel," where the preRaphaelite maiden is seen looking from her tower and her captor is a hooknosed witch, reminiscent of an allegorical death figure. And yet the evil and doom still are missing. In illustrations with a lighter touch, the drawing for "Rabbit's Bride" shows a Tenniel rabbit and a fox wearing plastic-rimmed glasses, not entirely justified, and seemingly anachronistic compared with the other drawing.

The Juniper Tree deserves praise for bringing more of the stories of the brothers Grimm before the public with accuracy and completeness. But the illustrations clearly do not "transcend everything he has done until now," as the blurb on the dust jacket claims.

King Grisly-Beard, with illustrations by Sendak, uses the text from the Edgar Taylor translation of 1823, the first edition in English of *German Popular Tales.* The illustrations take the bottom half of the page, with the text along the top. An interesting device is a pair of children in modern dress on the frontispiece approaching an impressario who asks them to dress up in the parts of the story. Then the illustrations proceed through the text with these same costumed children entering the story and making brief comments about the story in comic book bubbles above their heads, perhaps a device to make the book accessible to the young reader on his own or for the very young child to follow along with the pictures when read to. The illustrations themselves are in a comic-strip style and follow the main action of the plot to its end in which the selfish proud daughter of the king is taught humility by having her husband, the king, take various humble disguises until she makes the right choice and he reveals himself as the king à la the frog prince motif. The two children then resume modern dress and walk off along on the backpiece saying to themselves how good they were in their roles.

The Damp and Daffy Doings of a Daring Pirate Ship by Guillermo Modillo is a picture book with no text. It has a highly imaginative series of brightly colored drawings of pirates building their ship, launching it, encountering and sinking another pirate ship, while a reclining sea monster on the bottom half of the page (underwater) bemusedly watches the action and then goes after the winner, only to be repulsed by an arrow and left up-ended on the bottom of the sea as the victorious ship sails away. And yet no sooner is this accomplished than the pirates find themselves sinking and taking refuge on a treasure island they had only moments before looted. Then they build a new ship. Excellent telling of the story through pictures alone, good continuity and humorous irony achieved through each hope of success leading instantly to another disaster. The pictures are of sufficient color and interest to compete with children's cartoon shows on television. Perhaps the outstanding color is because of its publication in Holland. American publishers seldom achieve this quality of color reproduction.

Number 24 by Guy Billout, also a Harlin Quist Book, is a nonsensical, uninteresting book with airbrush drawings of a man waiting at a sign with 24 on it, with each vehicle that approaches him—an auto, a bi-plane, a rowboat, being smashed by a larger vehicle until the bus number 24 approaches, with the front cover showing that the bus also will be smashed. Not funny even in terms of slapstick.

Millicent the Monster by Mary Lystad with pictures by Victoria Chess, another Harlin Quist Book, is highly derivative from *Where the Wild Things Are,* with Millicent a female version of Max saying to her little brother that she will "eat him up"; she continues as a rebellious child with rudeness to various characters (the pictures on the page facing the four line text) until after a series of adventures she returns home to a warm meal and a loving mother. Interesting as a crib from Sendak.

The Supreme, Superb, Exalted and Delightful, One and Only Magic Building by William Kotzwinkle with illustrations by Joe Servillo is an excellent example of a picture storybook in which the woodcut illustrations are an integral part of the effect of the book, the verbal elements and the visual playing equally important roles. The colors of black, red, and orange are varied to intensify the mood of the illustrations as the story proceeds. The story tells of an oriental emperor who scorns the work of the humble worker, Old Ridgepole, who is given menial tasks while the building of the Castle of Pride continues until lightning strikes the palace and burns it; in the devastation Old Ridgepole's hut is found to have been transmuted into gold and magnificence amid the rubble of the vain emperor's strivings. The drama of the story is marvellously extended by the illustrations, particularly in a full two-page woodcut of the conflagration, orange and red, followed by the completely black drawings of the aftermath. A good integration of visual and verbal.

Perhaps the complete banality of Leo Politi's book *The Nicest Gift* is well suggested by its treacly title. Politi fails as both writer and illustrator. The setting of the book is in the barrio of East Los Angeles and never did a ghetto shine with such luster and greening of many plants and happy peasants. The book in general has an ingratiating tone of "sharing cultures" with cute translations of Spanish words for the gringo, obvious in the opening lines:

> On the outskirts of Los Angeles, in the neighborhood known as the Barrio, Carlitos lives with his father and mother. His dog Blanco lives there too. *Blanco* means "white" and Blanco is a white dog.

Later we learn that the children there "like to play *caballito.* Caballito means little horse."

Such fawning and social white-washing is unworthy of a winner of the Caldecott award and certainly of a writer who himself lives in a great city where the reading proficiency of ghetto children is in the range of 3%. Surely he should possess a greater social conscience than to indulge in the saccharine portrayal of his neighbors and his city. The book (almost majestically) misses the point of the special quality and problems of Los Angeles and is an anachronism in a day when children's books such as *Sounder* do confront racial realities head on.

To end on a more positive note, *King Stork* by Howard Pyle, first appearing in 1887, is now brought out in a new edition with illustrations by Trina Schart Hyman. The style of illustration is nostalgic, somewhat in the format of the Volland Mother Goose, with the text of the story outlined in black in a rectangle in the lower third of the page and illustrations covering the rest of the page. The illustrations create a scenario which the verbal text lacks as a drummer boy comes marching along the road (at the beginning of the adventure) and meets an old man sitting by the side of the road. What is lacking in descriptive detail in the story is well supplied by the illustrations, an outstanding example of how a picture storybook should work. The encounters and detail of place and time lacking in the words are carried out in the page drawing. The placement of the story line is almost in the nature of a subtitle to a film and the two work together in such a manner that their meanings fuse and blend into a speaking picture.

William Anderson

Other Words, Other Ways

Eskimo Songs and Stories. Translated by Edward Field. Illustrated by Kiakshuk and Pudlo. Ages 6 and up. (Delacorte Press/Seymour Lawrence, $5.95).

In the Trail of the Wind. Edited by John Bierhorst. Illustrated with period engravings. Junior High and up. (Farrar, Straus and Giroux, $4.95).

The Enchanted Orchard. Selected and adapted by Dorothy Sharp Carter. Illustrated by W. T. Mars. Junior High and up. (Harcourt Brace Jovanovich, Inc., $4.75).

The Golden Shadow, by Leon Garfield & Edward Blishen. Illustrated by Charles Keeping. Junior High and up. (Pantheon Books, $5.50).

Word Hoard: Anglo-Saxon Stories, by Jill Paton Walsh and Kevin Crossley-Holland. No illustrations. Junior High and up. (Farrar, Straus & Giroux, $3.75).

King Arthur in Fact and Legend, by Geoffrey Ashe. Many photographs and illustrations. Junior High and up. (Thomas Nelson Inc., $4.95).

The Etruscans (Everyday Life Series), by Ellen MacNamara. Many photographs and illustrations. High School and up. (G. P. Putnam's Sons, $5.00).

In our shrinking world, where children of all ages are becoming acquainted with other cultures, either through actual travel or through television and other media, the books reviewed here perform a valuable double function: they present to us the imaginative sensibility of another culture and at the same time preserve and enlighten our traditional heritage, whether specifically as English-speaking Americans or generally as human beings of the 20th Century. A young person who read all seven of these books would be richly rewarded, enlarging both his store of "straight" information and the range of his or her imagination.

The most delightful book here is Edward Field's *Eskimo Songs and Stories,* a charming and moving collection of poems based on songs and stories printed by the Danish explorer Knud Rasmussen. Handsomely printed, the poems are accompanied by colorful, dramatic prints by Eskimo artists Kiakshuk and Pudlo. Field's translations are simple and direct, rather like his own poetry, and will give different pleasures to children of different ages (and adults too). The "warmth and earthy humor" of the Eskimos shine through the book; children will love poems like "The Raven and the Gull Have a Spat":

> RAVEN: You dirty-white slob of a gull,
> what are you plumping yourself down around here for?
> You're no match for me
> so better not start anything, big boy.
>
> GULL: Who's trying to tell me what I can't do?
> When the streams run free of ice in spring
> who goes spear-fishing with his beak? ME!
> That's something you can't do, short bill,
> and never will.
>
> RAVEN: Oh yeah? But when it's freezing out
> you have to stay home, crying from hunger,
> You're pecking bones while I'm eating berries,
> So what did you say I couldn't do?

There are poems about hunting, sickness, hunger, family affairs, traveling, animals, and work, along with the story poems involving legends and magic. This book will be loved by readers of any age; because of this, it reminds me of its poem "Magic Words," which ends like this:

> That was the time when words were like magic.
> The human mind had mysterious powers.
> A word spoken by chance
> might have strange consequences.
> It would suddenly come alive
> and what people wanted to happen could happen.
> All you had to do was say it.
> Nobody could explain this,
> that's the way it was.

In the Trail of the Wind, edited by John Bierhorst, is also a strong book, but for a more limited audience, mainly high school students and up. The poetry and incantations from various Indian tribes (Navajo, Sioux, Crow, Iroquois, etc.) as well as from the Incas, Aztecs, and Eskimos, are fascinating and informative, but because they are done by different translators they lack the unified style that distinguishes Field's book. *In the*

Trail of the Wind is illustrated with period engravings that generally will appeal more to older readers than to children.

The book is divided into thematic sections on Home, War, Death, Dreams, etc., and many of the poems are short, with a haiku-like effect:

> What shall I do? My man compares me
> to a wild red flower.
> When I have withered in his hands,
> he will leave me.

Many of the most successful are prose-poems, incantations and prayers, including the title poem from the Navajo:

> It was the wind that gave them life. It is the wind that comes out of our mouths now that gives us life. When this ceases to blow we die. In the skin at the tips of our fingers we see the trail of the wind; it shows us where the wind blew when our ancestors were created.

There are over 125 poems in this collection, taken from over 40 languages, giving the reader a good sense of the richness and diversity of our poetic heritage from the Indian cultures of North and South America.

Dorothy Sharp Carter has collected and translated 22 stories and folktales from Central America in *The Enchanted Orchard*, which is in some ways like a good prose companion-piece to *In the Trail of the Wind*. Like Field's Eskimo poems, the book has a unified sensibility at the center, which adds greatly to the reader's enjoyment. Sparsely but well illustrated by W.T. Mars, *The Enchanted Orchard* has all the traditional appeal of fairy and folk-tales, added to the novelty of the Indian perspective. There is even a Tio Rabbit, who has some of the mischievous quality of his WASP brother Peter. This book, with its magic orchards, hands of fire, stories of revenge and intrigues, is written in clear and straightforward language that can be enjoyed by all ages.

The Golden Shadow is a re-creation of the Greek legends by Leon Garfield and Edward Blishen, with sensual and striking drawings by Charles Keeping. The authors have formed one long narrative centered around a wandering story-teller and the myth of Heracles (Hercules).

The story begins with a fisherman overhearing a conversation between Themis and Thetis, when Themis foretells that Thetis will "bear a son who will be greater than his father," and ends with the prophecy fulfilled in the violent love-making of Thetis and Peleus (whose child will be Achilles, though the book ends before his birth). The myths are ingeniously tied together; for example, the fisherman tells the story-teller of his overheard conversation, and the story-teller in turn describes it to Peleus who then goes seeking Thetis.

The story-teller is a fascinating character, a poet who seeks all his life to meet a god, always just missing, but arriving at various places where the gods have intervened in man's world (he is at Thebes reciting poetry when the child Heracles strangles the snakes sent by Hera, and thus gets involved in Heracles' story). Ironically, the first god he meets is on his death-bed, when Hermes the Messenger comes to take him to Olympus. *The Golden Shadow* is a fast-moving, very physical book that teen-agers in particular will appreciate.

The style of *Word Hoard: Anglo-Saxon Stories* is often a bit heavy:

> Cealla's temper snapped. "By all the gods, you brats deserve a flogging!" he cried. "I and your mother, Wulfrun, and your mother and father, Beorn, and yours, and yours, bend over plough and harrow in the fields day after day, slaving to bring in food for your greedy gullets, and you feckless and useless idlers will not even bring kindling for the fires!"

Nevertheless Jill Paton Walsh and Kevin Crossley-Holland have gathered vivid material in their eight stories from the Dark Ages (from the 400's up to 1066 and the Norman Conquest). I liked particularly the story of the miraculous blossoming of poetry in the cow-herd Caedmon: the authors catch beautifully the awe the old monks felt when suddenly the previously undistinguished Caedmon began to recite poetry in praise of the Lord and His creation. The other stories, too, succeed in conveying a picture of times that may have been "dark" but also had their dignity, suffering, visions, humor, and despair. Unillustrated, this book is most suited for high school students.

King Arthur in Fact and Legend by Geoffrey Ashe is a scholarly presentation of the "British myth" of Arthur and his Knights of the Round Table. Through the use of old literary and historical texts, archeological discoveries, old maps, and a great deal of shrewd guessing, Ashe tries to get at the "truth" behind the legend.

He begins by tracing the beginning of the Arthur story from Geoffrey of Monmouth's *The History of the Kings of Britain* (1135-1140) through various poetic embellishments by writers like Chrétien de Troyes to Malory's famous *Morte d'Arthur* (on which almost all re-tellings, including T.H. White's *The Once and Future King,* are based), published by Caxton, the first English printer, in 1485. Ashe then gives a valuable, succinct summary of Malory's work; and the rest of the book is devoted to finding the facts behind the legend. His investigation, which concludes that Arthur really lived and was a great war-leader (not a king, however) against the Saxons early in the sixth century, will intrigue anyone already interested in the Arthurian stories, though it is perhaps too "dry" to appeal to younger readers or non-Arthurians.

The Etruscans by Ellen MacNamara differs from the rest of the books reviewed here in that it is primarily a history text-book designed for young scholars. Profusely and well illustrated, the book documents clearly and in detail what the ancient region of Etruria was like. Located in what is now Tuscany, the lovely section of Italy lying roughly between Florence and Rome, the Etruscans had a high and influential civilization of prosperous city-states, reaching its height between the seventh and third centuries B.C. The book is handsomely done, very well written and organized, tracing through archeology, art, and written documents a solid picture of a fascinating people and their times.

Peter Meinke

Athens at War, by Rex Warner. Decorations by William Stobbs. All ages. (E.P. Dutton & Co., $4.95).

When I was growing up, the ancient Athenians were very wonderful people who invented democracy, carved a lot of marble statues wearing fig-leaves (I'm ashamed to say I never questioned the sculptors' knowledge of Genesis) and spent a great deal of time walking in the sun and asking difficult questions. Such sketchy bits of ancient politics as came my way never seemed to be about the same wonderful people, but I thought that was because I was more interested in art and sunshine than in politics.

The Spartans however, had invented a state rather like my own boarding school and were not very imaginative. They were only happy when returning from battle with their shields or on them: and I never did understand why they combed their hair before being defeated by the Persians, except that there seemed something insulting about it, like a cat washing itself while you try to talk to it. They invented one revolutionary idea, which was vaguely linked to our having daily gymnastics.

When I came, late in life, to realize that art and sunlight are conditional on politics, I read Thucydides, and the shock was terrible. I had lived (largely underground) through a world war, and now read every day in the current news of the slow destruction of Indo-China; and here, like a backdrop to all the slaughters were the golden people grabbing for land and trade, uttering unctuous justifications of imperialism and, to the limits of their non-technological ability, "laying waste" or "devastating" their enemies' dwellings, farmlands, crops. They were, after all, no better than we; the limits of destruction were marked only by the bounds of possibility.

If *Athens at War* had existed in those days, I might have been better educated for that future which is now the present. In this abridgement of his original translation of Thucidydes' *Peloponnesian War* (Penguin, 1954 and many times thereafter) Rex Warner has omitted many of the complications of that war, but simplified nothing of its meaning. Ironic, clear-eyed beyond despair and the edge of tragedy, Thucydides still speaks; despite the compression of material and the addition of necessary explanations, the translator's elegance of style remains.

The moments of high and deliberate drama are kept—it is mostly narration which has been abridged—and it is this rather than anything in the attitude which renders the book more appropriate for children than the original. It is more consistently appealing to the instinct for drama—and this, of course, is where false dreams of history begin. ("Boredom is the force in life which histories always omit," said Robin Fox, writing about, of all people, Alexander the Great).

Yet the scenes so graphically described have none of the imperial coziness that made my visions ludicrous. We see the plague in Athens (p. 40); we hear the shameful debate at Melos (p. 110); and we end with the soldiers of the Sicilian expedition crowded together, dying in the stone quarries at Syracuse (p. 167).

To those of us who are not young, these scenes are intolerably full of ghosts and echoes. To those growing up in a world already inured to future shock, this dark vision of our likeness across the millenia may be the best foundation for true understanding of the wonders that sprang from the ancient world—from man himself. They were not better than we; yet they had the ability to create which we so desperately need to believe ourselves capable of—a vitality which in art, in literature, in politics, in the record of its own shame negates the terrible ending of the Sicilian expedition.

> They were utterly and entirely defeated; their sufferings were on an enormous scale; their losses were total; army, navy, everything was destroyed, and, out of many, only few returned. (p. 168)

Barbara Rosen

Two Books from Scandinavia

Great Swedish Fairy Tales. Selected by Elsa Olenius. Translated by Holger Lundbergh. Illustrated by John Bauer. Ages 9 and up. (Delacorte Press, $7.95).
It's Raining, Said John Twaining. Translated from the Danish, and illustrated, by N. M. Bodecker. (Atheneum, $4.95). Contains 14 old Danish nursery or nonsense rhymes; text combined with mostly full-page colored illustrations.

Great Swedish Fairy Tales is a handsome well-bound book on heavy paper, with good print and wide margins, and with a wealth of exceptionally imaginative illustrations. The tales and pictures tell of legendary creatures from the evergreen forests of the north, the trolls, elves, and giants, with their very human foibles, and their contacts with princesses, princes, and all sorts of ordinary children and adults. The tales were written by nine of the best loved children's story tellers in Sweden, and were published with these same illustrations in various publications, in the early part of this century. John Bauer, who himself spent much of his childhood in and near the great forests, was a superb painter and draughtsman, as well as a man of imagination and vision, and his illustrations communicate with adults as well as children.

The stories have been translated with a fine ear for naturalness of idiomatic expression in English, as well as with a distinctive style which will help enhance a child's appreciation of good literature. It is gratifying to one who has read less successful translations in the past that Mr. Lundbergh has avoided the pitfalls of too literally translating Swedish idiomatic expressions. Over-literalness, especially in dialogue, causes characters to seem odd in ways not intended by the author, and this effect is particularly alienating to young readers, subliminally if not consciously, because they cannot relate to the characters as do native children in the original language.

At the same time that the book makes use of an extended and imaginative vocabulary, its style remains simple and uncluttered. It is readily understandable by young as well as older children in dialogue, action, and context; such a book enhances a child's ability to comprehend material that does not "talk down to him," enriching his vocabulary and enlarging his imaginative capacity. The illustrations add an ambience of mystery and wonder as well as giving form to characters and places. There is humor in the stories, too, which serves to lessen the fearsome aspect of the ill-natured trolls and giants, who are so often laughably naive and foolish in ways appreciated by children. They can usually be outsmarted, and thus the child feels a certain superiority to them.

This is a book that children and parents will treasure together.

The other book, *It's Raining, Said John Twaining,* containing fourteen old Danish nursery and nonsense rhymes, is brightly and imaginatively illustrated on each of its 32 pages, most of the pictures full-page in size. The rhymes deal with rabbits, cats, odd doings of grownups, and princes and princesses with strange nonsense-names that are a challenge to say without a mistake. Whether these rhymes, translated and read to a child with a different folk culture and language background, will be as much enjoyed by that child as they are by children reared in the original culture and language may be questioned. Nursery rhymes often include words and nonsense syllables that simply by the juxtaposition of sounds communicate humor or other emotional qualities in the native culture. For English-speaking children, the nursery rhymes that they have learned in the English language have become already a part of their background, as they are likely to have heard them either spoken or sung from their infancy. And as this is likely to have been the case with their playmates and schoolmates as well, those rhymes become even more meaningful to them in the social context.

However, as experience has shown with some of the French and other foreign nursery songs which have become a part of our heritage, rhymes from other ethnic backgrounds can become accepted and loved here, particularly when they are sung.

Certainly, children will respond to the bright pictures and to the whimsical humor of *It's Raining, Said John Twaining,* especially if their parents read the rhymes aloud with patience, and refrain from rushing over the nonsense syllables and repetitions at too fast a clip. The children themselves will help decide which newly-heard nursery rhymes will become a part of this nation's heritage.

Doris G. Carlson

Perihan's Promise, Turkish Relatives, and the Dirty Old Imam, by Helen Chetin. Illustrated by Beth and Joe Krush. (Houghton Mifflin, $3.95).

At this time in history, when internationalism in children's literature can be a great force for good, books which claim to deal in depth with foreign cultures must be considered from points of view other than the purely literary. Authors, editors, reviewers, librarians and teachers must be alert to expressions and situations which strengthen dangerous stereotypes, and to supposedly factual information which is wrong or misleading.

There have been few books for children which offered to open a window on Turkey, and therefore *Perihan's Promise* is initially welcome. If the jacket copy can be trusted, it is at least to some degree a reflection of the author's own life. Perihan's parents have been divorced; her mother (an American) is now married to an American in California and her father (a Turk) lives in Canada. If, as appears to be the case, Perihan's mother is the author of this book, her choice of details and of incidents may be examined to determine whether bias is present.

The title itself, incorporating the term "dirty old Imam" is unfortunate in its slickly commercial double meaning. Granted, there may be "dirty old" imams, just as there may be "dirty old" preachers, "dirty old" priests, and "dirty old" rabbis, but it is unlikely that Houghton Mifflin would have countenanced any of the three latter terms in the title of a child's book purporting to reflect *American* culture. (And it is open to question how an imam could be *literally* dirty, since he performs ritual ablutions five times daily). The play on words is used at the expense of national and religious dignity, and at the expense of our children's understanding, since they may never meet an imam at all except in this book.

Alerted to bias, the reader takes note—among many possible examples—of the following: "And, I silently added, that my mother hated it [life in Turkey]" (p. 3); "... I thought that, compared to the Imam, Frankenstein's monster was harmlessly clumsy and Dracula merely gallant" (p. 33); "Kadri, Haleh's fiancé. . . . comes to the house almost every day. He just looks over the situation, gives Haleh the once over as if he's making sure all the parts are still there, then disappears" (p. 45); and "There's something I want to tell you about Sukriye, though maybe this isn't the right time. You see, she farts a lot, very loud and nonchalantly. Of course, she can't hear it. But no one else does it like that. At the same time, they never indicate to her that she shouldn't" (p. 48). The book, presented as a diary of a fourteen-year-old American-Turk teenager written during a summer visit to her father's family in rural Turkey, seems rather more a form of therapy for the author than a genuine contribution to children's literature.

As is true with too many American books about foreign cultures, much more emphasis is given to "exotic" features—the sunnet dugunu (circumcision "wedding" [literally, "feast"]), the annual mattress-fluffing, a wedding and elopement, even an earthquake—than is devoted to the day-to-day events that make life in any country real and identifiable to young readers. The tenor of the book, a breathless tone, suggests that Turkey is as sensational and as "far-out" as Perihan herself terms it, and as—alas—most American adults, including teachers and librarians, fancy it to be.

Several expressions dropped in as "explanations" are quite misleading. Two instances will suffice: On page 48, Ms. Chetin says, "... twenty-five *kurush* [like cents]"; actually, there are 100 *kurush* to a *lira,* and there are at present 14 *liras* to the American dollar, so a *kurush* is less than a tenth of a cent, a considerable difference from the figure given. On page 117, the author states, "He was standing in the mosque yard by the little fountain where people wash their feet before they go inside." Actually, Moslems, before they enter the mosque, wash three times, not only their feet, but their faces, their eyes, their nostrils, their ears, their hands, and their arms up to the elbows. A Moslem who washed only his feet would invalidate the entire service for all those participating. In the interest of honesty, an author offering a piece of information should expect to furnish the truth or else not deal with that particular point at all. In such cases, half a loaf is worse than none at all—and most readers will never have a chance to check this half-loaf. In short, our children deserve a squarer, fairer look at rural Turkey than the text of this book affords.

The pictures—lively sketches—by Beth and Joe Krush are responsibly done and delightfully suggestive of both the scene and the spirit of Turkish village life. Apart from the costume given to the Imam (page 32), which includes a fez long outlawed in

Turkey, the details are well handled, and offer a genuine window on Turkey, a window badly needed by today's readers of all ages.

Barbara K. Walker

Uri Shulevitz, Illustrator and Writer

The Fool of the World and the Flying Ship. A Russian tale retold by Arthur Ransome. Illustrated by Uri Shulevitz. (Farrar, Straus & Giroux, $4.95).
Rain, Rain Rivers. Written and illustrated by Uri Shulevitz. (Farrar, Straus, & Giroux, $4.95).
The Magician, by Uri Shulevitz. An adaptation from the Yiddish of I.L. Peretz. (The Macmillan Company, $3.95).

Many picture books currently available are mediocre, humdrum, and lifeless, with no real substance of text and with illustrations that are coy, contrived and otherwise poor. The literary text of a picture book should have enough literary quality to stand without illustrative support. Illustrations, on the other hand, should complement and elucidate or extend a well-written text, but remain subordinate to it. Although writing and graphic style varies greatly from individual to individual and from book to book, the best picture books result when there is a harmonious blending of text and illustration; which means that the style of the writer and that of the illustrator must be compatible. When author and illustrator are one and the same and when the writing and graphic talents are both exceptional, an exceptional book should result. *Rain, Rain Rivers,* written and illustrated by Uri Shulevitz, is one such book and so is *The Magician.* But Mr. Shulevitz also excels as an illustrator of books written by others. As proof of this, he was awarded the coveted Caldecott Medal in 1969 for his illustrations of *The Fool of the World and the Flying Ship,* a Russian tale retold by Arthur Ransome.

The late Mr. Ransome is one of the most admired and influential writers of works for children and *The Fool of the World* provides further evidence of the validity of our respect. During his stay in Russia as a foreign newspaperman during the Bolshevik Revolution, Mr. Ransome collected the Russian folktales which he retold and published in 1916 as *Old Peter's Russian Tales. The Fool of the World and the Flying Ship* is from the 1916 collection. It is a fascinating story, presented by Ransome with dignity and humor; while designed to delight and entertain the young, *The Fool of the World,* to use a Lockean expression, may also "afford useful reflection to a grown man." Be that as it may, Ransome's story furnished Uri Shulevitz with an excellent base for his illustrations. His line and wash drawings for *The Fool* are colorful, bold, spirited, and spontaneous. They command much of the space of each page or double page. Lively, dramatic, exaggerated, and vigorous, the Shulevitz illustrations never obscure or lessen the vitality of Ransome's text; on the contrary, they complement and enhance it. The author's text, the artist's illustrations, the end papers, page design, and book cover make *The Fool of the World and the Flying Ship* a near perfect example of the excellence which should characterize picture books for children.

The versatility of Uri Shulevitz as an illustrator and his own competence as a writer is amply apparent in his *Rain, Rain Rivers.* This book is as perfect an example of the harmonious blending of text, illustration, and design as is *The Fool,* but the poetic and wistful nature of the Shulevitz text requires less vigorous and bold illustrations than those of *The Fool.* Ostensibly designed for a very young audience, the text of *Rain, Rain Rivers* is brief and the illustrations absorb much space. The subdued blues, greens, and yellows of these illustrations are in perfect harmony with the textual tone of *Rain, Rain Rivers.* The alliterative language, the imagery, and the delicacy of color and illustration combine in a sensitive, nostalgic effect, suggesting the dreaminess experienced by children on a rainy day.

The Magician reveals yet another side of the artistic talent belonging to Uri Shulevitz. Here his black and white cross-hatch drawings anticipate a style of illustration which he later uses for Isaac Bashevis Singer's *The Fools of Chelm. The Magician,* adapted from the Yiddish of I.L. Peretz, is a very short tale of a travelling magician who comes on foot to a little village on the eve of Passover. After a final miracle the magician, who is really the Prophet Elijah, goes on his way—but not before being captured for earthly immortality by the magic pen of Uri Shulevitz. His illustrations, lively and humorous but innocent of ridicule, occupy the first half of each page of *The Magician.*

It is refreshing and reassuring to discover in one artist such great diversity and flexibility as is evident in the three works of Uri Shulevitz presently considered.

Charity Chang

The Greentail Mouse, by Leo Lionni. Illustrated by the author. Ages 5-8. (Random House, $4.50).

Growing up is akin to being a grown-up in that both states share the harrowing frustrations of daily life. The ability to cope is what determines how a person will provide for his survival. Children are instinctively interested in this aspect of life because they know that a mastery of it is essential to their own development.

The field mice in *The Greentail Mouse* live in a visually stimulating world created for them by Lionni's imaginative use of gouache. Inspired by a city mouse's description of Mardi Gras the field mice decide with the spontaneity of children to have their own Mardi Gras. The ingredients for the festivities are streamers and confetti along with music, dance and big scary masks. The mice are so involved in their celebration that their ability to distinguish between reality and fantasy is diminished. They are lost in a world dominated by the ferocity that their masks invoked. Lionni magnifies this terror by the use of a double page spread with a dark murky background. Not wanting to be mean, he soon relents and brings on a strange mouse who is capable of relieving the mice of their torment.

Blue skies and soft clouds cushion the return of the field mice to reality. The horrors of their fantasy are neatly burned into oblivion with the masks. Greentail, however, is left with a constant reminder of that awful celebration. In her enthusiasm for Mardi Gras she had painted her tail green. The paint she used must have been indelible because no matter how hard she tries she can never get her tail clean.

People have wonderful ways of dealing with bad memories. Rather than regarding her tail as a scar or talking about her painful experience Greentail chooses to tell other mice that her green tail is the result of a festive occasion. Although this may not be the best way to cope with painful thoughts, it is what many people do.

But, when writing for children, I feel the author has an obligation to show them how to deal constructively with problems or fears that are raised in his story. Lionni takes the easy way out by allowing Greentail to hide her fear behind bright colors and cheerful words. Greentail merely exchanges a scary mask for one with an artificial smile, and the attractiveness of the new mask has the potential of fooling children into believing that prettiness and happiness are interchangeable.

It is a shame that a beautiful book was compromised for a slick ending.

Iris Finkelbrand

I Will Catch the Sun: A Story for Grown-ups and Children, by Nephtalí De Léon. Illustrated by the author. (P.O. Box 5186, Dallas, Texas: Trucha Publication, $2.00).

This deceptively simple story, the latest publication of one of the Southwest's most promising Chicano authors, deals realistically with the harshness and ridicule that barrio-Spanish-speaking children all too often must endure in some schools. Nephtalí uses the barrio-Spanish-English spoken in many Chicano homes; and he represents in his work various Chicano foods and customs. Most important, however, he credibly captures the intuitive genius of all children, transcending narrow ethnic boundaries to celebrate the human spirit that permeates all ages and all ethnic traditions.

Nephtalí achieves these goals through his heroic child, Raul. The story contrasts Raul's home life with his school experiences. At home, little English was spoken and it was easy to ignore, while speaking Spanish was fun and his tongue had no difficulty with words like *tortillas* and *enchiladas*. At school, however, his teacher scolded him for speaking Spanish, and no one explained the meanings of unfamiliar English words like "astronaut" and "scientist."

One day the teacher asked her students what they wanted most of all, and Raul courageously declared that he would catch the sun. The students laughed loudly and ridiculed Raul. The teacher also laughed. After several days of repeated humiliation, Raul observed nature and guessed at a credible way to catch the sun. In a dramatic demonstration, Raul not only redeemed himself to himself, but also vindicated himself to his classmates and teachers.

Larry Tjarks

On Their Own: A Review of Three Books

The Nothing Place, by Eleanor Spence. Ages 10 and up. (Harper and Row, $5.50).
Ox Goes North, by John Ney. Ages 10 and up. (Harper and Row, $6.95).
Nilda, by Nicholasa Mohr. Ages 10 and up. (Harper and Row, $5.95).

Since the reading of fiction is a process of identification, books for children must present identifiable characters and problems for the young reader. To achieve this kind of identification the main character must usually function independently of parents and adult figures. This is especially true in "middle and older" books, and the reason is quite simple—children moving into adolescence need to define themselves as autonomous beings, independent of adults. In becoming independent they also become critical of the world adults have prepared for them to enter. For the writer working with such material there is a need to probe the tension between the adult behavior and the critical adolescent's understanding of the adult world.

Today there seems to be an abundance of books showing characters groping towards adolescence and a distressing world. The three books briefly discussed here are examples of emerging adolescents on their own.

Eleanor Spence's *The Nothing Place,* set in dreary suburban Australia, is a good example of the "on their own" theme and the problems which somehow by the end of the book they must come to terms with. The main plot centers on Glen, a new kid in town who has recently suffered a hearing loss. As this loss becomes permanent the solution seems quite simple—buy the kid a hearing aid. But such a simple solution doesn't occur to Glen's parents, teachers or doctors.

In the hands of a less skillful author, *The Nothing Place* would be a boring story, but it is not. What saves it is the many characters and subplots that keep the reader's attention off the simple and easy solution to Glen's problems. But the flaw, and it's a major flaw, comes when one considers why the parents, not only Glen's but Lyndall's also, never do what is obvious. And one suspects it's not because the adults don't have time nor love but because Ms. Spence wants to keep spinning a story. She has placed her characters on their own, but she doesn't give us enough information to let us know why the adults failed to act. It is not enough to show mothers trying to keep pace with their housework and office schedules, or fathers hiding behind newspapers and television. That may keep the story going, but in the end Ms. Spence writes herself into a corner.

Moving from the new middle class of Australia to the ugly rich of Palm Beach and the cold rich of New England one finds a more successful treatment on the "on their own" theme. John Noy's *Ox Goes North* is a sequel to *Ox: The Kid At The Top.*

Ox Goes North is the story of Ox Olmstead, a fat, lazy, rich kid whose family sends him off to a Vermont camp as a way of getting rid of him for the summer. Ox has been made cynical by money and, more important, by the adults he has come into contact with. He has learned from his father that everything is washed up and nothing can be done to halt the decay in which modern life is sinking.

The novel strips away the New England social facade and lays bare the moral decay and apathy of most of the adult characters, and thus the adult world which Ox must enter. The author's handling of this theme is successful; care has been taken to show why Ox is isolated.

At times the story threatens to become a rich Hardy Boys adventure with characters moving in and out of the action to keep the plot together; to drive the get away car, to provide more money when the first thousand is spent and to blow up the bad guys. But in the end we are left with the ugliness and folly exposed. And it is Ox who exposes the adults' failure to do or even see what is humanly right and just. We are left with an angered anti-hero whose adventures, and rescue of Campbell, only serve to alienate him further and reaffirm his cynicism.

The jump to *Nilda,* by Nicholasa Mohr, takes us from the white rich to the Puerto Rican poor.

Nilda is the story of Nilda Ramirez; it is set in Spanish Harlem between July 1941 and May 1945. It is a sensitive, well written and powerful story of a 10-year-old girl's growth into adolescence. Nilda is on her own because no one else survives. She must not only grow into adolescence, but she must learn what it means to be Puerto Rican and poor in America. She must face cruel nuns, teachers who teach her to speak Spanish with an Irish accent, social workers and of course the police. At the same time she must come to grips with a poverty that kills her step-father and eventually her mother. She must understand the crime and drugs that take her brother. She must understand why her girl friend got pregnant and the threat that pregnancy means to her. She must also try to understand the larger world with its world war that her other brothers go off to fight in as good Americans.

At times the odds against Nilda, or any child, seem overpowering. At the end of four years her survival is still in doubt; one hopes she survives because as a reader one is so involved in her life, but even as the novel closes one can not be sure.

This is an outstanding first novel by a new writer and one hopes that this book will receive the recognition it deserves.

Ray Anthony Shepard

Fiction, Fantasy, and Ethnic Realities

Nilda, by Nicholasa Mohr. (Harper and Row, $5.95).
Reggie and Nilma, by Louise Tanner. (Farrar, Straus, and Giroux, $4.50).
To Walk the Sky Path, by Phillis Reynolds Naylor. (Follett, $4.95).
Felicia the Critic, by Ellen Conford. (Little, Brown and Co., $4.95).
The Nothing Place, by Eleanor Spence. (Harper and Row, $5.50).
Head in the Clouds, by Ivan Southall. (Macmillan, $4.95).
Ox Goes North, by John Ney. (Harper and Row, $4.95).
Timothy the Terror, by Ruth Cavin. (Harlin Quist, $1.50).
Hubert, by Wendy Stang and Susan Richards. (Harlin Quist, $1.25).
Something New Under the Sun, by Patrick Couratin. (Harlin Quist, $1.25).
Go, Go, Go, Grabote! by Nicole Claveloux. (Harlin Quist, $1.50).
Alala, by Guy Monreal. (Harlin Quist, $4.95).

I have yet to see a children's book which is not without a message (nor a big people's book, for that matter). The charge of didacticism has frequently been one means of dismissing entirely the books for adults which espouse a cause, dictate morality, or in explicit ways attempt to influence opinion. But with children's books didacticism is apparently not a factor which ostensibly determines the quality of the work. If it is accepted that children's books are by virtue of their character didactic, then it would seem to me that we should pay very close attention to their messages, for the argument which holds that the quality of a work inheres elsewhere than in its content will hardly allow us to deal with children's books except in a surface way. Some might argue that a book can be good no matter what its message, but I could not imagine that anyone would make that argument for children's literature. Clearly some messages are better than others.

Of the dozen books to be discussed here Nicholasa Mohr's *Nilda* is the most significant. It describes the life of Nilda Ramirez from her tenth to her fourteenth year as she grows up in Spanish Harlem. The author's view is an insider's view and is to be distinguished from views which might not be so intimately informed about the subtle meanings of the experiences narrated. But more importantly the author has such a good grasp of the social dynamics involved in her tale that it tells not only a story which in many ways typifies the life of the poor in Spanish Harlem, but it describes as well the plight of the urban poor everywhere. It recognizes the role institutions play in sustaining poverty, and it shows the extraordinary difficulty of breaking out, even for the strongest, most sensitive, and most intelligent. There is no pity here, for the author is too much aware of the humanity of her characters and of the other implications of pity to be in any way condescending. There is insider's humor, gentle, and in no way degrading. (An example is the scene in which the aged aunt summons the police because the grocery owner will not take her numbers bet.) All in all *Nilda* is what I would call a significant book, a touchstone by which others may be judged.

The titular characters of Louise Tanner's *Reggie and Nilma* are a black housekeeper and her son. On the second page of the book a certain event is described as being "before the time when everyone modeling a sweater or using a mouthwash was black." Prior to this the narrator says, "Nilma was my colored nurse—I know you mustn't say it that way now, but that is what she was..." Since the author is apparently unaware of the negative implications of these statements, we might expect to find other evidence of lack of understanding on her part, and we are not entirely disappointed. The author's problem is that she interprets the events of the narrative in a wholly personal way, not realizing that there is far more at stake in the experience described than her personal loss when her relation deteriorates with Reggie. The author expresses a sense of guilt and even responsibility because of the impingement on the lives of Reggie and Nilma of racism. Yet she fails to understand the fault of the situation which allows her to have her "colored" mammy. She indeed accepts *that* fact without recognizing the inequality built into the circumstance itself. Many of the experiences narrated in the book by Kim, the fourteen-year-old teller of the tale, are heart rending, but the final statement of the book, "Maybe this is the way it has to be . . ." reveals the author's (I *mean* author—not narrator) implicit assumption of the inevitability of the status quo despite the narrator's closing statement, "I don't like it and I never will." To equate Reggie's deterioration with growing older is to confuse the social and the natural.

To Walk the Sky Paths (Phyllis Reynolds Naylor) is about the conflict in the life of a ten-year-old Seminole boy between the traditional ways of his forbears and more modern, American ways. Since the problem is set up this way in the book, the author has good opportunity to indicate attitudes about both poles of the dilemma, and this she does, showing the advantages and disadvantages of both. She has sympathy for the ways of the Indians, and she shows scorn and disdain for some aspects of modern American life (mostly the ill manners of tourists and prejudiced whites). She indicates a good and convincing knowledge of her subject. Everyone, however, would not agree that, all things considered, the young boy is better off choosing modern America. The grandfather's dying at the end represents a value judgment which is at best questionable. The danger of this book is clearly seen if its implications are imagined as being translated into public policy. The argument of the book is that it is in the best interest of Indians to be integrated into American life. I do not think all Indians would agree.

Felicia the Critic is a light, ephemeral thing whose conclusion is somewhat ambiguous. Felicia is a young girl whose orientation is toward problem solving of a practical sort. The question the book asks is whether criticism is good. The answer is that criticism is sometimes good and sometimes bad, but the author, Ellen Conford, does not draw the line as clearly as it might be drawn. She seems to believe that one should not be critical if criticism may prove embarrassing. Surely we should wish other criteria than this, for criticism, even at Felicia's level, stems from the impulse to order the disorderly, to create proper proportion, to make just the unjust. I do not find it the least bit humorous that Felicia should finally write the President telling how the country might be made better. Of course carping criticism or personal criticism should be discouraged, but the implication that one should endure rather than risk embarrassment by criticizing (though in truth not a *clear* implication of the book) seeks the basest conformity.

Eleanor Spence's *The Nothing Place* is chiefly interesting because of the sense of place conveyed of a newly developed, small suburban community in Australia. It would probably be less interesting to anyone who knows such communities. The problems with which it deals are somewhat commonplace; its characters are typical of youngsters everywhere of a comparable socio-economic status. I will resist the temptation to draw from the title in evaluating the book.

Ivan Southall's *Head in the Clouds* is likewise by an Australian author. It is somewhat humorous in its descriptions of its central character's attempts to work magic on the school children who pass him on their way home but do not notice him. But one wonders whether such gratuitous ill will on Ray's part is justification enough for the enmity he bears against the children. It is a funny book for those who do not take humor seriously but a slight book finally.

Ox Goes North by John Ney is interesting in its conception of its main character, Ox, "the kid at the top." He is wealthy, intelligent, anti-intellectual, and unlearned. The character carries the story, and there is some awareness expressed on the author's part of the deeper implications of what he writes about. But for whatever reason, he does not indicate explicitly enough what those implications are. Is his relationship to his parents, for example, a function of their immense wealth or of their personalities? What does it mean that Ox's freedom to move about the country—his freedom in general—is a function of his great wealth? Is the implication that wealth and social status do not really matter, but that the real question is where your heart is? Are the central problems of the world problems of the disposition of the heart? The author seems to say as much. There is a great deal in the book about power and its exercise, but I find the author's conception of that subject and ultimately of what happens to people and why somewhat unsatisfying.

Timothy the Terror, Hubert, Something New Under the Sun, Go, Go, Go, Grabote! and *Alala* are all books in the Harlin Quist series, books unusually fine and interesting in their printing, illustrations, and format. *Timothy the Terror* is about a little boy who is picked on by his sisters until he achieves power to overcome them. It is a nice simple little story about Timothy and his black family. The story is told in the first person and in dialect, and its dialect is its most problematical aspect. Its English is intended undoubtedly to be black English. As such, one wonders about the stereotypical elements of character which of necessity arise in this situation given the values attached to language in our society. Authors often indicate attitude through the use of dialect and this, coupled with the primitivistic elements of the story give rise to questions regarding the author's conception of the characters. I am reminded by the cover, illustrating a little black child standing in a lion's mouth, of Little Black Sambo. Through sympathetic magic Timothy derives his power from the jungle beast. What does it all mean? I am not convinced that its meaning is salutary.

Hubert and *Something New Under the Sun* are both intentionally slight books. *Hubert*, subtitled The Caterpillar Who Thought He Was a Mustache, has as its theme that one should not be what he is by nature not. This may be a good or a bad message. It is a good message if it means that horses can run faster than men and that turtles cannot fly. Obviously we should recognize the limitations of our physiological characters. But if it means that social roles should be equated with biological roles, then its message is not so innocent as it appears. Since the book begins with Hubert being criticized by other caterpillars for proclaiming that he is a mustache, "Everyone knows that a caterpillar is a caterpillar and only a caterpillar," there seems to me the implication that the book is about social roles, the specific nature of which is not clear. I admit, however, that my interpretation here might be somewhat open to question.

Something New is about dull and unimaginative people who are unwilling to step for one moment out of their accustomed routine. It says in effect that one should consider the possibility that there *is* something new under the sun. A simply told, uncomplicated fable.

Go, Go, Go, Grabote! is the least charming book I have ever encountered. It tries to be amusing and utterly meaningless. It must have been inspired by Da-Da, though Da-Da is infinitely more interesting. Its message is that the world has no meaning, is chaotic and unordered by nature, and that there are no limits which allow distinction between one phenomenon and another in either time or space.

Alala is about a little girl who keeps going inside a television set and interfering with the programs, changing their plots and dialogue. In one sense it has its "Grimm" side in that her parents, who have been so careful not to change channels while she is inside, finally do so to punish her. She is buffeted about the world in time and space and emerges never to enter again. Alala is a brown child of mixed parentage. She marries a Manchurian prince and they have children of all colors including a violet one. The illustrations are lavish in size and color and are as much a part of the book as the text if not more. At base the text is the traditional one about the disobedient child who grows up after she accepts the limitations and responsibilities of adulthood. It is, however, somewhat surrealistic in text and illustration. Its orientation is away from reality and toward dream and fantasy.

Donald B. Gibson

Birds and Beasts

Walter Chandoha's Pet Album, (Follett, $4.95).
The White Cardinal, by Griffing Bancroft. Illustrated by Charles Fracé. (Coward, McCann & Geoghegan, $4.95).
An American Ghost, by Chester Aaron. Illustrated by David Gwynne Lemon. (Harcourt Brace Jovanovich, $6.95).
The Death of a Wombat, by Ivan Smith. Illustrated by Clifton Pugh. (Charles Scribner's Sons, $5.95).

The photography in Walter Chandoha's *The Pet Album* is beautiful and should be appealing to children. For the most part, the text appears to be well thought out and puts a proper degree of emphasis on the child's responsibility towards a pet. As someone who has had much to do with animals both wild and tame, I did feel that there might have been mention of the fact that the wild animals which the child is being encouraged to feed can bite—*hard.* One doesn't want to dampen a child's enthusiasm but it should be tempered by a degree of caution.

I also take strong issue with the suggestion that the child "get a male and female rabbit . . . to see how baby rabbits are born." In this day and age when animal shelters are full of unwanted "pets" waiting to be slaughtered, no child or adult should be encouraged to breed *any* animal just to see the babies born. It is exceedingly selfish and most unfair to the animals to produce unwanted litters just to show one's child the "miracle of birth."

In addition, it was a disappointment to me to find such a careless taxonomic error as box "tortoise." It is unfortunate that a man who takes such lovely photographs cannot take the time to explain the difference between a turtle and a tortoise—and a box turtle is certainly *not* a tortoise.

In conclusion, I enjoyed the photography very much but felt that the text left something to be desired both in its outlook on "pets" and in its accuracy.

The White Cardinal, though a novel, is a first rate natural history book. It contains a wealth of details about bird life in a readily absorbable form. One who wanted to read the book for the story alone would enjoy it since the scientific facts are a well-integrated part of the story and are not pushed obtrusively at the reader.

The book is very much in the modern trend with its emphasis on preserving the species in the wild—or perhaps our views have simply come full circle, since this is how things were many years ago before "science" took over with its view that nothing could be understood unless it was cut up and sealed in a bottle.

The author seems to have done a thorough job of researching the details of the life histories of cardinals and their co-existing species. I found it all extremely interesting since, not being an ornithologist, many of the facts were new to me. Bancroft's presentation of these facts is excellent; he does not talk down to the reader but simply states things in such an uncomplicated form that they are readily comprehensible. A parent would not have to be ashamed to be caught reading this book for his own information.

Whether intentionally or not, *The White Cardinal* may also serve as an object lesson in pointing out that there are outcasts in the animal world as well as in the human sphere. It is sometimes difficult for children (and adults) to see the parallels between human and animal realms and this book is an excellent illustration of one of them.

An American Ghost is a fast-moving adventure story, yet one which is similarly full of points to ponder. The author leaves the conflict unresolved at the end. One is not clear about what use the boy intended to make of his newly-gained insights into man's dependency on creatures other than himself. Running through the book is Albie's discovery that the world does not exist solely for the good of man, nor does man have the right to make arbitrary, unthinking decisions about who shall live and who shall die. It is never implied that these decisions must not be made but only that they must never be made casually.

Aaron emphasizes the terrible problem of determining one's values by showing the boy at the story's conclusion faced with the first of a never-ending series of conflicts: the family he loved and had always depended on for sustenance becomes a deadly, uncaring enemy of the species that had temporarily served as his family. It is a striking contrast to the foreward where Albie is shown never questioning the casual killing of two Indians.

This is an exciting book and should hold the interest of the reader with no difficulty. However, it is not a comfortable book or one which will leave the reader steeled and sure of himself.

Death of a Wombat is even more disturbing because the author writes so brilliantly and unsparingly of disaster in the animal world. The word pictures are so vivid that the reader is transported to the Australian bush, seeing the sun rise, hearing the noises of the day's beginning.

Reading this book, one becomes each of the animals in turn, wombat, kangaroo, koala, dingo. The reader is so much a part of the scene that his nose wrinkles with the first acrid fumes of smoke; he feels the impact of the huge breathless mass of heat as the fire begins its advance. Casting his lot with one species, or perhaps with all, he flees from the fire and finally, inevitably, feels the waters of the river close over him, the heat gone at last.

The story has tremendous reality. One lives it rather than reads it.

My only criticism of the book, or perhaps of myself, is that, as a child, I would never have appreciated its beauty; the emotional impact would have been too strong. Of course, the level of sophistication in the average child is growing; but I wonder how many could fully appreciate *The Death of a Wombat*, the magnificance of its writing as well as its sadness. Surely this is more a book for all ages than just for young people. Certainly it had enormous impact on me.

Mary Fine

Clever Cooks: A Concoction of Stories, Charms, Recipes and Riddles. Compiled by Ellin Greene. Illustrated by Trina Schart Hyman. (Lothrop, Lee & Shepard, $4.95).

The retelling and/or reprinting and reassembling of old tales is a prevalent practice, but not everyone who attempts it does so successfully. In the hands of less gifted collaborators *Clever Cooks* could have been just another in the barrage of contemporary compilations. Fortunately this is not the case.

Clever Cooks is a delightful and diverse collection of some dozen or more stories about cooks or bakers whose culinary abilities lead them into troubles from which they are, happily, able to extricate themselves. Some of the stories are simply reprinted; others, retold. Ellin Greene as compiler has avoided the repetitive dullness that sometimes characterizes such collections. She has skillfully and tastefully balanced her selections with appropriate riddles, charms, and recipes. The opening story, for example, has to do with a woman flummoxing fairies. This story is followed by a recipe for Fairy Cake. The recipe, in turn, is followed by the charm "Come, butter, come," a recipe for butter cookies, and a suitable riddle.

The style and pace of *Clever Cooks* is light and lively and the supporting black and white drawings of Trina Schart Hyman are superlatively imaginative. It can be fairly stated that *Clever Cooks* is a satisfying example of harmony of text, illustration, and book design. The text has substance; the literary style has merit; the illustrations delight and enhance but do not intrude; and the book's design and page composition contribute to its overall aesthetic quality. *Clever Cooks* stands a good chance of survival.

Charity Chang

Two Books from the Jung Institute

The Problem of the Puer Aeternus, by Marie-Louise von Franz (1970).
Patterns of Creativity Mirrored in Creation Myths, by Marie-Louise von Franz (1972/3) (Spring Publications, Zurich and New York).

Marie-Louise von Franz was a trusted associate of Carl Jung and she remains one of his staunchest disciples. *The Problem of the Puer Aeternus* and *Patterns of Creativity Mirrored in Creation Myths* are essentially transcripts of lectures delivered by Dr. von Franz at the Jung Institute in Zurich between 1959 and 1962. Like the other books in the Spring Publications Seminar Series*—a series edited and compiled by Jungians—these books are of value to the student of children's literature when read in their proper context.

The Jung Institute Lectures are directed primarily at students of Jungian clinical psychology. The fact that a fairy tale or a myth or any other kind of narrative can, by way of Jungian analysis, reveal something of the problems of human psychology is of immense importance to the psychiatrist. But unless Jungian analysis or Freudian analysis or any analysis of literature is applied to literature by someone whose primary concern is the appreciation or evaluation of the literary work itself, the result is all too often the simplistic kind of literary interpretation which is to be found in the Puer Aeternus book in question here. Dr. von Franz does teach us much about the psychological problems of Saint-Exupéry and, by extension, of others who suffer from the Puer Aeternus (eternal youth) syndrome.* But for her *Le Petit Prince* is a cadaver to be dissected, while for many adults and children it is a living experience to be felt and appreciated.

Whereas *The Problem of the Puer Aeternus* is sometimes irritating to the reader whose discipline is not psychology, *Patterns of Creativity Mirrored in Creation Myths* is an engaging work, perhaps because in it Dr. von Franz concentrates on universal mythic motifs rather than on the interpretation of literature. If the literary critic avoids the all too prevalent tendency to confuse clinical conclusions with literary ones, however, the information supplied by Dr. von Franz in both books can be applied to literature—especially to children's literature and most especially to the fairy tale.

The work of Jung and his followers has helped many to get at the essence of those "mysterious chords" struck in works of art—those chords which move and attract us even in the absence of common knowledge or conscious experience. The theory of archetypes grows out of Jungian psychology, and nowhere are archetypal images and patterns less veiled than in the fairy tale.

For example, once we understand the "puer aeternus" type we should have no difficulty in recognizing it in the fairy tale involving the youth of mysterious or special origins who, by way of tests and trials, redeems a family or a society by uniting himself (or herself) with a royal person who is in some magical way revealed as his or her logical complement. The prince and the princess live happily ever after; they reunite the male and female principles—the Yin and the Yang. They achieve eternal youth. The ritual marriage at the end of the fairy tale (and at the end of 'adult' comedy) represents the mystic's ideal, the reunion of formerly deluded man with the universal and eternal reality. "Whereupon" writes Alan Watts, "the life which had seemed momentary would be found momentous, and that present which had seemed to be no time at all would be found to be eternity" (*Myth and Ritual in Christianity* [Beacon, New York: 1968], p. 236). Perhaps this is a partial explanation of the emotional attraction of the fairy tale. One could go on from here in the Jungian manner to bring into play "puer aeternus" figures of myth—Dionysus, Attis and others—who might lead us still further into the truth and vitality of the tale.

The importance of the creation myth to the fairy tale is clearly shown here too. Dr. von Franz amply illustrates the connection between creation stories and rituals of initiation and renewal. The creation myth can be seen as symbolic of an awakening into consciousness; it is a myth of chaos becoming life, of death leading to rebirth. It is a myth of losing the self to find the Self. The "puer aeternus" and creation myths are, thus, both myths of individuation—a process achieved by the hero and heroine of fairy tale. Through our awareness of these myths we gain further insight into the "mysterious chords" of the fairy tale and of all enduring literature.

David Leeming

*See, for example, von Franz's *Introduction to the Interpretation of Fairy Tales* and *The Problem of the Feminine in Fairy Tales*, both reviewed in *Children's Literature*, Vol. II.

** The Puer Aeternus neurosis involves a mother complex with complications. It is approached by Jungians by way of archetypal patterns found in the myth of the divine child of the Eleusinian mysteries—a myth Jung and Kerenyi thoroughly explored in their now classic *Essays on a Science of Mythology.*

On Children's Literature, by Isabelle Jan. Tr. from the French, edited, and with a preface by Catherine Storr. (Allen Lane, £2.50).

First published in France in 1969, this work is by a professor in the education department of the College Sévigné and Head of Studies at the French school of librarianship. Her thesis is that children's literature is a *genre,* but her primary focus is on certain writers and themes.

She adopts a familiar viewpoint—that childhood was discovered in the eighteenth century or somewhere at the beginning of the industrial age, and that this discovery, in turn, created a special children's literature. She does not delve into the possibility that there might be a relationship between the "discovery" of childhood and industrialism—that there might be an economic reason for separating those not yet ready for the labor market, and that this reason might affect the quality of the literature.

To argue that an entire field of literature is a genre is a tour de force that does not quite come off. Though these are charming informal essays, they cannot be compared in quality to some other work. For instance, her comment on Alice in Wonderland as never being the right size for her surroundings, while delightful, cannot be compared with the acute treatment of Alice in Donald Rackin's essay, "Alice's Adventures to the End of Night," in the *Publication of the Modern Language Association,* October, 1969.

However, with the current paucity of serious study of the quality of children's literature, Isabelle Jan's work is, all in all, a thought-provoking contribution to the field.

Francelia Butler

The Nesbit Tradition: The Children's Novel, 1945-1970, by Marcus Crouch. (Rowen & Littlefield, $10.00).

Marcus Crouch, Deputy County Librarian for Kent, England, is a respected critic of children's literature. This work only adds to his reputation for balanced and thorough analysis.

Humanists will especially welcome his introductory comment, which establishes the perspective from which the entire book is written: "I come more and more to the view that there *are* no children's books. They are a concept invented for commercial reasons and kept alive by the human instinct for classification and categorizing. . . . When a child has mastered the technique of reading . . . the world opens for him, and not one artificially isolated segment of it."

Mr. Crouch's initial effort is to isolate several defining characteristics of E. Nesbit's stories: "portraits of real, timelessly naughty children"; "incongruities which make for humour"; "magic applied to the commonplaces of daily life"; "the 'time' theme in historical reconstruction"; and especially "colloquial, flexible and revealing prose which was her unique contribution to the children's novel." To pinpoint these attributes as essential to E. Nesbit's artistic accomplishment is a valuable critical service in itself. But Mr. Crouch's contribution is even more significant as it enables him to single out writers and aspects of style for discerning and sometimes illuminating comment.

For example, he is able to include writers not usually thought of as children's authors among practitioners of the Nesbit traditon; one of those he notes is the distinguished British novelist and translator Rex Warner, who in 1936 wrote a story for the young called *The Kite,* about the international drug traffic. Crouch calls it "exciting and forward-looking."

Perhaps the most interesting aspect of the Nesbit tradition as Mr. Crouch defines it is his emphasis upon the vital role of humor. His high praise of the work of a well-known American writer makes plain the attitude he values most highly as the essence of the Nesbit tradition. His comments also convey a fair sense of the application of his critical outlook to specific works:

> Natalie Savage Carlson, an American writer who knows France and French ways, writes with an effortless lightness of touch. It all seems easy, but so vivid a picture of an interdependent society of children and adults cannot but be the work of a disciplined and very skilful writer. The dialogue is especially fine, capturing the fine inconsequence of children talking and of the logic of men like the merry-go-round man. When he was a boy he had always said when he felt miserable: 'When you are a big man you shall have a merry-go-round.' Now he is big and he has one, and he is sick of it. But he cannot sell it. 'How can I sell the merry-go-round that I promised to a poor, unhappy boy?'

Thus, economically, either by direct quotation or succinct comment, Mr. Crouch illustrates, extends, and refines a number of helpful critical observations about the many writers who wrote in "the Nesbit tradition" during the twenty-five year period, 1945-1970.

Francelia Butler

Two Catalogs

A Select Assembly of Notable Books and Manuscripts from the Allison-Shelley Collection of Anglica Americana Germanica. With a foreword by Philip Allison Shelley. (Pennsylvania State University Library, $5.00).
The David McCandless McKell Collection: A Descriptive Catalog of Manuscripts, Early Printed Books and Children's Books, by Frank B. Fieler, assisted by John A. Zamonski and Kenneth W. Haas, Jr. (G. K. Hall & Co., $32.00).

If well conceived, effectively arranged, and accurately annotated, exhibit catalogs, publishers' catalogs, and printed catalogs of private and other unique book collections can be of inestimable value to those who use them. The two considered here are both excellent.

The first catalog listed details more than a hundred rare, unique, and bibliographically significant items from the Allison-Shelley Collection at the Pennsylvania State University Library exhibited there on June 9-July 24, 1972. The material exhibited and described is limited primarily to British and American translations of German writings showing the impact of German literature and culture upon England and America. Of particular interest to scholars concerned with children's literature are pp. 89-101 of the catalog.

The second catalog enumerates all items in the David McCandless McKell Collection, which is predominantly a collection of children's books owned and housed by the Ross County Historical Society in Chillicothe, Ohio. In the McCandless McKell Collection are many historically important first editions of works of such writers as Jacob Abbott, L. Frank Baum, Frances Hodgson Burnett, G.A. Henty, and Rudyard Kipling, to name only a few. This important collection might have remained unknown, except locally, had not Professor Frank Fieler of the English Department of Ohio University in Athens, Ohio, with the help of two graduate students, cataloged the collection.

Users of the G.K. Hall printed catalog which resulted will readily recognize and appreciate the high standards and scholarly efforts used by Professor Fieler and his assistants in the preparation of the catalog. The logical organization of the catalog, the elucidating introduction by Professor Fieler, the source bibliography, and the extensive indexes all work together to assist the user. The McCandless McKell catalog contains a section for each of these categories: Manuscripts, Early Printed Books Before 1700, and Children's Books Dating from 1700. The value of the catalog is greatly enhanced by the rich and informative notes which have been supplied, when appropriate, for each item listed.

Charity Chang

Imagination and the Spirit: Essays in Literature and the Christian Faith presented to Clyde S. Kilby. Edited by Charles Huttar. (William B. Eerdmans Publishing Co., $9.95).

Two personalities overshadow this *Festschrift* anthology of essays: one is that of an inspiring scholar and teacher at Wheaton College, the other that of a great humane scholar and writer at Oxford, now no longer living. To Clyde Kilby, the teaching of English and the chairmanship of a growing and energetic English department in Illinois have been the major part of his life. Scholar, teacher, inspiring friend, "a faithful servant of the Lord Jesus Christ" (pp. 476-477), Clyde Kilby's influence is obvious throughout the pages of this anthology. Typically, Glenn Sadler (who contributes a perceptive and much-needed essay on "The Fantastic Imagination in George Macdonald") was first introduced to the work of Macdonald, not through lecture or seminar, but through devotional reading prefacing Kilby's class.

Kilby's personality is one half of the background to *Imagination and the Spirit*; the other half is the personality of C. S. Lewis. Kilby was a long-term admirer of Lewis' writing while the Oxford scholar was still alive: "Many evangelical students whom Kilby guided through the structure of Lewis' thought found the same vivification of the fabric of Christian ideas" (p. 472). His interest in Lewis' work had three important results. One was the meeting between the two men in Oxford, which led to a lively correspondence. The second was a useful interchange of material and unfinished projects, in which the handicap of Lewis' failing health was partly overcome by help from Illinois. The third, and perhaps the most important in the long term, was the continuing work of the establishment in the library of Wheaton College of an archive of C. S. Lewis manuscripts and correspondence.

Imagination and the Spirit will certainly contribute to the reader's awareness of a Christian tradition, and the writer's place in a Christian society; yet a sense of the boundaries of the imagination and the capabilities of the human spirit in exploring these boundaries stands behind the scholarship of these pages. Specifically, one may turn to the section on "Inklings and Ancestors," to the essays on Wordsworth and MacDonald, to two important essays by Alice Hadfield and Marjorie Wright on the fiction of Lewis and Williams, and to two equally important but specialized essays on Lewis by Walter Hooper and Corbin Carnell. For too long regarded loosely and at half-acquaintance as a writer of science fiction and the amusing if unintelligible *Screwtape Letters,* Lewis is revealed in these essays as an important writer of allegory and fantasy. His works yield richly to the scholarly investigation they receive—a true liberation of the imagination as of the spirit.

This liberation is perhaps the theme which will most attract those who teach children's literature. The writer's vision of reality is transformed in writing for children into a form of critical meaning: sometimes the meaning may be all but concealed, sometimes re-interpreted in a way which could be described as ". . . a poet's artistic diary of youthful dreams"—Glenn Sadler's description of Macdonald's *Phantastes* (p. 220). The artistic diary, like all diaries, will select what is recorded, and this makes all the more valuable the biographical insights which we can receive into MacDonald's life and its effect on the world of his art.

Professor Sadler combines information on MacDonald's youth, and the influence of Scottish scenery, with an investigation of the debt MacDonald owed to the German romantics—a linking of the "blue hills" of his birthplace and the impossible dreams of the *Märchen* which emerge transfored in *Phantastes,* "an imaginative journey into MacDonald's poetic unconsciousness" (p. 222). To perform such a journey, to illuminate the artist's vision, somehow to relate the world of fantasy to the reader's experience, must surely be the responsibility of those who teach "Children's Literature."

More material on C. S. Lewis is available in this collection, in a context which makes clear how his fantasy repays study on the same level as that of MacDonald. Marjorie Wright's valuable essay interprets his vision of cosmic order: "clearly defined regions organized by an intricate system of cosmic order—order, that is, which embraces the whole world in which each myth is set" (p. 259). To understand such order is to see, not rigid society, but "kingdoms full of life, movement, ceremony, courtesy" (p. 276). To read Lewis is to inhabit this world of Hierarchy, and yet at the same time relate it to daily reality.

This is not only a problem for the reader, for as Walter Hooper's fine biographical memoir will make clear, Lewis himself for many years had difficulty in reconciling the "outer" and "inner" worlds of his own mind "being lived over against each other, albeit at the same time" (p. 278). In early years, beset by religious doubt, and before his "conversion," Lewis found a great chasm between these worlds; but in the mature productions of the Narnian fairy tales this chasm has in part been bridged.

In the writing of fairy tales, relief is gained, but this is far from escapism. "No literature is less likely to give a person a false impression of this present world than are fairy tales" (p. 290) according to Lewis: by arousing and imaginatively satisfying wishes they liberate the spirit, but do not allow it dangerous freedom. We would give children a false impression of their world, argues Lewis, if we wrote for them of a fairy land with no dangers and no threats. They are born into a world of danger and violence, and "ought at least to hear of brave knights and heroic courage" (p. 291). Their world and their fairy tales will interact. They will not turn to the fairy tale for relief or escapism, but for commentary on their own experience, and for imaginative stimulus. Lewis, after all, admitted that marvellous literature evoked his desire for Heaven (p. 290).

And so the twin themes of this book are united in the writing about Lewis' fairy tales. The Christian experience of writer and teacher and the interest in the fantastic combine in C. S. Lewis, as in the Christian example of teachers like Clyde Kilby. To read in the world of fantasy is to pass "watchful dragons" but the countryside beyond the dragons is appealing. *Imagination and the Spirit* stands as a tribute to Lewis the writer and Kilby the teacher in their attempt to pass "watchful dragons" and lead others with them.

Ian Campbell

Poems of Robert Louis Stevenson, selected by Helen Plotz. Drawings by Charles Attebery. Ages 12 and up. (Thomas Y. Crowell Company, $4.50).
Dr. Hyde And Mr. Stevenson, by Harold Winfield Kent. Older Children and Adults. (Charles E. Tuttle Company, $10.00).

Robert Louis Stevenson died of tuberculosis at the age of forty-four, and (ten years later) so did Anton Chekhov. Despite the enormous differences between them, including Chekhov's greater stature as a writer, they had many things in common besides fragile health. Both were gregarious men, gifted with generous capacities for friendship and humor; both were cheerful, unostentatious humanitarians; and both had the particular kind of mind and manners which enables a grown person to get on well with children.

As to children's literature, Chekhov had firm views; here he is sending two dog stories ("Kashtanka" and "Whitebrow") to a friend for use in an anthology of works suitable for children:

> I don't like what is known as children's literature; I don't recognize its validity. Children should be given only what is suitable for adults as well. Children enjoy reading Andersen, *The Frigate Pallada*, and Gogol, and so do adults. One shouldn't write for children; one should learn to choose works suitable for children from among those already written for adults—in other words, from genuine works of art. (*Letters of Anton Chekhov*, ed. Heim and Karlinsky, p. 372)

In these terms, Stevenson's best poems perform a difficult triple feat: they are suitable for children; they are genuine works of art fit for adults; and they are about children, sensitive Romantic works about the helpless isolation and luxurious privacy of childhood ("Romantic" because the isolation and privacy are felt and cherished by the poet, too).

The selection, editing, design, and introduction of Helen Plotz's volume meet the requirements of Chekhov with taste and good sense. The book makes plain that Stevenson (again like Chekhov) is a less melancholy, less soft, and less twilight-bound figure than conventional opinion would have him. He has a charming, Lennon-McCartney side, as in the poem "My Wife and I, in One Romantic Cot," with its cool, poised closing lines:

> Harvests of flowers o'er all our garden-plot,
> She dreams; and I to enrich a darker spot,—
> My unprovided cellar; both to swell
> Our narrow cottage huge as a hotel,
> That portly friends may come and share our lot— My wife and I.

On the one hand, this tone is sophisticated, and on the other hand a quick-witted child will enjoy the gentle surprises. It is not necessary to know literary history to be amused by the couplet:

> My wife and I, in one romantic cot,
> The world forgetting, by the world forgot,

when it is picked up a few lines later by the amusing deflation of the rhyme word in:

> I pledge my votive powers upon a yacht.

The open, affectionate irony and the fresh use of tired diction are what call to mind the Beatles.

Even when treating the Romantic themes I mention above, Stevenson is not soft or false; retreat into the microcosm of childhood and fantasy is seen accurately *as* retreat; the consciousness of sickness is there in the brilliantly-chosen adjective in "The Land Of Counterpane":

> And sometimes for an hour or so
> I watched my leaden soldiers go.

And a consciousness that the word "pleasant" is somewhat sick, that the retreat into dreamy stillness and fantasy is somewhat sick, animates the poem's superb final stanza, with its hypnotic tense-change:

> I was the giant great and still
> That sits upon the pillow-hill,
> And sees before him, dale and plain,
> The pleasant Land of Counterpane.

Without inflating such poems, one can say that they are emotionally complex works of art about childhood, available to children. The retreat into fantasy and its microcosm is not seen in sweet pastels, and neither is the awakening into a large adult world—as these lines from "The Little Land" show:

> When my eyes I once again
> Open, and see all things plain:
> High bare walls, great bare floor;
> Great big knobs on drawer and door;
> Great big people perched on chairs,
> Stitching tucks and mending tears,
> Each a hill that I could climb,
> And talking nonsense all the time.

I will allow myself one more quotation, to demonstrate that Stevenson can use these same powers on subjects other than childhood. Here is all of "An End Of Travel," where like Landor he gives the nineteenth-century sensibility a chiseled, hard form we might expect from a Classical or Christian source:

> Let now your soul in this substantial world
> Some anchor strike. Be here the body moored:—
> This spectacle immutably from now
> The picture in your eye; and when time strikes,
> And the green scene goes on the instant blind—
> The ultimate helpers, where your horse today
> Conveyed you dreaming, bear your body dead.

Such tough simplicity, about spectacles and helpers so purely physical, is not easy.

Dr. Hyde and Mr. Stevenson re-examines the controversy between Stevenson and the Rev. Charles McEwen Hyde, D.D., a Calvinist missionary to Hawaii. Hyde wrote a letter derogating the Belgian peasant-priest Father Damien, who lived among the leper colony at Kalawao-Kalaupapa. Damien eventually died of leprosy, which Hyde (jealous of Damien's posthumous publicity) believed "should be attributed to his vices and carelessness." That is the only evidence which Hyde or Kent can adduce for Hyde's contention that "he was not a pure man in his relations with women."

Stevenson came vigorously to Damien's defense. Kent's book tries to rehabilitate Hyde and show that there were two sides: Damien was indeed "coarse" in manners and "dirty" in dress, as the Hyde letter complains, and Hyde never intended his letter for publication. On the other hand, there is no evidence that Hyde complained to the Protestant colleague who published the letter.

But the most damning evidence against Kent's man Hyde is Hyde's own prose as quoted in the book: priggish, mean, Pecksniffian, semi-literate, suggesting at times a vindicative repressed homosexual. There is no room here to quote Hyde's terrifying, self-righteous description of his expelling a boy he "learned to love," telling the boy that he could not expect to become a minister of the gospel because of his morally-tainting leprosy. But here is another sample of Hyde:

Accustomed as I was to the purity of a New England home, there yawned before me, in Hawaiian social and family life, an abysmal depth of heathen degradation, unutterable in its loathesomeness.

(p. 369)

It is heartening to see Stevenson cudgel such opposition; as a tough, effective man, in the world of controversy and action, he used his powers of language to defend his generous and humane convictions. Those same powers wrote his lines about "a child of air," and in such strength and variety there lies a hero-story "suitable for children"—in the words of Chekhov, whose efforts on behalf of the prison-colony at Sakhalin evoke similar feelings of admiration.

Robert Pinsky

Biography for Children

The Life and Legend of George McJunkin, Black Cowboy, by Franklin Folsom. Ages 10 and up. (Thomas Nelson, Inc., $5.95).

Rosa Parks, by Eloise Greenfield. Illustrated by Eric Marlow. Ages 6 to 9. (Thomas Y. Crowell, $3.75).

Black Woman: A Fictionalized Biography of Lucy Terry Prince, by Bernard and Jonathan Katz. Ages 12 and up. (Pantheon, $5.95).

Jesse Owens, by Mervyn Kaufman. Illustrated by Larry Johnson. Ages 6 to 9. (Thomas Y. Crowell, $3.75).

Carl Sandburg, Young Singing Poet, by Grace Hathaway Melin. Illustrated by Robert Doremus. Ages 8 to 12. (Bobbs-Merrill Co., $4.95).

Me and Willie and Pa: the Story of Abraham Lincoln and his Son Tad, by F. N. Monjo. Illustrations by Douglas Gorsline. Ages 6 to 10. (Simon and Schuster, $5.95).

Robert E. Lee, by Ruby L. Radford. Illustrated by Tran Mawicke. Ages 7 to 9. (G. P. Putnam's Sons, $3.39).

Thomas Carlyle's statement that "the history of the world is but the biography of great men" established a point of view that strongly influenced the writing of biography throughout the 19th Century and which, in large measure, still influences the writing of biography for children. Such an approach creates many problems, for the great man exists very much as a part of his own times and most young children have not developed the historical consciousness necessary to understand fully this relationship. As a result, authors are often tempted to fall into extremes in their portrayals of historical figures: they can give a scissors-and-paste treatment of the past which makes the temporal background of their subjects wooden, or they can so water down the background as to make the heroes of the books seem like people who exist in a timeless realm in which, but for the lack of electric lights and television sets, people seem very much as they are today.

Another problem is created by the fact that the lives of great men are often inner and, as such, are not filled with the physical adventures which make for the exciting, fast-paced narrative enjoyed by children. For example, Herman Melville's times on board a whaling ship and amongst the Typees are the stuff children love, but his long contemplative talks with Jack Chase between watches, his probing conversations with Hawthorne, and his lonely reading of Emerson, Shakespeare and Dante, which are infinitely more important to his development as a writer, would have to be glossed over in a story of his life written for youngsters.

A third problem in biographies for children is to be found in the fact that many volumes are commissioned for series and thus writers may be producing on demand studies about subjects for which they have little knowledge and sympathy. Moreover, an author may be limited by being forced to write within the format of a particular series. One suspects that these problems have created the weaknesses in three of the books under consideration here.

Grace Hathaway Melin's *Carl Sandburg, Young Singing Poet,* a volume in the Bobbs-Merrill Childhood of Famous Americans series, is frankly a dull book. One quarter of the way through it we have seen the three year old Cully climb aboard a buggy, ask his mother about a wagon with the words Chicago on its side, and live a generally nondescript life. Not until page 145 do we discover that he loves words and not until page 178 do we learn he wants to become a writer. The rest of the time he goes to school, delivers milk and papers, rides the rails, and gets arrested for swimming nude in the local pond. For a person with a knowledge of Sandburg's poetry, it would be possible to discover in his activities the "grass roots" origins of much of his poetry; but the book makes no attempt to trace the growth of his poetic impulses during his childhood. The life described appears as a very ordinary one, told in a very ordinary, almost dull style.

Mervyn Kauffman's *Jesse Owens* is one of the Crowell Biography series, an easy-to-read book, which follows the life of the great athlete through his Olympic triumphs and into the active time as a teacher and youth leader. While a book of this nature is restricted in the amount of in-depth analysis it can provide, one would hope to find more about the loneliness and agony that short-distance as well as long-distance runners feel. For example, we are told only that "later that year (1936) he was sent to the Olympics," and after a detailed account of his winning the long-jump only that "he won two races and a relay." The point about Jesse Owens' life is that he overcame poverty, racial discrimination, illness, and slick promoters to become a great athlete and fine citizen. Even a biography written for children six to eight years old should give more a sense of his achievement than is the case here. One suspects that Mr. Kaufman wrote this book on demand for the series and that he did not have the requisite involvement with the subject mentioned above.

Such is not the case with another in the Crowell Biography series, *Rosa Parks,* the story of a courageous black woman whose refusal to relinquish her seat on a Montgomery bus began the famous boycott which so changed the course of American history. Author Eloise Greenfield and illustrator Eric Marlow obviously have a deep feeling for their subject and have vividly captured the inner and outer struggles of a woman who, early in her life, determined that "I don't want to be pushed by your son or anyone else." The nature of southern white racism and the civil rights movement are clearly described for children of the '70's, to many of whom much of the background will be unknown. There are a few weaknesses. For example, just what is meant when we are told that Rosa's father had moved to another city? If it is divorce, it should be stated. Children are sufficiently aware of this social problem, and thus don't need to have it glossed over. Generally, the subject is well treated and Rosa Parks assumes a three dimensional quality not always found in series biographies.

Of the final series book, Ruby L. Radford's *Robert E. Lee,* a Putnam See and Read Biography, little need be said other than that the work is as limited in its treatment of its subject as it is in its vocabulary. Early in his life, Robert became head of the family, and learned to be kind and gentle to the sick—all this, presumably, as training for his war leadership. Of his entry into the Civil War, we are merely told that although he hated slavery his loyalty to his people was greater. While an easy reader does place limitations on the writer, one might have hoped that Ruby Radford had been a little less simplistic in her treatment of the war, none of the horrors of which are mentioned.

It appears that one must turn away from series to find acceptable juvenile biography, and such, at least, is the case with the books under consideration. *The Life and Legend of George McJunkin, Black Cowboy,* by Franklin Folsom, tells the story of a man who, born in slavery, grew to be one of the most respected men in the Cimmaron Valley. The general theme of the study is that McJunkin, although highly regarded, was always in search of total freedom. He found equality on the trail herd, was a second father to the sons of many white ranchers, and more than once won acclaim for his bravery; yet he never fulfilled his dream of owning his own ranch. In fast-paced narrative, Folsom vividly recreates the main adventures of McJunkin's life. Yet if one were to criticize the biography, it would be on the grounds that several of the incidents seem to be designed to foreshadow a major event of George's life, one which does not, however, arrive. It is almost as if the author wished his subject to be of greater historical stature than, in fact, he was.

Bernard and Jonathan Katz's *Black Woman* is a fictionalized biography of Lucy Terry Prince, who lived in Vermont in the 18th and early 19th centuries. Born in slavery, Lucy's freedom was purchased by her future husband, Abijah Prince. A clever woman, who learned to read and write in her teens and who composed a poem on the Indian Wars, she was stern in defense of her rights, appearing more than once before governing bodies to demand what she felt was owing her. Both authors have done a good deal of historical research and have, through narrative and dialogue, created a vivid picture of life two centuries ago. However, for a book designed for readers twelve years or older, one would have liked to have learned more of the inner thoughts of Lucy Terry Prince. Life was not easy for anyone in the pioneer existence of the 18th century, and when to these difficulties were added the struggles of a proud and defiant black woman, one surely has psychological drama of a magnitude that the socially and racially conscious teen-age readership of the 1970's would find compelling.

F. N. Monjo's *Me and Willie and Pa* adds another book to the ever expanding shelf of Lincoln biographies. This one purports to be written as it might have been by Lincoln's favorite son Thomas, or "Tad," who was eight when the family entered the White House, and who, the author tells us, was a "lonely little boy [who] was a very bad student, read poorly, could scarcely write, and spoke with a pronounced lisp or speech defect." Written in cadences which remind the reader of Huck Finn's language, the book begins on an ominous note: "When I look back, thinking about our time in Washington, most everything I remember is sad." With this introduction, one might expect the book to be a presentation of a young child's coming to terms with the puzzling and terrifying realities of war and death. But in large part, it is a recitation of the games and happy times that Tad enjoyed. In this respect, the story has considerable charm, a charm which is increased by the drawings of Douglas Gorsline, who has attempted—and generally successfully—to approximate the steel engravings of the 1860's.

To write good biography is difficult; to write good biography for children even more so, for the business of bringing subject and reader together creates a number of challenges which usually only the best of writers can successfully meet. Generally speaking, the writers of the books discussed here have not met these challenges. With the exception of the Rosa Parks book, the series biographies are simplified and simplistic, while the other studies never completely realize the rich potentials of their materials. Either the authors have underestimated the abilities of their prospective readers, or they do not have the abilities to probe the complexities of the people they consider and to present these complexities to a young audience. One hopes it is the latter.

Jon C. Stott

ChLA Notes

The Children's Literature Association is a nonprofit, membership organization formed in 1973 to promote serious scholarship and research in children's literature and publish these findings in the journal *Children's Literature: The Great Excluded* and at an annual conference. The first annual conference of the Association was held March 15-17, 1974, at the University of Connecticut. The ChLA is pleased that the conference was successful in achieving its goals.

The theme of the conference was "Cultural and Critical Values in Children's Literature." The Association hoped to achieve three things. The first, as is evident from the conference theme, was to examine critically various aspects and types of children's literature through the presentation of papers, panels, and workshops. Three panels focused on fields, other than teaching, which are concerned with the literature of children: publishing, writing, and reviewing. Representing the publishing industry were George Nicholson of Viking Press, Barbara Bates of Westminster Press, and Pat Connolly of Doubleday & Co. The authors' panel consisted of John Langstaff, Jean Fritz, James Haskins, and Feenie Ziner. George A. Woods of *The New York Times*, Robert Miner of *Newsweek*, Donald Reynolds, a member of the Newbery-Caldecott Committee, and Barbara Rosen of *Children's Literature*, made up the reviewers' panel. All three panels discussed children's literature from their particular viewpoints, and all agreed on the need for applying critical standards to the field.

Eight papers presented to the conference critically examined areas within children's literature. Paper topics were "Literary and Cultural Values in the History of Children's Literature" (R. Gordon Kelly, Univ. of Pennsylvania); "The Utopia of *St. Nicholas*: The Present as Prologue" (Fred Erisman, Texas Christian Univ.); "The Quest for Growth in Children's Literature" (Virginia L. Wolf, Univ. of Kansas); "The Tales of Manabozho: The Literary Traditions of the North American Indians" (Althea K. Helbig, Eastern Michigan Univ.); "The Social Odyssey of Diminutive Heroes" (Lori Clarke, Univ. of Utah); "Cotton Mather and His Children: Some Insights into Puritan Attitudes" (Carol Gay, Youngstown State Univ.); "Sacrifice in Wilde's *The Happy Prince*" (Jerome Griswold, Univ. of Connecticut); "For the Good of the Country: Cultural Values in American Juvenile Fiction, 1825-1850" (Anne S. MacLeod, Univ. of Maryland).

A second concern of the conference, to examine the teaching of children's literature, was reflected in informal discussion among those attending and by a panel devoted to this topic. This panel was made up of Dr. Irving Baker, School of Education, Univ. of Connecticut; Dr. Leonard Mendelsohn, Dept. of English, Sir George Williams Univ., Montreal; Dr. Francelia Butler, Dept. of English, Univ. of Connecticut; and Professor Glenn Sadler, Dept. of English, Point Loma College, San Diego. Many aspects of the topic were discussed; the panel agreed that there is a need to improve the quality of teaching in children's literature and thereby warrant the respect this area deserves.

This issue of respect was a third goal of the conference. The ChLA feels that children's literature is too often viewed as an insignificant area of literature without depth and complexity, which can be taught by anyone. The issues dealt with at the conference, the examinations made in the papers, showed this to be an erroneous viewpoint. As the conference program stated, if we respect the child, we must take his/her literature seriously, ensure that the literature merits respect in its own right, and respect the study of that literature. The conference was only one step in the changing of attitudes, but all who attended agreed that it was a significant step.

Following the conference, there was a meeting of the Executive Board of the ChLA. At the meeting the Board members voted to raise the membership fees due to rising costs. The new fees, effective March 17, 1974, are $14.50, regular membership; $7.00, student membership; and $20.00, institutional membership. The Board expressed regret that this increase was necessary. Among other business, the Board noted with pleasure that membership in the Association continues to increase rapidly, indicating that the Association is meeting widely felt needs.

With the increase in its fees, the ChLA hopes to be able to expand its services to its members. The past year has seen the accomplishment of some of the Association's aims; hopefully the coming years will see the full realization of its goals. The ChLA Executive Board wishes to thank the members for the support they have given to the formation of the Association, the presentation of the conference, the publication of the journal, and to furthering serious interest in the study of children's literature. The Executive Board solicits continued support in the coming years.

For membership information please write:

Anne Devereaux Jordan
Executive Secretary

The Children's Literature Association
P.O. Box 242
Storrs, Connecticut 06268

Areas for Research
(continued from *Children's Literature*, Volume One)

Values in the Folktales of India (or in Grimm)
Causality in Cumulative Verse and Folktales
Politics in "Rip Van Winkle"
The Shadow in Shadow Plays
The Unicorn
Birds or the Spiritual in Children's Literature
History of Drama in Relation to Children
Trolls in Norwegian Tales
Games as Children's Literature
Boundaries in Children's Literature
Violence in Children's Literature
Style and Content in Kenneth Grahame's *Golden Age* and *Dream Days*
Doubles in Children's Books
Use of Language in *Uncle Remus*
Techniques of Oral Narration
Ideology of *Orphan Annie*
Sign Language as Literature

Police in Children's Books
Old People in Children's Books
Literature for Gifted Children
Children's Literature and the Counter Culture
Canadian Animal Stories
Children's Literature and Ecology
Death in *Charlotte's Web*
Children's Literature in Colonial America
Cats in Contemporary Literature for Children
Lost Childhood in Song
Innerviews of fantasy
Migrant Workers in Children's Books
Socialization through Children's Literature
The Changing Image of the Dragon in Children's Stories
Tom Swift
Circles in Illustration of Children's Books
Jokes and the Smile in Children's Books
The Bible as Children's Literature
Louise de la Ramée ("Ouida") and *The Nuremberg Stove*
Henry Miller's *The Smile at the Foot of the Ladder* as Children's Literature
Superstitions in Children's Books
The Serious Undertones in Mother Goose Rhymes
Indians in Children's Literature
Mystical Intentions in "Jabberwocky"
Family Folklore as Children's Literature
Pornography for Children
Gypsies in Children's Literature
Loneliness in Grimms' Tales
Parents as Villains
Oral Fixations in Children's Books
Summer Camp Songs as Literature
Variants in Content of Certain Folktales as Reflections of Social Changes
The Theatre of the Absurd as a Source for Children's Plays
Japanese *Kyogen* as a Source for Children's Plays
Use of the Ancient Rhetorical Method of Imitation as a Way of Stimulating Creativity
Creative Dramatics for Children
Implicit Valuation of the Child in Medieval Literature
Implications of the Child as Audience in Medieval Literature
Children's Responses to "Adult" Classics
Oral Narration: Black Rhyming Language among Children
Family Relationships in the Books by Laura Ingalls Wilder
Sibling Interdependence in Nesbit's Books
The Cautionary Tale
Maeterlinck's *Blue Bird* as a Children's Play
George Sand's Puppet Theatre
Cultural Influence of Americans on Vietnamese Children
Peanuts as Children's Literature
Children and Nineteenth Century Moralistic Poetry
The Meaning of "The Wolf of Gubbio"
Feminism and Lang's "Color" Fairy Books
Symbolism in Tolkien's *Smith of Wootton Major*
Heroism in Tolkien's *Farmer Giles of Ham*

Values in Filipino Folktales
Image of the Black Male in Children's Books
Varieties of Distortion in Literary Fantasies
Poetry of Children in Agony
Changes in Beginning Readers
Women as Mothers in Current Literature for Children
Puppetry as an Added Dimension in Oral Narration
The Protestant Ethic in Contemporary Children's Books
Effect of Black Movies on Black Children
Reactions of Retarded Children to Selected Classics
Values in Irish Folk Plays
Literary Elements in "Rainy-Day" Activities
Sexism in Textbooks Used in Elementary School
Lions in Children's Literature
Eating as Reward and Punishment in Children's Stories
Unrecorded Appalachian Folktales for Children
Humor in Contemporary Children's Books As Contrasted With That in Older Classics
Stereotyped Characters and Situations in Children's Television Shows
Photography as a Way of Illustrating Children's Books
Themes of French Children's Songs
Astrid Lindgren's Writings for Children
Symbolism in Dr. Seuss
The Wind in the Willows and the Bible
Characters with Speech Defects in Children's Literature
Representations of God in Cartoon Shows
Morality in Yiddish Folktales and Poems
Humor in Children's Poetry
Jungian Archetypes in *Alice in Wonderland*
Values in Norwegian Folktales
A Comparative Study of the Reaction of "Normal" and
     Mentally Disturbed Children to the Same Literature
A Linguistic Study of *Winnie-the-Pooh*
Themes of Andersen's Tales
Television Commercials as Children's "Literature"
Cultural Transmission through Lithuanian Folk Songs
Heads in Folktales of Various Ethnic Groups
Psychological Analysis of Mother Goose Rhymes
Psychological Analysis of *A Child's Garden of Verses*

Contributors and Editors

Joan Evans de Alonso has recently retired as Professor of Spanish, Suffolk University, Boston.

William Davis Anderson, Ph.D., Univ. of Texas, is an associate professor of English, California State Univ., Northridge. His works on children's literature include *A New Look at Children's Literature* (Wadsworth, 1972).

Sandra Fenichel Asher has published a number of poems and stories for children.

Jan Bakker teaches in the English department of the Univ. of Tennessee, Knoxville.

Marcella Spann Booth, a specialist in modern poetry, prepared *From Confucius to Cummings: An Anthology of Poetry* (New Directions) in collaboration with Ezra Pound.

Ingrid Bozanic, trained at Columbia Univ., has made the study of traditional and modern Norwegian literature for children her special interest.

Bennett A. Brockman, Ph.D., Vanderbilt Univ., is a member of the Univ. of Connecticut English department. He is a student of medieval and children's literature.

Francelia Butler, Ph.D., Univ. of Virginia, is Professor of English at the Univ. of Connecticut.

Glauco Cambon, Ph.D., Univ. of Pavia, subsequently studied at Columbia Univ. on a Fulbright-Hays Fellowship. Professor of Romance and Classical Languages at the Univ. of Connecticut, he is widely known for his criticism of Dante and for his work in comparative literature.

Ian Campbell is a lecturer in English literature at the University of Edinburgh. His main teaching fields are English and Scottish literature since 1800.

Doris G. Carlson has taught English at Becker Junior College, Worcester, Mass., and contributes poetry and short stories to little magazines.

Charity Chang, head of the Serials Department, Wilbur Cross Library, Univ. of Connecticut, reviews children's books for various journals and for *The Hartford Courant.*

Mary Fine is a research biologist, Department of Biobehavioral Sciences, Univ. of Connecticut, who has extensive experience with nondomestic animals.

Iris Finkelbrand is on the staff of *Scholastic* magazine.

Rachel Fordyce, Assistant Professor of English at Virginia Polytechnic and State Univ., Blacksburg, specialized in children's theater and received her doctorate from the Univ. of Pittsburgh.

Stephen Howard Foreman is playwright in residence at the Univ. of Connecticut; his plays have appeared off-Broadway and on national television.

Martin Gardner, author of over a hundred scientific and critical works, is best known to students of children's literature for his *Annotated Alice* and his introductions to several of L. Frank Baum's *Oz* books. He also contributed some eighty short stories to *Humpty-Dumpty.*

Donald Gibson, Ph.D., Brown Univ., is the author of *The Fiction of Stephen Crane* (Southern Illinois Press, 1969) and editor of three collections of Black literature.

John Graham, Ph.D., John Hopkins Univ., is Assistant Dean of the College of Arts and Sciences, Univ. of Virginia. He has written extensively on problems of aesthetics and style.

David L. Greene is Assistant Professor of English, Piedmont College, Demorest, Georgia. He edited *The Baum Bugle* 1968-1973, and is co-author of the Introduction to L. Frank Baum's *The Master Key* (Hyperion, 1974).

Jerome J. Griswold is a doctoral candidate in English at the University of Connecticut, where he team teaches a class of some three hundred students of children's literature in the humanities program.

Father James Heisig, Ph.D., Cambridge Univ., is a Roman Catholic priest. He is an assistant professor of philosophy and religion at Divine Word College, Epworth, Iowa.

Ravenna Helson, Institute of Personality Assessment and Research, Univ. of California, Berkeley, is a Project Director of a study of critics and criticism in children's literature which is supported by the National Endowment for the Humanities.

James Hillman, Director of the Jung Institute, Zürich, is also editor of Spring Publications, Postfach 190, 8024 Zürich, Switzerland.

Father Walter Hooper is executor of the C. S. Lewis estate at Oxford. An Episcopal priest, he is assistant chaplain of Jesus College, Oxford.

Karen K. Jambeck is a doctoral candidate in medieval studies at the Univ. of Connecticut.

Thomas J. Jambeck, Ph.D., Univ. of Colorado, specializes in the study of medieval literature, particularly Chaucer and the drama.

Anne Devereaux Jordan is founder and Executive Secretary of the Children's Literature Association.

Helen Kay, author of some twenty-six books for children, is especially known for her *Picasso's World of Children* (Doubleday) and *Secrets of the Dolphin* (Macmillan).

Narayan Kutty currently teaches children's literature at Eastern Connecticut State College, Willimantic. He is particularly interested in comparing children's literature of East and West and in modern British literature.

Eva M. Lederer, Queens College, CUNY, is a librarian at the Univ. of Connecticut.

David Leeming, Ph.D., New York Univ., is the author of two books on mythology, *Wings* (forthcoming) and *Mythology: The Voyage of the Hero*.

Peter Meinke is a professor of literature at Eckerd College. He has published two children's books and regularly contributes poetry and criticism to the *New Republic* and other magazines.

Leonard R. Mendelsohn is an associate professor in the English department of Sir George Williams Univ., Montreal, and Principal of the Rabbinical College of Canada.

William T. Moynihan is Head of the English Department, Univ. of Connecticut.

Robert Pinsky teaches English at Wellesley College. Author of *Landor's Poetry* (Chicago, 1968), his poems have appeared in *Antaeus, Modern Occasions, Poetry,* and elsewhere.

Deidre Pitts teaches children's literature in the English Department, State Univ. College, Buffalo, New York.

Alexandra Placotari, a poet and member of the Hans Christian Andersen Jury, lives and teaches in Athens, Greece.

Richard R. Reynolds earned an LL.B. at the Univ. of Michigan and a Ph.D. in English at Notre Dame. An Assistant Professor of English at the Univ. of Connecticut, his special interest is in English literature of the eighteenth century.

Barbara Rosen, Ph.D., The Shakespeare Institute, Univ. of Birmingham, is author of *Witchcraft* (Taplinger, 1971) and co-editor of the Signet edition of Shakespeare's *Julius Caesar.*

William Rosen, Ph.D., Harvard Univ., is author of *Shakespeare and the Craft of Tragedy* and co-editor of the Signet edition of Shakespeare's *Julius Caesar.*

Lynne Rosenthal has recently completed the requirements for the doctorate in English at Columbia Univ.

Ellen Schecter Scaduto, Associate Editor, Scholastic Magazine, Inc., is producer-writer-editor of numerous filmstrips for children.

William E. Sheidley is Associate Professor of English at the Univ. of Connecticut; his field is Renaissance literature.

Ray Anthony Shepard works for *Scholastic* and has taught children's literature at City College and Hunter College in New York City. His latest book for children is a retelling of the *Conjure Tales* of Charles W. Chestnutt (Dutton, 1973).

Walter Scherf is Head of the International Youth Library, Munich, Germany, an associated project of UNESCO.

Justin G. Schiller is a collector and dealer in early children's books and graphics of the eighteenth and nineteenth centuries. He is founder of *The Baum Bugle.*

Judith Sloman, an Assistant Professor of English, Univ. of Calgary, Calgary, Alberta, teaches children's literature. Her Ph.D. is from the Univ. of Minnesota, where she specialized in Restoration literature. She is currently studying the development of the novel by women writers.

Barbara Smith is a doctoral candidate at the Univ. of Connecticut.

Jon C. Stott is Associate Professor of English, Western Michigan Univ., Kalamazoo. His special interests are American literature and children's literature.

Alexander Taylor, Assistant Professor of English at Eastern Connecticut State College, currently holds a grant from the Connecticut Commission on the Arts to assist his writing and translating. His stories, poems, and translations have appeared widely in the United States, Canada, England, and Denmark.

Larry Tjarks, Ph.D., Univ. of Nebraska, is Assistant Professor of English at Texas Tech Univ., Lubbock.

Kim Kurt Waller has written prize-winning poems, articles, and scripts for movies. She taught English at Briarley for some years and is now a fulltime writer.

Barbara K. Walker, Curator of the Archive of Turkish Oral Narrative at Texas Tech Univ., has lived and taught in Turkey, is the author of fifteen children's books, and has taught children's literature for many years. She leads a summer program on internationalism in children's literature.

Martin Williams, Director of the Jazz and Popular Culture Programs at the Smithsonian Institution, has edited L. Frank Baum's *A Kidnapped Santa Claus* (Bobbs-Merrill) and is currently working on some long-forgotten Gruelle magazine stories as additions to the Raggedy Ann chronicle.

William Wilson is an Assistant Professor of art history at Univ. of Connecticut.

Thomas A. Zaniello is Assistant Professor of Humanities, Northern Kentucky State College, Covington.